A Life

Worthwhile

Author Mike Jacobs

The Memoirs of
Squadron Leader W Jacobs
Royal Air Force

1937 – 1973

Whitley Bomber 1939

CONTENTS

Sgt. Bill Jacobs 1940

PREFACE
YOUTH WILL BE SERVED

By the time I left school in the summer of 1934 there was no doubt in my mind of what I wanted to do. I had an insatiable desire to fly and was already quite knowledgeable, so I thought, in this subject. Much of my enthusiasm, was it perhaps more imagined than real, had been generated by reading American pulp magazines, which were of dubious authenticity generally and not particularly accurate in those parts which were claimed to be factual, as I was later to discover. Some of these magazines have been retained as fortunate survivors of many changes of location over a period now exceeding sixty years. Other treasured books of those early days of boyhood interest and ambition have been lost (mostly stolen by borrowing), but some, published in the United Kingdom, have been saved in my library, more out of sentiment than anything else, some of them becoming valuable originals though somewhat tattered, whilst some of the lost titles have been re-issued in recent years by new publishers. A few of these newer editions are also to be found in my library, with many others acquired since my retirement from active RAF duty to provide a well-balanced library of aviation reading.

At about the age of twelve, I started to make model aeroplanes, but it was not until some years later that I experienced my first success with those that were intended to fly. I learned a lot about flight from models, and my fascination with them as both a hobby and a challenging sport has persisted throughout my lifetime. My enthusiasm was also fired by my reading of the air war of 1914-1918, of the so-called aces and their aircraft, events that were quite recent in our history and played a great part in our early upbringing. But as for getting into the air as a career, there was little hope. Financially, it was out of my grasp, and there was no local facility anyway. I was also keenly interested in the developing fields of electrical and wireless technology - the term radio was not then in general use.

I was offered initial employment as an apprentice by a small firm of electrical engineers who also had a shop selling wireless receivers and domestic electrical appliances. I was pleased to accept their offer, which, with an essential degree of application by myself, could have led firstly to a City and Guilds and London Institute qualification and, perhaps, eventually to membership of the Institute Of Electrical Engineers. I took to the work as a duck takes to water and, after some twelve months, felt there was little more that I was likely to learn with them. The work was a continuous round of house wiring, works installations, maintenance of motors and starters installed in workplaces, general repairs, and battery charging. Although offering secure employment in a good trade it obviously did not have any potential for future advancement to heavy electrical engineering. The repair of wireless sets other than valve changing was practically non-existent. Although I acquired a good initial electrical work experience, I soon found the daily round somewhat monotonous, and not surprisingly, my thoughts, never far from flying, returned to it now with serious intent.

I had acquired from the Air Ministry a booklet on the subject of 'Careers for Boys in the Royal Air Force', which is still among my possessions. I had the necessary application forms and had taken the first step of seeking my former headmaster's sponsorship. I had indicated to my parents my wish to enter as an Aircraft Apprentice in the trade of Wireless Operator Mechanic, which seemed to be the obvious choice for me. The period of training at Cranwell would be for three years, and after a further three years of productive adult service, I would have the opportunity of selection for NCO pilot training. This was what I wanted and it seemed a tailor-made opportunity for me. Unfortunately, I met with opposition from my parents, particularly my mother, who had visions of her only son mangled in a pile of wreckage. So I had to relent and applied for an aero-apprenticeship with Alliot Verdon Roe and Company. I was quite thrilled to find myself accepted and gave little thought to the travelling involved; the time of the train I had to catch to be at my place of work by 0800 hours is permanently engraved on my mind - it was 0613, and the journey included twenty minutes walking time. But I didn't mind, I was getting nearer to my goal.

The working week at that time was forty-four hours which normally included Saturday morning. Apprentices could work overtime with a legal restriction of two hours a week for those under the age of eighteen. I got home about 1800 hours, and on three evenings a week, from September to April, had to attend classes to study for the higher certificate of education required by the City and Guilds and London Institute as a preparatory qualification for admission to diploma courses in the engineering trades. The subjects included English, Science, Mathematics, and Engineering Drawing. I had already started this course after leaving day school and was in the second year of it. Home study was also a prominent feature. One was not considered to be a qualified engineering tradesman until reaching the age of twenty-one ("Done his time"- as the saying went) with a City and Guilds Diploma to prove it. In those days, apprenticeships required serious application and study, usually for seven years. Avro was a member of the Hawker-Siddeley Group of companies, and aircraft in production at that time were Hawker Hinds for Persia, Avro Tutors for the

RAF, the Avro Rota, which was the Cierva Auto-Gyro made under licence and, on the main production line, the Avro Anson. Mention of the Anson brings to mind a little ditty frequently heard on the Anson assembly line; it was sung to the tune of 'The Ovaltinies', a popular Sunday morning commercial programme broadcast from Radio Luxembourg sponsored by the makers of the beverage Ovaltine. The words were: -

We are the Anson fairies,

Happy men and boys.

We work all day in Avro's workshops,

When the buzzer goes the work stops.

When we are tired and weary we go and have a scow.

We all know Professor Dobson,

Old man Rigg and Mr Thomson,

May they all grow old with knobs on,

Happy men and boys.

(Dobson - prominent member of Roy Chadwick's design team. Rigg and Thomson - production managers. Scow - waste some time in the toilets, where a man was employed to ensure we didn't waste too much of it).

Whilst I was happier to be among aeroplanes and those who made them, the hankering for flying was still there, I wanted to get airborne, and I was not going to be satisfied until that ambition was achieved. Quite unexpectedly, the answer to my dilemma came in the form of a change in parental attitude. One day, my father, always more understanding of the youthful desire for a faster action lifestyle, told me that he had been discussing the matter further with my mother, who had now indicated her consent, reluctantly, to my entry into the RAF, and he suggested that I should re-submit my application. It was then about April 1937, but as I had already gone through the initial stage for entry as an Aircraft Apprentice I thought it would be a straightforward matter. However, on writing to the Air Ministry, I was informed that by the time of the next entry of Aircraft Apprentices in August, I would be past the age limit of seventeen years. The same letter advised me of an alternative which, as I was keen to fly, would, subject to training achievement and selection, guarantee immediate employment on flying duties on completion of technical training. I could enter under a training scheme that had been introduced in 1934 and present myself for final selection in September 1937, which was only a month later, and I would just make the age limit of seventeen years and three months. The entry conditions were identical, and as I had the necessary educational qualifications for AA, it was simply a matter of going through the nomination procedure again. Air Ministry also explained that whilst the technical training would be for Wireless Operator, it would be possible at a later date to take the conversion course to Wireless Operator Mechanic, which would put me exactly where I would have been with the earlier entry as an AA, and possibly without any loss of time. Furthermore, my initial training would be with the apprentices at Cranwell except that it would be of sixteen months duration instead of three years.

So, I had to get a move on. Firstly, my former headmaster's nomination again, but this time on the new application forms, followed a little later by an interview with three elderly members of the local education authority who seemed convinced that I was planning to run away from home. One member said that my signature looked remarkably like my father's and, after questioning me at length in regard to the same, required me to produce an on-the-spot specimen signature. I began to fear that they were going to delay the process for further written confirmation of parental consent. However, they obviously gave their endorsement as I shortly received from the Air Ministry the necessary instructions regarding pre-entry medical requirements and documentation to attend the final Entry Selection Board at RAF West Drayton on the 20th September. This would take a working week commencing on that date, which was a Monday. No bother, nothing in the world would have stopped me.

Chapter I
Youth Entry and Training

Arrival was made easy from being met and assembled at the London destination railway station, from where we were escorted to West Drayton by rail and then on to the RAF Reception Establishment by road.

I have no clear recollection of what happened immediately after our arrival at RAF West Drayton except that we seemed, somewhat strangely, to be put together in the small dormitories in groups that formed the basis of our future friendships. But I shall never forget the next morning, which started with what seemed to be a never-ending session of running around in our birthday suits or waiting wrapped in a blanket at the behest of medical officers, mostly civilians, who seemed to be everywhere in unlimited number. West Drayton was the home of the Central Trade Test Board who, besides being the authority governing training standards and examinations, was responsible for assessing our suitability for technical training and particularly for our chosen trade. In this department, it was explained to me that my choice of the wireless trade, whilst offering the best opportunity for flying duty was, because of its technical complexities, the most difficult of the three choices available to youth entrants; the other two being armaments and photography. They did, however, seem to be suitably impressed with my previous work experience as an electrical apprentice and aero-apprentice.

There were interviews with RAF officers, much be-medalled, and all specially chosen members of the flying branch. On mentioning my hope of eventual selection for flying duties, I was left in no doubt that flying was a privilege to be earned rather than expected. Motivation was obviously high on the agenda, and I was questioned at length and in some detail about my interest in the flying service, its history and traditions, also the notable personalities I had learned of in my reading. Model aircraft figured in discussion, and I was asked particularly about the world war types of which I had claimed to have made scale models. The last day was spent mostly waiting to be told of selection or failure and I found myself in a rather anxious state as the time passed into late afternoon. However, I was called at last and told that I was accepted for training as a Wireless Operator and would proceed to Cranwell the next day. Then followed the induction procedure and, with three others at the same time, I took the Oath of Allegiance to King George the Sixth, His Heirs, and his Successors. A brief word of congratulation from the attesting officer, a stern reminder of our future responsibilities as members of the Royal Air Force, then a hand-shake. We were then put through the final documentation procedures and allocated our service numbers; mine was 551757. All our numbers started with 55 that were the block of numbers allocated to our type of entry. Those of us who had been selected were a very happy band of youths that evening.

Nothing was done at West Drayton to create false impressions of things to come. The conditions were, to say the most, basic but thoroughly hygienic. I do not remember seeing any non-commissioned personnel other than the aircraftman orderly whose only job seemed to be the cleaning of our dormitory and ablution facilities. No doubt he had other duties. He was friendly, communicative, and most helpful. But for all his kindness he got into his bed one night to find that he had several grasshoppers as bedfellows. The grassed areas of the camp were teeming with them, but I hasten to add denial of any involvement with this cruelly youthful prank. There were also apprentice clerks from their nearby training school at Ruislip getting hands-on experience with our documentation procedures, and escorting us in parties to wherever we were required to go.

I don't suppose any who were there will ever forget the short rotund officer who was occasionally seen walking around the camp. He wore a naval beard, and it was rumoured that he had been branded on the chin whilst held prisoner by the Germans during the war. Good enough, perhaps, for youthful imagination, but I suspect very far from the truth. He was Group Captain Vivian Gaskell-Blackburn, a former naval officer who, I imagine, had been permitted to retain his beard on transfer from the RNAS when it was amalgamated with the RFC to form the RAF on 1st April 1918. The dining room, which never seemed crowded or boisterous, was furnished with wooden tables and forms that were scrubbed white. Food was plain, plentiful, and quite acceptable to our eager appetites. The breakfast marmalade and teatime jam were placed on the tables in soup plates and were a great attraction for the multitudinous wasps, but they did not diminish our enthusiasm for eating. Ablution facilities were basic and for ordinary washing purposes, consisted of a zinc-lined trough with loose metal basins and a centrally located hot water source. There was, of course, a bathhouse where one could have a hot bath in the evening.

The morning of our departure came at last - Friday. We were addressed by the bearded Station Commander who, after adding his own congratulations on our selection, told us, more or less, what we had already been told by a letter from the Air Ministry. He went to some length to explain the career that was being offered to us. He mentioned that some of us, quite early in our service, would probably be recommended for training as Air Observers when we would have the rank of corporal. Some of us would eventually be selected to continue our service to the maximum of twenty-four years. I must say that I experienced a great feeling of pride. After a jolly lunch, we met Warrant Officer Bill Hoy, who had come from Cranwell, where he was to be our Wing Warrant Officer, to escort us to our training location. He had the squarest shoulders that I have ever seen; so square they seemed quite unnatural. He had a most commanding voice and manner. Under his supervision, we entrained for Sleaford. Then, by road to RAF Cranwell, where we were deposited adjacent to our accommodation in East Camp.

CHAPTER II
RAF CRANWELL
ELECTRICAL AND WIRELESS SCHOOL
NO.3 (YOUTH ENTRY) WING

On alighting from the vehicles we found ourselves in the space formed by the two lower legs and the horizontal bar of the 'H Type' barrack block that was to be home for many of us for the next sixteen months. We were greeted by a rather frightening cacophony of catcalls from those already resident; "Rookies, get some in, you'll be sorry" and other raucous noises delivered in the manner of youths who had the advantage of a little experience. Every window, top and bottom, on either side of us was crowded by cheeky-faced youths, all shouting and grimacing. We were to behave in like manner in our turn.

I found myself, as Air Ministry had told me, in the same location as I would have been had I arrived a month earlier as an Aircraft Apprentice. We were sorted in alphabetical order to our squadrons. I was in 'B' Squadron No.3 Wing which occupied the barrack block adjacent to the point of our arrival. Aircraft Apprentices were in the neighbouring barrack blocks occupied by Nos. 1 and 2 Wings; we shared the same mess hall, places of instruction, and instructors. We wore the same brass identifying sleeve badge of a four-bladed propeller in a circlet - a device worn initially by RFC technicians - and our hats and caps had a distinguishing coloured band in the squadron colours; for 'B' Squadron No.3 Wing, these were red and navy blue chequers.

We were kitted-out during the next morning (Saturday) with the station tailor in attendance to ensure good fitting with a little room for growth. There was never any problem in getting replacements for garments outgrown. A smart appearance and good deportment was of the greatest importance, and woe to he who did not measure up to the required standard. After a few days of feeling miserably homesick, I began to settle into the routine and to feel that I was doing what I wanted to do. We soon felt privileged to be members of the Royal Air Force and that there was a place for us in its future. We were well clad, well fed, and looked after by hand-picked instructors, mostly old enough to be our fathers, in fact, mostly fathers themselves. Although discipline was strict it was fair, and not the repressive type. No one was ever bullied or humiliated by instructors. Each squadron had a commanding officer of flight lieutenant rank specially selected from the flying branch. 'B' Squadron had Flight Lieutenant Jones, a tall, distinguished-looking officer whose office was located on the upper storey of the block. We seldom saw him except for Saturday mornings when he was on parade at the head of his squadron. The one authority mostly in direct contact by day was the squadron flight sergeant, who was the squadron disciplinarian, physical training instructor, drill instructor, our administrator, guide, and mentor. He was Flight Sergeant Harry Wade, small, pugnacious with a nose that looked like it had been filleted. I never saw him display signs of anger; he raised his voice only to be heard. He had the happy knack of being able to deal with serious situations in jocular manner, but one was never left in any doubt about his meaning. I liked and respected him very much and felt his reciprocation. He was assisted by a corporal in drill and physical training and in the administrative role by boy NCOs, who were locally promoted to be the sixteen leading boys in the squadron and from whom the eight corporal boys were eventually chosen; I was to hold both these local ranks in due course. The training at Cranwell, as at all the youth training establishments, was comprehensive, comprising general service training, physical training outdoors and in the well-appointed gymnasium, technical training for our chosen trade, and continued general education with emphasis on mathematics and science appropriate to the technical side of our wireless training. It was thorough, and it was good, not unlike a boarding school with a background of good order and military discipline and the same sort of pranks practised by high-spirited youths wherever they are to be found in number. I vividly remember one very cruel prank that was perpetrated a few weeks after our arrival, about the Guy Fawkes time of November 1937. There was one boy who, from the very beginning, was clearly a misfit. His physical development was not as advanced as that of the majority. He seemed to be a little younger than the average and was awkward at drill, and in technical training was having great difficulty. Whilst he could have been as much as twelve months younger than the average had he been accepted at the minimum entry age of fifteen and a half, I doubt it. The average age for entry selection was about sixteen and a half to avoid the obvious problems if training was completed much before reaching the age of eighteen, the legal age for entry to adult service. To be sent out younger than eighteen placed special responsibilities on the receiving unit. I was quite unaware of the developing plot, which resulted in his best boots, always on display under the foot of his bed, having the toes blown out by fireworks of the rather powerful Thunder Flash variety. The culprits were soon brought to task, and strict disciplinary action meted out. The boy himself was removed, presumably after consultation with his parents, who were no doubt advised that he had been found to be an unlikely subject for whom they should exercise the option of free release before the expiration of

5

the initial three-month period. I am sure it was the best thing for him, as he clearly did not have the makings of a successful career in even the lowliest RAF trade.

The Trade training instructors were mostly civilian, some former RN and RAF with a good many members of the RAF Education Branch that was entirely civilian staffed. The barrack room atmosphere was generally of a high standard, and friendships were quickly formed. Bullying or acrimony was soon dealt with by the boys themselves, usually the boy NCOs who were quick to intervene and use their authority. Mostly behaviour was good and responsible in character. Boys were selected from stable family backgrounds, generally of the artisan class, each with the higher secondary level of education required for those chosen to be future long-service technical warrant officers and senior NCOs. Any who did not match the standard was soon spotted and quietly removed from the scene, usually being offered the option of voluntary discharge. Boys found unable to grasp the complexities of wireless technical training were offered the choice of being sent to Eastchurch or Farnborough to try armament or photography or, if over the age of seventeen and a quarter, offered a lower level of training commensurate with their re-assessed ability. The initial selection process ensured that this action was most unusual.

Our barrack blocks were of the 'H' type in plan form, consisting of two floors, each having four dormitories on the two sides connected by wide central corridors giving access to toilet, bathroom facilities, and the dormitories. Each of the eight dormitories accommodated some forty boys. Before entering the dormitory, one passed through a small square ablution area which was furnished with some twelve porcelain wash-basins, each served with hot and cold water taps, the area being separated from the dormitory by the entrance door and short partition walls which broke the view of the two banks of basins. Quite civilised, really, by comparison with what we had experienced during our short stay at West Drayton. Along the length of the dormitory, there were four wooden topped tables, each with two wooden forms all the wood was scrubbed white. The floors were covered with standard brown linoleum that shone like a mirror. The effect was of a thoroughly clean and hygienic atmosphere wherein there was a high degree of essential order and disciplined living. A corporal boy was in charge of each dormitory and usually occupied the small room at the entrance, known as the bunk; his two leading boys had their bed-spaces at each end of the dormitory. The boy NCOs were in complete charge during non-working hours and were at all times in a position of responsible authority.

The dormitories were furnished with iron beds of the Macdonald type that were made in two pieces so that the foot could be pushed under the head. The unyielding bed base was of interwoven broad metal straps, and the mattresses consisted of three horsehair-filled biscuits. We had four blankets, two sheets, and a pillow that was round in cross-section and also stuffed with horsehair. Beside each bed was an open-fronted wooden locker, and above the head of each bed, fixed to the wall, was a steel locker with lockable steel doors; this contained our kit. Each working day, the routine required the beds to be closed-up. Biscuits were piled so that the front edges were aligned with the front edge of the bedstead. The bedding, folded to a standard pattern, was placed on top of the biscuits with the sheets sandwiched between three blankets and the fourth blanket, folded lengthwise, wrapped around them. The whole bundle was then displayed with the folded edges neatly displayed to the front and the pillow placed on top. Wooden locker placed in line with the foot of the bed with knife, fork, spoon, mug and other items of small kit laid-out on the shelves in conformity with the standard layout. Best boots and gym shoes were placed under the foot of the bed. Everything was perfectly aligned along the whole length of the dormitory. Our kit in the metal locker was likewise laid-out in a standard pattern. Webbing equipment, kit bag, and rifle were hung on pegs under the wall-mounted locker. The dormitory was left in this state throughout the working day, thus making inspection easy.

We were, of course, required to maintain a very high standard and the linoleum was expected to have a good shine each morning. To achieve this, it was essential to sweep and shine ones allotted bed-space daily, but polish was usually applied only once a week. There were no electric floor polishers in those days. We used things called 'bumpers' which were long-handled polishers with a very heavy hinged polishing head. These were used to good effect to produce the daily shine. Friday night was 'bullshit' night when everything in sight got a good cleaning whether it needed it or not, the linoleum being given special attention. Soft floor polish was evenly applied by hand using a suitable cloth, usually a piece of old blanket, and the shine was obtained by the energetic use of the bumper, the final shine being applied with a piece of folded blanket under its head. Summer or winter, it usually entailed getting oneself into a lather of sweat. Having polished the floor, we then protected it by walking about with pieces of folded blanket under our footwear. As each boy was responsible for his own piece of the floor, it is easy to imagine the shouts of objection produced by any departure from the established safeguards.

Saturday morning marked the end of the working week when we had a full kit inspection and parade. So our personal kit and equipment also received special attention on Friday evenings. Webbing equipment had to be blancoed using the tables specially provided in the bathhouse. The numerous brasses, buckles, etc., had to be polished, rifles cleaned and polished, brass butt plate shining, bayonets burnished and scabbards shining with heel-ball, wooden lockers scrubbed, everything had to be clean. The dustbin, which occupied its allotted place outside the entrance door, had to be burnished, the unpainted handles and rims of the two adjacent fire buckets were also burnished. It may seem totally unnecessary to go to such ridiculous extremes, but the effect of filthy essentials such as these in the obvious best location outside the entrance door to the dormitories was not only seen to be disreputable but also quite out of keeping with the standard of cleanliness and order required. There was no need for disinfectant; there was no infection, just absolute cleanliness and good hygiene. There were, of course, other things to be cleaned such as the windows, bath and toilet facilities, the tables and forms to be scrubbed, these chores being allotted by roster detail devised and administered by the boy NCOs.

After the Saturday morning kit inspection, it was time for the ceremonial parade. The enormous parade ground of East Camp was well filled by the three wings that together produced something like two thousand youths in full marching order with rifles and bayonets. The youth entrants had their own brass and pipe bands and buglers —all usually on parade. It was only on these parade occasions that one really came to appreciate the numbers actually under training. The parade was very demanding with its routine inspection by the parade commander, usually, the officer commanding the school (Group Captain J H Simpson during my time), followed by the salutes and march-pasts in column and line abreast, advances in review order, in fact, the full complement of parade manoeuvres. The Electrical and Wireless School dwelt in the shadow of the RAF College, the commandant of the college being also commandant of the whole station. Not surprisingly, there were common standards. Our weekly ceremonial parades were identical to those of the college, and on the last Saturday of each month, our parade was taken by the commandant himself (Air Vice Marshal J E A Baldwin) and took the precise form of the passing-out parade. We were glad when it was all over for another week, and we could get out of our gear, have some lunch, and relax for the remainder of the weekend. Of course, there was always swotting to be done and plenty of sporting activities to take part in.

Saturday evening was time for the weekly visit to the station cinema, always anticipated, particularly if the lead actress was a well-known glamour-girl. Sometimes, we also went on Wednesday evenings if studies and finances permitted. The cinema seemed to be a particular responsibility of the station warrant officer, who was known as 'Pecker Smith.' He was always to be seen at the top of the entrance steps where his presence was sufficient to ensure Good Order and Air Force Discipline, also an unpaid entry that, if one is to believe the claims of some boys, he did not always accomplish. The cost of admission was four pence which was a large slice of our weekly pocket money. We were paid nine pence per day, which is five shillings and three pence per week, the equivalent of twenty-six pence in our modern currency. Of this, we actually received two shillings a week, ten pence today, the balance being kept for us until we went on leave. We had to provide our own soap, toothpaste, metal polish, boot polish etc., but we seemed to manage all right. We occasionally got a measure of financial support from home and usually came back from leave well stocked with the basic essentials. There was also the occasional parcel of mother's baking. We were well provided with the necessities of life and really wanted for nothing. With a bit of sensible financial control, we managed on our two bob a week and could even afford the occasional cup of char and a wad at the YMCA.

The cinema was, of course, also used for the presentation of excellent plays and concerts produced by the station's amateur dramatic society. There were also talks and lectures by visiting personalities one of whom I found particularly interesting and remember well. He was a diplomat from the German Embassy, typically Teutonic in build and appearance. His name was Von Rinteln and his subject - 'The Zimmerman Telegram.'

There was always a Sunday morning church parade for which one was detailed in rotation, as the church was unable to accommodate the full complement of each religious denomination. Of course, one could always attend the evening services, but the church parade was obligatory when detailed according to denomination. Church parades required us to march dressed in best blue, and we were always led by one of the bands. By comparison with other parades, it was relaxed, but marching to the usual high standard was expected. Our daily work routine required us to march to classes and between places of instruction. Marching was the responsibility of the boy NCOs and there was no nonsense as adult NCOs were always on the lookout for any deviation from normal standards. The instructional buildings covered a large area and consisted mainly of a bewildering number of wooden huts, most of which dated back to the earliest days of the RNAS, and were used by the RAF college from 1920 until the present college building became available in 1929. It was in one of these huts, and on the adjacent south aerodrome that we received instruction in visual signalling - flags and lamp - under the tutelage of an instructor known to all as 'Willie Wink,' formerly of the Royal Navy and so called because of the little flashing light he used for indoor instruction. This considerable expanse of huts was dominated by the only brick building that was formally called the Technical Block, but better known as the 'Taj Mahal' because it always looked so pristine in its white paint. This is where we came to grips with the technical equipment that we were required to know thoroughly and operate efficiently. The instructors in this block, and in the neighbouring wooden 'Electrical Block,' were RAF personnel of corporal rank. These were the only uniformed technical instructors and were, as one would expect, well-experienced with the latest equipment in operational use.

Wednesday afternoons were dedicated to sport, and one was expected to take part in some organised activity, be it rugger, soccer, team training, fencing, gymnastics, or whatever. Cross-Country running was popular, but there was no opportunity for scrounging. The gymnasium was well-appointed, and there were always willing instructors for boxing and other indoor sporting activities. The vast expanses of the grassed aerodromes provided, at their eastern extremities, space for ample sports pitches with goalposts set in ground-sockets so that they could be conveniently removed for safety when flying was taking place. The Cranwell Stadium was located just beyond the western boundary of the north aerodrome; here the Cranwell Tattoo was held annually, and the stadium was the venue for many RAF and Inter-Service sporting activities. There were frequent evening Boxing Tournaments at which our own Flight Lieutenant Jones seemed always to be the appointed referee. He was obviously keenly interested and had a thorough knowledge of the RAF Boxing Association rules. These required that only the contestants should be in the ring during the actual sparring when absolute silence was expected. The referee was positioned at the side of the ring and slightly above it. Spectators were permitted to offer the usual encouragement between rounds, but during bouts, conduct was generally of the highest calibre. Otherwise the fight was stopped and offenders removed to be effectively dealt with.

For a youngster of my inclination, Cranwell was a place of great wonder. Historically, it dated back to late 1915 when the Admiralty, seeking suitable flying training sites for the Royal Naval Air Service, acquired some three thousand acres of land to the west of Cranwell village. Bisected in the east-west direction by the road from Sleaford to Nottingham it lent itself conveniently to the creation of two aerodromes, one to the north of the road, the other to the south. Accommodation, both working and domestic, was developed between the south aerodrome and the road commencing with the construction of West Camp. The building of East Camp, on the same side of the road, soon followed and was thoughtfully separated from West Camp by the clever use of the natural landscape. In naval tradition, the establishment was named as though it was a ship, and RNAS Cranwell became known appropriately as 'HMS Daedalus'. Whilst both aerodromes were used for flying training, the north aerodrome, on which only technical buildings were built, was also the location chosen for naval airship and balloon training and is commemorated to this day by the continuing use of the name 'Lighter Than Air Road' for the main access road to it. An Electrical and Wireless School was established at Cranwell in May 1916, and the RNAS Boys Training Wing came into being during 1918. Following the amalgamation of the RNAS and RFC on 1st April 1918 to form the RAF, a School Of Technical Trailing (Boys) was formed. In May 1921, this became the Boys Wing, Cadet College until October 1925 when it was renamed No.4 (Apprentices) Wing, continuing until January 1936. The

RAF Electrical and Wireless School was transferred to Cranwell from Flowerdown, Wiltshire, in August 1929. Established custom required that youth training should be segregated from adult training and this was conveniently achieved by the use of East Camp with its existing accommodation facilities, as the new RAF College buildings were, by that time, available.

It is probably appropriate to mention that the segregation policy was not only based on age difference but the object of youth training, which, being to train boys for long-service careers and advancement to the senior NCO ranks, was somewhat different in character to the training provided for adult recruits who were initially recruited to short-term engagements usually of seven years. These offered no prospect of advancement beyond the attainment, by trade test, of the top trade classification of leading aircraftman. Re-enlistment to twelve years, which was a pre-requisite to the maximum pensionable engagement of twenty-four years, was very selective and based on a personal service record of the highest order.

The south aerodrome was used almost entirely by the college, but the north aerodrome was the flying training site for the Electrical and Wireless School. Here we did our initial flying training in the Vickers Valentias that served as flying classrooms. Later, in the rear cockpits of the Westland Wapitis and Wallaces, we were left to our own devices. Here, it was simply a matter of success or failure, so different from the warm, cosy environment of the classroom or wireless cabin. The noise also produced an entirely different effect from that which was artificially applied to headphones during ground instruction. The wireless equipment was installed at the back of the cockpit and required one to get down on the knees to operate it. The transmitter and receiver were held in their mounting frame by cord-elastic to minimise shock effect, but vibration was always present, often making it a problem to set the receiver tuning dials, which had an aggravating tendency to wander off tune. Some resorted to the use of a dab of chewing gum as a means of jamming the dials, but this was not popular in view of the messy result, which the next user had to tolerate. The proper way was to use the hands; even if one was writing - using the message pad on the right knee - it was possible to hold the radio frequency tuning dial on spot tune with the left hand or follow any tendency the received signal may have had to wander; wireless transmissions were not very stable in those days. We were fastened in by what was known as a monkey chain, which was, in fact, a length of stranded cable anchored to the cockpit floor and attached to a ring at the lower back of the parachute harness. This allowed one to stand and move around as much as the Scarff ring mounting (for the machine gun) on the rim of the cockpit would allow. There was no voice communication with the pilot and instructions were passed by message-slip handed over the dividing fuselage decking.

Nothing much had changed since the war. In fact, the Westland Wapiti had succeeded the wartime deHavilland DH9A and had been designed so that DH9A components could be incorporated as a matter of economy. The only real advancements were to be found in the increased power and efficiency of engines, whilst wireless equipment, due to advanced design techniques, was reduced in size with increased efficiency, now enabling aircraft to carry both transmitters and receivers, thus making air to ground communication possible, whereas the wartime aircraft had been able to carry only a transmitter albeit of considerably greater size and primitive design. There was considerable extraneous noise, from the engine and slipstream besides the atmospheric noise that was generally found as a component of wireless reception in aircraft. Whilst many did not enjoy the flying side of the training, I revelled in it and somehow managed to complete all the airborne exercises without the problems that seemed to attend the efforts of others.

During September 1938, we were to hear something of the so-called Munich Crisis. The Prime Minister, Neville Chamberlain, returning from Munich after talks with Adolph Hitler, emerged from his aircraft waving a piece of paper and proclaiming "Peace in our time." Hitler had been making a series of territorial claims in an effort to regain territories lost to Germany by Allied conditions imposed after the war. Apparently, Chamberlain agreed not to interfere with the latest claim for the return of the Sudetanland but had made it quite clear that any attempt to regain territory in Poland, with whom we had a Treaty of Friendship and Alliance, would result in war. He had taken Hitler's word on this in apparent good faith. In the event, he had bought the United Kingdom a little more time to prepare for war. Shortly after this, a second Electrical and Wireless School was formed at Yatesbury and named No.2 E&WS whilst Cranwell was renamed No.1 E&WS. Our training courses were shortened by two months, and my course designation was changed from 9B1 to 8B11. This meant that we would now pass-out in November 1938 (8/11) instead of January 1939 (9/1). The change had no apparent effect on the training routine, but I suppose there was some reduction in time spent on drill and other non-technical periods. Bearing in mind that for my entry, the two months included the loss of the Christmas and New Year leave period, there was, in fact, no significant effect on training by the reduction of the course length.

Also, on the north aerodrome, where the hangers were still identified by their original RNAS designation of shed, there were two sheds, 'J' and 'K', which housed instructional airframes, many of which were of considerable antiquity. One of my greatest delights was the privilege of getting into these to handle equipment from earlier times and let my mind run riot as greater meaning was given to my remembered reading of pioneering exploits.

In due course, I became a leading boy and proudly wore the identifying miniature single chevron on both sleeves. Subsequently, I was promoted to corporal boy with double chevrons, and with this local rank - there were only eight per squadron - I was to learn something of great value to me in my early adult service - responsibility, together with a little experience of administration and disciplinary duties of the kind expected of junior NCOs. Passing-out time soon came around with its attendant anxieties. The minimum pass mark was forty per cent, with the ability to send and receive Morse at eighteen words per minute. This was the norm, and the majority passed-out at this level with the trade classification of Aircraftman 2nd Class, (AC2). For Aircraftman 1st Class, (AC1), a pass at sixty per cent with Morse at twenty-two words per minute was required, and for Leading Aircraftman, a pass at eighty per cent with Morse at twenty-five words per minute was the highest accolade possible, except that one was required to serve twelve months satisfactory adult service before being granted authority to wear the coveted propeller badges of the LAC and receive the pay for that trade classification. The examinations, which lasted about a week were, as always, conducted by the Central Trade Test Board brought in from West Drayton and included all subjects in both theoretical and technical aspects, also practical applications. To gain advancement from AC2 to AC1 and progressively to LAC after completing initial training required one to be recommended for examination by the Central Trade Test Board involving a week at West Drayton, it was not easy to make progress in the aircraftman classifications unless one was prepared to apply oneself to serious study and preparation. The standard required of technical tradesmen was understandably very high. However, I was fortunate enough to obtain a pass above eighty per cent with the requisite twenty-five words per minute in Morse and, therefore, passed-out as Aircraftman First Class. (Leading Aircraftman on probation). I was also awarded the prize for Best All-Round Boy - a handsomely bound volume embossed with the Royal Air Force Crest in gold. Entitled 'Living Rough' by the well-known author Kenneth Mackenzie, it has survived to become a treasured possession in my library.

I was selected for flying duties together with twenty-odd others, about twenty per cent of the entry strength. We were permitted to nominate three choices of station for our first posting, and I chose two where there were Army Co-operation squadrons and one Bomber station as it was at these that air observers, my next step, as I then saw it, would be required. I got the bomber choice and was posted for flying duty with No. 102 (B) Squadron, then based at RAF Driffield, East Yorkshire. When I said goodbye to Harry Wade, he said to me, "let's see you back here soon for the conversion course". I remember not feeling very interested at that time, but I sometimes wish I had done it, although it is difficult to imagine what effect it may have had on my subsequent career.

I look back on Cranwell with great affection. I wanted to go there; I went there and did what I had chosen to do. I liked it, and without any conscious effort to do anything outstanding, I had the satisfaction of passing out with a place among the very few top-scorers. It was soon to stand me in good stead, but there were dark days ahead which, in our youthful enthusiasm, we were unable to discern, not that we gave the slightest thought to it. So I left my RAF Alma Mater on the 24th November 1938 and, leaving the dormitory of which I had been privileged to be the Corporal Boy-in-charge for the duration of my time spent in that exalted rank, I was delighted to see as I passed the full-length mirror in the ablution area, written boldly in soap 'Good luck, Bill.' It was a mild day for November, as I recall, and I was pleased to find on arrival at Sleaford railway station that I had AC2 Arnold Oddy as my travelling companion; he was posted to No.77 Squadron also at Driffield and sister squadron to 102 from which it had recently been re-formed. We arrived at RAF Driffield in the late afternoon, having walked, in full marching order with full packs on our backs and kit bags on our shoulders, from the railway station, a distance of about one and a half miles. After all, we were eighteen years of age and no longer boys as we had been on our awakening at Cranwell that morning.

CHAPTER III
PEACEFUL SKIES AND REARMAMENT

On the 24th November 1938, I joined No. 102 (Bomber) Squadron - later to become No. 102 (Ceylon) Squadron - at Royal Air Force Station Driffield. I was posted for duty with 'B' Flight. The squadron was, at that time, commanded by Wing Commander C F Toogood, 'A' Flight by Squadron Leader S S Murray, and 'B' Flight by Squadron Leader Parker. The squadron, together with its sister squadron, No.77, was part of No.4 Group, which was the only Night Bomber Group in the RAF; in fact, the only night bomber element in any of the world's air forces.

I had been trained as a wireless operator in the Boys Wing of the Electrical and Wireless School at Cranwell under an Expansion Scheme Programme, introduced in 1934, intended to train boys between 15 and 171/4 as Wireless Operators. I had passed out as a prize-winner with the highest possible trade classification and had been selected for flying duties, my next objective was to qualify as an Aerial Gunner, thereby ensuring continuing employment as a member of an aircraft crew, progressing to Corporal Air Observer after three years, and subsequently to Sergeant Pilot after a further four years. After a total of twelve years flying duty, it was intended that tradesmen, that we all were at that time, would be returned to their basic trade duties in the rank they would normally have otherwise attained. (It should be noted that employment as members of aircraft crews, being of a temporary nature, carried only acting rank above trade classification. It was not unusual to be returned to aircraftman classification after periods of flying duty. The term 'Aircrew' had not yet been introduced, and one was simply posted 'for flying duty' or for duty as a 'member of an aircraft crew'. The maximum engagement at this time was twenty-four years. Such was the career opportunity for boys selected for flying duties, but we were technical tradesmen trained for long-term engagements and future advancement to the warrant officer and senior non-commissioned ranks. From these boys, it was intended to select the nucleus of the future requirement of flying personnel, as then envisaged, to crew the increasing number of squadrons planned for the expansion scheme. I was eighteen years of age and events were to alter the career plan for most of us.

RAF Driffield was a new station. Built to a standard pattern for the additional stations required under the expansion programme, a little work still had to be completed in the domestic areas. The new style barrack blocks, a more compact two-storey 'H' Type, were located on one side of the parade ground with the dining room and NAAFI adjacent. The barrack rooms were smaller than at Cranwell but furnished in a more relaxed and modern style to accommodate twelve men.

Of course, the daily routine required some degree of similarity with the morning work parade and personnel being marched to their places of work after roll call. The aerodrome was the usual large grassed area with four hangars to house the aircraft of the two squadrons, with a fifth hangar, to the rear of them, for major aircraft maintenance as part of the station workshops organisation. Very few aerodromes had runways, these being found at very few locations where they were necessary due to unusual features of the ground condition. There were no runways at Driffield, the only hard surfaces being the tarmac aprons in front of and around the hangars.

The day after arrival, I went through the routine arrival procedure, drew my flying clothing and parachute, was allocated a flying-clothing locker, shown the locations of essential services, and introduced to those with whom I would need to have frequent contact. I was shortly ushered into the flight commander's office and was greeted warmly enough. I was then handed a file and told to read the contents. I found myself reading an 'Order Of The Day' issued by the Air Officer Commanding-in-Chief, Bomber Command. The order went to some length to explain the importance of the wireless operator's role in bomber aircraft and pointed out that an aircraft had never been lost due to failure of the Signals Service. Having read it, I was told to read it again and then sign the attached certificate to indicate my having read and understood it. I felt my chest expanding somewhat at the enormity of this new responsibility. The importance of the wireless member of a bomber crew is, perhaps, best explained by stating that we did not have any cockpit aids to navigation at that time. There was no radar, and navigation by maps, charts, rulers, dividers, course and speed calculators, etc., was at best rudimentary. But we did have wireless direction finding, a system that depended very much on the skill of the wireless operator for its value to navigation. Used to good effect, a wireless operator could bring the aircraft to an overhead position at any station equipped with the facility. As an aid to navigation, the wireless operator could, provided wireless communication was possible, obtain bearings using ground stations and actually fix the position of the aircraft. Also of great use to us was the maritime rotating wireless beacons primarily intended for the use of coastwise sea traffic. With the aid of a stopwatch, the directional transmissions of these beacons could be used to obtain reasonably accurate bearings. There were several of them convenient to the North Sea and English Channel.

The squadron had just started the process of conversion from the Handley Page 'Heyford'- the last of the biplane bombers - to the Armstrong Whitworth 'Whitley.' Not surprisingly, there were many tales of 'Heyford' events, and I was soon given a first-hand account of what were undoubtedly the squadrons, perhaps the RAF's, worst peacetime catastrophe. I well remember the news to which the nation awoke on the 13th December 1936 when it was reported that several bomber aircraft had come to grief on the Lancashire/Yorkshire boundaries. Little did I realise that within two years, I would become a flying member of the squadron involved. RAF Aldergrove (now Belfast airport) was a well-used venue for bombing and gunnery practices over nearby Lough Neagh. On the previous day, seven Heyfords of 102 Squadron left Aldergrove in formation bound for their base at RAF Finningley and encountered fog with severe ice accretion conditions over the mainland.

Only one aircraft, piloted by Sgt Biddulph, arrived without incident. The other six fared as follows:

K4864 Sgt Williams crashed at Gainsborough.

K5188 P/O Gill-Murray force landed ten miles north of York and proceeded to Finningley next day.

K6900 Sgt V C Otter crashed into hills at Hebden Bridge. Sgt Church, LAC Clements and AC 2 Bodenham were killed. Sgt Otter was seriously injured, sustaining extensive burns to his face. (He was later posted to 77 Sqn on its reformation but was still undergoing frequent specialist treatment for quite sometime after my arrival at Driffield).

K4874 F/L Villiers and crew were forced to abandon their aircraft, which became out of control due to ice jamming the controls. F/L Villiers, P/O Tomlin, and AC Mackan landed safely by parachute, the latter sustaining slight injuries. The aircraft crashed near Oldham with no damage to property.

K4868 S/L Attwood (then squadron CO) force landed at Disley SE of Manchester and proceeded to Finningley next day.

K6898 P/O Clifford turned over, attempting to force land at Disley.

Handley Page presented their prototype HP38 design as the 'Heyford Express Bomber' (the production version was designated HP50), not because of its speed but because of the rapidity with which it could be refuelled and re-armed. The main part of the bomb load, consisting of ten 250 lb bombs, was contained in the thickened centre-section of the lower main plane, which was low enough to permit loading from ground level, whilst smaller bombs of 120 and 20 lbs could be loaded in light series carriers outboard of the main bomb cell, the doors of which were held in the closed position by cord elastic (bungee), as were the bomb doors of the Whitley. Access to the interior was through a hatch in the underside of the fuselage above the trailing edge of the lower wing, and one had to climb up using foot, and hand holds protruding from either side of the rear wing-supporting vee struts. I remember the sad case of a wireless operator who tried to enter whilst carrying a large 40 ampere-hour capacity accumulator, two of which were needed to supply the electrical and wireless systems. These accumulators were very heavy, and to move them in and out safely, one really required a helping hand from an assistant stationed in the hatch. However, this chap thought he would go it alone and, much to his embarrassment, lost his grip of the accumulator that fell straight through the lower main plane bomb cell, causing extensive damage.

The squadron did not yet have a long history. It was formed following the decision to intensify the strategic bombing campaign against long-range targets in Germany and was in action in France by September 1917 as a night bomber squadron equipped with FE2b aircraft. Its service in France was quite distinguished as indeed were some of its officers: Captain W J Harvey describes some of his experiences as an observer in his book "Raiders of the Night Sky" written under the pseudonym Nighthawk. Lieutenant J E P Levyns, one of several South Africans who served with the squadron, describes his experience as a pilot during the last two months of WW1 in his American-published book "The Disciplines of War."

The squadron was disbanded shortly after the end of WW1 but had been reformed on 1st October 1935 at Worthy Down by the usual expedient of taking a Flight from another squadron, in this case, No.7 (Heyford) Squadron. No. 102 Squadron had a full complement of Heyford Mark IIIs by the end of July 1936. In September it moved to Finningley, to Honnington in July 1937, thence to Driffield in July 1938. In June 1937, 'B' Flight became the nucleus of No.77 Squadron on its reformation, which thereby became a sister squadron. At the time of my arrival, 'B" Flight was still in the early stages of re-building, and the Whitleys held were Mark III with an odd Mark II. Conversion was not completed until the early spring of 1939, the Heyfords being progressively transferred mostly to 97 and 166 squadrons at RAF Leconfield. Although the squadron had a full complement of Whitley IIIs quite early in 1939, there was a shortage of flying personnel, and I have a recollection of what I then considered to be an awesome task in my personal responsibility for the routine inspections and servicing, at squadron level, of the wireless and electrical installations of two Whitleys, also a Heyford up to the time of their final disposal. The personnel state was progressively improved throughout the summer of 1939, and we were just about up to full strength by the declaration of war on 3rd September.

Aircraftman First Class Dennis Mackan was given the task of introducing me to the squadron routine, and I remember him with great affection for his warm friendship and help. Dennis was one of the longest-serving members of the squadron. We became good friends, and I was soon integrated and declared fit for crew duty. There were squadron and station duties that we all had to perform in addition to our normal flying and servicing tasks. One of these duties was that of Duty Signaller that a squadron wireless operator had to do, by roster, whenever night flying took place. Being a night bomber station, flying was on the agenda most nights when weather permitted. On such occasions, the Duty Pilot and the Duty Signaller were in charge. There was no Air Traffic Control organisation in those days, but a Duty Pilot was always present in the Duty Pilots Hut whenever flying was taking place. During the day, he was responsible for ensuring that the ground indicator indicated the landing direction and other signals related to winds and weather hoisted on the staff adjacent to the hut. For night flying he was on the aerodrome with the Duty Signaller. There were no runways, and a flare path had to be laid using gooseneck paraffin flares. A large flare known as the Money Flare, about three feet high and four feet in diameter, made of cotton waste held together in a stout wire basket and soaked with paraffin, was placed at the approach end of the flare-path. The Duty Signaller had two Aldis Lamps, one with a green lens, the other with a red lens. He and the Duty Pilot were stationed by the Money Flare, onto which paraffin was poured whenever an aircraft was about to land. The procedure was for an aircraft taxiing to the flare path to flash its aircraft identification letter on the upper and lower identification lights using a keying device in the cockpit. Seeing this, the Duty Signaller would call out, for example - "S for sugar on the ground, Sir". If all was clear, the D/P would respond with "S for sugar on the ground a Green," and the D/S would then flash 'S' with the green lamp sighted on the aircraft cockpit. A pilot wishing to land would likewise flash his letter, but this time, the D/S would call out "L for London in the air, Sir," and would be instructed to flash a red or green depending on the state of the circuit, Although Duty Signaller could be a rather cold stint, even when wearing fur-lined boots and Irvin flying jacket, and also very smelly due to the burning paraffin, I really quite enjoyed it.

One station duty that I particularly hated arose in that winter of 1938/39 through the activities of the IRA, who planted small explosive devices in several GPO pillar-boxes over a wide area of the country; there was also some concern for the security of military installations. We had to mount standing patrols, day and night, covering the working areas of the station. It was a two hours on, four-hours-off job during a twenty-four-hour stint starting at 0800. Initially we were armed only with a police truncheon and patrolled singly. Later, we carried rifles without ammunition at night and patrolled in pairs; the object of the rifle was to go through the loading motion, hoping that the challenge of "halt who goes there" accompanied by the sound of the bolt action might serve to bring any intruder to a state of submission. What a miserable duty it was, particularly on a cold, windy night with only the occasional feeble light and the hangar doors clanging eerily. Aircraft were always kept in the hangars at night when there was no night flying, and whilst this made the duty less exacting, it did nothing to ease boredom and tension on those initial one-man patrols.

I retain a vivid recollection of another occasional duty that one could be called upon to do at short notice. All RAF stations are required to assume automatic responsibility for crashed aircraft in the station's defined area. In December 1938 I was detailed, with two others at short notice, for Crash Guard duty at a country location a few miles from Driffield. We were taken there by vehicle and relieved to find that the site was conveniently close to a farm house where there was likely to be a degree of sympathy for us during our miserably cold task of guarding a Heyford, which had been obliged to force-land in a field of Swede turnips. The field had been ploughed so that the turnips could be easily gathered, and the ground was, as one would expect at that time of year, in a very muddy state. In fact, we found ourselves ankle-deep in the clinging damp earth. We had, of course, been provided with gumboots to wear for the duration of our stint but found that they showed a marked reluctance to accompany us as we moved around. The Heyford was upright on its landing gear that, surprisingly, had withstood the landing and the short run imposed by the ground condition. It was, of course, up to its main wheel axles in mud with its large wheel spats full of the stuff. The pilot had obviously done a wonderful job in putting the aircraft down with no visible damage other than that inflicted by turnips, which were everywhere in wild profusion, including many lodged in the aircraft itself. The farmer and his wife were warmly hospitable and we were well plied with tea and bacon sandwiches that were most welcome as the RAF seemed to have overlooked our need for any form of sustenance. This was the only crash guard I ever did and it stays in my memory because of the cheery disposition and sympathetic concern of those good Yorkshire farming folk.

Yet another cold task in winter was that of Compass Swinging. It was particularly cold for the crew member, usually the wireless operator, who had to work behind the aircraft, enduring the added discomfort of the chill factor caused by the slipstream of the propellers as the aircraft went through a standard series of compass headings using its engines to manoeuvre. The necessity for compass swinging is to check the effect on natural magnetic deviation caused by the aircraft itself, and any equipment that may have been added to it. The deviation is determined by the use of a calibrated compass mounted on a tripod located about fifty yards behind the aircraft and sighted along the aircraft centre-line at each chosen compass heading. When the aircraft is settled onto the required heading, according to the aircraft compass, the second pilot, standing head and shoulders out of the cockpit roof emergency exit, signals by hand for the member behind the aircraft to take the check bearing. This is passed back using simple arm movements to indicate the numeric reading of the landing compass, as the tripod-mounted instrument was known. Thus was created the compass deviation card, always to be found mounted on the instrument panel above the magnetic compass, and so essential in making allowance for deviation when setting the required course to steer.

The transition from the Heyford - really only a generation removed from its WW1 predecessor - to the more advanced Whitley was soon seen as an expensive problem needing specialised conversion training, particularly for pilots. Incidents about the time of my arrival included a fatal crash of a 77 Squadron aircraft (K8963 actually on the day of my arrival), which lost height on take-off due to raising the flaps too soon, and a 102 Squadron aircraft landing on its belly, resulting from failure to lower the retractable undercarriage. There were similar accidents throughout No.4 Group, which then had six squadrons equipped with Whitleys or in the process of conversion. The need for specialised conversion was satisfied initially by the introduction, early in 1939, of a Group Pool Scheme that was a personal initiative of the Bomber Command C-in-C. For No.4 Group, the scheme came into being by designating the two resident squadrons (Nos. 97 and 166) at RAF Leconfield as the Group Pool. Similar pools were formed in the other four bomber groups. Since pilots could not be converted without other crew members, particularly a wireless operator who had to be carried by regulation, I found myself attached to 97 squadron from 20th March to 15th April 1939, during which time I managed only 2 hours and 5 minutes in Heyfords which, for me, was something of a waste as I had already logged 56 hours in 102 Squadron Whitleys. However, one must bear in mind that these were early days, and the Leconfield squadrons were still flying our old Heyfords. After these two squadrons were themselves converted to the Whitley, the scheme soon became effective, particularly in orientating newly qualified pilots to the Whitley. From Group Pool, I went directly to No.2 Air Observers School at Acklington in Northumberland where, on two-seater Hawker Hinds and Whitleys, I gained a distinguished pass in aerial gunnery and returned to the squadron on 13th May wearing my much coveted Winged Bullet.

Our introduction to the Whitley was really quite gentle until we had a full complement of aircraft towards the end of February 1939. It was not until late January that we were able to try out the new Vickers 'K' guns in the front and rear positions and the twin Browning's in the mid-under turret; the guns had only just become available. By February, however, we were doing lots of bombing and gunnery exercises, any amount of familiarisation trials, day and night cross-countries, and plenty of circuits and bumps, both dual and solo. Mentioning solo reminds me to add that a pilot was not permitted to fly alone in bomber aircraft, as any emergency situation arising would almost certainly require assistance. It was desirable that the aircraft should be in contact with base by wireless and, in the event of a diversion, able to fly to another location. It was, therefore, standard practice for a wireless operator to be carried to provide for communication, navigation by wireless direction finding, and other emergency situations. In regard to our bombing exercises, it is appropriate to add that we were not permitted to drop high explosive bombs or even practice bombs on land bombing ranges due to government restrictions based on public concern. We bombed wooden rafts anchored in the sea in designated bombing areas using small practice smoke or flash bombs. Therefore, we were unable to get any night bombing practice.

Other activities in the remaining days of peace were directed at showing off our new aircraft to the public and other interested parties from overseas. For instance, on 27th February 1939, after demonstrating our ability to fly in formation to the Air Officer Commanding No. 4 Group (then Air Commodore C H B Blount), we proceeded to RAF Northolt in formation. There, we were required to demonstrate the Whitley's capabilities by doing a formation fly-past for the benefit of an Arab Delegation, followed by their inspection of the entire squadron. The formal part of the show took place on the 1st March, and we returned to Driffield via Bassingbourne, Scampton, and Finningley next day. The annual Empire Air Day had for many years been the means of showing the RAF to the public and for the 1939 event, on 20th May, I was with a detachment of three aircraft at Ringway (Manchester), where we did two formation fly-pasts to the acclamation of a very large crowd of spectators.

During June, our numbers began to increase as personnel were posted in from their basic training schools, quite a few came from the recently established Group Pool at Leconfield. Among them was a young Pilot Officer, Jimmy Warne, whose name I mention, as it will be of particular interest to the members of my family. I had the pleasant duty of introducing him to the electrical and wireless installations of the Whitley on what was one of those unforgettable, glorious summer afternoons when one would think we ought to have been airborne. But knowing all about ones' aircraft is a very important pre-requisite to flying for any newly joined squadron member.

Throughout May 1939, the pace of squadron training began to intensify. On the 11th June we went to Catfoss for the annual Practice Camp that extended into the early days of July; it was a most useful training session for both flying and ground personnel. An incident that I witnessed during this camp highlights the increasing danger, at that time, of not having an air traffic control system in touch with aircraft by wireless. The RAF had recently acquired North American Harvard aircraft for pilot training and some of these had been converted for drogue (target sleeve) towing. One beautiful afternoon, I was on the tarmac apron prior to a sortie as a Harvard was taxiing out for take-off. The Harvard turned into wind and started its run along the grassed surface, apparently unaware that a Whitley was just about to land on top of him. Providentially, the Whitley over flew the Harvard, whose pilot then took the only action possible, which was to abandon take-off. But unfortunately, it was now in the tail well-up attitude and going too fast to permit braking without causing itself to nose over into the ground with a collapsed under-carriage. Although a serious accident was averted by the action of the Harvard pilot, he should have given way to the landing Whitley who obviously he did not see before turning for his take-off run. It was during this practice camp that I had the pleasure of flying with the aforementioned Pilot, Officer Jimmy Warne, on a long cross-country flight.

By August 1939 with the situation in Europe looking very grave, we became involved in a short period of intense activity to test the Home Defence Organisation. I took part in what we called Dummy Raids on the 6th, 7th, 9th and 10th August. We were supposed to be friendly on our first outbound run towards the Dutch coast and enemy on the first return to the East coast and out again, then friendly on the final approach to our own coast. Of course, we were not permitted to cross the Dutch coast, and the Dutch made sure we did not by identifying their coastline with brilliant illumination that we could see for miles and quite unmistakably read as 'NEDERLAND.'

We were close to war and if it was to come, let it. We were confident in our new equipment and in our ability to use it for the purposes of war. Together with Nos. 10, 51, 58, 76, 77, 97, and 166 Squadrons based at Dishforth, Linton-on-Ouse, Driffield, and Leconfield, we comprised No. 4 Group as it then was. As the only Night Bomber Group in the Royal Air Force, we were the forerunners of the Pathfinder Force that was later to become No.8 Group with 97 as one of its founder squadrons and many former personnel of the Group in prominent appointments. But this was three years into the future; meanwhile, we had to fight with what we had, and it was precious little as we were soon to discover.

CHAPTER IV
WAR OPERATIONS

So it happened that by the 3rd September 1939, I was a Leading Aircraftman Wireless Operator Air Crew (the correct formal title, not generally known, for what used to be called, and continued by default to be called, a Wireless Operator/Air Gunner). It came about in this manner: First of all, I should explain that on the declaration of war, the RAF was required to assume its planned war establishment. It did so by recalling to active duty its regular reserve of personnel who had reserve obligations as part of their engagements. Officers holding permanent commissions were recalled from retirement up to the age of sixty. The Auxiliary Air force, which to the RAF is the same as the Territorial Army is to the regular Army, was immediately mobilised and embodied, as was the RAF Volunteer Reserve, whose peacetime members took a little time to appear as they were mostly required to await individual notification to report to their emergency duty locations. There was also a progressive compulsory call-up of men over the age of eighteen who were given the opportunity to volunteer or were conscripted for war service with the RAFVR. All normal entry to the Royal Air Force (the regular service) ceased immediately, including entry to the RAF College, Cranwell, whose cadets under training were transferred to the service flying training schools to complete their initial flying training to wings standard. The entry scheme under which I had been trained and selected for flying duties also ceased, although the training of those already entered continued until the last pre-war entry completed training in 1940. All of this was done to implement the massive mobilisation plan that was designed to rapidly expand the RAF to its war establishment and had, of course, to provide for considerable changes in the rank structure. So far as long-term regulars were concerned, care had to be taken that they were not promoted to ranks from which they could not be reasonably reduced on cessation of the emergency, and it, therefore, became obvious that if the war went on for long enough that regulars would be overtaken by non-regulars who could be easily disestablished. In my own case, being close to the end of the probationary period, my reclassification to LAC was advanced to the 3rd September, thereby placing me immediately in position for any consideration of further advancement. Similar action was taken for other aircraftmen who had passed their examinations and were within a few weeks of completing the time requirement for reclassification. The Wireless Operator Air Crew trade category was introduced in January

1939 by Air Ministry Order with the object of creating a flying status for Aerial Gunners who, whatever their basic trade, would be required to transfer to the trade of wireless operator after retraining. The scheme seemed somewhat ill-conceived as it was clearly out of the question to conveniently retrain all, or any significant number, of part-time gunners without causing extensive disruption in the squadrons. However, the proposal was somewhat modified by adopting the more obvious step of creating a new flying category for wireless operators who would be remustered Wireless Operators (Air Crew) on becoming qualified Aerial Gunners. No further action was taken in regard to tradesmen in other trades who were qualified as aerial gunners until the summer of 1940. The new trade of Wireless Operator (Air Crew) did not attract any increase in pay, which continued as before, so that in my own case, I was paid four shillings and sixpence a day as aircraftman first class W.Op plus one shilling a day flying pay and sixpence a day Aerial Gunners qualification pay, A total of six shillings a day. On my reclassification as LAC the trade element was increased to five shillings. It was in this category that I went to war at the top of my trade, with a flying qualification, for the princely sum of six shillings and sixpence a day. There were many W.Ops and other tradesmen in the lower trade classifications of AC1 and AC2 who were paid less. I was fortunate.

On the 3rd September 1939, my logbook recorded a total of 155 hours 49 minutes, of which 46 hours 10 minutes was night flying. We had been standing-by for several days, and there was considerable activity in the hangars, particularly in altering the squadron identification letters on the aircraft from 'TQ' to 'DY'. Shortly after the Prime Minister announced the declaration of war over the wireless, we had an air raid warning and took to the shelters, but this was probably nothing more than a trial. The crews were restless, each wondering what we were waiting for, but the day passed without any indication of action; little different to any other Sunday apart from enforced inactivity and an unusual quietness no doubt related to tension.

The morning of Monday 4th September, brought great activity in the Flights of both 77 and 102 Squadrons, and it soon became apparent that we were to do our first show this night. Details of aircraft and crews were posted in the Flight Authorisation Book during the afternoon: Raid DM82 Whitley III K8958 Crew P/O Bisset, P/O Kierstead, Sgt Lees (Obs), LAC Jacobs (Wop), AC Killingley (Rear Gunner), ETD 2359. The fuselage forward of the mid-under turret was crammed with large parcels of leaflets wrapped in course brown paper tied with thick twine. Access, normally difficult enough because of the retracted ventral turret, was now extremely difficult through the narrow alleyway between the parcels on either side. At the evening briefing, we were acquainted with the purpose of our mission, and the reader will understand our feelings at not being called upon to deliver anything more damaging than a good supply of paper and stout rubber bands on Germany's industrial heartland. However, maintaining strict wireless silence except in emergency until clear of enemy territory, we were to enter German airspace north of Holland and, avoiding neutral territory, fly southward, distributing our leaflets down the Ruhr Valley, into France and home across the English Channel.

By the time we crossed the enemy coast, we were at 15,000 feet, breathing oxygen. Horizontal visibility was good, but ground features were obscured, and navigation was by dead reckoning assisted by my wireless bearings obtained with the direction-finding loop aerial. Shortly before we commenced leaflet dropping, we observed a beam of light apparently aimed in our direction slightly below and to the right of our nose. It was certainly airborne, and Bill Lees gave it a burst from the front gun; it went out immediately, and we concluded that we had been the object of an attempted night-fighter interception. The lot of dropping the leaflets fell to P/O Kierstead and me; what a wearisome task it was. At 15000 feet, the outside temperature was about fifteen degrees below freezing on the Fahrenheit scale. We had to disconnect ourselves from the oxygen supply and were soon bathed in perspiration from the effort. The parcels nearest the flare-chute were discharged first to clear the surrounding area. Soon the thick brown paper and string became a problem until space was cleared into which it could be condensed out of the way. The parcels could only be moved with difficulty over the raised turret, and to reduce the effort of moving them to the flare-chute we had to partially lower the turret with consequent effect on airspeed and flying characteristics. The whole process seemed interminable and we were quite exhausted and perspiring profusely by the effort at that height. We then found that the turret would not fully retract due to frozen hydraulics.

I have read several accounts of leaflet dropping written by those not directly involved, and these, together with photographs showing individual bundles of leaflets being loaded, tend to create a false impression of what was entailed. I am not aware that individual bundles were ever loaded into aircraft, as to do so would have created a very unstable load. The leaflets measured 8.7/16 x 5.3/8 inches when folded to produce a four-page leaflet of that size. Five leaflets were placed inside each other, and bundles of these, about four inches thick, were secured by a stout rubber band located some two inches from one end. The secured end of the bundle was fed into the flare-chute so that on emerging into the slipstream, the loose end was presented to the full force, causing the bundle to separate and scatter immediately. The brown paper parcels weighed about thirty pounds containing eighteen, perhaps twenty-four, bundles, and these large cumbersome parcels had to be opened progressively as the drop proceeded.

With the dawn, we found ourselves above complete cloud cover. At about 0640 hours, having taken only occasional loop aerial bearings to check our dead reckoning and believing ourselves to be well clear of enemy territory, I broke wireless silence and obtained bearings from our own direction-finding system, and these, when quickly plotted, placed us close to Dieppe. Being anxious about our fuel state and the possibility of being unable to make our intended fuel stop at RNAS Ford on the West Sussex coast, we decided to break cloud and found ourselves over water with Dieppe just behind us. P/O Bisset decided to land immediately on a small aerodrome that seemed to be inactive but the only one we could see. On final approach, we thought it judicious to unload the guns, of which I was responsible for the two Brownings in the ventral turret that had to be lowered to bring the breeches into the unloading position. I found the turret was still frozen and was wrestling with it when we touched down. Looking aft through the small slit windows in the fuselage, I saw a blue-clad figure seemingly being thrown off the leading edge of the port tail-plane. I thought perhaps that this lonely sentry had performed the gallant but foolhardy act of throwing himself on the tail-plane in an attempt to arrest our speed and help prevent us from finishing the landing run in the boundary edge. He seemed to be unhurt, and by the time we came to rest with the nose almost in the boundary edge, he was some distance away, strolling nonchalantly with his rifle in the slung position. On reflection I find myself wondering if he was, perhaps, taken completely unaware in that sleepy and inattentive condition that usually attends one at the end of a long period of lonely night sentry duty. If so, he was most fortunate that he was not killed or at least seriously injured, as the port propeller must have passed close to him. Did he throw himself to the ground to be struck by the tail-plane as he tried to get to his feet? We shall never know. P/O Bisset did not see him after the tail wheel grounded because of the obscured view of the ground from the cockpit. Either way, he was very lucky. The aerodrome was otherwise deserted until twenty minutes later when a dozen or so French Air Force personnel, probably reservists, on bicycles, arrived from the direction of the town. Meanwhile, as I did not have the opportunity to contact base before landing because of the turret problem, I passed a coded message to Driffield informing them of our situation. We had been airborne for six hours and fifty-five minutes, our longest flight so far.

Refuelling from small cans by hand was a lengthy business. We were on the ground for three hours and thirty-five minutes being airborne again at 1030 hours. The turret had thawed-out while we were on the ground, and I was able to retract it before take-off as soon as we had the engines running, but now, due to atmospheric phenomena, I was unable to contact Driffield until we were halfway home, and had to request Abingdon to relay my messages. We landed at base at 1255 after a combined flight of nine hours and twenty minutes and an absence of almost thirteen hours. Thus, we ended our first operational flight. Whilst we had done nothing to harm the enemy war effort, it had been a great experience for ourselves, being quite unlike any of our night cross-country training exercises in terms of duration. The imposition of wireless silence had provided a useful test of navigational ability, and from this viewpoint, it was a model of dead reckoning assisted by wireless direction finding using the loop-aerial whilst flying over enemy and neutral territory. I took loop bearings on every identifiable transmission source, and before we broke wireless silence, we reckoned we were near Dieppe, as was soon confirmed. It would be wise to bear in mind, however, that weather conditions had been ideal despite total cloud cover over most of the route.

Our first losses occurred on the night of 8/9th September when two aircraft of 'A' Flight, with crews on their first operational mission, failed to return. S/L Murray in K8950 was shot down by flak near Kassel. We later learned that all crew members had survived and were POWs. (The first complete bomber crew to become POWs). Many years later, whilst researching for the purposes of this personal memoir, I discovered that they had foolishly overlooked the basic navigation essential of noting the time of setting course from base. They, therefore, had to guess, and later events proved that they were so much in error that they flew too far east before turning onto course for the Ruhr Valley. Eventually they saw lights that they triumphantly assumed to be Paris and set their course for home accordingly. Soon after, with the dawn, they realised that they were dangerously low on fuel (gauges were not accurate enough at a low fuel state to be relied on) and would soon have to land. They then encountered flak and were shot down. It seems that what they had taken to be Paris was, in fact, Berlin, which illustrates the degree of navigational error resulting from their initial and subsequent guesswork. This is, perhaps, an example of appallingly poor navigation and, even worse, an apparent total failure to obtain a wireless bearing check on their position, which would have been easy enough after their initial failure to note the time of setting course. However, they paid the price of their folly by spending the entire war years in captivity. They were fortunate to have been able to save their lives by executing a controlled emergency landing in the early light of day. The second misfortune affected F/O Cogman and his crew who got lost in K8985 and strayed into Belgian airspace where, under escort by two Belgian fighters, they were obliged to land at Nivelles. They were interned, and F/O Cogman returned to Driffield a few weeks later after managing to slip out undetected. The remaining crew were returned sometime during May 1940. I remember discussing their internment with Lofty Steele (Wop/AG), who told me they had been held quite comfortably in an ancient fortress from which they had been released when the German threat began to look ominous earlier in May.

We were now to start the long, monotonous period of near stagnation that became known as 'The Phoney War'. Much has been written about this period that, prudently, was put to good use in preparation for what was to come. There can be no doubt in the minds of any then involved who had the good fortune to survive later events of the disastrous outcome had we been committed to the kind of action our youthful enthusiasm foolishly envisaged. It was to be three months before my next operation, and this was the pattern for most. Actually, and this was not generally known, there was a kind of Bombing Truce. This came about because of an initiative on the part of the United States President, Franklin D Roosevelt, who appealed to the belligerent nations to avoid bombing targets where civilian lives would be at risk. The allied governments, needing as much time as they could get, were willing enough to agree, but the Germans did so only after showing initial reluctance. Prime targets making the most important contributions to the enemy war effort were obviously in the more populous industrial areas, and the problems involved in considering the lives of the workers involved in war production virtually made the bombing of any major industrial target impossible. However, for the time being, we were expressly forbidden to bomb any target, specified or at random opportunity, where civilian lives would be endangered.

There was enough non-operational activity to keep us occupied: air firing, practice bombing, cross-country, and local flying for the benefit of newcomers. In October 1939, we began to receive Whitley Mk Vs as replacements for our Mk IIIs. My first experience in this latest mark was on the 31st in N1386 - dual and solo for P/O Bisset. Replacement of the MkIII was quite rapid, most being transferred to the maintenance units at Kemble, Shawbury and St Athan. There was no Ferry Command at that time, and all the flying involved in the change over had to be done by the squadron crews, whose familiarisation with the new aircraft was also done at the squadron level. My last job in MKIIIs was at Shawbury in K8994 on 30th October as a passenger to collect K9014 with P/O Bisset. The latter was the second last MKIII to be produced and was allotted to 102 after previously belonging to 77. We had a full complement of MKVs by December 1939. There were, of course, several incidents, both operational and non-operational, during this relatively quiet period affecting both squadrons at Driffield. In particular, I remember the horrendous accident at Catterick when an 'A' Flight aircraft (K8996) with Sgt 'Acker' Gaut as pilot was assisting with the move of 41 Squadron on 18th October. With nine souls on board and a load of ammunition bound for Drem, the aircraft stalled on take-off and nose-dived from 100 feet, exploding on impact. All were killed except two of the passengers who, miraculously, survived but suffered injuries. Acker had made representations to Driffield about the load, indicating his reluctance to accept it, particularly as there was a starter trolley that he apparently considered to be a particular danger. It seems he was over-ruled. The aircraft was seen to take-off quite normally but, at about 100 feet, went nose-up and stalled. Presumably, there was a load shift causing a tail-heavy condition with total loss of control.

Towards the end of December, we started the Security Patrols over the Friesian Islands. The weather became our worst enemy although there were many incidents in which aircraft of No.4 Group experienced enemy opposition with, providentially, only little loss. Leaflet raids also continued throughout the winter. Apart from my own more fortunate experiences at this time, I recall two suffered by the same crew on two successive missions. On the night of 27/28 October P/O (Lofty) Long with P/O (Ken) Gray (both New Zealanders in the RAF) brought their aircraft (N1377) back badly damaged by flak. A month later, on the night of 27/28 November, the same aircraft and crew experienced the worst effects of the atrocious weather conditions to which we were exposed at the time. Severe icing conditions with consequent difficulty in maintaining height and an unfortunate lightning strike, which caused the fabric aft of the port wing main spar to strip, placed them in a serious situation. Unable to maintain height, it was a wonder that they were able to make it to the coast of East Anglia, where they made a successful emergency landing at Bircham Newton - a truly magnificent feat of airmanship for which both pilots were awarded immediate DFCs. The WOp/AG was AC1 F Hollywood.

My first Security Patrol was on 14 December in N1376 with F/L Owen. Raid DM176 Borkum and Sylt, take-off 1350 hours, duration 5 hours 10 minutes. My second on 20 December, again in N1376 with F/O (Birdie) Bisset, P/O (Ralph) Kierstead, Sgt (Bill) Lees, and LAC (Carl) Killingley, brought little relief from the monotony of these patrols. This was Raid DM192 Borkum. Nordenay, Sylt. Taking-off at 1900 hours for a flight of 7 hours 5 minutes, we were fortunate enough to spot some seaplane activity at Sylt and deposited our load in a two-run attack on a flare-path. We encountered only slight opposition from ground defences. Third patrol on 9 January 1940 in N1420, Raid DM209 crew as before. Nothing observed in the most atrocious weather that featured high winds and extreme turbulence. Ordinary navigation was impossible except for steering a compass course with little idea of the wind effect. It was essential to our safety to break wireless silence and for me to undertake considerable direction-finding activity. The weather produced the worst wireless conditions with atmospheric noise making reception just about impossible. However, I managed to obtain a series of eleven fixes on the homeward run and finally to get progressive courses to steer, which took us to Driffield. This situation, which made dead reckoning navigation virtually impossible, was a true test of the importance of the wireless operator and his ability to use the wireless service. (See my mention of the Order Of the Day by the C-in-C Bomber Command in the fourth paragraph of Chapter III). I was not to know it at the time, but I was later quietly informed that I had been cited for a distinguished flying award, the result of which received mention later.

During these patrols, we were under strict orders to bomb only targets of opportunity on the water and, at all costs, to safeguard against bombs falling on land to the peril of the civilian population, thereby infringing the Bombing Truce and giving rise to reprisal. Sylt was the exception, as there was no civilian population on the island. These missions were dreadfully monotonous and we suffered great discomfort in the extreme weather conditions and intense cold. The real purpose, of course, was to hamper maritime activity and, particularly, the mine-laying seaplane menace to our shipping in the North Sea, reasons not always appreciated by those involved.

The 26 January dawned bright and sunny with several inches of newly fallen snow on the aerodrome. Soon, it seemed that all station personnel were gathered outside the hangars. In line abreast about twenty-five yards wide, rank upon rank, they tramped across the field to flatten and compress the snow to form a runway. It was unusual, the like of which we had not seen before, but the reason was soon revealed to us when we were called to briefing in the operations room at the odd time of mid-morning. We were to fly to Villeneuve (code name 'Sister') in the Champagne and, from there, carry out leaflet raids on Prague and Vienna, principally to prove to the German population that Herman Goering was misleading them by his claim that the RAF did not have the capability to penetrate so deeply.

I had just been transferred to the crew of S/L J C Macdonald, who succeeded S/L Parker as 'B' Flight Commander during the last weeks of peace, and this was my first trip in that capacity. One of the responsibilities of the flight commander was to ensure that newly joined members were checked out, and this applied particularly to pilots, observers, and wireless operators. In this respect it was essential that he had the services of an operationally experienced wireless operator of proven ability to cope with navigation problems of the sort already described. The flight commander and myself thereby became the 'B' Flight operational conversion team, as it were, and I therefore found myself flying with different second pilots, observers, and second wireless operators who were being checked, perhaps without realising it. In N1380 (DY-R), we took-off at 1200 hours in clear conditions from that beaten down snow. Meteorological briefing had warned of worsening weather as we proceeded south but we got worse than we expected when we found ourselves in blizzard conditions. Navigational assistance was called for, and I tuned-in to our Medium Frequency Direction Finding System and on making my first transmission (pre-flight testing had been prohibited), I realised, to my horror, that all was not well with the equipment. Atmospheric noise was extreme and would have been only marginally less in the ears of the ground operators. My transmissions were so poor in signal quality that the ground stations could not determine bearings. The cause was easily diagnosed as a fault in the high-tension supply to the transmitter and, on stripping-down the motor/generator, I found a very badly neglected commutator on the power output side. It was this that was delivering an intermittent supply to the transmitter that, in turn, was emitting a harsh signal, not unlike that of the earliest spark systems, which was almost totally absorbed in the atmospheric background noise. Fortunately, I had a small piece of emery cloth in my flight tool kit, and I cleaned it up as best I could, but it was really a workshop job. Considerable improvement resulted and enabled us to proceed to our destination that we reached after a flight of 3 hours 30 minutes.

On arrival at Villeneuve, we learned that most of the force from No. 4 Group had aborted, and only four had arrived. The only other aircraft from 102 was probably N1381 with F/O McKay, P/O Pengelly, Sgt Pollit, LAC Jackson (Wop), and LAC Golding, who was a Fitter Engine/AG. Our own Crew included Sgt Masham as second pilot, Sgt Dawson as Observer, myself as Wop, and AC R Gates, my second wireless operator, as rear gunner. We also had F/O J Crockett of 77 Squadron flying as passenger for some other duty at Villeneuve. The other two aircraft were from either Linton or Dishforth, one of the WOp/AGs being AC (Titch) Henry, who was in the same entry as me at Cranwell. We were billeted in vineyard worker's accommodation at the quiet village of Avise.

Our intended stay was three days, but weather conditions in that now legendary winter of 1930/40 virtually froze us to the ground. To say the least our accommodation and messing arrangements were most primitive. We slept on straw-filled palliases placed on two long wooden platforms built along the length of the walls about twelve inches above floor level on both sides of a central corridor. There was one small coke-burning stove in the long, lofty room; its warming effect was barely noticeable. The water supply was from frozen horse troughs located nearby, and our water containers were made from four-gallon petrol tins with the tops removed. Not only did we carry water in these, but also had to use them as wash basins after heating the water on the stove top, a very lengthy process, or wash and shave in cold water. The mess room was located nearby in what had previously been some sort of store room. The place was unheated, and the food so miserable that we decided to take our nourishment in the two local cafes where we could obtain good food cheaply and enjoy it in warmth and comfort, usually in the good company of the locals and members of the French Army. For an occasional change of scene we visited the provincial town of Eperney, the centre of the wine industry in Champagne. We were able to travel to it quite conveniently by local train service and without the need for special authority. We found it a pleasant change from Avise.

Paris, of course, was too far distant to visit casually, but we did manage to arrange a long weekend pass for the two Driffield crews. Staying in the Hotel Moderne, located in the Place de la Republique, placed us conveniently close to all the usual sights, but many attractions, such as the Eiffel Tower and the Louvre, were closed for the duration of hostilities, all treasures having been removed from their normal locations to safe-storage. Places of entertainment were in full swing and we saw the current show at the Alcazar de Paris that featured the celebrated showgirl Josephine Baker. We also saw the film 'Vernon and Irene Castle" starring Fred Astaire and Ginger Rogers. (The Castles were a famous American dance-duo of the WWI era, and Castle himself was a well-known flyer who, after service in France, was returned to the US as an instructor, where he lost his life in a crash resulting from his own deliberate action to avoid collision with a student pilot who should have given way to him while landing). It was an enjoyable experience except for aching feet caused by walking around in flying boots, the only footwear we had.

It was the 22 February before we were able to do what we came for. Our Raid was CDM102 leaflets Vienna and reconnaissance Munich, take-off 2230. The two crews from Linton went on a similar mission to Prague. I shall never forget the effect of our pre-flight meal in a corrugated iron shed on the aerodrome with the stove glowing red half way up the chimney pipe. A meal of canned stew of a brand not previously sampled. I doubt if any of us experienced such raging thirst as was to attend us throughout that long flight.

In good conditions, we were able to pinpoint our route to Vienna that we found clear and not only bathed in moonlight with its famous features clearly visible but also brilliantly illuminated for our special pleasure. We leisurely deposited our leaflets, somewhat less this time, and turned onto a westerly course for Munich about 220 miles and slightly south of our outbound track. The weather, however, began to deteriorate, and we found the Bavarian capitol totally obscured by towering cumulonimbus. However, we were required to do a reconnaissance of this city and since we could see nothing but cloud, we decided to go down and have a look. In the next few minutes, we were to sample, for the first time, what must surely be among the most terrifying of war-time night flying experiences: whilst still in the towering cloud tops with the advantage of moonlight, trying to find a hole, we were subjected to considerable turbulence and buffeting which was to be expected? Loud detonations and flashes led us at first to believe that we were in electrical storm conditions until closer flashes and smoke puffs with diffused searchlight beams confirmed our true situation, and we knew that we had arrived. Down we went through that piece of hell and somehow managed to get below the cloud and heavy flak. The probing searchlights failed to locate us as we stooged around, having a good look at the city with its rooftops seemingly wet and glistening in the light of searchlights reflected from the low cloud base, and I can still see in my mind's eye the numerous rooftop windows; there seemed to be something quite eerie about it. There was some inaccurate light flak and, as we had discovered Munich to be adequately defended, and not having a target or anything to drop, we thought it propitious to leave the scene and get home to report. Heading west again we began our climb through those ominous clouds back to the smoother moonlit sky above. In the cloud tops, our watchful eyes caught a glimpse of something shining in the broken moonlight just off the port wingtip, and three voices yelled in concert over the intercom, "Balloon cable." How many we had not seen, we shall never know but looking upwards we could see those ghastly shapes above and before us. Mac sat there like a block of granite at the controls and we thanked God for that moon by which we were able to judge angles and pick our way through those deadly cables.

We had an uneventful flight back to base in clear moonlight above unbroken clouds and after judging ourselves to be out of German airspace, I was able to demonstrate the effectiveness of the French civil wireless system by contacting Le Bourget, the control station of their wireless direction-finding network, and obtaining an occasional check on our position. Finally, homing by wireless bearings on the RAF manned facility at Villeneuve, we touched down after a flight of 9 hours 15 minutes. Still with raging thirsts, we found the stove in the hut with its chimney pipe glowing red and were thankful for its friendly warmth and a mug of steaming tea. We were looking forward to a good breakfast but on being told, apologetically, that the day's rations had not yet arrived and there was only more stew, we told the duty cook what he could do with it, and got the lorry back to Avise where we spent most of the day on our straw-filled mattresses (palliasses).

Before returning to Driffield on 24 February, Mac congratulated me with the news that I had been Mentioned in Despatches by Air Chief Marshal Sir Edgar R Ludlow-Hewitt on 20 January for gallantry and distinguished service. He also gave me advance news of my promotion to corporal effective 9 February. We then did some local flying for the benefit of the French media and flew back to base.

On arrival, we discovered that all qualified aerial gunners had been formally awarded the new - brevet-type - flying badge introduced by Air Ministry Order in December 1939. So, there were some alterations to be done to my tunics and greatcoat by the station tailor. I now had some rank privileges and was allocated a room to myself with responsibility for the adjacent barrack room and the men occupying it, meals in a segregated section of the dining room, and use of the completely separate corporal's facilities in the station institute (NAAFI). Furthermore my daily rate of pay increased to eight shillings a day. There was some envy, perhaps resentment, among the other wireless section members in the squadron, many being senior to me in age and adult service but not the LAC classification.

But they were not ex-youth entrants, and although I did not fully appreciate it myself at the time, my unusual passing-out attainment at Cranwell was now beginning to have some effect at the highest selection level where the exigencies of the Service were necessarily the paramount consideration. One thing that was certain, however, was that the personnel establishment of the squadron had been amended to include the provision of a corporal in the trade of Wireless Operator (Air Crew), and I had been selected to fill it, presumably with the prior confirmation of the squadron commander. I now had to undertake administrative and disciplinary responsibilities appropriate to that rank within the squadron and station, besides the automatic responsibility carried by all personnel of non-commissioned rank at whatever rank level. Although we were now in a war situation, there was no noticeable change in our daily routine and attitudes to service generally, and I doubt if anyone, certainly not I, had given any thought to personal advancement beyond the trade classification of leading aircraftman. Our attitude tended to be vocational, highly professional, and responsible, and we knew that promotion to non-commissioned rank was slow and the best we could hope for in our flying career was progression, by selection, to Air Observer and subsequently to pilot with the acting rank of sergeant. Yet, without the remotest thought here I was suddenly a corporal albeit in the rapidly expanded war establishment. Had our perception of events been keener, we would have been better able to appreciate the effect on ourselves of things that happened immediately after the Munich Crisis of 1938, when direct entry schemes were introduced for the training of NCO observers and pilots both carrying the acting rank of sergeant on reporting for squadron duty; a move that was made to increase the numbers of flying personnel to fill a serious deficiency. These first direct-entry NCO flyers were posted to bomber squadrons a few weeks before the outbreak of war. Sgt Bill Lees, who was crewed with me for our first mission, was one of them.

My next operational mission was to become something of an historical event. The bombing truce previously mentioned was broken by the Germans on 17 March 1940 when aircraft attacking shipping in Scapa Flow dropped bombs on land, killing one civilian - on an aerodrome - and wounding seven others in a nearby village. On the 19 March, briefing was at an unusually early hour - about 1500. Now, we were to drop bombs deliberately on German soil for the first time. The government had authorised a reprisal raid to be carried out on the Friesian Islands seaplane bases, but only where there was no danger to nearby civilian population. Bomber Command had selected the mine-laying seaplane base at Hornum on the southernmost tip of Sylt. This was an important operation, being the biggest of the war so far, and the first intentional bombing of a German land target. Thirty Whitleys of No. 4 Group were to bomb first, followed by twenty Hampdens of No.5 Group. Other No.4 Group squadrons involved were 77, 10, and 51, the last two based at

Dishforth. Our feelings on receiving this news can be easily imagined. Now, we were to carry out our intended role, and our spirits were understandably high. By the time we were in the locker room, tension was being released with much noise, ribald, comment and song - 'Any Old Iron' seemed to fit the occasion.

First aircraft off was N1380 (DY-R) at 1745 with S/L Macdonald, W/C Burton (our new Sqn Cdr recently arrived to succeed W/C Toogood) coming along for his first trip, Sgt Masham as second pilot and bomb aimer, Cpl Jacobs as first WOp/AG and AC Gates as second WOp/AG and tail gunner. My logbook records 'Bombs dropped at 1953 hours'. Prior to the bombing runs, I had released flares to assist target identification and we had no opposition until we started our second run when we were hosed by multi-coloured light flak, mainly flaming onions. Flight time was six hours and five minutes, and we were back at base with whole skins just before midnight. We were the first to bomb on this historic raid and it was for this reason that I, unusually, recorded the bomb release time when entering the flight details in my logbook.

The next day, we learned that Dishforth seemed to be getting an unfair amount of publicity, with credit for the first on target going to the CO of 10 Squadron, who had been dubbed by the Press as "Crack 'em Staton" (W/C Bill Staton), who apparently was first of the Dishforth aircraft on target, having departed Dishforth at 1930 hours. As both Driffield squadrons had attacked earlier, 77 Squadron decided to remonstrate by delivering, stealthily by hand, some hastily prepared leaflets around Dishforth conveying the message - 'Congratulations to Crack 'em & Co (The heroes and leaders of Sylt) from an admiring Driffield'. We later received a very poetic response from Dishforth printed on toilet paper delivered by air. Copies of these leaflets are included in the end papers of these recollections. Shortly after, Driffield was invaded by the aviation press, and several photographs taken on this occasion are now well known. Also photographed was N1380, of which mounted sepia prints were presented to members of the crew by 'The Aeroplane' magazine; mine has been a treasured possession ever since, and a smaller copy of it is included herein.

A 77 Squadron crew had a most unusual escapade when returning from a leaflet job on Warsaw on 16 March. Being anxious about their fuel and believing they were well into France, they decided to land and ask the way. Approaching some local yokels in an adjacent field, they soon discovered that they were in the company of Germans. Quickly scrambling back into their aircraft (N1387), they were fortunate to get their engines started without difficulty and took-off under rifle fire from troops rapidly closing in on them. They arrived safely at Villeneuve, somewhat shaken by their experience. F/O Tomlin (already mentioned) was the captain and the WOp/AG LAC (Alf) Perry. (Allusion to this incident is jokingly made in the third verse of the Dishforth leaflet mentioned in the previous paragraph. It is the kind of situation that gives rise to many comments regarding the general uselessness of wireless as an aid to navigation, made by authors without personal experience and pilots without understanding of wireless who were too ready to condemn. In this case, the crew were unsure of their position but thought they were out of German airspace, they were therefore lost, and, being anxious about their fuel state had an emergency situation that would have justified breaking wireless silence. They had the means whereby they could easily have obtained their position and a course to steer for their intended destination. (See my own account of a similar situation that could have developed in the final stages of our return from Vienna and Munich on the night of 22/23 February).

Operational flying began to intensify during April as our efforts were directed towards the German occupation of Norway and shipping in the Scaggerack and Kattegat. On 11 April, during a night patrol, we located and bombed a convoy in the Scaggerack, obtaining a lucky strike on a ship of about 8000 tons, which, judging by the explosions, we thought to be an ammunition ship. This was Raid DM193 in N1420, take-off 1905 duration 7 hours 40 minutes, crew Macdonald and Co. The strike was later confirmed.

A particularly memorable operation was the bombing of the Luftwaffe occupied aerodrome at Stavanger on 15 April. Raid DDM201 in N1380 (DY-R). Take-off 1900, and we were first on target again. In brilliant moonlight, we flew up the fiord, the snow-clad hills on either side standing out in such stark relief that it seemed possible to reach out and touch them; we were flying low to evade radar detection. Turning right on leaving the fiord, we lined-up for our first low-level run across the base and laid our incendiaries among the technical buildings. If we caught them napping, it didn't take them long to react, for by the time we were half way round the lake in a wide circuit, we were being hosed by very intense light flak, most of which seemed to be coming horizontally from the surrounding high ground. It was like a gigantic fireworks display with everything brilliantly illuminated, not least ourselves, I imagine; the clear moonlight on the water below us, the white snow on the surrounding hills, red, yellow and white lines of fire streaking around us, and to the left our incendiaries burning brightly. I shall never forget the exhilaration of those moments, which somehow seemed to hold no danger for us, all fear suppressed by excitement, so much so that I found myself standing behind the pilot's seat - we were the only two in the cockpit at the time - and lifting up the right-hand flap of his helmet saying "Pretty isn't it?" to which I got the thumbs up sign. Under intense fire, we went in and dropped our heavy stuff to spread the fires. How we came out of that melee unscathed is quite unbelievable, as we must have been clearly visible. This was our first experience of light flak at low altitude and, looking back, I think we were very fortunate to get away with it.

On 19 April, a small force of No.4 Group Whitleys was positioned at RAF Kinloss on the Moray Firth for strikes against the more northerly Norwegian targets. On the 23rd, again with S/L Macdonald in N1386, we took-off from Kinloss in 2025 to give the Luftwaffe at Trondhiem some attention on Raid DDM283. Weather conditions were bad, and we found the target area completely obscured by low cloud and were recalled. 7 hours 35 minutes of hand clapping and foot stamping in the miserable cold.

At this time we lost two aircraft and their crews in less than a week. The first was N1383, with F/O Horrigan and crew all killed except Sgt Barr POW against Aalborg on 24/25th. Also, on 29/30th N1421 missing from Fornebu with F/O Murphy and crew POW except LAC Ellwood killed.

On the 10 May, I was promoted to the rank of Sergeant, to my own amazement, perhaps more than that of anyone else. A corporal of my acquaintance in 77 Squadron was likewise promoted, and LAC (Len) Bailey was promoted to corporal to fill the slot left in 102 Squadron by my own advancement. Truly astounding; I had been a corporal for only four months, yet here I was with senior NCO rank at barely twenty years of age. My pay was at the rate for my rank and basic trade of wireless operator - eight shillings and sixpence a day - plus my flying pay and air gunner's pay, producing the magnificent total of ten shillings a day. I was well received in the sergeants' mess, particularly by the pilots and observers.

The 10th of May was also a memorable day, marking the beginning of what was to become known as 'The Battle for France'. On this day the Germans began their advance through the Low Countries. Bomber Command was now to be committed to hindering the German advance on both fronts of the giant pincer movement one point of which was directed towards the Channel Ports, with the other in the East thrusting directly into France towards Paris. Lines of communication provided the main targets, and 102 Squadron played a part in yet another historical event - the first bombs to be dropped on the German mainland. In N1380, again with S/L Macdonald, on Raid DDM227, we left Driffield at 2130 hours for a sortie of 6 hours and 25 minutes, dropping our bombs on lines of communication targets leading to southern Holland.

There were several of these raids during May, and the targets, mainly road/rail junctions, were difficult to locate as they occupied such small areas. Considerable time had to be spent in the general area pin-pointing by the light of flares and precise bombing was, therefore, extremely difficult even when no ground opposition was encountered in the target area. Later in May, we met with increasing opposition from ground defences, particularly in the more industrial locations where they seemed able to predict height and course, in a most uncanny manner and pass us onto the next defence section. Flak became commonplace, being mostly of the box barrage type of which we soon became nonchalant as there was no way of avoiding it. To attempt to evade this type of fire by flying other than a straight course was futile simply because it was just as likely to fly into a shell as it was to be hit directly by one. But any accurate prediction was startlingly obvious, and violent evasive action was necessary with consequent loss of height. We were soon to experience early demonstrations of the effectiveness of the German prediction system, particularly when used against aircraft operating singly. With terrifying suddenness, we would find ourselves illuminated in a brilliant beam of piercingly blue-white light, the master searchlight, with which the larger calibre (97 millimetres) anti-aircraft batteries were synchronised. The radar device, which had so precisely directed the searchlight to the target, also directed the gun and a shell was already on the way. Immediate evasive action was therefore essential and this required the unhesitating initiation of a steep nose-dive and weaving out of the beam and the path of the shell. A good many aircraft received direct hits through hesitation in these situations; it was easy to freeze on the first occasion.

On the 16 May, we were able to see for ourselves the dreadful effects of the German bombing of Rotterdam. Our own bombing effort was now to be directed against the Ruhr industry and railways, our target for Raid FDM311 being Aachen, one of several targets attacked that night in the first strategic bombing of German industry of WW2. I well remember at the briefing for this raid the intelligence chap telling us about Rotterdam, which was to be our landfall on this occasion, but not to worry as we would be about 10,000 feet still on climb-out and that they could not possibly have anything in the area able to seriously affect us. We left base at 2157 hours and soon saw before us the raging inferno that was Rotterdam, with smoke rising densely above our height; it was truly awesome. Most of the smoke seemed to be coming from the seaward part of the city where the docks with warehouses full of butter and other edible fats had apparently been given special attention together with the petroleum storage installations. At our height, there was still some light, and four of us in the front end were looking at the scene below as we approached the pillar of smoke when, immediately in front of us and only a little below, there was a flash and the loudest detonation we had so far experienced; a near miss that would probably have been a direct hit only a split second later so much for not having anything there that could touch us at 10,000 feet. It must have been a flak ship. However, down went the nose into that pall of smoke, and we had no further hatred for whatever it was. We lost quite a bit of height and had to try to recover as much as we could before reaching the target. Other raids in which I took part in May were:

21 FDM363 N1499 Euskirchen Marshalling yards. 6 hrs 35 mins

23 FDM402 N1524 Eulnoye Road/Rail Junction. 6 hrs 20 mins

28 FDM435 N1413 Givet Road/Rail Junction. 7 hrs 35 mins

These targets were main points on the route of the German advance into the Low Countries and France. The latter target, Givet, situated on the Franco-Belgium border, was particularly well defended by mobile light flak batteries to defend the high volume of personnel and arms assembled in the locality. We had an uncomfortable degree of attention during our low-level attacks in the half-dark of night at this time of year. The captain on each occasion was S/L Macdonald and we had come to regard N1380 as our very own as it had been allocated to us. Of course it was not always possible to use it for reasons usually to do with routine inspection and servicing. On the 19th/20th May, whilst our crew was stood down, F/L Owen and crew who failed to return from a sortie on the Oise Bridge at Ribemont used it. The aircraft was shot down at low level and crashed about ten miles south of St Quentin. The crew: F/L DWH Owen, F/O DFS Holbrook, Sgt DHJ Barret, LAC RJ Newberry, and AC2 MD Dolan were all killed and lie together in the cemetery at nearby Brissay. A Videotape together with correspondence between me and Mrs Alma Crebbin (younger sister of AC 2 MD Dolan, the tail gunner) and Mr Mike Newberry (younger brother of LAC RJ Newberry - WOpAG) will be found among my papers relating to No. 102 Squadron.

Not surprisingly, increased operational activity gave rise to higher casualties but no more than the acceptable percentage loss rate. At the beginning of May, we still had a small presence at Kinloss in connection with the Norwegian business, and there was some final movement between there and Driffield. On 1st May P/O Ken Gray (previously mentioned), in N1500 carrying a small party of ground tradesmen back to Driffield crashed into a hillside at Insch, Aberdeenshire, and with the exception of one passenger, all on board perished. On 6th May, Sgt Masham and myself were instructed to proceed to Kinloss in connection with this crash. We were to fly the station Magister L8612 which would require us to refuel at Carlisle and Montrose. The Magister was not equipped with wireless and communication between front and rear cockpits was by the Gosport Tube system. About half an hour out of Driffield, we found a Hawker Hind in formation on our port wing with the WOp flashing us with his Aldis Lamp telling us to divert to Linton, where we learned that base had forgotten to tell us something more required of us. I mention this to illustrate again the pressing need for wireless communication for all aircraft.

On 19/20 May, we lost two aircraft to the enemy. F/S Graham Hall with my good friend LAC Jimmy McCutcheon, the WOp/AG member. I remember that one of the crew could not be found at crew transport time. The four other members arrived at the aircraft to find that he was still absent. As he had not put in an appearance by take-off time Graham decided to go one light and did the navigating himself as his co-pilot (P/O Glover) had only recently arrived and was on his first trip. The target was a synthetic oil plant at Buer and Graham did the bombing. Unfortunately a master searchlight illuminated them before Graham could get back to the cockpit where he found the co-pilot somewhat uncertain of his situation that required immediate evasive action. At this point, they were hit and suffered severe damage. However, Graham managed to restore a degree of control but they were obliged to abandon the aircraft in the vicinity of Goch. The co-pilot went first and Graham instructed Jimmy to ensure that AC2 Murray, the rear gunner, was out before he went himself. Arriving at the tail end Jimmy found Murray virtually wrapped in his parachute that he had apparently grabbed by the ripcord handle instead of the carrying loops. Of course, he was in a state of panic and asked Jimmy if he could hang onto him on the way down. But Jimmy told him to wait and dashed back to the cockpit, where Graham was still desperately trying to maintain height, and returned with a parachute. The absentee had placed his 'chute in its usual place in the aircraft before absconding, presumably to make it look like he had intended to come along. All were taken POW and spent the remainder of the war in captivity. On learning of Jimmy's selfless action, Graham ensured that the details were passed to the RAF authority via POW channels, and Jimmy was awarded a well-deserved DFM. After the war, Graham was awarded an MBE for services performed during captivity.

We also lost an 'A' Flight aircraft this same night with F/O Cogman (recently returned from internment in Belgium) as captain. Their target was at Duisburg but they crashed in Holland near Eindhoven. One member was killed, three taken POW, and F/O Cogman evaded capture. It is believed that he was subsequently drowned following the sinking of the SS Abukir on 28th May 1940. P/O Geoff Womersley of 'B' Flight in N1528 crashed in France without casualties to the crew, who were safely returned to the squadron. Quite a month for the squadron, and for the Command, but only a little taste of what was to come. There were, of course, several other incidents including plenty flak damage, forced landings and accidents on the ground.

At the beginning of June our attention was directed to industrial targets in the Ruhr with the occasional line-of-communication job. Now they started to fly the pants off us. In the first few days of the month, quite a number of new boys arrived and we began to feel somewhat overcrowded; among them was a dapper P/O by the name of Cheshire and another called Verran. Those of us who had been with the squadron since before the outbreak of war had no notion that these when properly settled in, would soon replace us as no set tour of operational duty had thus far been declared to us. But we had a lot more to do in that hectic month of June in which I did a further eleven missions with S/L PR Beare (known as Maxie after the famous heavyweight boxer), who had been promoted at the beginning of the month to replace S/L Macdonald promoted to Wing Commander and posted to command 77 Squadron still resident at Driffield.

My first operation in June was on the 3rd in N1471. Raid FDM466 Oil Storage Plant at Essen. Now we were to get a real taste of 'Happy Valley'. Our route took us over Rotterdam which we had seen burning on the 16th May. No smoke to hide us this time as the hatred came up thick and fast with searchlights for good measure; nose down and weave, loss of valuable height, and a long climb back towards the target area, which we found quite easily, as we could see what was waiting for us some time before we got there. The night sky was lit by probing searchlights, flares, exploding heavy flak, and those flaming onions which seemed to weave their way heavenwards so lazily until, at closer quarters, they looked enormous as the whole string of them passed with a mighty sound of rushing air, always seeming, mercifully yet nonetheless intriguingly, to be deflected by the envelope of turbulent air around the aircraft. (I never heard of anyone being hit by flaming onions, but I am glad I never had the experience of being hit myself, they were always close enough to be bloody frightening). Although horizontal visibility was good, the vertical was affected by industrial haze and I was called upon to add some of our flares to the illuminations: in flak conditions, this could be a most unpleasant task. In the darkened fuselage space between the centre section access passage and the rear turret was the flare chute. The flares were held in stowages on either side of the fuselage. About four feet in length the flares were not so much heavy as cumbersome in the confined space. The flare-chute had a removable extension, not unlike a coal scuttle, at the top of which was a pulley holding a length of thin steel cable with a hook at the free end to take the loop of a cord attached to the flare-striking mechanism. As the flare was released, the cable ran off the pulley to its full length and pulled the cord out of its retaining pocket, thus activating the fuse as the cord left the main body of the flare. The height at which the flare ignited was determined by a calibrated fuse-setting ring that had to be set whilst the flare was in the chute and before the removal of the safety pin. At the top of the chute was a handle that held the flare ready for release. It was easy enough when placing the flare, tail fins first, in the chute to let go whilst holding the flare with one hand and trying to close the retaining handle with the other, all in the feeble light of a hand torch. Add to this the effect of evasive action or normal buffeting, the noise of exploding shells, and the sickening stench of burnt cordite, and the reader will, perhaps, get some slight idea of what it was like to take station at the flare-chute. Periods spent at this always seemed to be agonisingly lengthy and it was easy enough to become quite exasperated as the aircraft circled back round each flare in an attempt to identify ground features, a difficult enough task even in the best conditions of night visibility without action from the ground defences.

However, returning to that scene above Essen in the first hour of 4th June 1940. I was no sooner at the flare-chute than we were held fast in a cone of searchlights that seemed to snap on to us instantaneously and we were immediately under fire. I could hear shrapnel peppering us as the nose went down and we started weaving. Eventually, we came out and resumed our search for the target. We found nothing as the result of the first flare and I was asked for another that I already had in the chute. The release technique was to pull the release handle with the right hand whilst giving the flare a good push with the left. I called out, "Flare gone," and we stared the turn, "Where's that bloody flare" came over the intercom and, with the next one cradled in my arms, I looked down the chute and saw, to my horror, that it was jammed across the mouth of the chute; I had not imparted sufficient impetus and the slipstream catching the tail fins had forced them back far enough to cause the nose of the flare to jam across the chute exit, a good arm's length from the fuselage floor. This situation posed a great danger in the event of ignition in the chute of a magnesium charge to the value of a million candle power, capable of causing serious structural damage and, most likely, fire. It had to be cleared, and I asked for speed variations and erratic movement but to no avail. Removing the chute extension and taking care not to further extend the cable attached to fuse cord, I reached down into the chute with my left arm and found I could just touch the rounded cap covering the fuse setting mechanism. I was unable to move the flare even by using my torch as an extension to my arm. Somehow, I had to get hold of it and pull it up the chute. My greatest worry was the possibility of ignition, and it seemed wise, therefore, to try to unhook the fuse cord from the cable. I removed my parachute harness and Mae West, slipped the Sidcot suit from my shoulders and took off my jacket. Now, with a bit of wriggling, I was able to get my shoulder further into the top of the chute and obtain a better grasp on the cap. I found the end of the cable, released the cord and knew that I was now fairly safe. Somehow, in sheer desperation, I found sufficient strength to pull the flare back up the chute a little way. I had thoughts of saving it but could not raise it more than a few inches, but enough to push it clear. All this happened in less time than it has taken to describe it in writing, and the rest of the crew, being otherwise occupied, were quite oblivious to the lonely struggle going on in the mid-fuselage. Perhaps it was better that way; it was certainly a one-man job. How long I was at the flare-chute, I do not know, neither do I know how many flares I released before I heard the bomb-aimer giving steering instructions for the bombing run to the target. This was the Command's heaviest attack so far and targets were fairly widespread over the industrial area. Flak had been sporadic throughout and this persisted during our first run. Our second run was attended by more intensive gunfire and we had to do quite a bit of weaving after bomb release. I believe it was on our return from this trip in the grey light of dawn we found that we had suffered quite a bit of flak damage. One shell had passed through the port aileron, leaving a jagged hole about sixteen inches across and presumably exploding above us; a good job it wasn't instantaneous. A split second later, it would have passed by harmlessly, a split second earlier, it would certainly have caused serious damage and a probable abandonment. A fairly large piece of shrapnel was also found in the casing of a flare stowed only a few inches from my head adjacent to the flare-chute. But this sort of thing was becoming quite commonplace. During the next seven days, we were on the transport systems again:

5 June N1499 FDM506 Bapaume.

8 June N1524 FDM? Westkapelle-Charleville-Meziers (Bombed transport).

10 June N1471 BDM56 Gournay - Cross roads.

(Note the changes in aircraft that arose due to damage, also the locations dictated by the German advance).

About the 10th June, quite unexpectedly and without prior notice, all wireless operators who were qualified air gunners were promoted, irrespective of rank or trade classification, to the rank of acting sergeant. Although the policy for the future rank of all non-commissioned flying personnel had, seemingly, been determined by January 1939 it had been kept under close wraps and was certainly not known among personnel at squadron level. In the few weeks prior to 3rd September 1939 we had some direct entry sergeant pilots and observers posted in and this, had we known it, was the first effect of the modification brought about by the need to speed up the manning process by the introduction of a direct entry scheme at the end of 1938. Early in 1940 in response to a call for volunteers for pilot and observer training, a number of us applied and were apologetically told by the station commander that the notice in station routine orders should have made it plain that anyone already mustered as WOp (Aircrew) could not be considered for retraining. Those of us who had entered as youths saw this as a breaking of faith since it was from youth entrants that NCO pilots and observers were mainly selected since the reintroduction of the Air Observer category in 1936. However, from the manpower utilisation point of view, it made sound common sense. This was the final implementation of the scheme whereby all flying personnel would have the minimum rank of sergeant. At the same time, the scheme introduced the trade of what was generally known as 'Straight Air Gunner', but not all ground tradesman who were part-time air gunners and had flown operationally up to that time were permitted to remuster to this new category. Here again, manpower utilisation criteria had to be applied arbitrarily in the selection process. This sudden increase in the senior NCO population of flying stations gave rise to considerable resentment among senior NCOs in ground trades and many who, after all, were basically ground tradesmen with only acting senior NCO rank for the duration of their flying period. It also caused initial accommodation and messing problems since sergeants' messes were not of the appropriate size to provide for the sudden increase. In the absence of prior information, stations had not made any preparations and, consequently, had quite large numbers of dumbfounded men who had attained SNCO status unexpectedly and should have been immediately afforded the perquisites of the rank by adequate and timely preparation as was rightly deserved. Makeshift arrangements had to be made and it was some time before things settled down. At Driffield re-commissioning a vacant wooden building, which had served as the initial service institute, provided another mess. Sleeping accommodation was provided in the airmen's married quarters, which had been vacated at the outbreak of war. This meant of course, that many of the newly promoted sergeants had to share rooms, but it was a great improvement for them. Those already members of the station mess, myself included, were apologetically required to move out and I must admit that we were rather disappointed at the serious reduction in the quality of what we found in our makeshift mess. I was allocated a single room in one of the married quarters that was no great comedown. It was, to say the least, most inappropriate, even for those who had not sampled the normal standard of a pre-war station. But they were, after all, however sudden, senior NCOs and were expected to behave as such, it was appropriate, therefore, that they should have been afforded the perquisites of the rank by adequate preparation. But this was war time and, although flying personnel were the main component in the discharge of a flying station's role, the final part of the implementation, which obviously had to be made in one move, should have received better thought and action in the planning stage. Aircraftmen flyers unfortunate enough to be taken prisoners of war were required to work in captivity that, had they been Senior NCOs, would not have happened. The new status took care of this and all aircraftmen flyers in captivity were promoted. It was at this time that the term 'Aircrew' came into prominence.

On the 11th June, about midday, still heavy with sleep, I was roused by someone, obviously in great haste, and told to report to the crew room immediately. It transpired that Italy had entered the conflict and we were to proceed to Jersey, in the Channel Islands, as a means of getting closer to Turin, where our intended target for that night was the Fiat works. What a glorious summer day it was as we left Driffield at 1430 hours, thinking somewhat disgruntled what we could have been doing at Bridlington on a well-deserved day off. In N1471, we left Jersey at 2100 hours for Turin. About two and a half hours out, still climbing to clear the Alps, we entered cloud and soon encountered severe turbulence.

Electrical disturbance was the worst I had ever experienced, and the noise in my headphones was unbearable. Fearing for my equipment led me to disconnect the aerials, and in doing so, I suffered superficial burns to the fingers of my right hand. It became agonizingly cold, and we soon felt the depth of its penetration. The cloud seemed without top as we struggled laboriously for height. We now heard ominous bumps as of something striking the aircraft and soon deduced that ice was being flung off the propellers. The captain asked me to shine the beam of the Aldis Lamp along the leading edges of the wings and we could see the ice building up despite the action of the pulsating de-icer boots. The ice formed with great rapidity and soon we could see it building up thickly over the leading edges, and we began to wallow very badly. We descended rapidly as low as we dared but there was no improvement in our situation, which was now of extreme hazard. The fear we all shared was aggravated by the effect of the arctic conditions, and there was now ice inside the cabin, it was quite impossible to keep still. To me, the navigator seemed to be performing the wildest gyrations, and I have no doubt that he thought the same of me. Maxi was fighting with the aeroplane to keep it airborne, and what the poor sod in the tail was doing only God knows. We were obviously not going to make it this trip and reluctantly decided to abort. After dropping our bombs safe we staggered round to return to Jersey. We found that most crews had experienced the same as ourselves and only a few had miraculously avoided it and found the target. Seemingly Turin was clear and with no blackout. We were airborne 5 hours and 55 minutes and, after a short rest, were airborne again at 0700 hours for Driffield, thankful to have that cruel experience behind us but, nevertheless, disappointed at the failure of our mission.

On the 14th in N1524 - BDM609 Rheydt. 17th again in N1524 - BDM 640 Oil Refinery Gelsenkirchen. 19th in N1524 - BDM? Marshalling Yards at Schwerte. All pretty much the same pattern with searchlights, flak all round, and noticeably accurate at Gelsenkirchen.

We lost Sergeant Masham and crew, all killed in N1499 against Bottrop on the night of 18/19 June. Mash had been our second pilot for some time and got his own crew and N1499 after his last trip with us in that aircraft on 5/6 June to Bapaume. My logbook records that Maxie and I flew to Manston in it at the later date of 21st to recover P/O McArthur and crew, who had belly-landed there with flak damage. We could not have used N1499, but the Flight Authorisation Book must have shown it erroneously as it was from that source that logbooks were completed usually as much as several days later. Having regard to the intensity of our operational activity, our losses were, perhaps, no more than was to be expected, but the strain was beginning to show. France had fallen, the British Expeditionary Force had been miraculously evacuated, and there was a feeling of great sadness, something close to a feeling of defeat. What had it all been for?

On the 24th, we did the Rhonengin Works at Mannheim. This was BDM725 in N1524 –a very rough trip with dense clouds over the target area, lightning, searchlights and intense flak. No.2 Group Blenheims had been on this target during the day, and the Germans were very trigger-happy. We had to stooge around quite a bit and get down dangerously low, where we got a large dose of concentrated light flak; not so exhilarating now as that brilliantly lit scene at Stavanger. It was bloody fearsome, to say the least, but our minds were occupied with the task at hand. After 7 hours and 15 minutes, we landed at Stradishall, gasping for fuel.

On the 27th June in N1471 - BDM? We visited Duisburg, another hot spot, but the story is very much the same now. The 29th June took us to an Ammunition Factory at Hochst for Raid DM756. We derived some real satisfaction from this one. The area was heavily defended and we got the hot reception we had come to expect: the usual flare dropping and searchlights with intense flak as we went in low to give the bomb-aimer a good look, the detonations from our own bombs and explosives in the buildings, the resulting fires all contributing to a scene of apparently wide destruction.

During the period of the Battle for France (10th May to 29th June for the purpose of this narrative), I was engaged in sixteen operations and logged a total of 104 hours and 50 minutes operational flying for the period. Most of the pre-war squadron flyers had done about the same, and I doubt if crews were ever called upon to make that kind of effort; more than half of what was to become an operational tour in less than seven weeks. At this time, nothing had been declared as to what an operational tour would be, and we did not think of such a thing, but rather that we would simply carry on for the duration, or earlier as fate might determine, which would, of course, have been absolute nonsense. However, I seem to recollect that the yardstick used to take the first of us, and subsequent crews, off operations was 200 hours. Initially, this approximated to 25/26 missions in the twin-engine aircraft, but when the four-engine types came in, they were found to be capable of approximately thirty missions in the 200 hours, and this became the norm for the rest of the war.

Driffield was bombed on 4th July at about 2215 hours. Most of the aircraft were away on another mission, but we had been washed-out by a last-minute technical failure. A stick of four bombs in the domestic area caused minor damage and one death. Unfortunately, I happened to be too close to one of them and collected a few superficial wounds that were sufficient to keep me on the ground for a month - repaid in my own coin, as it were. However, I was due to go on leave the next day and managed to persuade the medical officer that I was fit enough to travel and get attention at home. I couldn't fly anyway so what was the use of staying there? While on leave, I received word from my good friend

George Maughan that I was posted, with most of the pre-war members, to 19 Operational Training Unit at Kinloss as part of the initial training staff. Returning to Driffield on 18th July, I found that I was the only one on the posting list remaining and was to proceed forthwith. I did not wish to leave and made an appeal to Maxie Beare, who told me in a very positive way how fortunate I had been to survive the initial onslaught - the intended role of the regular force under the defence strategy then extant - and was now required to pass on my experience to others, at least for the time being, and to be rested for a period of at least six months. I left Driffield feeling somewhat depressed and, after a miserable overnight rail journey, arrived at Kinloss to be reunited with friends from 102 Squadron and many others from Linton On Ouse and Dishforth. As Maxie had told me we were to have a rest while training others to follow us in No.4 Group. But that is another story.

CHAPTER V
THE TOOLS FOR THE JOB

Many writers have commented about the unreliability of aircraft wireless equipment. Some have questioned the usefulness of the wireless member of the crew. It is my opinion that these were poorly informed. Most were not there and, at best, were totally ignorant in regard to the development of wireless technology. During the early part of my time with 19 OTU, there was the most embarrassing incident in which a junior officer pilot, an instructor with operational experience, in the presence of others, actually referred to his wireless operator as a useless passenger. Here, perhaps, was a typical example of the source of much of this adverse criticism: crew captains themselves. (Remember, a bomber pilot had to be accompanied by a wireless operator at all times). The pilot was ordered to make an apology before a large assembly of the units' flying personnel and one can imagine his feeling of regret for his ill-considered and hurtful words. He was shortly and quietly removed from the scene of his humiliation. In the summer of 1947 I bumped into Johnny Crocket in St James Street, London. His most pleasant greeting was, "Good Lord! Bill, my last memory of you is of that frightful trip to Villeneuve when you had the wireless in bits all over the floor." What a picture such an innocent and well-meant statement is likely to produce in the mind of the uninformed reader of today. Actually, I had the greatest respect for Johnny Crocket who had seen much of me since that memorable event, which I shall never forget. I served as his senior squadron wireless operator for quite a lengthy period when, as a squadron leader, he commanded C Squadron of No. 19 OTU at Kinloss, which obviously was not his first memory of me on the occasion of the chance meeting in London.

The standard aircraft wireless equipment in use at the beginning of hostilities was the combination of Receiver Type R1082 and Transmitter Type T1083. Both were compact, soundly constructed and perfectly reliable if properly maintained and used competently. The receiver was little more in circuit design technology than the ordinary domestic receiver of the time, employing five thermionic valves. The power supplies were, in fact, identical to battery-operated receivers powered by a two-volt lead-acid accumulator to heat the valve filaments, and a one hundred and twenty-volt dry battery to provide high tension to the valve anodes (plates). The receiver also had a set of coils of which two were required for each segment of the frequency range covered by the receiver. The transmitter was of the Tuned Anode/Tuned Grid type with 'High' and 'Medium' frequency band capability. Each band required two fairly large plug-in coils: one for the Master Oscillator circuit and the other for the Power Amplifier circuit. Power for the transmitter was provided by a motor-generator powered by the aircraft's twelve-volt supply. (It was this item of equipment that caused me such trouble on that trip to Villeneuve. It arose due to neglect, over a lengthy period, on the part of the wireless operator responsible for daily inspection and maintenance - not myself in this instance, as the aircraft was not assigned to me; I was detailed to replace the usual operator at the last minute whilst he actually flew on this mission with the crew from which I had been transferred that day and in the aircraft for which I had been responsible for daily inspection at the beginning of that day). Altogether, the wireless equipment provided adequate general-purpose communication within the wireless range then feasible in the light of technological development.

The R1082/T1083 equipment was progressively replaced, commencing in the summer of 1940, by the T1154/R1155 that, since it had to perform in the same atmospheric conditions, did nothing to improve communication. All it did, by the use of advanced design techniques, was to eliminate the use of ancillary batteries and plug-in coils and provide a receiver with an approximately calibrated scale showing frequencies in kilocycles and a transmitter with integral tuning coils that could be pre-set by a system of click-stops. There was also provision for a degree of frequency stabilisation by means of plug-in crystals that were about ten times larger than those in use with modern transistorised equipment. But in 1940, miniaturisation was yet to come, and these new sets were somewhat larger than those they replaced, although the receiver valves were much smaller than those in the R1082.

What is not generally understood is the effect of natural phenomena on wireless transmissions at that time. Although these phenomena still exist, technology has advanced to such a degree that equipment can now be designed to operate at frequencies where their effect is of little or no consequence. In those days, operating frequencies were between 250 and 10,000 kilocycles (kilohertz in modern electronic parlance - to perpetuate the name of Gustav Hertz, the inventor of the Hertzian Cycle). At the lower end of the scale, medium frequency we called it, we had to use a trailing aerial two hundred feet long. For the higher frequencies, a fixed aerial mounted between fore and aft masts on top of the fuselage was used. At these frequencies, electrical disturbances in the atmosphere were picked up by the aerials and amplified by the receiver so that the wireless operator was almost constantly straining to hear over the combined noise of atmospherics and noise produced by the aircraft itself. Atmospheric noise was frequently of such intensity as to seriously reduce effective range. As regards range, one should understand that transmissions at these frequencies were more readily affected by terrain features causing absorption, screening and deflection, whilst natural phenomena in the ionosphere causes reflections from the Heaviside and Appleton Layers, giving rise to what is known as 'Skip Distance'. My experience of 5th September 1939 illustrates this. Shortly after 0700 hours I had no difficulty in contacting Driffield on 3625 kilocycles from the ground at Dieppe. The distance is only some 320 miles, yet three and a half hours later, I was unable to make contact, before take-off or when airborne until the distance had been approximately halved. What had actually happened was that the ionosphere had risen since the early morning thereby shortening the length of the 'Skip Distance'. There was nothing wrong with the equipment; it was due entirely to limitations imposed by natural phenomena. As previously mentioned, personnel entered for 'The duration of hostilities' were not trained for long-term engagements and I doubt if the basic training of war-entry wireless operators included more theoretical knowledge than was absolutely necessary. It was, in my opinion, misunderstanding, or ignorance, of these phenomena, and a large measure of simple neglect - loose or dirty connections, badly soldered joints, etc., that were the real Gremlins said to affect aircraft wireless and electrical systems. Worst of all, perhaps, was dampness and condensation, particular hazards for aircraft kept in the open.

A Direction Finding Loop was an essential part of the aircraft aerial systems. This enabled bearings to be obtained from the aircraft on known transmissions. It was particularly useful during the long periods of wireless silence when it was usual to take bearings on identified transmissions as a means of checking dead reckoning navigation. Here again, poorly informed writers have pointed out the risk of taking a reciprocal bearing. Of course that was possible, but one would have to be lost to such a degree as to not know which side of the aircraft the ground station was located. The greatest problem when a gearing was in the fore and aft direction and doubt about having passed over the source of the transmission, but an experienced operator would be able to quickly resolve this doubt. Let the reader fully appreciate that the wireless operator in these early wartime activities, besides providing the communication link, was the only navigational aid to dead reckoning that was seriously affected by unreliable wind forecasts over Europe and our natural inability to see in the dark. I never forgot that C-in-C's 'Order Of The Day,' which I was required to thoroughly digest on my first reporting for duty with 102 Squadron.

In the Whitley Mk V, the installation also included a Transmitter/Receiver Type TR9F similar to the type used in fighter aircraft. This provided Radio Telephony over a range of about thirty-five miles in good conditions and was remotely connected to the pilot's position so that by the use of a flexible cable system, he could work the Transmit/Receive switch of the set to which the wireless operator could connect him directly. The facility did not provide more than voice communication.

The French had a good Medium Frequency D/F System similar to our own civil one from which it was separated by only ten kilocycles. One night in June 1940, when the German advance in the east was beginning to look serious for Paris, I had recourse to use this system, in conjunction with our own, to fix our position. I called Le Bourget (call sign FNB) and was asked to transmit so that bearings could be taken and, in quite normal manner, was given a set of co-ordinates. I immediately heard another station sending 'Bum' 'Bum' 'Bum,' it was Tours (call sign FNO), still well south of the ground battle, tipping me off that the Germans were on the frequency having captured some of the systems stations, no doubt including Le Bourget. I have reason to be grateful to that vigilant unknown friend who passed me a bearing from Tours, which, when plotted with one from our own system, was obviously genuine. Had it not been for that intervention we might have accepted a 'Spoof Fix' and, if we had been totally lost, proceeded to disaster.

One final comment about equipment: Since no mechanical or electrical contrivance is infallible, only the highest standards of manufacture, servicing and maintenance are acceptable for RAF airborne equipment. Inspection and acceptance is the responsibility of the Aeronautical Inspection Directorate whose inspectors are usually based at manufacturer locations for the period of any major contract work. Component and wiring failure within transmitters and receivers was, in my experience, remote. Detection of such isolated failure was, with minor exceptions, unlikely in the air, and spares were not carried, not even spare valves. The action of dismantling a transmitter or receiver for fault diagnosis was, therefore, illogical. Failure of loose external wiring and connections, particularly the intercom-microphone-telephone system with its complicated switching arrangement into which the wireless installation was also connected, was not so remote and could only be minimised by thorough routine maintenance. Obviously, wireless operators were trained to detect and rectify faults likely to be experienced in the air (I certainly was), and at 19 OTU, in-ground and air training exercises, we used every possible device to this end. I am sure the same applied at the other OTUs, but instruction is only as good as he who gives it and he who receives it. As a pre-war regular trained for a long service career, I have always been a keen advocate of 'Preventive Maintenance', and I cannot subscribe to any suggestion that wireless equipment provided during the 1939-1945 period was in any sense unreliable because of poor design or manufacturing standards. The human element was, of course, the greatest single factor; has there not always been a tendency for mankind to blame the tools provided for the job?

CHAPTER VI
AIRCREW

At this juncture, it seems appropriate to offer a brief explanation of the manner in which the RAF selected and trained personnel for flying duties between the two world wars.

When World War One ended in 1918, the infant Royal Air Force was not only the world's largest air force in terms of personnel and aircraft. It was the only independent air force in the world; independent that is of any control by the Navy and the Army. The politicians, not surprisingly, were concerned with the restoration of the economy after a war that had been costly in terms of manpower and finance. The United Kingdom was in serious debt, particularly to the United States. Anyway, after a 'War To End All Wars', surely the only need in the way of defence was for token forces, and as for the RAF, why not merge the Army and Navy functions with their respective forces, thus making for further economy. Of course, both Navy and Army hierarchies supported this, and thus, against this opposition and the financial stringencies imposed by successive Governments, began the long struggle to maintain an independent Air Force as an essential instrument of Air Power. After the post-war reductions, the young Service with Sir Hugh Trenchard (so passionately involved in its creation) now at its head as Chief Of Air Staff, but with hopelessly inadequate resources, seized the opportunity presented by the creation of British Government responsibility for the control of the mandated Middle East territories previously occupied by Germany and the Ottoman Empire (Turkey). Principally, these were in what are now Iraq (Mesopotamia), Iran (Persia), Palestine, Jordan, and the Arabian Peninsular (now Saudi Arabia and the Trucial States). Also there was a continuing need to protect our interests in the Suez Canal Zone providing, as it was intended to do, a vital trade shortcut to the Far East. There was also the continuing problem of the troublesome North West part of our Indian Empire. All this provided the opportunity, seized by Trenchard, to demonstrate the full potential of Air Power, in an Air Control Function, with resulting economy against the full employment of Army and Navy resources. Full use had to be made of existing WW1 aircraft until the end of the 1920s, and other economies had to be made in the employment of personnel. By 1923, the role of the Air Observer had long been regarded as mainly the defence of the aircraft against attack from the rear. Thus was born the idea of replacing the observer with an Aerial Gunner selected from suitable ground tradesmen, and training all pilots in aerial navigation such as it then was. The resulting economy in terms of manpower utilisation will be apparent, whilst in financial terms, the abolition of the observer - usually an officer or sergeant, and his replacement by a lowly aircraftman performing a dual role for a trifling addition (one shilling and sixpence a day whilst so employed) to his basic pay, needs no further comment. However, such was the need for economy in all things RAF and, in the light of my own long experience, I can say that an acute awareness of the Public Interest in terms of financial expenditure has always attended the day-to-day working of the RAF.

The Aerial Gunner identity badge of a Winged Bullet in brass to be worn on the upper right sleeve was introduced in 1923. By this time, air-to-ground wireless communication was essential to the Air Control function of the RAF overseas, and therefore, the trade of Wireless Operator was prominent in the selection of aerial gunners. Thus, became the WOp/AG, but remember, he was basically a WOp also engaged in a normal ground wireless trade function. Part-time AGs were also required to undertake High Level bombing and photography, and the full extent of the economy gained by these measures in the overseas theatres will be appreciated. Of course, the same system was applied throughout the RAF and continued into the late 1930s.

The rise to power of Adolph Hitler and the emergence of the German Luftwaffe brought the Government of the day to its senses, though only partially, and in 1934 a measure of expansion for the RAF was authorised. The obvious need for the modernisation of squadron equipment required consideration for the provision of personnel and their training to crew the increased numbers and types of aircraft to be introduced, particularly for the larger bomber aircraft envisaged. The proposals included the reintroduction of the Air Observer category and a scheme whereby youth entrants between the ages of fifteen and a half and seventeen and a quarter were to be trained in the basic trades of wireless operator, armourer and photographer under conditions broadly similar to those for Aircraft Apprentices, and from whom would be selected the nucleus of the future requirements for flying personnel as then envisaged. The three trades were, of course, directly related to the former Air Observer role that was to be re-introduced in 1936, as it was, in fact. From these trades it was intended that the majority of future air gunners would be selected, with the trade of wireless operator being mainly preferred as the obvious choice for conversion to Air Observer after further training. Airmen selected for flying duties would be paid the standing addition to basic pay of one shilling flying pay plus sixpence a day qualification pay whilst so employed; that is to say - whilst held against a squadrons authorised strength of air gunners and not, as stated by many writers, applicable only to days when actually employed on a flying duty. From these personnel, it was intended to select, after three years productive service as air gunners, the future Air Observers who would be employed in the rank of Acting Corporal. Since wireless training was technically complex and lengthy those already mustered in the trade of wireless operator were as prominent in the selection process as was the case following WW1. After seven years of productive flying service, the scheme provided for further training, by selection, as Airman Pilot with the rank of Acting Sergeant for a further five years, after which an airman was to be returned to his basic trade in the rank he would normally have attained. A Corporal Observer was to be paid the combined pay of nine shillings a day, and Sergeant Pilots twelve shillings, eleven shillings, or ten shillings a day depending on their basic trade. It was, of course, possible for airmen in other categories, particularly former aircraft apprentices, to be selected for part-time flying duties including Airman Pilot. But airmen in these categories would be returned to their basic trade duties after six years.

The Munich crisis of 1938 gave further impetus to the expansion by the creation of direct entry schemes for the training of pilots and observers for short-service engagements in the acting rank of sergeant. In January 1939, an official 'Policy and Conditions of Service for Aircraft Crews (other than pilots)' was laid down. The main effect of this was to create a full-time employment basis for all air gunners who were also to be wireless operators, those who were not being required to remuster. (Thus was born the new full-time trade of Wireless Operator Aircrew, although pay and trade classifications remained the same). The undesirable effect of re-training airmen who were not already wireless operators was soon the subject of amendment and part-time AGs, were permitted to continue until mid-1940, when most in skilled ground trades were taken off flying. Others in semi-skilled and unskilled trades were offered continuation as what we then called 'Straight AGs.' The cloth flying badge 'AG' replaced the 'Winged Bullet' sleeve badge in December 1939, but many continued to wear it throughout the period of obsolescence. In June 1940, all wireless operators who were qualified air gunners were awarded the rank of acting sergeant, irrespective of their trade classification, with special rates of pay, although in my own case, already holding that rank, I continued to be paid as a sergeant in my basic trade plus the combined flying and gunners pay which was, of course, advantageous. When I was later promoted to flight sergeant I had to be awarded an extra shilling a day to make it worthwhile accepting the promotion. Thus, by June 1940, we had an all Officer/Senior NCO Aircraft Crew Structure, and it was at this time that the term 'Aircrew'', in its applicability to flying personnel, came into general use.

Chapter VII
Instructor

I limped into RAF Kinloss during the morning of 20th July 1940, feeling very sore as the wounds in my left side were not yet fully healed. I had spent a miserably uncomfortable night in the train; there were no seats available, and I had to make the best, with many others, of the standing space in the corridor. After the overnight journey from York, I was tired, miserable and very sad at having left Driffield and 102 Squadron. However, there were many old friends and acquaintances from Driffield and the other stations of No. 4 Group, who had arrived at Kinloss during my leave of absence.

First thing was to get myself accommodated and cleaned up, then see the medical officer who, finding my wounds still open, grounded me pending further examination. The Chief Instructor did the only thing he could do with me and put me to work in the ground school that was still in the first stage of formation. So I was to be a lecturer for a while! I didn't mind as I had always felt at ease in front of small audiences and was able to hold my own on technical subjects in my particular specialist field.

No. 19 Operational Training Unit was still in the early formative stage and we were the initial instructors. A few students had arrived and there were sufficient aircraft for flying instruction: Ansons for continuation of pilot training on twin-engine aircraft, navigation training for observers, and air firing for gunners. There were Whitley Mark III aircraft for advanced training of pilots, observers, wireless operators and gunners. These now being surplus to operational squadron requirements following their replacement by the Whitley Mark V.

One of the first jobs to be done in the Ground School was the installation of demonstration equipment and this kept us quite busy for two to three weeks between giving occasional random lectures. The entire ground-training scheme was rather makeshift until the classrooms were completed to plan, which they were in good time for the arrival of the regular intake of students.

Construction work at Kinloss had started some time before the outbreak of war as the station was part of the RAF peacetime expansion programme. However, when it was seen to be impossible to complete it as intended, the remaining work was carried out to a temporary peace standard with the result that only the technical buildings were of permanent brick construction. Other buildings were of wooden construction with space heating mainly by solid fuel stoves. This meant that in winter conditions, personnel had to return to cold rooms after working hours, frequently entailing lengthy flying details, having to light fires and trying to maintain a reasonable degree of warmth with a totally inadequate weekly fuel ration. This was to become a common situation at most United Kingdom locations, the worst examples being the war expansion operational flying stations constructed to war standard, mainly utilising Nissen-type buildings of corrugated iron construction.

The station was initially in Training Command, with the principal resident unit being No. 14 Flying Training School. However, when Germany occupied Norway practically without resistance in March 1940, the station became listed as a vulnerable prime target, and 14 FTS was hastily re-located. The station was then allotted to Bomber Command as an Operational Training base, with the capability to become fully operational, if required, by the rapid conversion of the OTU to form at least one bomber squadron. Apart from No. 19 OTU, the station had to provide for No. 45 Maintenance Unit, which, being a lodger unit of Maintenance Command, was self-supporting, requiring only accommodation and messing facilities. No. 45 MU was, however, a large unit for which permanent (brick-built) working accommodation facilities had been provided to peacetime standard and, since it was an aircraft repair and storage unit, also had several grass-covered hangars widely dispersed around the northern perimeter of the aerodrome. Its brick-built administrative and store buildings were the envy of the station that had to make do with the wooden type buildings for many years into the post-war era. They were, of course, superior to the temporary type erected to serve for the duration of the war.

There were many instructors who had a hankering to be returned to operations and some made nuisances of themselves in requesting this. They were told by the Chief Instructor (the unit commander) that they were screened from operations for a rest period of at least six months, during which, in the instructional role, they were to pass on the benefit of their operational experience to others. At this time, the instructors were all regulars and my own view was that we should go along with the system. Our superiors at the highest command levels had to be trusted to determine how best to employ us, and we were, after all, members of the Royal Air Force (the regular force), as distinct from the non-regulars who were entered into the Royal Air Force Volunteer Reserve for the duration of the emergency only. As such the war, however distasteful to everyone, was very much a part of our careers, rather than an intrusion to it. As a regular entered initially for a long-term career, my view was that I should do as I was directed, unless there were grounds for serious objection. There was always a proper course for airing personal opinion in matters affecting one-self and however much I disliked having been taken off operations, I found nothing wrong with the idea of taking a respite from it. As Maxie Beare had so forcefully pointed out to me on my departure from 102 Squadron, a rest period was essential. Although we may not have recognised it ourselves, we were all affected to varying degrees by the undue strain of it that was bound to have an effect on operational performance.

Although not formally declared fit for flying duty, I seized the opportunity, on the 2nd August, for a weekend in Yorkshire and to re-visit the No. 4 Group scene. I learned that Flt Lt Harry Budden was to make a return visit to Dishforth and to give it an official look, it had to be authorised as a training flight. So I picked myself a student wireless operator and went along as his instructor. I enjoyed a good break of four days in the company of old friends, among them John Moutray, who had been posted to 102 Sqn in July 1939 and was placed under my personal direction during his initial familiarisation with squadron work. He was posted to 51 Squadron at Dishforth in March 1940 and was just about at the end of his tour of operational duty. John was a Canadian in the Royal Air Force and we formed a lasting friendship from our very first meeting. I shall mention him again much later in my memoirs. Also at Dishforth with 51 Squadron were another two Canadians in the RAF – F/Os Bisset and Kierstead, with whom I was crewed at the outbreak of hostilities.

Towards the end of August, I was pronounced fit for flying duties and was immediately seized by Squadron Leader Johnny Crockett, OC 'C' Flight, to be his Senior Wireless Instructor. The flying part of the unit was organised into four flights. Each intended to be of the same numerical strength (Nine aircraft) of the flights in the Whitley operational bomber squadrons. Each flight was commanded by a Squadron Leader, 'A' Flight consisted of the Anson aircraft, and the others - 'B', 'C', and 'D' having the Whitleys. As the unit grew rapidly the flights were soon re-designated 'Squadrons'.

My new role required the performance of duties other than flying, an office and clerk coming as part of the job. My flying activities were mainly short-duration local stints - mostly checking flights for personnel and filling the standing order requiring a staff wireless operator to be carried at all times. We were also engaged in trials of a recently devised ground-controlled landing technique known as 'ZZ' Landings. This entailed the use of the ground wireless direction-finding station and required a very capable airborne wireless operator whose task was to keep the pilot informed of an un-ending series of courses to steer at specified heights. The technique was to bring the aircraft overhead, then send it out on a pre-determined course, turn it onto a final approach course with decreasing heights until the aerodrome was visible. All done by means of bearings obtained on transmissions from the aircraft, frequently interrupted by the courses to steer from the direction finding (D/F) station with height variations. All instructions to the aircraft were given in Morse code, the WOp passing them to the pilot over the aircraft inter-communication system. The duty pilot located in his hut on the aerodrome was in overall control and in direct contact with the direction-finding operator by telephone to ensure that the intended pattern of the landing was applied. It is appropriate to mention that we had no runways at this time but were, nevertheless, required to land in specified widths of the aerodrome according to the wind direction. The widths were changed from time to time to facilitate the recovery of the ground condition. There was, as yet, no radar, no instrument landing system, no Air Traffic Control system controlled by ground radio, and no cockpit aids to assist approach and blind landing. The Lorenz Beam Approach system was, however, soon to be introduced into the RAF as the Standard Beam Approach System (SBA). The trouble with the 'ZZ' system was the time taken for the ground D/F station to obtain bearings and pass the duty pilot's instructions to the aircraft. It was too slow to be impressive to the pilot of an aircraft descending through conditions of poor visibility, but it was all we had and was put to use as required in the short term before the introduction of SBA. We certainly put a lot of hard work into the trials at Kinloss. My pilot throughout was a F/Lt Kerr, who was a well-known Imperial Airways pilot pre-war and had experience with the early Lorenz system but seemed rather impatient with 'ZZ' and the time taken between instructions from the ground.

By late summer of 1940, we were in full swing with the training programme and course intakes were beginning to take on a regular pattern. Flying activity intensified and the Whitley Mark III was soon replaced with the Mark IV, of which only a limited number had been produced as a step to the introduction of the Mark V. The Mark IV was identical to the Mark III except for the replacement of the Armstrong Siddeley Tiger radial engines with the Rolls Royce Merlin in-line engines. It was this engine that saved the Whitley and prolonged its operational life as the Mark V and subsequent versions to the end of the war, although it was phased out of service with Bomber Command, as the squadrons were re-equipped with the four-engine heavy types, particularly the Handley Page Halifax and the Avro Lancaster.

As flying training increased, so the accident rate increased. Minor accidents are difficult to remember, but one of the most horrific major accidents will forever haunt my memory. This happened quite early in the life of 19 OTU - on 7th November 1940, in fact - when a Whitley MkV (N1440) returning from a routine training exercise suddenly nose-dived, from a low altitude, into the nearby town of Forres. All five members of the crew were killed instantly, and it is miraculous that there were no casualties on the ground as the point of impact was in the small backyard of a house in the most densely populated part of the town. The house itself sustained only minor damage. A small plaque commemorating this crash was recently installed by RAF Kinloss and is a prominent feature on a nearby wall just off Tolbooth Street. The fact that damage was confined to such a small area testifies to the steepness of the nosedive. The cause of the crash has often been the subject of local debate and conjecture. I can only recount the more informed opinions among us at the time. One member of the trainee crew had his wife resident in the locality of the crash. The Whitley was notoriously prone to slipping into a nosedive if turned too steeply, and particularly if any attempt was made to tighten the turn with the use of the elevator. This is what was generally believed to have happened. The pilot instructor was F/O Painter, who I had known with 102, and I cannot think that a pilot with his operational experience would have carried out such a manoeuvre at low altitude. The other staff member on board was Sgt (Pip) Lewis also formerly of 102 Squadron. My own feeling is of a foolish act of sheer bravado that cost five valuable lives. Sick with the sadness of this event, a friend, Larry Donnelly, and I decided we would visit Nairn, hoping that a change of scene would help us to forget it for a while. Nairn is fifteen miles west of Kinloss and was, even in wartime, served by a reasonable bus service from Forres. The journey from Kinloss to Forres was always a problem, usually to be solved only by a walk of thirty minutes. For me, the day's sadness was soon dissipated. Little did I know that the girl I met on this occasion would become, as she still is (February 2001), my wife of sixty years.

So the eventful year of 1940 drew to a close. It had been a sad year for those of us who started the war from its very beginning. The dreadful winter of 1939/40, the concentrated effort that had been thrust upon us since the German advance through Belgium and Holland, our vain attempt to frustrate that advance, the retreat to the Channel coast and the miraculous evacuation from Dunkirk, the fall of France and our feeling of desolation and isolation. Our ineffective pounding at German industry, the increasingly effective flak at the low levels we were required to fly. Our removal from the operational scene, albeit to train others to follow us. But I was twenty years of age, had survived so far, and was very much in love. I really had a great deal to be thankful for. Christmas 1940 came and went. I spent as much of it as my duties would allow in Nairn, which I was, of course, visiting whenever possible, and sometime in March 1941, Rosemary and I announced our engagement. We didn't wait long to fix the date of our marriage and settled on the 10th May 1941 for our marriage to take place in the Nairn Old Parish Church.

By the end of 1940, the intensity of the flying activity at Kinloss and the effect of it on the surface of the aerodrome was a matter of concern, and there was talk of a satellite aerodrome soon to be opened at a site alongside the main road and the River Findhorn on the western boundary of Forres. I remember taking several looks at this location and doing the occasional dummy landing approach to it that, because of prevailing winds, would have to be done over the town from the easterly direction. It was hardly an ideal arrangement for flying training as there was a high ground feature (Cluny Hill) dangerously close to the line of approach, but the terrain to the south was flat as far as Findhorn Bay and the Moray Firth. The western boundary of the site was somewhat higher as the ground rose from the course of the river that changed direction at this point. It was not a serious take-off problem as long as there was no loss of power, a risk that was considered and accepted.

The satellite facility came into use during the early spring of 1941 when 'C' and 'D' squadrons, with their student crews at advanced training level, were required to make maximum possible use of it. The ground surface was grass and whilst its length was adequate for take-off and landing, the width was of little use other than providing a means of spreading the surface wear and tear. The controlling elements of both squadrons remained at Kinloss and their aircraft were generally detailed to commence the day's flying activity from there, landing at Forres between sorties. The final landing was made at Kinloss thereby alleviating the problem of moving personnel by road. A mobile workshop facility was provided for servicing personnel and a small Nissen hut served as crew room for flying personnel. This also provided office accommodation for an officer in charge of the flying activity, usually a senior flight lieutenant, and myself as senior wireless instructor. There was no requirement for sleeping and messing accommodation at this early stage.

We usually referred to the site by the name of Balnageith, the farm through which access was provided, although it was officially Forres and shown on the Bomber Command location map as the Forres satellite of RAF Kinloss. My involvement, during the mid-1990s, in the creation of a memorial sited on what was the northern perimeter of the satellite brought an awareness of a somewhat resentful attitude on the part of certain members of the local population who seemed to believe that the site was, in fact, a Royal Air Force station in its own right, and should therefore be referred to as RAF Forres. This opinion was generated by would-be historians whose researches had concentrated mostly on Operations Record Books, probably the most frequently quoted as historical sources. These, although official records are only as good as they were made by those who had the unfortunate task of writing them in addition to their many other primary and more important duties. The RAF is not in the business of writing its own history, although all established units are required to maintain records of their operational activities. Maintaining the Operations Record Book (Form 540) can be quite a chore that is frequently reduced to absolute basics, taking on somewhat monotonous formats with comments on occasional unusual happenings.

During the summer of 1942, when the strategic bombing campaign started to intensify, Bomber Command had to be reorganised. The old No.6 (Training) Group, the controlling formation for all Bomber Command Operational Training Units, became No. 6 (Canadian) Group, Bomber Command. The command's operational training then became the responsibility of three new formations namely: 91, 92, and 93 Groups. RAF Kinloss became a station of 91 Group and 19 OTU a unit of that group. The pressure was now on to produce more flying personnel for the increasing size of the command with its larger multi-engine aircraft. Like most other OTUs the Kinloss-based unit had to be expanded, and additional accommodation provided for the increased student element. The Bomber OTU satellites were intended to provide for the evacuation of the OTU so that, in the event of the parent station being rendered inoperative, the vital training could be continued with minimum adverse effect. RAF Kinloss was a station of the permanent RAF, and any consideration of war expansion had to be related to envisaged post-war requirements. Therefore, the evacuation facilities at the Forres satellite were utilised, with an added measure of improvement, to provide temporary accommodation and messing facilities for students at the final stages of their operational training. Being of a temporary nature and bearing in mind the short duration of use by individual students, the facilities were obviously Spartan in character. Sleeping accommodation was widely dispersed in inconspicuous locations in the wooded areas on the south side of the aerodrome. It is the impressive size, in numerical terms, of this temporary accommodation that tends to create in the non-professional mind that these satellite locations became a fully blown RAF Stations of the war establishment. The Forres aerodrome did in fact, remain a satellite of RAF Kinloss, designated primarily for the use of 19 OTU, and as such continued to be used by 'C' and 'D' Squadrons to reduce pressure on the facilities at Kinloss until training ceased in 1945. If it had become a war establishment station, then it would have had an Establishment Document with a Policy Statement of its own, with responsibility for keeping the usual station records that would now be available to the public. My own enquiries made to the Public Records Office, Ministry of Defence Air Historical Branch and RAF Museum indicates that Forres was a satellite throughout its existence. I was, however surprised to find some admitted misuse of RAF terminology by the present generation of operatives at these civilian manned and run historical sources. Of course, one has to make allowance for them being mostly without professional RAF training and therefore likely, by unintentional default, to convey false impressions to those seeking what they believe to be historical fact. Those employed in these places seem to find comfort and protection in the conditions by which information is made available, responsibility for any inaccuracy being disclaimed. The operational records relating to this satellite should be found in the documents of RAF Kinloss, the station of which it was a satellite and the principal user No. 19 OTU.

Rosemary and I were married as planned on the 10th May 1941. My old friend of 102 Squadron days, George Maughan, did me the honour of acting as my Best Man, and Rosemary's close friend, Mabel Bailey, was the Bridesmaid. We had our wedding reception at the Royal Hotel, at that time one of the town's principal hotels, on Nairn High Street. It was an excellent event attended by many friends, RAF and civilian. After a brief two-week leave spent visiting our parents, we started our married life living-out in Nairn at Rosemary's grandfather's home at that time was known as 'Thistle Cottage' on the town's King Street. I travelled to RAF Kinloss by bus, train or bicycle;-whichever was most convenient for day or night flying. Frequently, when night flying from Forres, I would cycle from Nairn, do the required night flying programme, and cycle back home in the early light of day. Throughout the summer months, the period of darkness was very brief in the north, and I do not remember a flare path being necessary at Forres. If a night landing had to be made, it was usually made at Kinloss. Of course, it was often necessary for me to work during the day at Kinloss and, on being warned for a night flying stint, go home as early as transport facilities permitted, have a rest, and then cycle to Forres. There was no compulsory minimum rest period between flying periods at that time, just common sense. In September 1941, I was awarded a second Mention in Dispatches. I was also promoted to the rank of Flight Sergeant. On this occasion, however the promotion was in the recently introduced aircrew trade structure, and since I was already being paid more in the rank of sergeant in my basic trade, it was necessary to increase my pay by one shilling a day to ensure that the promotion brought a pay advantage.

By the autumn of 1941 I was again claimed by the ground school and spent my days lecturing. The winter of 1941/42 was a rather unpleasant time of travel problems. It was difficult to use the public transport systems, which were not timed to suit the routine working day of the RAF, but rather the convenience of the civilian population, as was right and proper. I made frequent use of the bike, but the weather was not always suited to that mode of transport; wind, rain and snow being particularly unpleasant companions. However, the winter passed into the spring of 1942 when there seemed to be a rather unpleasant feeling of impermanence amongst the instructional staff. By the summer of 1942, most of the pre-war RAF flyers had either been killed or were languishing in prisoner of war camps. If like myself, they had been fortunate enough to survive, they were being dispersed to other work where their experience could be used to good effect. Of course, we were too young and impatient to readily grasp what was happening in high places where the makers of policy and strategy determined our lives and careers. Had we been gifted with their wisdom and charged with their responsibility, it would have occurred to us that the time had come for action to preserve what was left of the pre-war Service for post-war continuity. Members trained for long service engagements, the so-called potential 'Lifers,' like myself, were expensively trained assets, and in the best interests of the Public, having done the initial job of holding the situation until the nation's manpower resources were mobilised and trained for war service, we should now be diverted to other pursuits where experience could be utilised to good effect with perhaps a better chance of survival.

The break-up started gradually as members of the old 4 Group squadrons were posted to seemingly unusual appointments. There were the beginnings of new things like Air Traffic Control, Heavy Conversion Units, and Special this and that. Some departed for training in various flying related appointments. As for myself, I was called for an interview by the Chief Instructor and invited to consider appointment to a commission in what he described as Special Signals. He showed me a letter that sought suitable regular personnel of my experience with a tour of operational flying duty behind them, capable of dealing with several situations at the same time and, otherwise suitable candidates for appointment to commissioned rank. Although I was under no obligation to accept this proposal, emphasis seemed to be on the fact that I was a member of the Regular Force and that, as such, a change in career plan was contemplated. The nature of the special signals duties was not spelled out in any detail, and my assumption was that they would be of the type found on any typical station. How wrong could one be in making such an assumption? However, off went the necessary papers recommending my appointment to a commission in Special Signals employment, which would place me in the Administration and Special Duties Branch, whereas most signals officers of my acquaintance were in the Technical (Signals) Branch. I was soon to be enlightened.

Chapter VIII
A Rustic Interlude

As previously mentioned the RAF underwent considerable re-organisation during the summer of 1942, with particularly effects in Bomber Command. In August I found myself posted to the headquarters of the newly formed No.92 Group located in the delightful Buckinghamshire village of Winslow. What a difference from normal station life. The headquarters occupied a large manor house and the appurtenances thereto. I was billeted at the local grocer, a very fortunate choice for me, and my duties were connected with the Group signals function but not in any special sense. As already mentioned, two other new OTU groups (91 and 93) were in the process of formation and, of course, No. 8 (Pathfinder) Group, but at that time, Donald Bennett was at HQ Bomber Command in a provisional appointment labelled 'Senior Officer Pathfinders.' As for my commission, I did not give it much thought tending rather to regard it as something that had already been filed and forgotten and unlikely to eventuate. It was a pleasant situation with time for sporting activities. I played some cricket in what was left of the season and football in the early autumn. I had found suitable accommodation and was able to bring Rosemary, who was pregnant with our first child, to live out with me in a delightful thatched cottage with the owner, Miss Annie Rowe. We were able to have our dog and were happy to settle down blissfully to village life in wartime Britain. Things certainly seemed to have taken a most unusual and fortunate turn.

At the close of one beautiful early autumn day, Rosemary and I, together with the dog, were taking a pleasant evening stroll along a narrow country lane close to the headquarters. It was dusk, almost dark when we heard the noise of galloping hooves approaching from the direction in which we were walking. It seemed like a frightened horse that had got out of its pasture and, being somewhat afraid we hurriedly got into the convenient roadside ditch that providentially was dry. I was concerned for our situation on this narrow road, particularly with a pregnant wife and a dog that seemed intent on bolting. However, the thundering hoof-beats drew level with us without faltering and passed us by in the direction of the main part of the village. We saw no sign of a horse or other living creature. Taking a known shortcut into the courtyard of the mansion house, we entered a small outbuilding that was set aside as a bar; we certainly felt the need for a drink. On relating our experience to the small company present, we were told of the ghostly phenomenon that had haunted that road at dusk for ages. For us, it was quite an unforgettable encounter with the equine spirit world.

One of the interesting tasks I was required to perform was the setting up of a monitoring section to maintain surveillance over the wireless frequencies used by the stations within the group so that infringements of wireless discipline could be reported for corrective action. This was a serious matter as a poor discipline could easily result in the leakage of information to the listening enemy. I was allotted a decent size room for the project and soon had the required numbers of wireless receivers installed. But throughout my remaining time at HQ.92 Group there were no other personnel but myself to do the monitoring job. Of course one man can only listen on one frequency at any time, but I did report a good many cases of poor W/T (Wireless Telegraphy) discipline on most of the Group's Operational Training Unit frequencies. No doubt, the facility was fully manned as the headquarters developed to its intended strength.

Personally, I found my time in Winslow quite pleasant with garden fetes in the grounds around the headquarters. Quiet relaxed evenings with my wife, mixing with the friendly locals. Life seemed to be good, perhaps too good to last. About the beginning of October, I was summoned to the Air Ministry address in London and found it in the bowels of the earth close to Whitehall. I was interviewed by two young officers who looked like they had just emerged from a military tailor. They were clearly of the type referred to as 'Boffins' and seemed rather ill at ease. They introduced topics for discussion relating to my operational flying experience, the fact that I was a regular, and matters of a technical nature relating to wireless, direction finding, etc. I gathered that I was undergoing a selection process in connection with the recommendation made before I left RAF Kinloss.

I returned to Winslow feeling unsure as to what had happened, somehow, it seemed rather mysterious and I had a feeling of uncertainty. However, in a few days' time, a signal was received from the Air Ministry to say, "Flight Sergeant W Jacobs posted to Newbold Revell with effect from (?) October 1942 for training as W/T Intelligence Officer." Where and what the hell was Newbold Revell? Never heard of the place. However, my respite from the real war was obviously near its end. I had to go where I was ordered, and other arrangements had to be made for Rosemary and the dog. She would go to my parents until after the baby was born and then return to Nairn in her own time.

CHAPTER IX
W/T INTELLIGENCE

I arrived at Newbold Revell in the Warwickshire countryside on the due date. It was quite close to Rugby, the railway station, for it being at the sleepy little village of Brinklow. A short walk along a canal footpath brought me to a large mansion house in extensive grounds. This was RAF Newbold Revell. It was, to say the least, a very gloomy looking place surrounded by Nissen huts that were the sleeping quarters, even for senior NCOs. The mansion house containing the administration and training classrooms was, however, comfortably heated. Thank goodness it was here that the Senior NCOs' mess was located, also our ablution facilities where we could, if we were lucky, take an occasional hot bath in the five inches of water allowed, a practice adopted nationwide as part of the fuel economy measures.

I found a very mixed bunch of individuals but very few regulars. Mostly they were volunteers who had been selected for employment in intelligence work and instantly promoted to sergeant rank. They were here to be trained in various aspects of mobile field intelligence work. There were very few, not more than three others, who had operational flying service. Some of them were much too young to take their place as senior NCOs among trained regulars, and they were very obvious. Among them was Sergeant Lord Derwent, who was in his early forties, an extremely nice person who integrated well. Another was Michael Marks, the son of the Michael Marks of Marks and Spencer. Also from M&S was Sergeant Lionel Abrahams a junior manager and very comfortable in his new role. But whatever they had been in civil life they were all well educated and had something worthwhile to offer. There were many teachers with useful degrees in mathematics and, of course, foreign languages, including some who had been specially sent by the RAF to study at the School of Oriental Languages. We would have to wait until we got to where the action was to see how they made out. Of course many of them never really got to the shooting war.

So, the training commenced and I found myself among those who were to learn about the German Luftwaffe and the Italian Regia Aeronautica, which seemed to be the obvious choice for me, or was it? I was quite looking forward to a spell in the Middle East theatre. Our usual instructor was Sergeant (Lofty) Fyfield, who had recently returned to Home

Establishment from a tour of duty in the Middle East Theatre. He was a regular and certainly seemed to be well acquainted with his subject in both German and Italian aspects. About two weeks into this area of intelligence training I was suddenly, and without explanation, switched to Japanese and the Japanese Army Air Force. There were now essential differences regarding language and how, in terms of wireless telegraphy, the language, with its syllabic structure embracing symbols and sounds far in excess of the twenty-six letters of our European alphabet, was adapted to Morse code. It was essential that we had a good grasp of the structure of the Japanese language without necessarily being fluent in it. I was one of a select few whose sole purpose would be to take intercepted messages and, by inference, based on operational flying experience, determine what was meant and present that information so that it might be used to frustrate the enemy's intention. It was, of course, understood that we would be in operational situations and that intercepted messages would usually be in high-grade cipher that could not possibly be broken in a field environment. To break these ciphers required the use of sophisticated tabulating machines, and even then, success was limited. Clearly, in the tactical situations, information had to be obtained by other methods and inference was the best answer particularly if it could be supported by other means, such as wireless direction finding, radar, etc.

Training came to a somewhat desultory end about mid-December 1942, and the unit was closed for a few days over the Christmas period. We were granted leave, and I spent a few days with Rosemary and my parents. Returning to Newbold Revell before the end of December, classes resumed in a rather half-hearted manner. During the first few days of January 1943, all but myself were instructed to prepare for departure to the Personnel Transit Centre at Wilmslow in Cheshire, where two Mobile Wireless Units were being assembled for service in the Far East Theatre of Operations. They departed on or about the 8th January, leaving me to share the Senior NCOs mess with the few members of the unit staff. I did not think other than that I was waiting for instructions for posting to the Officer Cadet Training Unit, particularly as I seemed to be the only one undergoing training prior to appointment to a commission. However, on the 17th January I formally requested an interview with the commanding officer in connection with my posting for training as a W/T Intelligence Officer. The result was certainly startling. I was summoned to the general office and instructed to proceed to Wilmslow the next morning to join 376 Wireless Unit. My commission would follow in due course.

I left Newbold Revell shortly after breakfast the next morning and travelled by rail from Rigby to Wilmslow, where I arrived about mid-afternoon. Here I discovered that I was due to embark with 367 Wireless Unit the next day, 19th January 1943. I was hurriedly issued with tropical kit and was soon at the same state of preparation as the others. We were allowed a last night out and I was determined to see Rosemary, who knew nothing of this latest development. There were lots of men going to Manchester for their last night out in the United Kingdom for what was likely to be a long time. I had to travel ten miles north of the city to Heywood, where my folks lived and I would have to make the additional journey by bus. It was sometime after 7 p.m. when I arrived to find Rosemary and my father at home. Regrettably, mother was out and unable to be contacted. However, I had two hours or so with Rosemary, who was naturally upset at the thought of my being overseas at the time of her confinement but taking the coming lengthy separation with calm dignity. At this time, the tour of duty overseas was, as it had been before the war, for a period of five years. For non-regulars, of course, it could be less but only if the duration of the emergency was less. So, the prospect was not very bright for the wives of regulars and non-regulars alike who had to stay at home waiting and praying for the return of their loved ones.

All too soon, the time came for me to leave and Rosemary accompanied me to the bus stop. We were the only ones there, and the bus seemed to arrive almost immediately. We said our last fond farewells and I got onto the bus, staying on the rear platform watching her cross the road, soon to disappear into the distance of the dark, unlit streets. I felt completely devastated and empty. Arriving at the Manchester terminus I knew I had precious little time in which to walk to the London Road (now Piccadilly, I believe) railway station to get the last train to Wilmslow. I arrived on the departure platform with no more than five minutes to spare. The train seemed to be crowded with RAF personnel, most of them at the windows saying their parting words to parents, wives, and sweethearts. As I walked along looking for a likely spot, I was comforted by friendly voices calling, "Hey, Bill! There's room here". I was among friends in the same situation as myself, but somehow they seemed to be making lighter of it than I was, which cheered me somewhat, and I found myself trying hard to join them in their enforced merriment.

CHAPTER X
A LONG SEA VOYAGE

The next morning, the 19th January 1943, dawned bright and sunny but quite cold. After breakfast we were assembled and conveyed by bus to the railway station and put on a train to some undisclosed point of embarkation. It turned out to be Liverpool that we had, of course, anticipated. Here we were quickly passed through a thorough checking and documentation system and arrived at the gangway appropriate to our accommodation on the ship. It was a rather good-looking vessel with the name 'Duchess of Richmond.' Conditions were rather crowded, but at least we had three-tier bunks with comfortable mattresses. The senior NCOs' mess deck was well-appointed and even had tablecloths on the long room-length tables. The ship, being one of the Canadian Pacific liners, was victualled in Canada and we had the rare treat of real butter and other foodstuffs strictly rationed in the UK. We had a promenade deck to ourselves, all in all, quite a good deal by comparison with a lot of the aircraftmen who were located on the lower decks, sleeping in hammocks in dreadfully overcrowded conditions. It was a Royal Air Force transport and had a Wing Commander Jones appointed as Officer Commanding Troops. He was none other than the officer who, as Flight Lieutenant, had been my squadron commander in B Squadron, No. 3 Wing at Cranwell during my time there in 1937/38. By the time for 'Lights Out' that night, we were still in the dock, but on rising next morning, we found ourselves tied up in the River Clyde opposite Gourock. Conjecture had it that we were waiting to join the convoy, and we waited until sometime that night, for when we saw the first light of the next day (the 21st) we were in heavy seas somewhere off the north of Ireland. Soon, we turned south into what has become known as one of the worst North Atlantic gales on record. It blew for days, how many I cannot remember, but I do remember the sight of the almost deserted mess deck and the wetted tablecloths to help keep the crockery from flying all over the place. I didn't miss a meal for I was among the very few who were spared the misery of seasickness. I spent as much time on deck as was possible and found a strange delight in the gigantic waves, which alternately raised us to a height from which we could see most of the ships in the convoy at various levels then plunged us into the depths of a trough from which we could look up and see only, and above us, the ship that was nearest to us. The 'Drunken Duchess' as our ship was now called, pitched and rolled, and creaked and groaned, night and day, but somehow I managed to eat and sleep without difficulty as we were rocked in the cradle of the deep.

Eventually, we ran out of that dreadful tempest and into calmer waters. Now, we could see the escorting destroyers fussing about on the edges of the convoy, shepherding the strays that had got too far out back into the safety of the pack. We had an occasional Sunderland flying boat above us, probably from Gibraltar, doing routine submarine patrols. We soon saw the Canary Isles quite close and the convoy slowed whilst there was some activity by small craft from the islands to the commodore ship. We soon came to Freetown in Sierra Leone, a name that had always intrigued me, and I felt quite excited as we entered the large harbour basin. All the buildings on shore seemed to have corrugated iron roofs that were red with rust. We had all manner of water-borne merchants alongside us. Boats with natives who would dive to the floor of the harbour, if they thought it worthwhile, for coins thrown over the side. Whilst watching some of these antics, my cigarette case fell out of my shirt pocket but I could not encourage anyone to recover it for me. I suppose it still lies where it fell, perhaps protected to some degree by its silver plate. We stayed a night in Freetown but there was no chance of going ashore, for we were off into the Atlantic again the next morning. We soon crossed the Equator and witnessed the traditional ceremony put on for us by the ships company. There was much time for reading and no shortage of good reading material. There were occasional concerts, and interesting talks, all organised by volunteers from among the passengers. During my time on board I attended lectures and learned elementary Military Urdu. The time passed quite quickly. We had duties to perform: orderly sergeants, guard commanders, lookouts, etc. There was a ship's newspaper that provided us with snippets of news from home and the war zones, the ship's progress, etc. There was no need for boredom.

After some five weeks sailing, we came to the South African port of Cape Town, overlooked by the massive Table Mountain. We were permitted shore leave the first evening and were disembarked early the next morning. After saying goodbye to the Drunken Duchess we were entrained for a suburb called Retreat, where we found a very large transit camp run by the South African Army. It was well appointed having regard to its size and the considerable numbers catered for. The Warrant Officers and Senior NCOs Mess was the largest I have ever seen, but the food was good, and the bar prices modest by comparison with the UK. The weather was glorious and public transport to places roundabout was plentiful and cheap. The locals were very friendly and hospitable. I found Cape Town and its environs most attractive and developed quite a fondness for it. There were plenty of cultural activities with places to visit and lots to see. Unfortunately, the cable railway to the top of Table Mountain was out-of-use for the duration. With the amount of shipping movement it was not surprising to find everywhere constant reminders 'Do Not Talk of Ships or Shipping.' Whilst at this location, I was privileged to attend the local premiere of the film 'Dangerous Moonlight' with its accompaniment of the now famous classical 'Warsaw Concerto'. On this occasion, I literally bumped into Corporal Alistair Mackintosh from Nairn. Known by his nickname 'Sandy,' he was the clerk to whom I referred in my mention of my work as Johnny Crocketts'senior wireless instructor in C Squadron at No. 19OTU, Kinloss. He had been fortunate enough to get himself posted to a cosy little number outside Cape Town and actually had a nice little suburban flat in Wynberg. I was sorry when the time came to leave this delightful place and return to the grim reality of war.

We left Retreat after about three weeks and embarked in the small liner 'Dilwara,' an appropriately sounding Indian name, if we needed one to indicate the direction of our final journey by sea. What a lovely ship. I actually had a very comfortable cabin that I shared with Reg Pullen. By RAF trade, Reg was a 'Clerk Code and Cipher' and had been selected for duty with the special intelligence units. He was not a cryptographer but dealt with the codes and ciphers used for routine messages passed on our own communications networks. He was a Cornishman and a very pleasant companion. I was to get to know him very well and we became very friendly. Our next port of call was Durban, and although we stayed on board, we were allowed shore leave on one occasion only. A small party of us thought we would walk into town after lunch but somehow took the wrong direction and finished in what was obviously the most desirable residential area. It was mid-afternoon, and I don't think we saw a living soul as we trudged endlessly in what we thought must be the direction to the main part of the city. Time, hunger and tiredness caused us to retrace our steps back to the ship and we were glad to enter its shade and our quarters in time for the evening meal. I retain a vivid memory of being at our cabin wash basin in a deep alcove with an open port hole above it. I was washing my hands and gazing idly at a seemingly deserted dockside when a black figure appeared with his head at the same height as my own. To my complete surprise, he muttered softly, "I kill you." I was glad of the short distance between the ship and the dockside that guaranteed my safety, although he did not make any threatening gesture and seemed to be unarmed. I left the open porthole and took a few moments to recover in Rug's company.

We stayed only one full day in Durban and sailed north, passing, in due course, Mombassa seen clearly in the distance on our port side. We spent hours, or so it seemed, watching the flying fishes as they soared above the surface of the sea, effortlessly keeping pace with the ship. We were not escorted by destroyers during this last part of our sea journey, so had nothing to view but the unchanging seascape. Our course altered to the northeast for the final stage of our long round-about sea journey, and it was mid-March 1943 when we first saw the Gateway of India forming the magnificent back-drop to the harbour of Bombay. We had arrived at last about nine weeks after leaving Liverpool.

CHAPTER XI
THE ROUTE TO ARAKAN

It was hot but not unpleasantly so as the heat was quite dry at this time of year. We were soon disembarked and transported to the transit camp at Worli, a most pleasant seafront location outside Bombay. It was a large tented camp built around centrally located administration and messing facilities in commandeered permanent buildings. It was comfortable enough for the short time we were likely to be there. I did not particularly care for Bombay and was glad when the time came to move on. We were there for about seven days and during the last few days of March, we entrained for Calcutta.

This journey was really something, believe me. The Indian troop trains were notorious for their lack of comfort, and this was a typical example of bare wooden seats and drop-down platforms for sleeping. Thankfully, we had been warned about the need to equip ourselves with a lightweight mattress and pillow, also bed-sheets. They were easily obtained; in fact there were plenty of merchants around the Worli transit camp with stocks readily available. Together with our standard issue cape-cum-groundsheet and two blankets, these became an essential part of our kit, providing an indispensable bedding roll that went everywhere with us. It was hot as we wearily puffed our way from west to east across the middle of India. The only way to keep reasonably comfortable was to fully open the windows to let the hot, dry wind of our passage through the compartment. The nights were long and anything but conducive to healthy, restorative sleep. The hopelessly inadequate toilet facilities for morning and other ablutions were quite beyond description. There were scheduled stops for meals usually served from station platforms onto our issued enamel plates, but these were nothing to write home about. We survived but were glad when we arrived at Calcutta's Howrah railway terminal.

No transit camp here. We were obviously expected, and arrangements had been made to ensure a degree of isolation. We moved straight into a suburb of desirable residences and occupied several of them conveniently adjacent to each other, sufficient to provide adequate messing and sleeping accommodation. There were no other residents, service or civilian, to be seen, and I had the impression of a sizeable take-over of valuable private property. We had the standard Indian Army beds (Charpoys-wooden frame with a criss-cross open weave of rattan rope) to sleep on. The basic daily ration was the same for everyone, but we had our own cooks and could supplement the rations for officers and senior NCOs by the purchase of extra-messing supplies, which could be purchased locally according to the degree of willingness of the members of the two messes to pay for them. I liked Calcutta; its main thoroughfare—Chowringhee—was most attractive. Forbidden to the multitudinous beggars, it was a delight of modern shops and air-conditioned cinemas on one side, whilst the opposite side was taken up by the pleasant green area of the maidan that included the cricket ground, beyond which was the racecourse. Firpo's a large, well-appointed restaurant offering good food in a pleasant atmosphere was very popular with officers and senior NCOs. We had a nice set-up but for me, and a few others, it was to be short-lived.

Obviously, we could not do any useful work at this location so far behind the war front and we had to move forward. After a few days another senior NCO and myself were detailed to proceed, with an advance party of twenty men, to a forward area location to superintend the setting-up of our initial operations base. We had with us Pilot Officer Philip Barnard who would stay a few days to make initial contact with the military authorities with whom we would need to have close liaison during the initial stages of settling ourselves in our pre-determined location.

CHAPTER XII
IN THE FIELD

It was now early April and the temperature was rising rapidly with a noticeably high humidity. The advance party left Calcutta by train for a rail point called Sirajgunge on the western side of the Ganges and Brahmaputra delta. It was a miserable place with nothing but a few huts and a wooden ramp down to the water. A small lighter took us out to a waiting steamer, to which we were soon transferred. We spent an uncomfortable night as we steamed eastwards across the delta, managing as best we could on our bedrolls lay out on the deck. Arriving at the other side of the delta early next morning at Chandpur in East Bengal, we found a troop train waiting for us and we were soon on our way to Chittagong, the Forward Area Main Base for the East Bengal/Burma sector of the war zone. Chittagong was our railhead and it was as far as it was possible to go by rail in the direction of the shooting war. Not surprisingly, the town and its surrounding area for several miles had become a militarised zone. There was every conceivable Army and Air Force unit present all, seemingly, located with infinite care and precision under Army jurisdiction so far as location and control were concerned. This military base was well dispersed and barely evident in the general appearance of the town itself, where there was little to attract anyone other than the railway station, which was busy only at routine arrival and departure train times. The town centre was wide, uncrowded, and surprisingly tranquil. There was nothing to attract service personnel. Although the military presence over a widely dispersed area was overwhelming, the indigenous civilian population, predominantly Muslim, had not been disturbed. There were no British or other white civilians. Otherwise, commercial activity seemed to be quite normal. There was a noticeable lack of restaurants and other facilities that would be attractive to the troops. Situated on the northeastern shore of the Bay of Bengal, Chittagong was a seaport of some logistical importance, but unfortunately, its docking facilities did not permit sea-going vessels to berth alongside. Anchorage for these vessels was some distance from the docks and, because of the shallow waters, transfer of loads had to be undertaken by lighter.

The war situation was one of stalemate following the surrender of Singapore and the British withdrawal from Burma to the Indian frontier, only a few months previously. The tactical plan was to stabilise the situation on the Indo/Burma border to prevent the Japanese from entering British India and to maintain that situation until the war in Europe permitted the logistical effort needed to support the offensive action needed to drive the enemy out of Burma, Malaya and Singapore. We were under the operational control of Headquarters No.224 Group, RAF which, commanded by its Air Officer Commanding, Air Vice Marshal S F Vincent, was responsible for tactical operations in the sector. Our intelligence masters were, of course, located with Headquarters India Command, a long way behind the war, in New Delhi. Our sister unit, No. 368 Wireless Unit, had been deployed in the vicinity of Comilla, where it was conveniently placed to cover Japanese air activities beyond the Imphal Plain, an important feature of the Northern Sector where the Japanese were most likely, as was the case in our own Southern Sector, to attempt to gain initial footholds on Indian soil.

We were taken to an ideal location for our particular line of work. It was a few miles south of Chittagong on the road leading to Cox's Bazaar and other places, Maungdaw, Buthidaung, Ratmalana; to mention just a few, that were to become well known on the western side of the Arakan. The site was on top of a small hill obviously chosen with thought for wireless reception. The top of the hill had been levelled a good many years ago to make a site for a large bungalow of typically British colonial taste but apparently deserted for some considerable time. The site was quite extensive and adequate for our purposes. There was also a long outbuilding consisting of several rooms typical of those used for servant quarters and storage. An immediate need was conveniently met during our first two days at the site by converting, with a little help from the Garrison Engineer, one of these rooms into a suitably secure armoury for our weapons. Each man was armed with a Sten gun, and the two SNCOs had pistols. Personal arms were both an encumbrance and unnecessary responsibility in our present situation. All these rooms would eventually be put to good use. The bungalow had a bathroom with primitive plumbing, which, of course, did not work. There was, however, a standpipe outside the bungalow, which had an ordinary domestic tap through which only a tiny trickle of water would flow even when it was fully opened. But at least it provided a water supply of sorts for the time being. Apart from the bathroom, the other rooms in the bungalow were in reasonable condition and would provide cover for the advance party until other accommodation could be built. There was a small room opening directly onto the front veranda, in which my SNCO colleague and I installed ourselves. On the Garrison Engineer's location map, the site was identified by the name 'The Fenneries', perhaps the name given by its original owner, who may have come from the English Fenlands!

Pilot Officer Barnard returned to Calcutta after three days and we were left to the delights of our new surroundings. We had a cook (LAC Scholefield) at the party, and he was in possession of essential field kitchen equipment of the type fired by paraffin pressure burners, rather like giant blowtorches. We set him up in the end room of the outbuilding, nearest to the bungalow, which he could use for food preparation; his cooking gear was just outside. We were on the garrison ration strength, and food supplies came to us through the good offices of the Royal Indian Army Service Corps. A field latrine had already been prepared by the Garrison Engineers sufficient for present needs, and so located that it could easily be extended before the arrival of the main element of the unit. Water, the obvious real problem, was clearly our number one priority. For drinking, the tap water had to be boiled and, after cooling, transferred to Chargoyles-wetted bags made of thick, closely woven canvas. These were hung outside where they could catch any movement of the air and were the most efficient coolers. For the collection of water, we used empty tin food containers, each capable of holding about two gallons. To overcome the problem of the trickling tap we devised a makeshift system of split bamboo to form short lengths of gutter linking a line of containers so that the water overflowed from one to the next in line. In this way we ensured a ready supply of water for cooking and for a good sluice down at the beginning and end of the day. Unfortunately, we had not been warned about the effect of washing with cold or insufficient water, and we soon found ourselves suffering the dreadful consequence of prickly heat. For most, this took the form of an itching, prickly rash on the shoulders, back and chest. A most irritating complaint, particularly troublesome at night and difficult to get rid of in the prevailing hot and humid conditions of the jungle summer. The heat rises very quickly during April, and by the end of May, an average daily high slightly in excess of a hundred degrees Fahrenheit, with very high percentage humidity, is quite normal. The prickly heat rash is caused by sweat-blocked pores and is not helped by washing in cold water, however pleasant that experience may be. Hot water on tap was a commodity we had to learn to do without and since necessity is the mother of invention, I later resorted, whenever possible, to making a small fire from split bamboo to heat my meagre water ration for the evening wash. It was most effective. I never had prickly heat again.

The need for a daily change of clean clothing was also a problem attending the scourge of prickly heat. However, there was no shortage of local labour and we soon had a laundry facility in place with an efficient dhobi wallah recommended to us by the local military authority, who ensured minimum security risk. Unfortunately, these locals had the same water problems and our clothing was washed in one of the many stagnant pools created for common use in most places throughout the Far East. We soon developed a sour-smelling odour that was associated with the Indigenous population and military personnel alike. Although the service was speedy and our laundry was returned immaculately ironed, it had the feeling of not having had a final rinse in clean water; this was something we just had to accept. Of course, the native methods of washing anything was to take it to the local pool and, without the use of soap, give it a good bashing on a convenient hard surface, then dry it wherever it could be conveniently hung on bushes or spread on the ground. Drying was also a problem as it took a long time in the humid atmosphere in shade and undercover, although drying in direct sunlight was usually easy enough. Another contributory problem to our personal discomfort in this unfriendly climate was, in my opinion, inadequacy in the provision of our clothing. At this time, the RAF scale of clothing did not include vests and, whilst wearing a vest did not meet with general approval, I soon found a ready supplier of good quality short-sleeved cotton vests from the itinerant merchants who occasionally called to sell their wares, which were carried, in enormous bundles on their heads. They must have walked considerable distances to find us. My own feeling was that a cotton vest would readily absorb perspiration and, in the same way, as our water coolers worked using the principle of cooling by evaporation, would have a cooling effect rather than retaining body heat by their additional insulation. Furthermore, it would be easy to wash a vest thoroughly oneself and dry it quickly in a sunny spot. It did the trick for me and the prickly heat became an unpleasant memory. Some time later, vests became general issue for all RAF personnel in the theatre, but they were, of course, dyed jungle green. There were other unsatisfactory features of our uniform clothing. We had been issued with the Wolsley Solar Topee that, although effective as a protection against intense sunlight on the head and neck, was heavy and uncomfortable for long use. It was a development of the tropical headgear first used at the beginning of the century. We soon noticed that occasional visitors were wearing the lightweight topee of civilian pattern, and we soon adopted this preference that, of course, had to be done at our own expense. They were readily available – it was amazing what the native mendicant traders could provide. The topee had a pugree (hat band) similar to that used on the official pattern hat to which our RAF Colour Flash could be easily attached. We were learning fast. Shirts were uncomfortable as they were made of heavy drill material with long sleeves that had to be rolled up during the day. Again, at our own expense, most of us adopted short-sleeved bush jackets that were made to measure by a visiting tailor (Dhurzi Wallah) with amazing speed. The material, being of the Aertex type, was light in weight; and made a great improvement to our personal comfort and appearance. The British Forces had not yet adopted jungle green and all uniform clothing was of standard khaki colour. Boots were issued as standard for all non-commissioned ranks, although senior NCOs were permitted to wear plain-fronted shoes that, of course, I already had. Shoes were permitted for junior ranks in overseas theatres but at personal expense. Again the considerable resource of the mendicant traders was used to good effect by those who were willing to pay.

Our food was, to say the least, miserably monotonous. It consisted mainly of canned commodities, usually in bulk packs. Dried vegetables were mainly potato, cabbage, and onion, all completely dehydrated. The potato was sliced and looked like pieces of black-streaked ivory, whilst the finely chopped cabbage and onion were quite beyond description. Reconstituted by soaking in water, they were most unappetising. There was, of course, the inevitable bully beef that came in seven-pound cans from which it emerged, already reduced to a stew-like consistency by the heat. Bully beef and, of course, the ubiquitous baked beans became our preferred staple diet. There were vile sausages that existed by the name of 'Soya Links.' Soya seemed to be their only constituent and they were quite without taste. I was once offered one boiled by the cook who wanted to demonstrate their enormous size after immersion in boiling water. Rice, with weevils of course, was plentiful, and curry powder provided the opportunity of an occasional variation in the preparation and presentation of bully beef. There was an occasional issue of bread baked in the Army field ovens, but it too was of unappetising appearance and taste. It was grey in colour with dark streaks, smelled musty and filled with weevils that were always present in flour and rice, etc., stored in tropical conditions. The bread tasted sour and was not popular. Most preferred the hard-tack biscuit that came in sealed containers and, although hard on the mouth and not unlike dog biscuits in taste, were fresh and contained additives that made them nourishing, usually with a few weevils for good measure. There were occasional tinned pilchards and dried fruit. Milk was of the evaporated kind. Dehydration had not yet reached the powder stage. The cook's life was not a happy one, but whilst coming in for a large amount of unjustified criticism, most appreciated the limitations imposed on them by the lack of variety in the ration commodities. To counteract the deficiency of fruit and vegetables we had to take a daily pill of vitamin 'C' (Ascorbic Acid) and, to ensure a sufficiency of salt, a concentrated salt tablet. Another daily pill was to become known as The Yellow Peril, Mepacrin, a malaria suppressant. Mosquitoes of the Anopheles variety were in constant attendance during the hours of darkness when slacks and long sleeves were no deterrent. We had a ration of cigarettes donated by some charity, but these, being in packets of ten, were so damp that they were difficult to light and even more difficult to draw. We were soon introduced to the 'Humidor,' a container with a small capsule of silica gel in the lid. But, as these could only be obtained in Calcutta, we had to wait for a purchase opportunity to arise. We also had an occasional beer ration, a particularly vile brew that came from the Solan and Raniket brewery in northern Assam. I am sure it was made from vinegar and boot polish, with a component guaranteed to give one a seriously sick headache. Once was enough for me, and thereafter, anyone could have my ration.

After only a few days at our new location and a couple of visits by a Garrison Engineer warrant officer, squads of native labourers arrived to commence the building of our additional bamboo huts (Bashas). They worked with surprising rapidity and it was most interesting to see them preparing the raw bamboo to make all the components on the spot.

Of course the raw material was available in unlimited quantity, but none of it was taken from our immediate surroundings. They went out into the deeper jungle and returned laden with prodigious loads of long bamboo trunks, all carried on the shoulders. Their only tool seemed to be a sharp chopping implement of the machete type, and all joints were tied with bamboo suitably stripped to a convenient size for the purpose. There were no nails or other fastening devices. Everything was made from bamboo right there on the spot. Doors, window shutters, woven bamboo stripping for the floors, mostly laid directly on the ground, and of course, tiles for roofing. Quite amazing. They were obviously working to a plan and placing standard pattern structures in designated locations. There were four large bashas for the junior ranks sleeping quarters, one for the senior NCOs, a mess building for the men and a smaller mess for the senior NCOs, and a basha to serve as an office for the CO, adjutant and a sort of orderly room and communication shack. Spaces for our mobile technical vehicles were left in places where a measure of concealment, a most desirable feature, would be assured. We did, of course, have to keep a careful eye on progress to ensure that what was being done met our requirements, but I never found myself in serious disagreement with the Garrison Engineer's plan.

Rosemary gave birth to our first-born son, Michael Anthony (inaccurately recorded by the registrar as Antony), on the 18th April 1943, in the maternity ward of Manchester Royal Infirmary. My first news of this happy event came to me by a Forces Telegram a few days later. This was an excellent service that worked with remarkable efficiency. It was most expeditious, with regard to distance and the restrictions imposed by war conditions, being a combination of telecommunications, as they were at that time, and the British Forces Postal Service. The telegram actually finished its final stage to my remote location by post, and as it was only a few days after the event, must have been passed over most of the 'black dividing sea and alien plain' by landline and wireless telegraph. Of course, it was only allowed in emergencies such as births and deaths. It was, however, comforting to the forces, particularly those in the field, to know that news from home was taken at the highest level as a serious consideration affecting morale. For ordinary mail, we had a system of Air Mail Letters on flimsy lightweight paper, also available to the folks back home from local post offices, this too was reasonably rapid utilising the Forces Air Transport Routes wherever they were able to operate with safety. Personnel movement by air between the United Kingdom and the overseas war theatres was, of course, restricted to the most important war considerations and usually to official couriers, escorts conveying highly classified documents, and high-ranking officers in the discharge of duties which required their attendance at conferences.

One day, towards the end of April, a dispatch rider rode into our clearing with a large envelope addressed to me. He had brought it from Headquarters 224 Group. On opening it, I found, to my delight, two large photographs of Rosemary with Michael in her arms shortly after the birth. They had been taken in the infirmary by photographers of the Daily Mirror who carried a short story of my enforced absence. My Mother-in-Law had some influence on this, being conveniently located in her specialised nursing work. She was in touch with influential people who had a son serving in RAF India Command. He was in the United Kingdom on duty and would convey the photographs. He was, in fact, Wing Commander Geddes, son of Lord Geddes, a prominent politician. Surprisingly, he was serving on the staff of Headquarters 224 Group, so it was an easy matter to ensure the envelope got to me safely. I was later able to see him briefly during a visit to Chittagong and thank him for his kindness.

Although the site was ready by late May, it was July by the time the main party arrived. Apparently, our mobile vehicles were still at sea, and the CO had decided to stay in Calcutta, where there would be less boredom for the men than at our forward location without the means to provide productive work. For those of us in the advance party, their arrival was a blessed relief. However, within a few days, arrangements had been made for the senior NCO element of the intelligence section to go on a familiarisation tour of the organisation in our rear. This would provide us with useful background knowledge and afford us a well-deserved break with an opportunity to see Northern India, an experience I had always hoped for, particularly as our intended tour was to take us to the North West Frontier with short stopovers in Calcutta and New Delhi.

So, after three months supervising the arrangements for setting-up our initial forward base, a party of six senior NCOs, including four who had arrived with the main party, with myself being the ranking senior in charge, left on a stiflingly hot and soggy July day, for more pleasant locations, without much idea of what we were likely to find when we reached them.

Chapter XIII
Hindustan

The first part of our long journey was at least familiar. We were taken up to Chittagong by road. Railway to Chandpur, and then the weary steamer crossing to Siragunge, and on to Calcutta by that dreadfully uncomfortable troop train with its bare wooden seats. Just outside Calcutta was an old Indian Army encampment appropriately named Barrackpore. Although predominantly Army, there was a small RAF Intelligence Section, which provided transit facilities for RAF intelligence personnel. There was, of course, a much larger Army Intelligence presence. The place was at least civilised. There was plentiful running water, good laundry facilities, baths, and showers, and good messing arrangements, although the basic rations were no better than we had now become accustomed to. There were, however, small restaurants outside the garrison within easy distance by rickshaws, which were always available. We soon lost the forward area smell, and our dhobi was returned with enough starch in the slacks to make them rattle. What a great difference; there were even electric ceiling fans wherever one went. There was a cinema only a few paces from our accommodation. We spent a pleasant few days at Barrackpore. I met an old friend who was in the same entry as myself at Cranwell; he was Sergeant Jack Hyde, who was fortunate enough to be on friendly terms with Sergeant Brian Stocks. Brian was from Bradford, where his father was a prominent person in the wool industry. He also had an uncle resident in Calcutta. After getting ourselves sorted out, we were able to make several trips to Calcutta, where Brian's uncle had a well-appointed apartment on Chowringhee. He introduced us to Firpo's, a first-class air-conditioned restaurant also centrally located on Chowringhee, Calcutta's main thoroughfare, where there were also air-conditioned cinemas and plenty of fine shops. I had time to see more of it than was possible during my initial stay in April, and I put it to good use, making such purchases as were necessary to improve my future well-being. Of course the acquisition of a Humidor to keep cigarettes dry was on top of the list. We stayed at Barrackpore for a week or so, made good contacts and saw something of the work that was going on there. It had all been very pleasant.

On the day of our departure, we were conveyed to Calcutta's Howrah station to continue our tour to the next stop, New Delhi. As the train was due to start, a panting figure dressed in civilian-style khaki drill slacks and bush jacket of the kind worn by upper class Indians, opened the door and asked if he could ride in our compartment. There was ample space for us four occupants and as he seemed to be a pleasant enough person and well spoken, we welcomed him. He was travelling to his home at Jullunder and was a Christian Missionary serving in Calcutta. What a thoroughly pleasant and interesting person he was. Davindra Dosh was his name, a missionary to his own people, well-educated and able to discourse over a wide range of topics. What a wonderfully fluent speaker he was, and well, I remember discussing the poetry of Rudyard Kipling and tales of India in bygone days, particularly the North West Frontier. He gave me a pocket edition of the New Testament that is still among my souvenirs. I was sorry when we arrived at Jullunder in the small hours of the next day when he had to take his leave of us.

Arriving in New Delhi, we reported to the Rail Transport Officer (RTO) and told the clerk on duty that we were on our way to the Wireless Experimental Centre at Anand Parbat. This seemed to cause some confusion, as his immediate response was, "Where the bloody hell is that"? On being told that it was an Army establishment somewhere outside Delhi, he looked through some sort of directory and said that the place we wanted was probably Ramjas College, which I said sounded like the sort of place such an establishment would be located. He then made a telephone call and, after confirming our expected arrival, arranged for transport to be sent for us. It took at least two hours to arrive, and we were tired and weary when we eventually arrived at our destination in the tremendous heat of early afternoon to find that there was no hope of a meal until evening. It certainly was hot, with a shade temperature about 115 degrees Fahrenheit, but dry and quite a change from the humidity of the East Bengal/Burma frontier. The Wireless Experimental Centre occupied a wide expanse of land somewhat west of Delhi in what is now the state of Rajasthan. Arid and barren, it was located at the western edge of the Thar (or Indian) Desert. It occupied numerous permanent buildings of late nineteenth-century design, built to withstand the climatic extremes of high summer heat and winter cold. We were housed adjacent to the Senior NCOs' mess (obviously of recent origin) in single rooms probably occupied initially by the college students. The accommodation was built in the form of an open rectangle to which there was only one wide entrance. Two storeys high, with access doors to the rooms under wide shady verandas on the inside the square, the sun never shone directly on the front walls of the rooms. The outer walls were not shaded but were built to provide insulation against the stifling heat of summer and were about three feet thick. Our arrival had, in fact, coincided with what was being referred to as 'A Heat Wave,' with a high of 132 degrees of shade temperature actually recorded during our stay.

An officer of colonel rank commanded the establishment. Only a few RAF personnel were present and, like their Army counterparts, were of sergeant rank to which they had been appointed by virtue of their employment on intelligence duties. There were no RAF officers, all RAF personnel being integrated under Army command; a contingency for which there was provision under the relevant sections of the Army Act and the Air Force Act. There were also a good many women, mostly Anglo-Indian, of the Women's Auxiliary Corps (India) known as WAC (I) s, employed on clerical duties within the various intelligence departments. Housed in their own compound, where they had their own mess and recreation facilities, they were seldom seen outside of normal working hours. The intelligence work was carried out in what had been the college proper. This occupied a large area within its own high-walled compound the entrance to which was guarded so that one had to produce a personal pass to gain entry.

Outside the security areas, there was ample space for sporting activities on the hard-baked ground, but there was not much sport during the summer as the heat was too great for exertion other than essential walking. There was a large swimming pool but water problems prevented use during the summer months. Anand Parbat was a small village just outside the main compound with nothing to attract personnel. There was no public transport and New Delhi could only be reached by hiring a horse-drawn rickshaw of the two-seat type, which was usually available, but the distance was really too great unless one could get away for at least the latter half of the day. So we did not really have the opportunity to view New Delhi, but what we were able to see of it during our journeys between the railway station and Ramjas College certainly seemed most attractive.

We stayed at the Wireless Experimental Centre for a week or so and left with the feeling that it had been a waste of time. We saw a British Army Intelligence Establishment comfortably situated a long way from the fighting front, where a lot of people, including a few RAF, seemed to be having a very easy war. It was not a scene that I cared for, and I was glad to leave it and get on our way to India's North West Frontier Province.

We left Delhi by the early morning train for Lahore, where we would have to make a night-stop. Soon we were rolling across the wide-open spaces of the Punjab in the great heat of summer. The trains were not air-conditioned and the only way to gain relief was to open the windows and let in the hot blast. At least it was dry heat, not unlike that from a furnace. Away from the troop train routes east of Calcutta, the Indian railway system was quite civilised, and one was able to enjoy some comfort in the higher travel classes. Our SNCO status ensured that degree and the coach compartments had upholstered seats, albeit thinly padded under green material resembling leather. There were problems with infestations of bugs that had to be taken into consideration, and for this reason, deep soft upholstery was unsuitable. Compartments on the long-distance trains were designed to accommodate six passengers in generous space. Sleeping facilities for six were provided by a simple arrangement whereby the backrests of the seats could be raised, on their hinges, and suspended by chains to provide three additional sleeping spaces. It was desirable to use one's own bedroll on the bed-space thus provided. There were no dining facilities on board, but the railways had efficient catering systems whereby passenger requirements could be telegraphed to the pre-arranged meal stop. If the meal had to be taken on the train one could rely on the ordered meal being brought to the compartment by a smartly clad bearer calling "Jacobs Sahib" or whatever. Curry was, of course, the favourite and undoubtedly the safest and best. At some stops, passengers left the train to take meals in the station restaurant where this facility existed, usually at the larger main-line stations.

So our long journey proceeded across the wide plains of the Punjab, Patiala, Ludhiana, Jullundur (Davindra Doshs' hometown), and Amritsar. It was well into the evening when we arrived at Lahore. The RTO arranged transport to take us to the Revnell Services Club located in the city, but comfortable and well run, it provided us with good sleeping accommodation and excellent food. It was, of course, extremely hot and we were content to stay in the club and get to bed early.

Continuing our journey the next day, we were relieved to find, after a few hours, the scenery becoming more rugged and a noticeable climatic change bringing some relief from the heat of the plains. A short stop at Gujarat, then, after crossing the River Jhelum, on to Jhelhum itself. It was late afternoon when we arrived at Rawalpindi and knew that we were now in the Frontier Province. We stayed on the train until we reached Taxila Junction, where the line divided, one branch going to the railhead at Peshawar and the other to the end of the line at Havelian. We were to spend a long, miserable night at Taxila. The station was deserted until, seemingly from nowhere, appeared three small boys who insisted on guarding our baggage, in exchange for a small financial reward, of course. There was a dim light at either end of the platform, but beyond that, nothing but a faint outline of hills. Such buildings as there were on the platform were closed and locked. No sign of any facilities for passengers obliged to wait for the morning train to Havelian. The boys seemed intent on being of assistance to us as guardians of our luggage and we thought it better not to antagonize them by refusal, so we tried to converse with them using our limited knowledge of the Urdu dialect, which was the adopted language of the Indian Army. We got on surprisingly well and picked up quite a lot of grammatical knowledge. Their presence helped to while away the long, weary hours until they decided they had earned their reward, and indicated that they would have to go. We gave them a five Rupee note and I have always remembered that I was the one who knew the correct Urdu expression (sub kewarsti) meaning for all.

It was now sometime after midnight and comfortably cool. We decided to open out our bedrolls and lie down rather than sitting on them. There was little chance of sleep as the mosquitoes were a nuisance here as they were anywhere in India. We were also afraid that if we all went off to sleep, we might have our other baggage stolen. It was not uncommon for the unwary to be quietly dispatched for the acquisition of their belongings. So we managed to while away the time until dawn with our own conversation of this and that. Eventually, a tired-looking official arrived and, engaging him in friendly discourse, actually got him to produce some tea in a most disreputable teapot. It was our first fluid intake since the previous midday, and we had not tasted solid food since then, either. We were ravenously hungry, but there was no hope of breakfast at Taxila. We were glad when our train puffed its way into the station and we were soon on our way to our final rail destination at Havelian, where we arrived about mid-morning. Here, we were relieved to find a small station restaurant of sorts that dispensed more char (tea) and offered us egg sandwiches, which we were glad to accept, and felt more contented as we awaited the transport that we had requested from the Army Depot at Abbottabad.

The Wireless Experimental Depot (WED) was, like the Wireless Experimental Centre (WEC) at Anand Parbat, a British Army establishment. There were no resident RAF personnel, nor was it involved with the war on the Indo/Burma borders, but rather the activities in, and beyond, Afghanistan. It was a much smaller unit, located in pleasant surroundings with that tranquil atmosphere that is reminiscent of peacetime. We certainly had the feeling of being far removed from the reality of war. The encampment was of substantial wooden buildings that had a pre-war appearance. The working area was fenced with controlled admittance to official pass-holders only. The accommodation was excellent, providing each of us with individual rooms and shared bathroom facilities. We had servants (bearers) to take care of our personal needs. My bearer was Ghulam Haider Khan, who would quietly enter my room in the morning, lift the edges of my mosquito net, and had my face lathered and shaved before I was properly awake. Not a word until, a minute or so later, he put down my mug on the bedside locker with the words "Char, Sahib." I shall always remember his wicked-looking razor that had been honed so often on its leather strop that the blade was worn to almost a spike. It was all very civilized after our forward area experience. There were a few married quarters occupied by families of unit personnel who had obviously been there since before the war. A nice little garrison church lent a touch of charm, and the whole scene, with the surrounding hills and pleasant climate, had a calming effect. It seemed like an easy war for personnel fortunate enough to be posted to this location.

The lowest rank in the place was sergeant. There was a well-appointed mess where one could relax in comfort, although there were very few members. The commanding officer was a lieutenant colonel and other officers seemed to be very few. I often found myself wondering what went on in this place. But that was none of my concern. I saw nothing of the working side of things other than the administrative processes. I had heard about an Indian Wireless Intelligence Service (IWIS) to which the Wireless Experimental Depot apparently belonged, but seemingly distinct from our own military intelligence organization. So why were we here? Certainly not to become acquainted with the function of the place, but pleasanter pursuits as we were soon to discover.

A detachment of six sergeants from our sister unit 368 WU arrived the next day and we were pleased to have their company and an increase in the strength of the RAF complement. We were soon gathered together in a lecture room, where we met an elderly lieutenant colonel who was to become our guide and mentor throughout our stay. I formed the opinion that he was probably a retired officer who had spent most of his service with the Indian Army. He seemed to be very knowledgeable about artillery and had probably been recalled from the Retired List and appointed to duties appropriate to his age. He was certainly well past the normal age for Active List duty in forward areas. A fatherly figure, he had an easy manner that made for a pleasantly relaxed atmosphere whenever we were in his company. We were to do many interesting things under his tutelage; he seemed to have the essential quality of making all learning interesting.

One of his early talks dealt with cryptography, something we were unlikely to have time for in our own envisaged tactical situations. I remember one exercise he produced which required us to break a simple transposition code. It was very simple once the essential clue had been spotted, and this I did quickly before anyone else, seemingly very much to his astonishment, not least my own. I have always remembered it and feel inspired to record it here. The coded message was as follows:

ESEE HCRE TSEC UOLG SADE RSAW NARS REDL UOHS SIHR EVOT AHTR IAHE HTDN ASEE NKEH TTAY DNAB DNAN AMYL GUNA SAWE HHOD NAEZ EERB AROF GNIL TSIH WDOO TSNA BILA CEHT FORE PPIK SEHT

This is one of the simplest types of code. It is the simplicity of it that tends to make it difficult for the uninitiated. Reading it backwards from the end where I was fortunate enough to spot immediately the initial three-letter word 'the' written backwards. Continuing from here the message reads:

"The skipper of the Caliban stood whistling for a breeze and oh he was an ugly man and bandy at the knees and the hair that over his shoulders ran was red as Gloucester cheese".

Of course, there are numerous ways of codifying messages, but all codes are easily broken, be they of the transposition or substitution types. Such codes, when used, have to be changed after very short intervals of time and used only for low-grade information. Cipher is a different matter employing the use of numerals, but here again, it is easy enough to decipher if sufficient messages are available to enable an expert in the language concerned to spot recurring numbers and determine which letters of the alphabet they represent. But with ciphers produced by electro-mechanical machines, recurring numbers are insignificant, and since each message is a separate cipher entity, they are virtually unbreakable. Certainly, it is a complete waste of time to attempt code and cipher breaking in a tactical situation unless one is in possession of the basics by which the messages are encoded or enciphered. Cryptography was not a front-line pursuit but rather one for quieter places where lengthy study could be applied to determine method, and machinery might be used as a means of relieving mental effort and tedium. Information gained from successful decodes of high-grade cipher messages is, therefore, usually of historical value only but often helpful in creating the picture of the enemy organization. Little did I know that the fortunes or misfortunes of war were to bring me into closer contact with long-term intelligence work.

Whilst at Abbottabad, we were to do many other interesting things under the guidance of our amiable lieutenant colonel. We were taken to the Indian Army artillery depot at Kakul, where we received instruction on the employment of animal transport, mules were still used to pull artillery pieces, and it was always likely that we may have to use them for our own future transport needs in jungle warfare. We also visited the Ghurkha depot and became acquainted with these famous soldiers from Nepal who we were to meet later in the field. We were invited to join them for an evening celebration of some feast or other at which we witnessed the rather gruesome scene of ritual slaughter. In this, one of the Ghurkhas had been selected, presumably, it was his turn to decapitate a goat with a larger than-ordinary kukri of the two-handed type. The goat was tethered, and he was required to do the job with one mighty swipe, which he did. Thereafter, the assembled company drew their individual weapons and set about a small herd of goats gathered in a nearby enclosure. The air was filled with blood-curdling yells, and blood was gushing everywhere. No doubt, it was a useful way of providing the depots' requirement of goat meat for a few days whilst ensuring weapon practice for the troops.

We had many delightful excursions into the hills combined with map reading exercises and the art of cartography. There were horses for us to ride. We also had, for most of our company, an introduction to field telephone systems and an opportunity to operate the field telephone exchange used in the Wireless Experimental Depot itself. This was, of course, old hat to me as my initial training included this essential field equipment, which I could have been called upon to install and maintain as part of my signals trade responsibility.

It gave us all the feeling of being a long way from the war; in fact, it was quite like a peacetime situation. Of course, there was no conscription in India and no food rationing for the civil population; at this distance from the war zones, there seemed to be little, if any, thought about the war on India's Eastern Frontier. Our pleasant interlude was about to end. We were now into September, and our colleagues from No. 368 Wireless were recalled to their base near Comilla, and we knew that our call would come soon. Just a few days later, we received our orders to return to unit.

We were transported to the station at Havelian and arrived at Taxila Junction in time for the train from Peshawar to Rawalpindi, Lahore, and finally New Delhi, which we were not scheduled to reach until early afternoon the next day. Arriving at Delhi on time, we reported our presence to the RTO who confirmed our departure time for Calcutta the next morning. Unfortunately, he was unable to make any arrangements for accommodation for the night, and we would have to do the best we could within the confines of the station. He directed us to a wide balcony above the front of the station, where he said we could spread our bedrolls and sleep without fear of molestation. So we left our gear in his charge and went off to explore New Delhi.

We took a couple of horse-drawn Tongas and asked to be put down in the city centre, a very pleasant feature called Connaught Circus. Designed by the famous architect Sir Edwin Lutyens New Delhi, it is truly a masterpiece of architectural design on a large scale. Connaught Circus occupies a huge central area with an attractive green centre with pathways, flowerbeds, and peripheral flowering trees inhabited by flocks of chattering parakeets providing a colourful display. From the circus, like the spokes of a wheel, radiate wide avenues giving access to the cities many other features, both ancient and modern, to delight the eye and excite the imagination. The Vice-Regal Palace, with its prominent monument to Queen Victoria set in an expansive and impeccable frontispiece. The Quitab Minar, a piece of ancient India providing a fascinating idea of early experiments in measuring time by using shadows and the movement of the sun. The well in this location was also of considerable antiquity, with its water level about thirty feet below ground. Small boys would dive into this for a small reward. It was amazing that they were able to do so without hitting the sides and killing themselves. Climbing out of the well by the footholds between the huge chunks of granite forming the slippery sides was itself a most awesome challenge.

We spent a very interesting afternoon that was marred by a torrential downpour from which we had to scurry for shelter. We had a good meal in one of the restaurants on Connaught Circus, Nirullas I think it was, and returned in the early evening to the delights of the railway station, itself quite a magnificent edifice. It was quiet as we prepared ourselves for the long night. Our thin mattresses provided small comfort on the hard concrete floor of the balcony, and we had to improvise, using pieces of baggage, to arrange our mosquito nets so that they were clear of our bodies. The station was quiet for most of the night which passed quite peacefully, although hot and sultry. We were able to take a good morning ablution and after breakfast in the station restaurant, it was soon time to board the train for Calcutta and settle down to a dreary two-day journey. We arrived in Calcutta in time to catch the troop train to Sirajgunge, and after a jolting ride on the now familiar hard wooden seats, we were soon aboard the steamer that would take us overnight to Chandpur and then on to the railhead at Chittagong.

CHAPTER XIV
RETURN TO REALITY

We were reunited with our comrades of 368 WU just seven days after leaving Abbottabad. Not surprisingly, we were travel sore and in need of a good clean up and a long sleep, but it was well into late afternoon, and we were not expected to do other than rest for the remainder of that day.

After a most enthusiastic welcome, we were quickly brought up to date with events during our absence. The place looked the same as we had left it, but our mobile equipment had arrived, and installation was far advanced. Two three-ton vehicles, each containing eight intercept wireless receivers, and another one providing our mobile office facility, were discreetly parked under the cover of trees. The electricity-generating vehicle, also of the three-ton type, was located close by. These four vehicles were absolutely vital to our operational effectiveness.

Of the four large bamboo huts (Bashas), it was found that two were sufficient to provide adequate sleeping space for the men, and one was available for their off-duty use. Nicely placed in seclusion on the edge of the clearing, overlooking the wide jungle-clad expanse to the south, the senior NCOs' basha was identical to the junior ranks quarters. Our mess was an addition to the main dining area, but it was hopelessly inadequate for our number and would have to be replaced, which it soon was. It then gave us a small dining space and a reasonable size anteroom, as much as could be expected in the circumstances. Most pleasing of all, perhaps was the inclusion of a small degree of electric lighting within the limit of the spare capacity of the generating equipment. This provided an aid to bed location in the sleeping huts and sufficient illumination in the messes and off-duty areas. Of course, it was essential to adhere to commonsense rules regarding blackout during the hours of darkness. We were very fortunate to have this facility due entirely to being able to generate our own electricity supply with a modicum of spare capacity beyond that required for our operational needs. The field kitchen arrangement was the same except that there were more cooks to produce more of the same old monotonous menu.

Additional small bashas had been built to provide offices for the unit CO (Squadron Leader Fred Julian), The Adjutant (Flying Officer Norman Gain – nicknamed Larry after the boxing champion). The unit Disciplinary NCO (Sergeant Harry Edwards) had an adjoining office, and a small communications terminal had been established where Sergeant Reg Pullen had his Typex machine, essential for the encryption and decryption of our own high-grade cipher communications. This hut also housed a small field telephone exchange. We were well organised, virtually a very small RAF station built of bamboo in the jungle.

The problem of the dripping water tap was seemingly beyond resolution. Therefore, we had to be supplied through the field water system, whereby a daily delivery was made by tanker. A small two-wheeled tank on-site held sufficient water for the daily drinking ration. This was topped up each day, and for other purposes, we had a daily delivery amounting to half a bucket per man. Water rationing was severe, and waste was a serious offence. We soon learned how to make the best use of it. I continued my practice of making a small fire of bamboo to heat my remaining water in the early evening and, with it, give my body the best possible sponge down. In this way, I managed to ward off the dreadful, prickly heat rash.

Our operational work started with a rush of activity to search for the enemy wireless frequencies within the range of our reception capability. Our intercept wireless operators soon had us heavily laden with encoded and encrypted messages of doubtless Japanese origin. The message texts were of no immediate value to us, but of greater importance was the identity and location of the sender and the recipient. In this way we could gradually build up the enemy channels of communication and his order of battle. In the tactical situation, there was no time for code cracking, this was a job for those located in the rear, much farther to the rear. Such messages were sent back to the Headquarters wallahs serving in the safe luxury of New Delhi.

Our portable Wireless Direction Finder was located in a carefully selected position a short walk from the main unit location. This consisted of a lightweight pre-fabricated circular hut to house the installation and provide a reasonable degree of operator comfort. Of course, it was atrociously hot inside, but an essential electric fan helped to circulate the air. It was well hidden from air and ground but isolated enough to provide a rather lonely outpost for those who had the misfortune to work in it. The facility was usually kept very busy during the daylight hours and was normally operated by one man. During the long night watches, however, it was thought wise to have two operators in the interest of security and to provide company. The facility was in direct contact by a dedicated field telephone. A most essential part of location by wireless direction finding is to have at least two stations widely separated, each capable of taking bearings on the same transmission. To facilitate this, we had a wireless link with our sister unit located at Comilla, a hundred miles or so north of us.

So with ample intercept and direction-finding facilities, we soon had the locations of the enemy ground stations on our part of the front, and many at much greater distance. Our map of their wireless communications network grew with each passing day, and their attempts to safeguard their organisation by sending and receiving transmissions on two different frequencies and changing frequency at dusk soon became obvious to us. The intercept operators developed familiarity with the enemy operators and were able to identify them by their personal Morse-key habits. Most of the locations were at places where we knew there were established airstrips, and with information from other intelligence-gathering sources, we were able to relate information acquired by ourselves with the enemy units at those locations.

The Japanese Army in Burma was their Third Gun (Army), and its air component was the Third Koku Gun (Air Army). The organisation and disposition of the units of the Koku Gun was our concern. By the end of 1943, we were as familiar with the Third Army Air Force as the Japanese themselves. We knew the call signs of individual aircraft, the identity of the units to which they belonged, and even the names of many of their flying personnel and unit commanders. If an aircraft made a wireless transmission, it was almost certainly intercepted and, given sufficient time, located by direction-finding technique. Their enemy was certainly listening and it was surprising what useful information they gave away by careless talk. The Japanese wireless operator was as vulnerable in this respect as any other.

The monsoon season came and went. With its arrival, front-line road conditions denied movement of vehicular traffic. Since the temporary object was to keep the enemy out of India, our front-line Army and Air Force elements made their seasonal withdrawal to prepared positions. From these they were able to continue to hold any attempted enemy incursion and knew that they had a safe withdrawal option if necessary. The enemy was permitted to occupy positions vacated by our own forces but found only the atrocious ground conditions that made our own withdrawal desirable. The Japanese would be pushed back to their former positions with the next dry season. Our own inability to mount an offensive into Burma but to concentrate, for the time being, on keeping the enemy out of India had given the Japanese plenty of time to prepare well-defended positions. It was known that they were deeply entrenched into the hills of the Arakan and that close combat techniques would be necessary to displace them.

The monsoon ended and while it broke the heat somewhat, it did nothing for the humidity. Then, at sundown on an evening about mid-November, it was suddenly quite cool and we felt the need for warmer clothing. The cool season had come at last and with it blessed relief. About this time, I was affected by a rather painful attack of, what seemed to be, arthritis of the left shoulder. I got the medical orderly to give it a rub with a greasy concoction of the kind used by athletes for strained muscles. Its main component was the oil of wintergreen. It did the trick, for the pain was gone by next morning.

As the unit was now settled into its provisional location and seemed to be operating smoothly, I thought it appropriate to mention again the matter of my appointment to a commission. I had mentioned it to the adjutant before we arrived in India, and it was now eleven months since I had been told, before leaving Newbold Revell, that it would follow me. He was, like all the other officers of the unit, in the Service for the duration of hostilities and seemed to show little or no regard for the regulars for whom the war was very much a part of their career rather than an unfortunate interruption. His attitude seemed to be that if there had been any substance in my claim to have been recommended in the first place, the matter would have been satisfactorily concluded by now. I was left in an angry and resentful feeling of having been falsely treated, that someone had blundered back at Newbold Revell. My not having proceeded to Wilmslow with the unit in the first place, then left without any information for several days and, on making a formal request to see the CO, ordered to proceed immediately to the overseas dispatching centre in such great haste. I now felt that I had been gotten out of the way before someone's blunder was discovered, that I was not where I was initially intended to be. I soon formed a good idea of how the blunder came about and who was responsible. For the time being, there seemed to be nothing I could do. I took an early opportunity to mention it casually to the unit commander, whose attitude was like that of the adjutant with whom there had obviously been discussion. He seemed rather unconcerned, and I felt hopelessly in the hands of wartime incompetents somewhat removed from RAF general administrative processes. As there was nothing I could do for the time being, I tried to dismiss the matter from my mind and get on with my job at the senior NCO level, where there were a few other regulars of similar rank, although none initially entered for long service careers.

It was close to Christmas, and my mind, like most others, I suppose, was more than ever back home. I was sick with longing to be home with Rosemary and our baby son. There were, of course, others whose wives had been left to the experience of first birth in the absence of their husbands in distant places. My friend Harry Edwards shared this agony with me at roughly the same time. Michael was now five months old and a healthy wee boy.

Christmas came, and we tried to make the best of it in our lonely outpost on India's eastern frontier with Burma. The memory that lingers prominently in my mind of that first overseas Christmas Day is the pleasant change in our diet, but only for that day. Higher Authority had clearly increased the daily ration allowance and the Royal Indian Army Service Corps had put it to good effect by providing half a small duck for each officer and man. Of course, our cooks had to do the roasting using their usual field cooking equipment, and it has always been a wonder to me how they did it. The duck was tough, but the taste was different, and everyone tried to make it a special occasion. How RIASC managed to procure enough ducks to provide for the forward area garrison is quite beyond my imagination. The officers and senior NCOs served the corporals and aircraftmen who also had a special ration of beer, but it was the usual vile Solan and Raniket brew that I hated the taste of and the unpleasant after-effect. It seemed to be specially produced to put one out of useful action with a severe headache for several hours the next day.

So! 1943 passed quietly into history. For me, it had been a momentous year. One that started with the sadness of having to leave my young wife with my child, and depart for far-off places. The birth of my first-born son at Easter Time brought a great deal of joy mixed with resentment at not being with my wife at that time. But such is war, and I was only one of many, regular and volunteer alike, to be called upon to bear this personal joy mixed with sadness. I had seen a lot of India and enjoyed a good stay in the North West Frontier Province. I had visited many other places and had become quite familiar with the geography of Northern India. I had also had the early experience of the summer climate in the war zone of the East Bengal/Burma frontier. The news from home had steadily improved as the Bomber War increased in intensity, and our impression was that Germany was taking quite a lot of punishment that must surely have had some early effect. The Russians seemed to be getting the measure of the German invaders in the cruel winter, and the prospect of the Allies getting back onto the continent in 1944 seemed quite promising.

In our own neck of the woods the stalemate situation was little changed. There was some slight build-up of our forces in the forward area and with the improving weather, there was some skirmishing activity before us as our front-line troops sought to regain their previously held positions, giving themselves space to consolidate for whatever was planned for offensive action in 1944. This sort of action was, of course, a waste of life and effort and produced no long-term gain. As for ourselves, we had the enemy Air Force dispositions secure. We knew the locations of their flying units in Burma. We even knew the names of many commanders and pilots, the call signs of their aircraft and ground stations, the frequencies they used night and day, and were familiar with many of their bad habits that provided us with a lot of useful intelligence even before trying to read their intercepted wireless messages. Somehow, 1944, from its beginning, seemed to hold greater promise that we might soon lose our unfortunate feeling of being the forgotten Army that had to wait until things improved on the home front and our own. We had the new feeling that the waiting was coming to an end.

Of course, we knew that the enemy would also have offensive action in mind before the 1944 monsoon. After all, he had now been held at the eastern gate of India for more than twelve months and knew that the British would have to push him out of Burma and Malaya in order to protect their eastern interests. His forces were disposed like a huge pincer with open jaws spanning a tract of territory rather more than a hundred miles wide. In the north, the jaw of the pincer rested dangerously close to the Imphal Plain. The southern jaw threatened East Bengal, the possession of which would give him complete dominance of the Bay of Bengal. This, together with the Bengal/Assam railway, probably formed his main interest in British India. It would have been an extreme vanity for him to covet the entire sub-continent. One thing that was obvious to us in the southern sector was the perilous situation arising for ourselves in the event of a successful thrust by the enemy in the north in an attempt to close the pincer. We would find ourselves, as we were already, with our backs to the sea and without the means of withdrawal further into India. On the plus side, however, we were in a friendly country, whilst the enemy was threatened by the intense hatred and active guerrilla opposition of those he had to continually suppress by a cruel occupation regime that could only intensify the hatred. His lines of communication were lengthy; he was a long way from home, and the Americans were giving him a hard time in the Pacific Islands, depriving him of his stepping-stones, as it were, but paying dearly for each hard-won victory. But we had no doubt regarding his military strength and capability that posed a threat to ourselves on India's eastern frontier. Although we were feeling better about our situation, we knew that we still did not have the capability to sustain a major thrust against the Japanese on our front.

One other important factor that is easy to overlook in our stalemate situation is the overriding effect of America's political interest in the maintenance of their supplies to the Chinese National Forces under Chiang Kai-Shek. This important lifeline was the so-called Burma Road that wound its weary way through perilous mountain terrain into China from Lashio in Northern Burma. Following the fall of France in 1940, the British, now without the support of its European allies, had been obliged to close the Burma Road under the threat of severe reprisals by the Japanese. It was this enforced action that led to the creation, by the Americans, of a volunteer flying unit under the direction of the retired USAAC Colonel Claire Chennault to fly these essential supplies from Assam into China over 'The Hump' as the air route over the eastern part of the Himalayas had come to be known. Fearing that Chiang would use their supplies to fight Mao Tse-tung instead of the Japanese, the Americans had also placed General Stilwell at the disposal of Chiang Kai Shek as advisor in the creation and training of additional fighting units for the Chinese National Army.

The Japanese had taken Burma by April 1942 primarily to close the Burma Road and deny Chiang Kai-Shek of his much-needed supplies. Because this road started so far in the northeast of Burma at Lashio, General Wavell, Commander in Chief of the India Command, and General Stilwell decided that they would adopt an immediate object to retake central Burma. This plan involved a replacement for the old Burma Road. The new route was to start at Ledo in North Eastern India and terminate at a convenient terminal for the Chinese Nationalists located at Kunming.

During September 1943 there had been a reorganisation of our 14th Army. Field Marshal Lord Wavell had become Viceroy of India. General Sir Claude Aukinleck had been appointed CinC India Command, and the 14th Army was now under the command of General Sir William (Bill) Slim. Whereas we had been in the old India Command, we were now absorbed into the newly created South East Asia Command under the overall control of Admiral of The Fleet Lord Louis Mountbatten as Supreme Commander Allied Forces, with General Stilwell as his deputy and headquarters in Ceylon (now Sri-Lanka). A large part of the14th Army had been busily engaged in North Burma to make it possible for the Chinese to take a more effective part in that important sector. With that accomplished, General Slim could now direct his efforts to driving southward to clear the Japanese out of Burma. It is perhaps pertinent to mention the rather unusual Brigadier General Orde Wingate, who, with his small force known as The Chindits (a long-range penetration group), was trying, with marked success, to demonstrate how the Japanese could be defeated by an army trained specifically in jungle warfare. The participation of The Chindits, with their infiltration tactics, did much to disorientate the Japanese and was of particular value in this early fighting and continued to be throughout the entire campaign. But there was a long way still to go and many tough battles to be won.

It was during the opening weeks of 1944 that we found ourselves presented with the unusual opportunity to take ordinary leave. This came as a surprise as such a possibility arising in our forward area situation had not occurred to us. We were encouraged to take it, but where could we go other than to Calcutta, where there would be some sort of private club facilities for officers and senior NCOs. For the junior ranks, there was the question of personal funds: whilst travel would be free and a small allowance would be payable in lieu of rations, the cost of accommodation, food, and entertainment would be beyond the capability of most. As far as the senior NCOs were concerned, we were encouraged by the CO to take the opportunity whilst it was available. During the coming summer, our second in the theatre, all members of the unit would have a two-week break at our allocated hill station (Shillong) in Northern Assam. Here the junior ranks would be able to take a leave break at an organised RAF facility without expense to themselves. For us, more fortunate senior NCOs, the unexpected leave opportunity was too good to miss, and three of us decided to take a longer look at Calcutta, but we were restricted to one week only, and of course, our respective sections would have to carry on without us, so I was the only one from my section. Harry Edwards, the unit disciplinarian came, and I think Bill Friend, our senior technical NCO, was the other. The other senior NCOs would take their turn progressively in parties of similar size.

Travel arrangements, the route and mode of travel were now all too familiar and nonetheless off-putting. Calcutta had little to offer beyond its main thoroughfare – Chowringhee. We found our suggested senior NCOs club in the pleasanter part of the city known, I think, as Tollygunge. It was run by elderly ladies, obviously, members of the large British community still remaining in Calcutta. The accommodation was good, as was the food altogether a pleasant change from our usual field conditions. There was always Firpo's restaurant on Chowringhee, a good air-conditioned cinema where, I remember we saw Judy Garland in "The Wizard of OZ". The Kardomah café was a pleasant venue in the square at the bottom of Chowringhee, close to the Clive of India memorial, for morning coffee and afternoon tea. But I cannot resist mentioning the bugs in the wicker chairs that found the bare spaces between our shorts and stockings. There was also cricket on the maidan on the open side of Chowringhee and beyond it, the racecourse where the jockeys all seemed to have well-known British racing names. I had only one little flutter on the tote and then, unsuccessful and disinclined to gambling anyway, called it quits.

It was pleasant to stroll along Chowringhee in the winter sunshine with its quality shops, well-appointed bars, and a noticeable absence of beggars, who were strictly prohibited. Behind, and running parallel with the main thoroughfare, was Dharamtala Street, where one saw the real India with its decaying buildings and open-fronted shops with all manner of merchandise spilling out onto the pavements. A wonderful smell of spices here and there but disgustingly nauseous smells elsewhere. "O! The stenches in the byway" (as Kipling wrote in his poem Christmas in India). Beggars everywhere, many of them small children intentionally horribly crippled in infancy and committed to the life of begging as a livelihood. Chowringhee was just a façade. Whilst we were strolling on the last day of our stay a small dog made a great fuss of us. She accompanied us to our club and simply refused to leave. She was still there the next morning and seemed to be seeking kindness. She was a nice wee dog about five hands high at the head, white and brown in colour and very dainty. We decided that the easiest way was to take her back with us and make her the unit pet.

We got back to our jungle base much better for our short break and found things unchanged. We christened the dog Chowringhee, a name to which she readily responded.

She was well-behaved and was made welcome wherever she went. Of course, she was well-fed and the only dog in our tight little world. She slept on the floor of our bamboo basha between Harry Edwards and myself and was usually in the company of one or the other of us. She never made any attempt to wander off and was excellent company for a rather tame mongoose that also sought our company from time to time. A useful animal to have around where snakes were occasionally to be found in secluded corners.

As regards entertainment, there was little of it other than what we were able to devise ourselves. But it really is surprising the amount of talent that can be found in the smallest company of men thrown together in circumstances such as these. Initially, we were limited to general knowledge quizzes between teams chosen at random. Of course we did not have the facility of a piano or other musical instruments. Gathering together in the evenings brought out talents for poetry and song without music. Larry Gain, the Adjutant, had a particularly fine baritone singing voice and was quite capable of tuneful renditions, without musical accompaniment, of the more classical old English songs such as 'Who is Sylvia' and 'Angels Guard Thee.' Others had repertoires of lengthy poems like 'Dangerous Dan Magrew,' 'The Pigtail of Li Fang Fu,' etc. I was able to draw on a few from Rudyard Kipling, whose work, during his time spent with the British Army in India, had interested me for several years. Then there were the more bawdy ballads in which several members seemed to specialise; a young officer, Flying Officer Lumgair, had a particularly amusing version of 'No More I'll Go A Roving, (with you young maid),' one verse of which I remember ran – 'I put my hand on my girl's breast, and the wind from her A... blew nor' nor' west,' a roving, a roving, no more I'll go a roving, no more I'll go a roving with you young man. This sort of ditty was well-liked among the lower ranks, and officers who were brave enough to offer it soon gained easy popularity thereby.

A self-help stage, erected by a few enthusiasts at one end of the junior ranks recreation hut, was to prove very useful on limited occasions. During the cool season of 1943/44 it was decided to present a concert of all ranks wishing to volunteer their talents. I offered to do a couple of numbers. One, based on the Indian Rope Trick, found me dressed in typical Indian garb with a genuine Indian flute, playing whilst a rope ascended to the roof. It was, of course pulled up to a point where a strong hook had been fixed, and a small Bengali child hidden to come down the rope, hand over hand, at the appropriate time. That went down very well, as also did my rendition of a poem that I composed based on the well-known comedian Stanley Holloway's comic adventures of 'Young Albert Ramsbottom at the Whipsnade Zoo.' This I converted as follows:

There's an RAF unit in't jungle, that's noted for hard work – and fun, and Mr. and Mrs. Ramsbottom had had to send their young Albert, their son.

100

Now Aircraftman First Class Ramsbottom, in topee and shorts, quite a swell, still had his stick with the horse's head handle. Remember, it were't the finest that Woolworths could sell.

Now Albert had heard about fight sergeants, how they were ferocious and wild, and seeing Chiefy in a recumbent posture one day, well, it didn't seem right to't child.

So Albert, the brave little feller, not showing a morsel of fear, took his stick with the horse's head handle and stuck it in't flight sergeant's ear.

You could see that the flight sergeant didn't like it, and giving a kind of a roar, he fell in young Albert between two men and marched him to't guardhouse door.

Next morning, young Albert was marched in front o't CO trembling and shakin wi' fear, and't flight sergeant told't CO what young lad had done, and proved it by showing his ear.

Now look here Ramsbottom said't CO, this thing that tha's done it's all-wrong, and seeing as how it were't flight sergeant you chose, well... I award fourteen days.........at Shillong.

I was also able to recite 'The Green Eye of The Little Yellow God.' On one concert occasion, Harry Edwards and I did a combined number in which I was on stage reciting, and Harry came into the audience pretending to be a posh drunk who interrupted the proceedings with every possible drunken contradiction of what I was saying as I tried to struggle through the poem. The whole thing finished in an uproar of delight from the troops.

There was a young airman called Les Buckland who could do an incredible imitation of Arthur Tracey, popularly known as 'The Street Singer', and had actually made a most realistic street lamp to lean against, in the manner of the artiste himself, whilst singing his signature tune – 'Marta.' I also have a compact disk of Arthur Tracy singing some of the repertoire for which he became so well known.

We had a portable gramophone with a few records of popular music of that era. I became quite sentimentally attached to the singing of Deanna Durbin, The Ink Spots, and Paul Robeson. I have recently added a few compact disks to my music collection and these include some of these sentimental tunes. The gramophone was passed from hut to hut. How we managed to keep it playing on the limited supply of needles remains a mystery.

We were now into February, and there was a positive indication of increased air activity that also tallied with reports of hard fighting on the ground at the northern end of the

Arakan as the Japanese were, seemingly, trying to break out in an attempt to skirt around our forward positions in a flanking movement to our north. It was seen to be an attempt to reinforce their forces facing our own prepared positions at Imphal and Kohima. I had the afternoon shift on one particularly memorable day and, towards the end of the afternoon, after collecting the latest batch of intercepted messages from the wireless vehicles, I spotted among them one that had recognisable features. So much so that I was able to read it almost as though it was in plain English. Although it was in the Japanese operating code, it told me unmistakeably that the commander of the 7th Hikodan, a flying brigade operating in our part of the front, had arrived at Magwe, about 180 miles east of Akyab island, and was scheduled to depart at 0700 the next morning. I summoned the CO on our unit field telephone system. He quickly came over to the mobile office, agreed with my inference, and informed our tactical group headquarters (224 Group), who said they would have a couple of Hurricanes in the Magwe area at the appropriate time. A successful strike resulted in the aircraft being shot down shortly after take off. It was reported to be completely destroyed by fire without evidence of survivors. Whoever authorised that signal was very foolish for, whilst it could be read by a trained Japanese wireless operator without the need for decoding, It was just as easy for me, with my own experience and specialised training, to read it. We were also listening out for the aircraft the next morning and intercepted its take-off signal, but nothing further. I guess the 8th Flying Brigade was a sadder but wiser bunch of aviators that night. Needs one to know one. That was the reason for my being there.

On another occasion, but much earlier in the afternoon shift, I thought there was unusual aircraft wireless activity well to the south of us. I kept a careful watch on it for a little while and plotted its progress by our direction finding facility. It was obviously coming in our direction and I guessed it was making for Akyab or, perhaps, for the port installations at Chittagong or even some other target further north where the Bengal/Assam railway was a prime target as it was the route by which supplies for the Chinese Nationalists was transported for airlift over the 'Hump,' or via the Ledo road. I alerted 224 Group, who directed their radar to make a concentrated search of the southern sector. They also scrambled a Hurricane squadron to patrol Akyab and soon confirmed the interception of a large Japanese bomber force south of the island. There was a tremendous fight at high altitude out of normal vision. We could hear it plainly and saw several flaming aircraft plummet out of the heavens to crash in the jungle. Sadly that which we saw quite plainly was one of our own Hurricanes crash flaming into the jungle close to us; there was no parachute. Strangely, we did not hear any sound of exploding bombs and, in the absence of a further report from 224 Group, concluded that the raid had been thoroughly routed with the surviving aircraft scooting back to base with their bombs saved for another occasion. We had achieved a comfortable measure of air supremacy by this time, and it was comforting to see a demonstration of it.

It was during the month of February, I think that we had the rather disconcerting news that the Japanese, noted for their infiltration tactics, had infiltrated the 5th (Indian) Division Headquarters defence box in darkness and put a large number of the sleeping headquarters staff to the bayonet. Those who were fortunate to survive were found miserably desolate in the jungle the next morning. We were left wondering that if the enemy could get through a divisional defence box, what were our chances? Although we were some distance from the actual scene I can record that we spent many anxious nights for some time thereafter.

However, the war in Burma was certainly looking much better as the Allied forces, against bitter opposition, gradually turned the tide against the enemy in their most northerly positions. Now, they were able to direct their effort to the next objective of central Burma and southward generally along the course of the Irrawaddy River on its course to Rangoon. But that objective was about seven hundred miles distant, and the 1944 monsoon season was only a matter of three months away. During March, the 5th (Indian) Division was redeployed from the Arakan sector to the Imphal/Kohima sector, where there were indications of developing heavy attacks. There was bitter fighting on our own part of the front where the enemy was well dug into carefully prepared positions in the Arakan Yoma, but they were held by our own positions along the Buthidaung-Maungdaw line. Buthidaung is just inside Burma, immediately south of Cox's Bazaar in East Bengal (now Bangladesh), from which it is separated only by the India/Burma border. Maungdaw is about thirty miles northeast of Buthidaung.

About this time we had a change of unit commander. It was quite unexpected and had obviously been kept under close wraps. The new CO was a much younger officer with a rather dashing manner. He had previously been employed on aircrew duties and wore a flying badge the same as my own. Where Squadron Leader Julian went I never did discover. I saw him the night before his departure when he came to make his farewell visit to the night watch that I happened to have that night. It was well after midnight, and it was obvious that he had taken rather too much to drink. This was unusual and, as spirituous liquor was not normally available, certainly not to the men who had to be content with a meagre monthly ration of inferior beer. He must have gone to unusual lengths to acquire it for a farewell drink with the officers. He was rather emotional, I thought, and his behaviour generally did not impress the men. On leaving, he was rather overfamiliar and said that I was a damn fine chap to which I would have had no objection had it been done at a more appropriate time in the right place. Where he went to, I have no idea, but he was not seen again in the theatre and was probably posted back to Home Establishment on age grounds; he must have been fifty years of age or thereabouts.

The new CO was Squadron Leader Power, who, resembling his namesake (the actor Tyrone Power) in general appearance, was immediately referred to by the men as 'Ty.' He was instantly popular and had the ability to put one at ease without undue familiarity or loss of dignity. During his first conversation with me, to which I was summoned as the ranking senior NCO in the Wireless Intelligence Section, he questioned me at some length about my service background and seemed genuinely delighted to discover that I was a regular. He told me he was also a regular entrant but had entered as an adult well over average age. Completing his training just after the start of the war, he had flown, like myself, as a Wireless Operator/Air Gunner with Bomber Command. He was commissioned early and, after completing a tour of operations, had responded to the same invitation as myself seeking volunteers for special wireless duties. Since he had spent much of his early life in the Orient, mostly in China, he was an obvious choice for duty in the area of Japanese Army Air Force intelligence. He was interested to learn that I had entered into this particular branch of intelligence for training as a W/T Intelligence Officer and wanted to know what had gone wrong. I gave him a full account as I knew it and left him in no doubt about my feelings at having been, seemingly, deceived into volunteering for something that had not transpired, particularly in terms of my career as a long-service regular. I felt that if I had been found unsuitable for appointment after training, I should have been told so and given the opportunity to return to my chosen RAF trade to get on with my career instead of being told the commission would follow whilst, at the same time, being disposed of in obvious haste in what seemed like an attempt to cover an administrative blunder. He said he would certainly take the matter further and keep me informed. He did, in fact, send it for me a few days later to make sure he had my case details correct.

April came, and with it, both temperature and humidity were rising rapidly. The Burmese summer was taxing enough for anyone who had to work through it, and it certainly did nothing for those who had to engage in armed combat. The monsoon, when it came, only added to the misery of all who had to endure exposure to the elements in field conditions. The fighting to the north of us began to look dangerous for us in the south as the Japanese mounted attacks against our positions, which denied them access to the Imphal plain. The enemy did, in fact, cut the road to Dimapur, thus denying the defending forces of their supply line. Supplies had now to be dropped by air, and it looked as though it was going to be a long battle. Air dropping off supplies now became widespread as the offensive action gathered pace. The supply of our own rations was also changed, and strangely enough, we found great satisfaction in the variety that the change made to our diet. Each ration pack contained breakfast, lunch or dinner for fourteen men and was packed in a stout waxed cardboard box in an open framework crate that supplied enough wood to make a fire if needed for heating the food. The supply system, however, frequently got the meals confused, and we found ourselves with all-day breakfasts, lunches, or dinners. However, they were generous in that they provided an ample supply of dry cigarettes and boiled sweets. Tinned fruit was a most welcome addition, as were all other components. Altogether, from the feeding point of view, we found ourselves agreeably better off. It was possible for our unit cooks to make much-improved meals, and of course, there was the easy option in the event of central cooking arrangements being difficult or impractical. By March, the important towns of Mandalay and Meiktila had fallen to the Allies. Akyab and Ramree were recaptured by units of the Commando Brigade as the airstrips on these islands would be essential for the air supply of our forces engaged in the rapidly developing conflict in central Burma.

May passed, and June brought the full heat of summer. The shade temperature at midday was seldom below 118 degrees Fahrenheit, with humidity of about ninety-five percent. The fighting continued with undiminished fury as casualties mounted. We had reports of a Japanese breakthrough onto the Imphal Plain, but they were by all accounts getting a good beating. It later transpired that the Japanese had been intentionally drawn onto the plain to get them into the open, where they would be deprived of their known ability at jungle warfare. The ruse worked, and they soon found that without the jungle cover, they were no match for the kind of fighting to which our forces were more accustomed. They put up a most determined attack, however, for which they paid heavily. But the siege was to continue for some time yet. We had been working very hard to keep a check on the enemy dispositions in the north of Burma. These were changing rapidly as it became necessary for them to up sticks and go – they were certainly being obliged to move, but we had the measure of them.

I was surprised and delighted to be told that it was my turn to take a break at Shillong, our hill station in northern Assam. Off I went with a small party for fourteen days of pleasant coolness, so I thought! The first part of the rail journey was all too familiar from the railhead at Chittagong as far as Chandpur. Then, the line took us farther north to Sylhet Bazaar (on the Bengal/Assam extension), where we arrived in the early morning. From here, we were taken by road in lorries up the precipitous one-track road to the halfway crossing point at Cherra Punji. Here, we had to wait for the convoy coming down the hill to this location, the only point at which north and south-bound convoys could pass. The food available to us at this only stop was proffered by small boys who came out of a large building with buckets of boiled eggs, calling "boil eck, sahib, boil eck." The air was filled with the acrid stench of boiled eggs and the ground was covered with eggshells. Cherra Punji is said to have the highest rainfall in the world situated, as it is directly exposed to the full effect of the monsoon. Climatically, it is ideal for tea growing and the whole beautiful pattern of hillsides was covered by a most luxuriant growth of green vegetation. We arrived at Shillong in the late afternoon and after a shower, what bliss! I felt wonderfully cool in slacks and shirt with a woollen pullover as protection against the unaccustomed coolness. The evening meal, served by waiters in a properly appointed sergeant's mess, was a great treat. I even had a couple of whiskies, what a privilege to have a bar facility again, even though spirits were necessarily rationed. Feeling pleasantly tired and relaxed, I went to bed early. I was asleep instantaneously and slept soundly.

Came the dawn, and I awoke to find that I had a dreadful pain in my chest. Thinking that I had been lying in an awkward posture, I lingered in bed, hoping that the discomfort would pass. It did not and I decided that I had better rise and take a shower and shave. I was having great difficulty walking, every step being shear agony. Perhaps some breakfast may help, so painfully, I crept across the mess to find that I couldn't manage more than a cup of tea. I decided that I was rather ill and needed medical aid. With great difficulty I walked to the station sick bay and was seen by the RAF station medical officer. With his stethoscope to my chest he said, "Come on, Flight Sergeant, breathe, your breathing is so shallow I can barely hear a thing." I just could not do any better, and he told me that I probably had Malaria and would have to be admitted to the British Military Hospital on the hill station. He summoned an ambulance that took me back to my quarters to collect my gear, then onto the BMH, where I was confirmed as a malaria case despite my having faithfully taken the compulsory daily dose of malarial suppressant tablets throughout the whole of my time in the forward area. I was given the first shot of raw quinine, and that I found dreadfully unpalatable. This was to be my treatment, three times a day for the first two days. Then, twelve days on an oral treatment of a quinine derivative drug called Pamaquin. What had caused the attack, I do not know. Perhaps the mere fact that I was carrying it in a suppressed state, the climatic change somehow allowing it to emerge.

For the first two days, I was pleased to be left alone with the occasional drink and the dreadful quinine. On the third day I was feeling a little more human as movement returned to my lungs. Then, about midday, we were told that the hospital had to be evacuated of all patients who were fit enough to be moved. Apparently, there had been tremendous casualties at Imphal and Kohima that were beyond the capacity of the facilities immediately in the rear of the battle zone. Those of us declared fit to move would be moved down the hill to Sylhet that very afternoon and then transferred to an ambulance train, which would take us to a BMH somewhere in the Indian Central Command. The ambulance convoy was well organised. I was on a stretcher that was fixed in the vehicle, and I had a quite comfortable journey. At Sylhet, the ambulance train was waiting and this was sheer luxury by comparison with the usual rolling stock used on this section of the Bengal/Assam railway. I had assumed that the train would have been routed all the way to our undisclosed destination in Central Command. But with the light of the next morning, we found ourselves in a railway marshalling yard. Questions were being asked about our location, and none of the patients seemed to know, nor were any members of the staff available to provide the answer. Putting my head out of the window at the side of my cot, I took one look outside, smelled the air, and said this is Chittagong. Yet I was somewhat bewildered. If this was Chittagong, why had we come to the southernmost end of the Bengal/Assam railway line? We were supposedly bound for Central Command, a long way to the north by way of Calcutta. To reach Calcutta would require a sea crossing from Chandpur to Siragunge. Why come south of Chandpur?

There was obviously something amiss as it was mid-morning before any of the trains medical staff appeared. They confirmed that this was indeed Chittagong, where we were to be hospitalised temporarily in the Forward Area BMH, awaiting early transfer to the Central Command BMH at Dehra Dun. I was now four days into recovery, and my own plan formed immediately. There was no way that I was going to Dehra Dun, which was about a hundred and fifty miles northeast of New Delhi and a thousand miles or so, in a straight line to the northwest of Chittagong, just to take a pill a day for the next ten days. Absolutely no way, the whole thing was sheer bloody nonsense. My own unit was easily accessible only a few miles forward, and that was good enough for me. I could take the pills there under the supervision of the unit Medical Orderly. Well, they saw the sense in not sending me to Dehra Dun but stubbornly insisted that I should remain in hospital care for my remaining treatment, for which they would send me to the hospital's Ambulatory Malaria Camp.

So in the company of another malaria patient, a young private soldier of the Royal West Kent Regiment, I was transported to the Ambulatory Malaria Camp located somewhere in the Chittagong area. By outward appearance, it could not have been more miserable than it turned out to be. It was, of course, the usual collection of bamboo huts (bashas) at the base of a small hillock with the ever-present jungle all around. The camp kitchen arrangement was on top of the hill with the patients' accommodation at the base. There was no lighting and no ablution facility. There were no medical personnel; the young soldier and I were the only patients. On our arrival, the camp kitchen was deserted. An Army cook did arrive during the late afternoon to prepare an evening meal for us, but he was not required to stay overnight. He would return in the morning to make breakfast. He also mentioned that there was a routine daily visit by a medical officer from BMH, and the drill was for patients to parade at his office tent by 1030 hours.

To borrow some more words inspired by Rudyard Kipling, 'Night fell heavy, as remembered sin' and with it came the misery of the mosquitoes. We decided to take to our beds and the protection of our mosquito nets for what was to be a very long dark night. As the provision of bedding was not a feature of this medical establishment, I was using my own, with groundsheet, mattress, and my own two sheets laid on the standard Indian Army charpoy. I had been lying for only a few minutes when I began to itch in several places at the same time, particularly on my legs. The young soldier had an electric torch, an unusual but desirable personal possession (I often wondered how he acquired the essential batteries for it. I cannot remember having seen any since leaving the UK. Perhaps he had access to Army sources). However, I asked if I might borrow it to explore the cause of my discomfort and, to my absolute horror, found my legs covered with bugs. The damn things were everywhere, even crawling up the inside of my mosquito net. I was out of bed in a flash and under the waist-high tap of the only water supply that was just outside the basha. What was I to do? I had obviously selected a bug-infested charpoy and my bedding was now likewise infested. It was pitch dark, there was no light, and we were the only two souls in this apparently deserted place. There was not a sound of human existence, just the creatures of the night, particularly mosquitoes and bugs, against the background noise of the ubiquitous cicadas.

The young soldier seemed to have been more fortunate in his choice of bedstead as he said he was not affected. Perhaps he had become accustomed to such discomfort. There was no way that I could de-infest my bedding in the darkness, so I decided to get into my slacks and long-sleeved bush shirt, put on my bush hat, and somehow pass the night away. There was not even a chair to sit on, and I was reluctant to sit on either of the two unoccupied beds in the basha. So I stayed outside, where I had only the occasional facial attack by mosquitoes to worry about. It was a long, long night of about twelve hours spent mostly walking about in the almost total darkness. I ambled up to the kitchen area, where I found a bench to sit on and spent quite a long time there swatting the mosquitoes, and I suppose, I dozed occasionally with my head on my folded arms. At long last, dawn came, and I was glad to get under the tap again for an all-over wash followed by a shave, after which I felt a bit more human. Using the thin rope, used to secure my bedroll, I managed to rig a line outside on which I hung the infested bedding. The bugs would soon desert it when exposed to the hot sun. An examination of the charpoy revealed that it was alive with bugs at the joints of the wooden framework and at the many places along the sides and ends of the top frame where the rattan rope was bound to secure the criss-cross rope support for the mattress, or whatever one chose to lie on.

This was only my fifth day of recovery, and bearing in mind that only five days ago I could hardly breathe, I was not, to say the least, feeling too good, particularly after a sleepless night spent out of my bed, nor was I feeling well disposed to the BMH Chittagong Ambulatory Malaria Camp which, as a medical establishment for anyone recuperating from malaria was a positive disgrace, and someone was going to hear about it. After all, there was no excuse for unhygienic conditions in the forward area where effective measures were available simply by calling in the Garrison Engineer. I had no idea where the camp was located but knew that it was a good distance from BMH judging by the time taken to reach it by road. Neither did I know where BMH was in the widespread, but not densely populated, Chittagong area.

The duty cook arrived to cook breakfast for us, I am sure we could have saved him the bother. The medical officer turned up close to the appointed hour, but he didn't know what was waiting for him. He was an Indian doctor of the Royal Army Medical Corps with the start rank of captain and a very officious one at that. I judged that he had little knowledge of Service life and, I suspected, limited experience of medical practice. He was apparently without any form of documentation and clearly did not know my rank, name, and unit. He seemed to take an instant dislike at having to deal with a senior NCO of the RAF; no doubt being used to dealing with humble privates of the Army. He didn't even ask how I was feeling. With due deference, I told him of my nocturnal experience and left him in no doubt about what I thought of the medical establishment for which I believed he had a measure of shared personal responsibility. He was not the least concerned about the hygienic implications of the bugs and indicated no action to redress the situation for my immediate benefit or for the benefit of others to follow. He showed not the slightest concern for the well-being of the sick or his professional duty of care for those in his charge. I told him that, as my unit was in reasonably close proximity, and I would be more comfortable there for the remaining ten days of my recovery and treatment period, I would not be present at his next sick parade. He mumbled something about the consequences of taking the law into my own hands, and I then walked out of the tent, having noted the field telephone on the table. It was a pity that I had not previously investigated this tent situated on the dirt track at the entrance to the camp, but some distance from the huts, I could have sought refuge in it during the night. It seemed to contain the only chair in the camp and the only telephone. I waited until he had departed then, using the field telephone, which I found to be connected directly to the Garrison exchange, I had no difficulty contacting my unit, where I was fortunate enough to find my friend Harry Edwards on the Admin extension. I explained my predicament and the totally ridiculous nature of it, and asked him to inform the CO and, for God's sake, to send me transport to bring me home where I could take my daily pill without the prospect of another night like the last one, which would have been bad enough without the bugs. As I did not know my location I told him that our unit medic would be aware of it and be able to give directions to the driver. It was early afternoon by the time the CO's jeep came into the camp where I was waiting at the already-mentioned tent. Half an hour later I was reunited with the members of my unit and was able to fully describe to the CO the unfortunate events of my last five days. He understood that I was not feeling in the best of health but that my action would have been his own in the circumstances described. After all, I could finish the malaria treatment in the accustomed environment of the unit and would be able to enjoy the facilities that we had developed to suit our own comfort and convenience rather than the rudimentary basics of that from which I had chosen to desert, albeit after giving due notice of my intention. I was to take it easy for the remaining treatment time, help where I could at my own pace and time, and then take the next party to Shillong and enjoy the two-week break that uncontrollable events had deprived me of. I never did hear anything further about my self-discharge from Army medical care.

So, exactly two weeks after my first journey into northern Assam, I went up to the RAF hill station again. The morning of my arrival, I went to see the medical officer who remembered me. I told him that I was now feeling well recovered from malaria, and he ran his stethoscope over me and told me to revert now to the standard daily suppressant treatment of Mepacrine available at the mess. He was rather horrified at my account of what had happened after my arrival at BMH Chittagong. He was particularly concerned that I had not been transferred at that point to RAF medical care.

Feeling refreshed after fourteen days, mostly spent tramping around the Kassi hills and enjoying an occasional game of golf with a wonderful distant view of Mount Everest well to the north, I arrived back at our forward area location. The fighting at Imphal and Kohima ended during March 1944, with the Japanese suffering a thorough defeat that was to mark the beginning of the end of their Burma conquest. They were being pushed southward by our main thrust. Their western flank was also exposed to continuing attack as they tried to consolidate after their withdrawal from Imphal, and there was fierce fighting on all fronts as they made a determined effort to regain their losses. In our own sector, fighting in the Arakan now presented a difficult situation that was finally to involve selected elements of our forces, principally the Ghurkhas and West Africans, in close combat of the fiercest kind. Whilst the situation was decidedly much improved since the closing months of 1943, it was quite clear that the end was not yet clearly in sight. The fighting at

Imphal and Kohima had cost the Allies 17600 killed whilst the total Japanese casualties were something like three times that number if those lost due to privation following their withdrawal are included. Little wonder that the Allied Memorial at Kohima appropriately contains the words – 'When you go home, tell them that for their tomorrow we gave our today.'

Our unit workload was, not surprisingly, attended by the effects of the heightened activity, and we were hard-pressed to cope with it. But we certainly had positive evidence of developing Allied air superiority and its marked effect on the enemy, who seemed to have little in the way of effective opposition. The Hurricanes previously mentioned were now reinforced by Supermarine Spitfires, the North American Thunderbolt, and the Lockheed Lightning, all of which made an impressive contribution to the fighter and ground attack capability.

On the ground, there was also a noticeable increase in Army personnel close to our own location and we were soon to find troops from British West Africa encamped about four hundred yards from us. They were small in number, and we guessed they were possibly reinforcements for their own regiment fighting a little to our south. They had moved into a small clearing below our own, and one morning, three of us decided to stroll down to greet them. Their officers and senior NCOs were British and we enjoyed a mug of tea and a good chat with them. As we were taking our leave of them, there was some activity at the base of a palm tree where, in the tangled growth, some of the native troops had spotted a cobra – not a nice thing to have around – which they quickly despatched with their pangas; the deadly looking hand weapon with which they could decapitate a human with one swipe, and with which each was armed. They were not to stay in our locality for more than a few days. Halfway up the hill, I suddenly began to feel unwell and vomited. By the time we got onto our plateau, a distance of no more than four hundred yards, I was puking blood. With extreme pain in the stomach, I managed to get to the latrines, where I emptied myself whilst still vomiting. I somehow got back to my basha and, in a matter of only a few moments, completely lost control of bodily functions and was passing blood uncontrollably from mouth and anus. I was on the ground and, with each frequently occurring rigour of intense abdominal pain, accompanied by an involuntary arching of the back, I knew that I was seriously ill, as did my companions who summoned the unit medic. I think I must have quickly passed into a state of semi-consciousness as I have only broken recollections of what happened next. After what seemed to be a lengthy interval, I found myself on a stretcher fitted to the rear end of a covered truck. Since we did not have unit vehicles of this type, the medic would have had to intimate an urgent requirement to the motor pool. This would have taken a little time. My next recollection is of finding myself on the floor of a rather barren room in some sort of permanent building. It seemed rather like a kitchen as it had a sink and a tap. I was alone with a different RAF medical orderly who told me that the medical officer would be along shortly, but I have no recollection of seeing him on his arrival. I suppose I must have been in an RAF clearing station. I have no memory of my journey from there, but I clearly remember arriving at a familiar place where I had been before to have some dental treatment, it was the RAF Mobile Field Hospital.

I was taken in on my stretcher, still in dreadful pain and arching my back with every spasm. I recall a very tall medical officer who told me that he was going to put me to sleep. In reply, I asked for a drink of water first. Well! Said he, "We will have to see about that." Shortly, a nursing sister appeared with a small bowl of purified water. She said something about being able to give me only a tiny drink and that she did it with a spoon, just one single spoonful. Then she told me that she was going to put me to sleep, and off I went into blessed oblivion. For the next three days I have only the faintest recollection of being roused occasionally to have a tablet pushed into my mouth. Then, it seems that I was forcefully awakened and encouraged to eat thick, concentrated soups and jellies over a period of several days. Special light diet, mostly chicken and fish with thick soups and jellies, followed for another week or so, then fat-free foods until my discharge after three weeks. The male nursing staff told me that I had been very fortunate to survive as it had held very little hope for me at the time of admission. On the morning of my discharge, the Senior Medical Officer, whose attitude was most sympathetic, handed me the official hospital report, which read – 'This patient has suffered a severe attack of Bacillary Dysentery with marked toxic effects. It is recommended that he be posted out of the forward area to the Southern Deccan or Northern India for a recuperation period of not less than six months. He is granted three weeks prior sick leave at the RAF Hill Station, extendable at the discretion of the Senior Medical Officer'. He also told me that I had had a very close call and had only just made it to the MFH in time to be treated with one of the latest Sulphonamide Drugs, namely May and Baker 693 (M&B 693).

CHAPTER XV
A CLOSE CALL - AND THE CONSEQUENCES

So off I went again to the hill station at Shillong, this time the only member of my unit. It was well into September, and everyone else had been. There were not quite so many on leave at this time of year. I shared a bungalow with a Canadian pilot, Flight Sergeant Bob Owen, from Calgary. He was flying with a Thunderbolt squadron based quite close to us and, like myself, was on sick leave. I read in him the familiar signs of flying fatigue, and he readily admitted his feeling that good fortune must surely desert him before long. He was not morbid but typically quiet for long periods. I found him an excellent companion and we had many good walks together and most interesting conversations in the pleasant hills. His period of leave was extended before my initial three weeks expired. When my time came to see the MO at the end of my three weeks, I was pleasantly surprised when he told me that I was to stay for a further two weeks, after which he would see how my health was progressing. Bob and I enjoyed our extended stay together until his time came to return to the forward area. I felt quite alone after his departure as I had the bungalow to myself. My leave was further extended by another week, and I made the best of it. I was returned to my unit after an absence of six weeks, wondering what had been decided for me in the way of a posting for at least six months. I had a very good idea; after all there was only one place to which I could be posted and remain in the Wireless Intelligence Organisation in India.

I was posted, actually detached, as anticipated, to the Wireless Experimental Centre at Anand Parbat. I was not overjoyed by the prospect of six months at an Army establishment that had a small element of RAF personnel without an independent CO. It was now early November and although the season had not yet changed on the East Bengal/Burma frontier, I found arriving at New Delhi early in the day very cold. The RTO contacted WEC for transport and, as I knew that it would take quite some time for it to appear, I went to the station restaurant and had a passable breakfast. At WEC, I was surprised to find my old colleague from Cranwell's days, Jack Hyde, who was in the communications centre. He still had the rank of sergeant and seemed quite happy with his lot since leaving Barrackpore, where I had last seen him. Strangely enough, Sergeant Brian Stocks, his particular friend at Barrackpore, had also accompanied him. Jack and I were the only two regulars in the place, other than the sergeant major, whose name was Ireson. All other senior NCOs were of the instantly promoted type on qualification in their chosen Army or RAF intelligence functions. There were very few RAF personnel, the majority of them instant sergeants. I was assigned to a section under Captain Harris. A non-regular, he was always very polite to me, and we got on very well. I found myself responsible for writing the section of the Monthly Intelligence Report dealing with the activities of the Japanese Army Air Force, a task to which I was well suited in view of my previous experience. I was, of course, responsible for the work involved in gathering the information required and found myself initially recording that which I had been responsible for originating myself. So, my introduction to this new line of work was simplicity itself.

There were three other non-regular sergeants in the section, one of whom was Gordon Cairns. Somewhat more mature than the other two, Gordon and I were to become firm friends and have remained in contact ever since. We both have north-country backgrounds, and I suppose that has had something to do with it. The section also had a small element of Anglo-Indian girls employed on clerical duties. They were members of the Women's Auxiliary Corps (India). Mostly with typically British surnames, the one who was to be my main clerical assistant was Hazel Mathews. A demure and very polite young lady she was always most interested in Rosemary's accounts about the exploits of our baby son Michael. I well remember her mirth when I told her he had emptied his bowl of porridge over his head.

There were a good many sections of this large establishment involved in the creation of the monthly report. This was usually about an inch thick, covering all aspects of Japanese activity in the theatre. It was interesting to read and, I am sure, of great value to senior commanders, in other places, responsible for the future conduct of the war. Whilst I was sufficiently interested in subscribing to my part of it and found it to be an easy exercise, I was not happy in this place where I saw so many who seemed content to enjoy an easy war comfortably removed from where the real action was. It was necessary and important work that had to be done. Mostly the personnel engaged in it were drawn from the teaching profession. They were, no doubt, recruited especially because of their proven ability to assimilate, record, and dispense knowledge by means of the written word. It was, of course, work of the type that could only be done satisfactorily in the comparative peace of the rear areas. But for me, I yearned to be back where the real action was and felt my sojourn in this place to be out of keeping with my temperament as a young regular. I would be glad when my six months spell was expired, and I was certainly not going to do anything to extend it. Mostly, I got on quite well with the other personnel, both Army and RAF, but I had the feeling that they were not happy with me as the regular member of an otherwise temporary scene that they were part of only because an unfortunate event had rudely disrupted their civilian careers. Among these, I found an exception in the person of Harold Thompson, a sergeant in the RAF element. Again there was an immediate attraction to each other. Harold was another Northerner, a Lancastrian from Warrington, who had read for an arts degree at Manchester University. He had a little teaching experience at one of his local schools before being called for war service.

There was another department in the WEC Establishment where dwelt those who really considered themselves God's gift to the intelligence function. They were the so-called cryptographers who inhabited the holy of holies where Electro-Mechanical Tabulating Machines kept up a constant clatter, day and night, in an unending effort to break the enemy high-grade ciphers. The cryptographers seemed to spend their time poring over sheets of tabulations from the machines. But I never did hear of any success. We reckoned that our own machine cipher was undecipherable, why should we think the enemy product inferior? This line of work must have been quite soul-destroying, with little or no result for the most part. Those of us in the inferential type of intelligence work knew that it was mostly guesswork, but we were at least able to make inspired guesses based on personal experience in our own line of professional work, and we often had the satisfaction of being right. Inferential intelligence was what I was good at and I knew where it could be put to the best use with immediate effect, and that was in the tactical situation at the sharp end where I most wanted to be.

Christmas 1944 and New Year's Day 1945 came and went with little of any note worth mentioning. There were no Padres or churches in the WEC Establishment. I have no recollection of anything done to mark these days that are usually celebrated in the Christian calendar. There was a small number of RAF junior ranks employed in the communications centre. They were comfortably accommodated in a permanent type barrack block, and I remember making an effort to spend some time with them. They plied me with an Indian whisky concoction that was no more than raw alcohol coloured with an orange dye that left its colour in the bottom of the glass. In view of my lingering reminder of serious trouble in the digestive tract, I thought it wise not to be pressed into over-indulgence, particularly with this rather vile imitation of the real stuff.

Early in the New Year, February perhaps, the sergeant major decided to have a parade. He no doubt thought we needed smartening up and reminding that we were members of a fighting service. So the parade detail was published in local orders. On reading this I found myself immediately roused to anger. The names of the senior NCOs in charge of each of the platoons were, without exception, Army, with the remainder detailed to form the rank and file. There was, as already mentioned, a predominance of instantly created Army and RAF sergeants without whom there could have been no parade. I was not mentioned by name being regarded, no doubt, as one of the many. As I was, in fact, the only RAF senior NCO with the rank of Flight Sergeant (equivalent to the Army Staff Sergeant, of which there were none), I protested directly to Captain Harris and told him that unless the matter was corrected, I would not be on parade. The matter was corrected with astounding rapidity. In fact, that very evening, I was singled out by the sergeant major, who was seldom seen in the mess. Over a drink, he apologised to me and explained that he had no idea that there was a regular RAF senior NCO promoted by normal progression to my rank. I was, after all, the next ranking NCO to him, being but one rank junior to him. We got on quite well after that. The parade, when it came, was done without the officers (there were no RAF officers on the strength of WEC at that time), all platoons being commanded by Army senior NCOs, except that commanded by myself, which comprised all RAF personnel with some Army to complete, the required platoon size. I noticed that the left guides of my platoon were placed very close to the wall of a small building, the other platoons being unobstructed. I wondered if this had been devised intentionally to test my ability in drill commands as it would require the unusual initial command – 'Left Wheel, by the Right, Quick March.' I was well-schooled in drill movements at Cranwell; the parade ground held no terrors for me. On taking up my march-past position at the head of the platoon, I had time to warn the left markers and, on my command, the tight left turn was executed impeccably, and we were perfectly lined up for the march-past. All went well with my command – 'Eyes Right,' being given precisely at the first saluting marker as the left foot was passing the right. The Colonel took the salute. Why the other officers were not required to parade was the subject of intense speculation in the ranks. However, for me, it was a tonic to feel the warmth and respect of the RAF personnel, most of whom knew of my initial refusal to parade; this sort of news travels quickly through the ranks.

During March I was summoned to the Colonel's office to be advised that a certain Group Captain from Headquarters RAF South East Asia Command wished to interview me in regard to a commission. An office would be made available for his use at the entrance to the camp and I was to meet him there at 1330 the next day. I was there a little before the appointed time and was surprised to see him walk through the camp gates, the vehicle that brought him had been, presumably, left outside. He was rather older than I was expecting, and I formed the opinion that he had probably been called out of retirement. He was anything but pleasant, and I got the impression that he had been required to make a lengthy journey for a totally improper reason. In fact I was most surprised that he had been sent to see me rather than being summoned to the Command Headquarters myself, but this probably had something to do with an agreed division of responsibility for the provision of transport for the RAF Element. However he went into the office and told me, rather than invited me to come inside. The room was small, furnished with only a desk and chair; I was required to stand and was not even invited to stand easy. He was quite brusque but had obviously been supplied with full background details of my service and the details relating to my case, at least as passed by myself to local sources since arrival in the theatre. He left me in no doubt that he disbelieved me. In regard to the Air Ministry signal that I claimed was the authority for my posting to Newbold Revel for training as a W/T Intelligence Officer, I was questioned at some length. He asked me if I had a copy of it. I had, but I was not going to admit that I had since it may have provided him with ammunition to accuse me of wrongfully making illicit copies of classified information, so I told him I did not have a copy of it but had seen it and remembered its content clearly. He then suggested that I had taken note of the signal reference and date, and to this, I told him that I had. He wanted to know why it had taken so long to get the matter to this stage and I tried to assure him that it was not due to lack of effort on my part, although I had tried not to become a nuisance about it, particularly in view of my remote location and the apparent disbelief of the unit CO, action was, after all, his responsibility. I made particular reference to my last attempt with the more recently appointed CO, Squadron Leader Power, to which his immediate response was that he thought Squadron Leader Power was not qualified to make a recommendation. It was, however, obvious that Squadron Leader Power had seen fit to forward the matter. I did not attempt to inject anything extraneous into his questions but made sure that I included all I needed to say in my responses to them. The interview, more an interrogation really, ended with my feeling rather upset at being treated in this dubious manner, but I tried hard to maintain my composure under what I thought was an intentional attempt to break down my reserve. He dismissed me as peremptorily as he had greeted me. I must confess that I felt uneasy about the whole thing and prepared myself for the final termination of a matter that, after such a lengthy time, had left me feeling cheated and somewhat embittered towards this particular branch of the Service.

Very shortly after this a Flight Sergeant was posted in from the United Kingdom to be the NCO in charge of RAF Administration. It was now April, and with the temperature soaring quickly, we were back into tropical dress. The new member was feeling unwell when he arrived late on a Sunday, but we attributed this to his immediate move, seemingly without a period of acclimatisation, from Bombay to Delhi by rail, not a good experience in the heat of summer, albeit early summer. The next morning, he was decidedly ill and had to report himself sick. I saw him in the sick quarters the next day, Tuesday, covered in wet sheets with fans blowing onto him. He died that night and, as the only other RAF member of his rank, I was detailed as a pall-bearer for his interment at sunset on the Wednesday. He died of heat exhaustion. A few days later a Wing Commander arrived on appointment to the newly created post of Officer Commanding RAF Element, WEC. Also, the familiar figure of Flying Officer Norman (Larry) Gain from 367 Wireless Unit arrived to be the adjutant. Another Flight Sergeant, Jock Hendry, was posted in to replace the unfortunate recently deceased, was added to the headquarters staff. Jock, also a regular, and I were to become firm friends. It was good to know that we now had much-needed RAF representation with its own separate headquarters. A few days later, the new RAF CO sent for me and told me that he had received a communication from RAF South East Asia Command to advise that the matter of my commission had been forwarded to the Air Ministry for further action and that I could expect to hear more in due course.

The news from the European Front was good, and at long last, it seemed that the end of the war with Germany was in sight. On the Burma Front, great progress had been made during the winter months. Mandalay and other important centres of communication were in Allied hands and although the Japanese were still making a determined opposition, the Rangoon objective was now definitely in sight.

I was pleased to learn that Gordon Cairns and I were to go for a two-week spell of leave at the appointed RAF hill station for our location. This was at Chakrata in the foothills of the Himalayas some distance north of Dehra Dun. It was a delightful spot and so well organised with excellent facilities catering for all activities. Messing arrangements were of the very best and we spent a truly wonderful two weeks mostly walking in the delightful hills with wondrous views of the snow-clad mountains, which, at times, seemed so close that one could reach out and touch the snow-line. Although I was not aware of it at the time, there was a certain Jimmy Young on the entertainment staff of this hill station; he was, of course, the Jimmy Young who was to become very prominent over a lifetime career in British Radio. The climate at this time of year was simply wonderful at this altitude, but we could look to the south and see the plain beyond Dehra Dun and the heat haze that betokened the arid conditions to which we were shortly to return. The time passed all too quickly, and as I had anticipated, on my return, I was informed that I was to rejoin my unit (367 Wireless Unit) in the field. I was quite elated with this news.

CHAPTER XVI
BACK TO THE ACTION

It was now late April and there was news of a successful naval action against targets in the Nicobar and Andaman Islands. On 1st May, a battalion of the 5th Ghurkhas was dropped at Elephant Point south of Rangoon, where they overcame a small force of Japanese defenders and cleared the way for landing craft to enter the river and take Rangoon itself, practically without opposition, the enemy having withdrawn to positions in the dense jungle areas north of the city. The news from home was wonderful, with the expectation of an imminent German surrender.

I left the Wireless Experimental Centre at this exciting time. My travel instructions were designed to take me back to the forward area railhead at Chittagong, but I was to make the obligatory night stop at Barackpore before proceeding south of Calcutta. On arrival there, I was informed that 367 WU had been withdrawn at short notice from the forward area and were en route to Calcutta for embarkation in HMT Highland Monarch, where I was to rejoin them the next day. Arriving at the docks quite early I was deposited at the gangway of Highland Monarch to find 367 WU already embarked. I was greeted like a long-lost brother returning to the family. The CO gave me a tremendously warm welcome and introduced me to Larry Gains' replacement as adjutant; he was a Flight Lieutenant Bob Crawford, a totally different and much more appropriate personality who, like Larry, was a teacher in civilian life. Being of greater maturity and worldly experience, also a father, I found him a most likeable officer who recognised my own value as a dedicated professional at the senior NCO level.

Conditions aboard the ship were excellent. There was no delay in our departure, and we were soon out in the Bay of Bengal with the familiar landscape of Burma to the east. Rangoon looked as if it had been thoroughly sacked. Bomb damage was to be seen everywhere. Of course, it was but a few days, no more than seven, since the Japanese had been driven out. Their occupation currency, in all denominations of notes, was lying on the ground wherever one looked, and one had but to bend and pick it up for souvenirs. It was, I think, one of the first things I did after disembarkation. Also lingering in the mind is the sight of open sewers as we passed through the city streets. They had, I believe, been covered with heavy wooden timbers, which, to the deprived citizens and no doubt their enemy taskmasters, were the only immediately available source of fuel for the cooking fires.

We were transported to our allotted location, where we joined No.164 (Signals) Wing, which was to be our immediate superior operational authority for the next stage of the war in Southeast Asia. The location was quite extensive, taking in a large former police barracks that housed the Wing Headquarters proper and a good many additional buildings to provide messing and sleeping accommodation for the wireless units of which the two still en-route from their previous field locations would complete the Wing strength and unit re-grouping for the next operational stage. The whole occupied a large area situated between the Shwedagon Pagoda and the main road from Rangoon to the airfield at Mingaladon. The senior NCOs' mess was in a large house and quite adequate for the purpose. Our adjacent sleeping quarters were good enough. I had an adequately sized room without its external door that had presumably been removed for fuel. The Wing was under the command of Wing Commander Kimbrey, who, being unable to fill the vacancy in the wing personnel establishment for a Wing Warrant Officer, sought the assistance of Squadron Leader Power who, having lost his own disciplinarian, Harry Edwards, on promotion to warrant officer and posting to WEC, immediately volunteered myself. So, I became the Acting Wing Warrant Officer with a ready-made load of initial work to be done yesterday. Being a senior NCO in a technical trade, this kind of work was not in my professional line, and there were others, albeit junior to myself in rank, in the unskilled general duties trade who could have done the job. Not surprisingly, there was some animosity from one of these who I told that I would be pleased to hand the task over to him if he got the Wing CO's approval. I had to explain to him that as the NCO in charge of disciplinary aspects of his particular unit that is what he should do and let me, as the temporary Wing Warrant Officer, get on with the duties appropriate to the Wing. After all, the job only required one to have that level of general knowledge of RAF Administration and Discipline expected of all regular senior NCOs, irrespective of their trade.

The immediate operational task was to clear the Japanese from Malaya and Singapore. This task was to be known as 'Operation Zipper,' the localised preliminary part of a much larger operation that was being mounted after the end of the war in Europe from the United Kingdom by the newly created Tiger Force and designed to regain Allied possessions throughout the whole of South East Asia. Our part in this preliminary action was to set up our unit function in the vicinity of Kuala Lumpur, where the airfield was an essential pre-requisite to the success of the operation. We were to go into Port Swettenham behind the initial commando assault. Operational control was the responsibility of No. 226 Group with its headquarters located in Rangoon.

The wireless intelligence work at our new location was resumed as soon as we had our mobile facilities that had accompanied us in the Highland Monarch, so we were in business again very quickly. The enemy were very active to the south in the Malay peninsular and in the islands of the Dutch East Indies-principally Sumatra, Java, and Borneo. We knew where they were, and we knew who they were. Their time would come. The Japanese to our north in the Pegu Yoma continued to be a nuisance factor, but it was only necessary to contain them. They were at the mercy of the elements and the hostile, though sparse, population. They were completely isolated from their lines of supply and communication. We had only just beaten the monsoon ourselves to take the main objective of Rangoon, but it was now upon us, and the abandoned enemy in Pegu and a few other pockets here and there. There was nowhere they could go except east, where they were faced with the mighty Irrawaddy and Salween rivers. They would have been better off in captivity, but such was their nature and indoctrination towards the ignominy of defeat and capture. Just leave them to get on with it; there was no point in wasting life and effort on them. Very few of them did surrender, but many perished, trying to escape across the rivers. I suppose that many of them, in desperation, took what they thought to be the only honourable end.

Towards the end of July, I was summoned to present myself at Headquarters No. 226 Group where I was required for interview by the Air Officer in charge of Administration. Arriving at the appointed time, I was pleasantly surprised at the warmth of my reception by the AOA himself, a most genial Air Commodore, and his deputy, a Group Captain; there was also a Wing Commander. They obviously had received information from the Air Ministry that was advantageous to me. From their combined attitude toward me, I got the feeling that they thought some appeasement was essential. It was a most pleasant experience from which I departed with a feeling of walking on air. About three days later, Wing Commander Kimbrey called me into his office and congratulated me with the news that the Air Officer Commanding No.226 Group had recommended to the Air Ministry that I should be immediately commissioned in the field. I would, however, have to wait for the final Air Ministry approval

On the 6th August, I was conducting an early evening meeting of the members of the sergeants' mess, of which I was Chairman of the Mess Committee. In the middle of the proceedings, one of our number, who had been on duty, burst in with the news that an atomic bomb had been dropped on Hiroshima. Of course, I had to bring the meeting to a premature close, as this was something to celebrate, possibly heralding the end of the war. Three days later, we got the news of the second atomic bomb on Nagasaki, and later, about the middle of the month, the unconditional surrender of the Japanese. But it was not to be the end for us. I cannot remember the date precisely, but a few days later, a few of the fluent speakers of the Japanese language were given the task of bringing the aircraft of the Japanese commanders into the airport at Mingaladon for the formal surrender of the local Japanese forces. They came from places further south and were required to orbit Elephant Point south of Rangoon. From there, our fighters escorted them into Mingaladon. Other formal surrender ceremonies took place in Singapore and Tokyo, and the final formal surrender was on the 2nd of September.

The order of things intended was quickly modified during the last days of August. 367 Wireless Unit was now to proceed to the reoccupation of Hong Kong. Squadron Leader Power told me that Wing Commander Kimbrey wanted to retain me in Rangoon, but as I was really on the established strength of 367 WU, it was really up to me. I told him that as I was misemployed, I preferred to accompany my unit to play my intended role. There was no further mention of this matter. We embarked for Hong Kong aboard the Highland Chieftain – sister ship to the Monarch – and well up to the same good standard.

CHAPTER XVII
AN ORIENTAL INTERLUDE

We arrived in Hong Kong sometime during the first week of September, and I remember a rather painful experience on the day before our arrival. As we approached our destination, it was announced that there as there were possible health problems for us in Hong Kong everyone would have to be brought up to date with their inoculations. When I produced my pay-book to the medical officer, he said 'full house for you, Chief'. He gave me the first shot, left the needle in, and then shot another three vaccines through it. All were straight from the refrigerator, and I had quite a lump on my arm for a while. It was, to say the least, rather painful, and I had ship duty that night, which required me to report the ship all-quiet to the officer on bridge watch at midnight. I did not have a good night because of the pain and was still feeling the effect of it at breakfast, by which time we were tied up alongside a jetty in Kowloon harbour. Disembarkation was slow and we found ourselves waiting impatiently in the aft well deck. The CO's patience became exhausted awaiting the order to disembark, and as the men were getting restless in the extreme heat and humidity of the early afternoon, he told me to get them off and march to a position opposite the Peninsular Hotel at the top of Nathan Road which was our assembly point. I believe we were among the first contingent of RAF personnel in the re-occupation force. The Royal Marine Commando had entered before us. After an interminably long wait, transport arrived, and we were taken to our allotted location at Ho Man Tin Hill, where our accommodation was excellent but the location itself, whilst obviously selected with consideration for our wireless function, was not suitable because of other tall buildings around us that would have a screening effect. The Garrison Engineer told us to have a look around for ourselves, and he would take the necessary action to commandeer.

Our eyes were, of course, on the high ground on Hong Kong Island proper: the Peak. So the next day, Flt Lt Bob Crawford and I did a reconnaissance of a suggested location and found it ideally situated. It also had just the required amount of accommodation for all the unit requirements. Houses that would serve as Officers and Sergeants messes, a large block of flats to provide sleeping accommodation for the men, and sufficient space for workshops. It was necessary to dispossess a family from the house that we earmarked for the wireless section, but they were, it transpired, squatters anyway. It was all conveniently situated in a secluded spot with the name Wan Fung Toi off the Tai Hang Road that runs from Wanchai, over the peak – and the reservoir – to Stanley. It could not have been better suited to our needs, but it was a great pity that all the wooden doors and parquet floor blocks had been removed from the block of flats that looked as though it had just been completed and awaiting occupation when the war came to Hong Kong. On our reconnaissance over the wider area we found a good many properties that had been stripped of all wood; such was the need of the indigenous population for essential fuel. The owner of this block of flats was not a resident on the site, but we felt obliged to do the decent thing and inform him of our intention to requisition. We visited the Hong Kong Police, who, after considerable delay, told us that his name was Man Fat Wee (we immediately decided that a good way to remember his name would be to rearrange it as Wee Fat Man), resident at an address in the very heart of Hong Kong. They actually provided transport and an interpreter for us and we had good reason to give thanks for this gesture as we could never have found it ourselves. The address was up a seemingly never-ending staircase, and with the stifling heat and humidity, we were exhausted by the effort of the climb. Man Fat Wee was very wasted and his tubercular appearance betokened a short remaining life. He seemed unconcerned about our intention but agreed to meet us at the site the next day when we would arrange for a representative from the Garrison Engineers' Department to be present. He arrived at the appointed time and, through an interpreter brought by the GE, was told of the arrangements for the acquisition of his property. At this stage we were glad that the matter was taken out of our hands.

There was one other house in our Cul de Sac site that we had been advised to leave alone. It was owned and occupied by a rather prosperous-looking Chinese family, who seemed not to have suffered any privations under the Japanese. The husband and wife, with their daughter, in her early teens, obviously enjoyed some favour in the eyes of our own authorities as, perhaps, they had by the Japanese. The man was obviously of some local stature or was under observation. We found them hospitable and courteous. We were invited to take tea with them and this, served in typical Chinese fashion, made a delightful occasion for us. But I doubt if I could ever develop a taste for the Chinese variety of tea. Their young daughter, who had the western name of Angela was quite Anglicised herself with a good command of English. The parents had very little English and Angela did most of the talking. We seldom saw any movement outside the house except for Angela leaving in the morning and returning in the afternoon, presumably attending her place of learning. My own assessment was that the man was a successful merchant who had made his money before the war and had been clever enough to get it out of the colony before the Japanese came and, at the same time, retain the ability to offer inducements to appease the Japanese and gain a degree of favour and freedom from interference.

The unit was not at full strength as it had been necessary to leave a good many in Rangoon as, for some, return to civilian life was imminent because of age and length of service considerations. There were only two officers, the CO, and Flt Lt Crawford – I would be the third when my commission was gazetted. As for the senior NCO strength, there were five of us, of whom I was the senior. But the one with the most important job, for the time being at least, was undoubtedly Sgt Dickey Jones, the boss of the field kitchen that had been sited at the side of the Sergeants Mess so that the basement space could be utilised.

We had none of our technical equipment, and there was little for anyone to do except settle down and enjoy the relative comfort of our changed situation after Burma. I shared the pleasant main bedroom with George Courtney. Ralph Liversage and Jack Harrison shared another bedroom, and Dickey Jones, who had to rise earlier than everyone else, had a room to himself. We had a decent bathroom and a separate dining room. All this was contained on the upper floor to which access was gained by a wide curved staircase from the entrance hall. The landing at the top of the stairs was sufficiently spacious to easily provide two more bed-spaces if needed. The entrance door, giving direct access to the hall, was about ten feet above ground level with a wide entrance stairway. The basement, having been designed to provide the house kitchen facilities, was ideal for a ration store and preparation area adjacent to Dickie Jones' field kitchen just outside. We had good iron bedsteads, and there was no need for mosquito nets. My room had two panoramic windows with a magnificent view of the busy harbour below and, beyond that, Kowloon with the New Territories in the distance. Furthermore I was able to see the whole of our site. It was wonderful to see the presence of the Royal Navy in the harbour; HMS Anson was the largest vessel we saw; she was on station when we first arrived, and stayed for some time. Everyone was pleased to be here. It was such a welcome change. There were. Of course, some initial problems with water and electricity, but we soon had things satisfactorily organized. Dickie Jones had his essential field kitchen equipment. Whilst our rations were basically the same to which we were accustomed, there were now supplements of fresh vegetables such as fresh sweet potato that Dickey used to make a welcomed dietary change in the form of excellent chipped potatoes.

Other good news for the troops came in the form of the beer ration that was of better quality UK brands. Officers and senior NCOs also had a bottle of scotch each month, and of course, the cigarette ration was from the UK in sealed tins of fifty. This was more than we expected and it was surprising the speed at which these things were implemented. For the men in the flats things were not so good initially, but most were in separate rooms with a good bed, and we managed to procure floor coverings to compensate for the missing parquet blocks. Toilet facilities were adequate after the initial water problem was corrected and, all things considered, life was pretty good by comparison with our recent past. It seemed that it was to be some considerable time before we would be able to resume our normal professional work, but for the time being at least, there was plenty to keep us occupied in improving and adapting the site, and our living quarters to our use and comfort. Our daily life was, to say the least, leisurely.

Entertainment was a problem initially. When we disembarked at Kowloon and marched to our assembly point adjacent to the Peninsular Hotel, we saw not a single person after leaving the dockside. The streetcars were not running, and there was not a sign of any vehicular traffic or rickshaws. It was as though there was a state of complete curfew for the civil populace. It was, of course, the siesta period, although that would not have completely emptied the streets. I never heard that a curfew was in force, but there could well have been a restriction of movement during the first few days of our re-occupation when the Japanese were still being rounded up. However, both Kowloon and Hong Kong came to life very quickly, and it was quite amazing to see the speed with which shops, restaurants, and places of entertainment were opened. Naturally there were shortages at first, but the Chinese were to display their entrepreneurial ability as the whole busy scene seemingly came to life immediately. The electric tramcars started operating and one could hail a rickshaw easily. On our hillside, however, we found the rickshaw coolies reluctant to pull their fares up the hill that was too steep, so we had to walk. But they did condescend to seek our custom for the downhill journey. Our location was immediately above the Tiger Balm Garden, a fascinating display of lifelike, sometimes rather grotesque, life-size figures and animals in scenes from Chinese folklore. All in eye-catching colour and tastefully arranged in the expansive garden site provided at the expense of the wealthy Ah Boon Pah family noted for Tiger Balm ointment, famous throughout the East for its soothing properties when applied, particularly, to the forehead, to ease the headache. I found the garden quite fascinating and often enjoyed looking down on it from our advantageous position.

About ten days after our arrival in the colony, we received a signal from Headquarters No. 226 Group in Rangoon, which read, 'Flight Sergeant W Jacobs to be informed that his commission has been placed in the Reserve Pool pending the re-allocation of redundant General Duties Branch officers to other duties.' This meant that whilst my appointment to a commission had been approved, it could not be put into effect because of the considerable number of Aircrew Officers who were now unemployed as squadrons and other operational flying units were disbanded. These temporary officers had to be directed to other forms of work, including, if necessary, my own specialised work. The Service now had to reduce to its post-war establishment strength that, although vastly greater than the pre-war established strength, comprised a considerable manning surplus that would take time to dispose of before new officer posts could be created. The redundant officers could not all be released immediately for fear of causing serious excesses in the civil employment market. Therefore, there had to be a phased release arrangement. It was as simple as that, and I just had to take it. It was gratifying to know that my commission was in the bag after a trying period of more than three years from the beginning in 1942. Whilst there had been no suggestion of administrative blunder at any stage, I had a positive feeling that some had been revealed and amends were being attempted. Field commissions were, after all, the exception rather than the rule. Hard luck for me, though; had things gone as they ought, I would have had the rank of Flight Lieutenant (equivalent Captain) by this time, with likely advantageous effects on my post-war career.

The seasonal typhoon period came and brought its expected rough weather, followed by a sudden change in the hot, humid conditions to rather cold nights in November with occasional rain. We had not done any intelligence work since arriving in the colony. Our mobile field equipment was still in Rangoon, and there seemed to be little or no interest in higher places regarding the work aspect. We were just required to occupy the place and do our own thing until such time as plans were put into effect. For the majority, this was good enough. They were mainly volunteers or conscripts content to await their release, their job was done, and they simply wanted to get back to their homes, families, and civil life as quickly as possible. They were not seriously interested in the work aspect. There were only two regulars in our company and George Courtney was on a short-term engagement that had just expired. So all personnel had been notified of their release group except, of course, myself, being a long-service (potential lifer) regular with five years still to serve to complete my initial engagement of twelve years from age eighteen.

It was about this time that I received the news from Rosemary that her grandfather (George Douglas) had died. By the beginning of December it became quite cold after sunset and an overcoat was desirable outdoors. About this time we were informed by signal that I was to be repatriated to Home Establishment during December. I knew that the journey home would involve the long weary route to Bombay via Rangoon and Calcutta, but I had heard that the Royal Navy were willing to offer spare capacity in their vessels sailing directly to the United Kingdom, and was seriously contemplating such a possibility. However, it was not to be. My travel instructions were duly received from 164 Signals Wing in Rangoon. I was to be at the Bombay Transit Camp not later than 20th December, but was to report to164 Signals Wing en route. I took leave of my fellow members of No.367 WU in the late afternoon of the 12th December 1945 and was conveyed to the small RAF

Transit Hotel situated at the top of Nathan Road, Kowloon, opposite the side of the Peninsular Hotel. It was raining and miserably cold so having a last look around was out of the question. I spent the evening in the hotel where I seemed to be the only, and lonely, guest. My last night in Hong Kong was rather boring after the evening meal, so I went to bed as the only means of keeping warm.

A cold wet and windy dawn was breaking as I stepped out onto the broad pavement of Nathan Road at 0600 hours on 13th December 1945 to board the waiting car that was to take me to RAF Kai Tak. Our military air transport routes had been set up immediately after the cessation of hostilities and, so far, lacked sophistication. Aircraft used were, of course, those that had been used for operational purposes and were flown by the operational transport squadrons of Transport Command. Aircraft employed on the main routes were the ubiquitous Douglas DC 47 (Dakota) still in the parachute troop role with bare metal seating along the fuselage sides. Our route was to be Saigon, Bangkok, and Rangoon. We took-off from Kai Tak promptly at the intended departure time and. after a bumpy climb-out with the dangerous escarpment of the New Territories on our port side, settled on course in the calmer altitude of cruising height. I found it pleasing to be airborne again after such a long time – rather more than three years in fact. We were at Saigon by midday. Here I found it so hot in my home service dress that I had to prevail upon the crew to allow me access to the tied-down baggage so that I could get back into tropical clothing. They were most obliging and I was relieved to get into the lighter attire and enjoy a surprisingly good lunch. There was time for a look around the airfield where I found some interesting biplanes used before the war by the French Air Force. Regrettably, exposure to the elements had rotted most of the fabric from them and they were quite bare, but otherwise in seemingly good structural condition. There was also a long line of medium bombers surrendered by the Japanese.

The next leg of the journey passed in quiet boredom and we arrived at Bangkok, in fact the military airfield of Don Muang where we were to stay the night. The transit accommodation was pleasant enough in military type wooden buildings with good facilities. After dinner I took a gentle stroll to a local bazaar where there was, surprisingly, quite a lot of interesting things on offer among a profusion of junk. I spotted an attractive bracelet in Thai silver with small square links depicting Thai figures relieved in black enamel. (Amara work I believe it is called). I had my heart set on it, but had no local currency. The woman made me understand that she would sell it to me for cigarettes and, as I had a newly opened tin of fifty Players she willingly gave me the bracelet for them. As they were part of my free ration I considered it a good deal. The bracelet is still in Rosemary's collection. The next day, 14th December, we were to have the company of two Japanese prisoners. They had been deprived of their footwear and were manacled at hands and feet. Their escort was a British Army private armed only with the familiar Short Lee Enfield Rifle. They were, in typical fashion – particularly in the light of their circumstance – most polite and bowed with great ceremony and obvious contrition, to the seated passengers. One of the prisoners was unusually big for Japanese, the other of rather diminutive stature. It transpired that they were members of the infamous Kempai Tai – Japanese Military Police – who were renowned for their maltreatment of prisoners. They were being moved to Singapore where the War Crimes Trials were in progress. The big fellow was a Warrant Officer and may, according to what was being said, have been the notorious Teruchi, who was found to be responsible for cruelty to prisoners and subsequently executed by hanging. Arriving at Rangoon (Mingaladon), we were taken to the transit mess for a meal. We were now back in the area where field conditions were still the norm. The mess was an open-fronted bamboo basha with plain wooden tables and chairs. There was a servery of sorts at the closed end, and the food was obviously made from the field rations we were well used to. The Sergeant supervising the serving of the food just about exploded when the escort apparently requested food for his prisoners. "Get the bastards out of here, I don't cook for the bloody Japanese, do you think they would feed you?" Unfortunately, the responses of the escort were inaudible from where I was sitting, but he was obviously somewhat taken aback and very much out of his depth. "I don't care a tinker's shit where you've come from or where you're taking the bastards. Just get 'em out of here, now", roared the Sergeant. The escort turned away and one could see by his troubled countenance that he was completely lost for a next move. He did not have the authority of rank and, as he was not a Military Policeman, seemed to have been given a task that was quite beyond his capability and training. However, at this stage, he was relieved of further embarrassment by the sudden appearance of two British Military Policemen who, having missed the arrival of the aircraft and the disembarkation of the passengers, were looking for the Japanese POWs and their escort. They quietly, but without ceremony, removed them from the scene, and we were left to finish our meal in peace. Although the POWs should have been fed, they should not have been taken into the dining facility being used by ordinary passengers. The escort should have been met at the aircraft and relieved of his responsibility.

I had already contacted 164 Signals Wing by field telephone and, in due course, transport arrived to convey me. It was mid-afternoon, and the Wing Commander was expecting me. He quickly explained to me the reason for his requiring me to report to Wing Headquarters on my way to Calcutta. He wanted me to extend my tour of duty for three months and take on the role of Wing Disciplinarian with immediate promotion to the rank of Acting (Paid) Warrant Officer. Perhaps in that time, my commission would be gazetted. Unhesitatingly, I told him that, as a regular, I was not interested in employment outside of my own technical trade even though the promotion would obviously have to be in my own trade, also, I personally doubted very much if the commission would eventuate at that time. I had completed my tour of three years of overseas duty and was now in the homeward-bound mode. Furthermore, I was returning to a wife who had, like so many, been separated from her husband by the misfortune of war for long enough, and I had a son of almost three years whom I had not yet seen. I thanked him for his consideration, which I found most gratifying. He did not attempt to continue the discussion but said that he appreciated my point of view and agreed with it. He called in his Sergeant Clerk and told him to ensure that I was routed to Bombay, departing next morning and arriving no later than 20th December.

After a flight out of Burma to Calcutta with a night-stop in our Barrackpore facility, I was entrained for the last weary leg of my journey to Bombay, where I arrived on the due date of 20th December to see the troopship Reina Del Pacifico leave for Old Blighty. She was to be the last sailing for six weeks due to strike action by the United Kingdom Dockers. At the RAF Worli Transit Camp, I found several senior NCOs of my acquaintance, among them Harold Thompson from WEC and Jack Newell, not seen since Newbold Revell. My constant companion during the long, boring stay was, of course, Harold with whom I had formed a good friendship during our time together at WEC.

Christmas came, and Harold and I decided that we would celebrate it with a meal in Bombay on Christmas Eve. I did not care a great deal for Bombay, and I cannot remember the name of the hotel we patronised on that occasion. It was well frequented by British officers and senior NCOs who, like us, no doubt, were awaiting passage to the United Kingdom and longed for reunion with loved ones. After the meal, we went into the crowded lounge bar, where everyone seemed to be seated in comfortable settees. There was no bar as such, but a very efficient team of waiters provided excellent service. Harold and I decided that we would celebrate in style by ordering a bottle of champagne and were pleasantly surprised when a well- known vintage was offered. There were some rather astonished glances from officers seated nearby as two senior NCOs sipped champagne whilst they drank the local beer. The Christmas spirit seemed to be lacking somehow; no doubt the disappointment of having to spend an enforced Christmas in transit dampened the spirits of everyone. But had we been embarked as intended, we would have been at sea, but though still in transit, we would have been nearer home with each passing day.

January 1946 came and left me without any memories. New Year's Day was like any other for us. We spent most of our time walking during the days along the pleasant promenade at Worli and that is the only worthwhile memory I have of my time spent there. There was a makeshift camp cinema where we saw a few decent films. Tombola was a popular evening pastime for many but I never cared for it, preferring to keep my money in my pocket rather than risk losing it in the vain hope of increasing it by gambling. My old friend of Cranwell days, Jack Hyde, arrived from Rangoon towards the end of my stay at Worli, his company bringing a measure of relief to the monotony of our seemingly interminable waiting

At long last, the news came that the United Kingdom dock strikes were over, but we now had to wait for the ships to make the journey to Bombay. It was well into February before the first troopship appeared, and there was now a tremendous backlog of troops awaiting passage, with many already past the date of their intended release from service. Naturally, there was growing resentment and signs of trouble brewing among the lower ranks. There seemed to be an expectation that troopships would appear in sufficient numbers to clear the backlog immediately. But for some reason not easily understood at lower rank levels, the arrivals and departures had to be carefully arranged and managed to prevent utter chaos at Bombay and United Kingdom ports, also transit centres and railways. It was late February by the time my name appeared on the embarkation list for the Empress of Australia. It sounded rather grand, but we did not know what disappointment awaited us. I was pleased that Harold Thompson's name also appeared on the same list.

CHAPTER XVIII
HOMEWARD BOUND

We embarked during the early days of March. The Empress of Australia did not look quite as grand as we thought it might have been. We approached her from the rear and saw, first of all, a rather ancient-looking stern of the vintage that suggested a vessel of the early steamship era. Her name was cast into the upper stern member and picked out in gilt paint. Overall, she seemed to be rather tired-looking, and we began to wonder what we might find onboard. We didn't have long to wait. The senior NCOs were the first to embark, and we were shown to our accommodation immediately. There were, I suppose, about fifty of us, and all were to sleep on a small deck at the stern immediately forward of the rudder operating mechanism. The deck was completely bare except for a pile of hammocks in one corner. I will not attempt a description of the various expressions of disgust at this treatment of Senior NCOs which was only different from that of the lower ranks by its being on an upper deck rather than below decks. It did have direct access to the lower promenade deck on which, next to the accommodation, was a narrow ablution and toilet facility for our exclusive use.

Rigging a hammock was, for most, a new experience, but we soon got the hang of it. The most difficult trick initially was getting into the damned thing slung, as it was, just above head height. Each hammock had a rope that had to be attached to the slinging hook at the head, and by this means, one had to heave oneself off the deck and throw rear end and legs into the hammock. There was very little space between each hammock, but they were slung so that the middle of one was between the head and foot of the two on either side. We soon got used to the idea of getting into them; there was no option other than the hard deck. I found sleeping in a hammock rather comfortable actually. The morning ablution was trying as one had to hurry in the inadequate and crowded conditions. Our messing facilities left much to be desired and the, since the ship was victualled in the United Kingdom, the food was disappointing. However, we were on the way home at last and that was something to be thankful for. According to the best informed, there were some four thousand souls on board. Certainly, the ship was filled to capacity, whatever that was.

The vessel was said to have been the Kaiser's Yacht taken as reparation after World War One. She could well have been, but nothing of her former splendour was to be seen after her conversion to the role of Troop Carrier except, perhaps, her name in gilt paint on the stern.

We steamed westward across the Arabian Sea for our first port of call, Aden, a journey of about two thousand miles. Harold and I spent our days strolling around the promenade deck or sitting on it using our life jackets as cushions. He was the best of companions, and we thoroughly enjoyed each other's company. We spent hours chatting about this and that between periods of silence reading our books, of which there was no shortage as they were readily passed from hand to hand. At last, we saw the South Arabian coast on our right hand and soon entered the bustling port of Aden. Here, at the southern end of the Red Sea, the Aden Protectorate was the home of Headquarters British Forces Aden; a major component of the Middle East Air Force. The Aden command responsibility included the whole of the South Arabian Peninsula and East Africa, including Eritrea, Sudan, and Kenya; quite a slice of real estate employing considerable naval and military personnel with their ships, armour and aircraft in many ports and land establishments. We were, I suppose, fortunate to be here in mid-March when it was hot enough, but nothing like the dreadful heat and humidity that would rise quickly next month with the onset of summer.

After a night stop spent on board, we started the next long leg of our homeward voyage. We were pleased when the monotony of the Red Sea ended, and we entered the Suez Canal at Port Tewfik. We were now approximately halfway home, and one could feel the change in spirit of all personnel on board. There was greater interest in the passing scene, and at Port Said, we spent an amusing day watching the antics of the Egyptians in their so-called Bumboats, the merchants trying to sell their wares to potential customers at the ships rails on both sides using a simple system of ropes by which money was passed down first before the goods were hoisted up for examination at close quarters. They did not do much business, but it did help to relieve the boredom of life on board.

Now, across the Mediterranean with, spirits rising noticeably as each passing day took us ever westward. Each sighting of land brought speculation regarding our position, with Malta being a certainty for the majority. The temperature decreased steadily and the sea state became rough as we entered the Straits of Gibraltar. I have a vivid memory of standing in the forward well deck, watching the stern of the vessel rise far above us as the nose dipped seemingly below the heaving surface of the sea. Soon, we were through and heading northward into the Bay of Biscay on the last few days of our homeward run to Liverpool.

As we entered the estuary of the River Mersey, we took a pilot on board to navigate the ship to its allotted berth. Soon, someone noticed a yellow flag flying at the masthead, and it was confirmed that it was indeed the Yellow Duster to signify that we had a case of smallpox on board. This was bad news as it meant that the ship would be legally quarantined until the Port Medical Authority was satisfied that there was no longer any danger of spreading this highly infectious disease over the wide area to which the passengers would travel after disembarkation. As we were guided to our berth, it was natural, I suppose, that the passengers would crowd the side nearest the dockside, in this instance, the side nearest the site of Liverpool's famous Liver Building. A stern message over the public address system soon corrected the dangerous list towards the dockside. Sure enough, there was a formal announcement that the ship was under quarantine law, and we would have to remain on board until further notice. The effect of this was immediate and it takes little imagination to understand the feelings of men who had spent years away from home and loved ones. There were positive signs of mutiny among the men below decks, where the vast majority were wartime volunteers returning home for demobilisation.

We stayed on board that night, and after breakfast, the next morning, hope was generated by a message that an early outcome was expected to be made to the Medical Authority. It was early afternoon when we were told that we were to be allowed to disembark to a transit facility at which our quarantine would continue. This did nothing for the mood of the men as we were entrained directly for a short journey to Heaton Park on the north side of Manchester. We arrived on what seemed to be the wildest, wettest, coldest, and darkest night of the year. We were shown to a Nissen hut that was freezing cold and without any sign of fuel for the two lifeless black iron stoves. There were no blankets, sheets, or pillows for the beds and only one naked light bulb. This was the worst kind of misery for anyone, let alone anyone who returned from service in tropical climes. To say the least, the mood among our small company of senior NCOs in that particular hut was the worst imaginable. However, we were soon hailed by an authoritative-sounding voice and instructed to follow to the mess for a meal. We were taken into a brightly lit and warm building, which did much for our failing spirits. There were large numbers assembled, and soon, an officer of squadron leader rank appeared, apparently the CO, to address us. His mode was conciliatory as he told us that we would soon be served with a good meal, and by the time that was over, we would find our sleeping accommodation complete with bedding and fires lit. He apologised for the unprepared state of the camp that had been the Aircrew Despatching Centre for overseas locations and had closed shortly after the cessation of hostilities, and to which he, with his staff, had arrived only that day to set it up for use as a quarantine facility for the passenger complement of the Empress of Australia. He told us that he was unable at that time to tell us anything about the probable length of our internment but that we were strictly confined to the camp pending further advice. It was well into the evening, with a gale force wind and rain, when we returned to our billets, and, sure enough, they were different altogether, with the stoves giving off pleasing warmth and each bed with adequate blankets and sheets. We were tired, and tomorrow would be another day.

The next day was as bleak as its predecessor, but breakfast cheered us somewhat until it was apparent that there was no further news about our enforced restriction of movement. Heaton Park was a well-known recreational feature of the northern outskirts of Manchester and I had been here several times as a boy. It was on the bus route to my parent's home a journey of about half an hour. But Rosemary and Michael were in our own home at Nairn in the Scottish Highlands, and that is where I wanted to be. I found a public telephone and sent a telegram to let Rosemary know that I was in the United Kingdom and would send further news when we were released from quarantine. Telephones were not a feature of many homes at that time. As the day wore on with nothing to do other than take a walk around our new surroundings, we became restive. At least we expected to be informed of any, or no, change in the situation. By lunchtime, the situation was looking very dangerous among the aircraftmen. However, whilst the meal was still being taken, an announcement instructed everyone to collect a leave application form, complete it, and leave it in the box appropriate to the initial letter of his surname. This brought some hope until it became apparent that the action was intended to ensure that travel documents would be available for issue instantly when the quarantine restrictions were removed. Late the same afternoon, all ranks were summoned to the dining hall where the CO was waiting with a very business-like squad of orderlies seated at tables, each indicating a single letter. The CO told us that whilst the quarantine had not been formally lifted, we were to be permitted to proceed to our disembarkation leave addresses. He explained the early symptoms of smallpox, and we were to report immediately to our family doctor at the first signs of feeling unwell. We were free to go immediately, but told not to leave until we add full details of our railway timetables. In my own case, it was much too late to travel to Preston to connect with the train to the North. So I had to wait until morning, but I could quite easily spend the evening with my parents, who would be pleased to have an unexpected visit.

It was but a short walk to a gate that was conveniently close to a bus stop on my required route. After a journey of about thirty minutes I alighted from the bus and three minutes later entered my parent's home to find Mother preparing the evening meal. What a wonderful welcome I had. Dad arrived a few minutes later to be followed almost immediately by my sister, Irene. What a difference I saw in her after three years. Now twenty-one and engaged to be married to Colin, the only son of a successful bakery owner. Colin was absent still engaged in war service with the RAFVR, but was awaiting his imminent discharge. Their marriage was being planned for later that year. We spent a very pleasant evening together and I was sorry when the time came for me to leave and get the bus back to Heaton Park. The next morning I received my railway warrant and routing instructions to Nairn. They were, of course, by the shortest and least costly route but not the most convenient. I had to get a local train from Manchester to Preston, change there for Perth, then to Aviemore for Forres and finally to Nairn.

The station at Perth seemed to be deserted when I alighted from the train a little before 0700. I had some time to wait for the train to Aviemore and was pleased when two ladies came along and, to my great relief, opened a small restaurant facility. The ladies were seemingly members of the local Women's Voluntary Service, and the facility, very much as it had been throughout the war years, intended to serve the needs of travelling service personnel, now very much reduced in number. I had the most peculiar feeling of being totally out of place and unsure of myself. I suppose it had something to do with having spent the last three years removed from contact with the home environment. When one of the ladies asked me what I would like for breakfast, I felt at a loss to answer, I simply had no idea. I think she must have thought me rather strange. I could not get my mind away from the fact that wartime rationing was still in place and I could get only what was given. When she asked me if I would like a sausage, I was completely dumbfounded and found myself trying to think how long it was since I had a sausage other than the dreaded Soya links of our field rations. I think I said, "It's a long time since I had a sausage," at which she gave me a strange look, no doubt wondering where I had been. However, I had an ample breakfast of non-rationed foods such as spam, baked beans, and the sausage that was quite edible but with little taste of beef or pork, and a piece of fried bread, all washed down with the usual cup of tea sweetened with saccharine. It seemed to have been a strange experience, but it would no doubt take a little time to get back into the swing of being back in the home environment.

I was soon at Aviemore, where there was still plenty of snow on the mountains. It was still only the first week of April and quite cold. The connecting train for Forres came along without delay, and I started the slowest part of the homeward journey with the train stopping at every one of the many Highland stations serving the widely dispersed small settlements of crofters where the train driver and fireman seemed to know everyone and had something to be left with the station master for someone; a sort of unofficial delivery service. It was nice to hear the warm cheery greetings passed between them and their enquiries about this one and that one. The change at Forres put me on the last short leg home. Short obligatory stops at Brodie and Auldearn, and I was soon slowing down alongside the larger platform of Nairn, eagerly waiting to get out to embrace Rosemary and my wee son, who I could see were the only ones on the platform. I was some fifty yards from them when I got my things out and set them down. I heard Rosemary say, "There's you, Daddy," and Michael came running to me and said quite casually, "Hello, Daddy, we have a taxi waiting for you." I was completely taken aback, and all I could say in utter amazement was, "He talks." The taxi ride was only a matter of a few minutes, and we were soon in a cosy little kitchen with its cheery fire. Home at last. Home where the heart was.

My feeling of being ill at ease wore off after a few days of being like the proverbial fish out of water. I suppose it was quite natural after such a lengthy absence from familiar sights and sounds. Michael was a lively wee boy with a seemingly well-developed sense of adventure. He could do the disappearing act instantly and was usually to be found in the most dangerous of places – the harbour basin that seemed to be his main fascination and only a short running distance from his own front door. Rosemary had a worrying time trying to keep him in safe custody. He was an accomplished escapist with an unending list of escaping devices that defied all attempts to keep him behind railings and fences. At the age of three, he was a well-known personality in the community, and it was quite common to hear one of the local wives at the door calling out, "Here he is, Mrs Jacobs," when Rosemary was not even aware of his latest escape attempt. The harbour master often brought him home with a stern admonition that his near frantic mother found rather upsetting.

In due course I received my posting instructions by mail. I was posted to RAF Chicksands. This was, as I expected, the most likely place to which I would be assigned as it was the only prominent signals intelligence location remaining in the post-war home establishment. It was another large country estate with a mansion house (Chicksands Priory) as the central feature. It was, of course, built during the war years, but the buildings were, unusually, of the pre-war temporary type of wooden construction intended to last much longer than the corrugated Nissen huts. The Commanding Officer was none other than Wing Commander Kimbrey of whom I took my leave at Rangoon in December 1945, six months earlier. I was pleased to learn that he was no longer looking for a Station Warrant Officer – there was one of appropriate grade already in post. Working accommodation was good but the living and messing arrangements for senior NCOs was well below peace standard, but this was to be a common feature of many places for some time after the war. Shift work was the normal order of things on the work scene and my task was to ensure that the wireless intercept arrangements were kept working as intended although I had no specialised training of what was being intercepted. Sufficient to say it was not in languages of my experience, nor did that aspect of the job seem to be important. I found it very boring and regarded myself as being grossly misemployed except for my technical appreciation that became useful during equipment failure. This was not for me and I had no intention of letting it be so. Like the proverbial bad penny Jack Hyde, my old Cranwell colleague last seen in the Bombay transit camp, turned up on posting but was employed in the station communications section. Nice to have friends in other places.

I was at the place only a few weeks when, during July, I was informed that my name was on the Preliminary Warning Roll for duty overseas. This time I was to be posted to RAF Habbaniya for intelligence duties. This well known location was situated on the lake of that name on the course of the River Euphrates in Iraq (formally Mesopotamia). I was to proceed on embarkation leave immediately. Before doing so, however, I thought it appropriate to point out to the Higher Authority that I had only been in the United Kingdom for a matter of three months, and a signal was sent to this effect. An immediate response by signal pointed out that I was the only person of appropriate rank and experience available, all others were awaiting release after completing regular engagements or war service. It was simply a case of 'if you can't take a joke, you shouldn't have joined.' I arrived home unannounced much to Rosemary's delight. She knew that I had lots of leave due – twenty-eight days end of war leave and another twenty-eight days of ordinary leave for 1946. But with that uncanny intuition that wives seem to possess, and without questioning, she seemed to read my thoughts and suddenly said unhappily, "You're going overseas again, aren't you?" My admission brought the anticipated response of outrage and indignation at the treatment of a regular who had only recently returned from three years of war service overseas to a wife and small child born in absence during that service. It did seem rather shameful and inappropriate no matter what the manning considerations. However, she stoically accepted the situation and understood that with a little more than four years of my initial engagement of twelve years still to serve, there was nothing I could do about it.

Returning to Chicksands, I was advised that the Adjutant wished to see me. I was surprised to learn that a communication had been received from the Air Ministry about my commission still in the Reserve Pool. If I wanted to proceed with this, I was to submit the Form of Application and Recommendation again to provide an administrative vehicle for the normal, rather than field, process of commissioning to proceed. The Wing Commander was delighted to do the necessary and forward the recommendation without delay. I mentioned to him my fears that I would probably find myself in the same situation experienced after leaving Newbold Revel in 1943. He thought this unlikely in the changed circumstances of post-war administration. He suggested that I might go on leave again while I had the chance to use up some of my considerable accumulation. So off I went for another three weeks. After all August, and I understood that there had been some measure of reversion to the pre-war trooping seasons whereby movement to hot climates took place in the winter time, starting October, to allow a reasonable period of gradual acclimatisation prior to the onset of the overseas summer. So, being the subject of PWR notification, I guessed I had until October before movement by sea.

During this period of leave, which extended into September, we were able to attend Irene and Colin's wedding ceremony. What a splendid affair it was, and to the delight of all, Michael was a handsome wee page in his kilt and sporran. Rosemary was beginning to accept the inevitable threat of another separation and I remember one very light-hearted event that we attended whilst still in the Manchester area. This was a visit to an early post-war event at Belle Vue, a leisure complex on the south side of the city. This was the Dirt Track, as it was then called, where motorbikes competed in races over a track that was covered with oily dirt. The riders were seldom in the saddle as, using a special stirrup into which they placed their right thigh and slid their heavily metalled left boot along the track, they forced their machines around the bends in skidding turns without slowing their engines, the rear skidding wheels sending up the black earth mostly over the unfortunate rider behind. There were usually four machines in each race, and we found the whole meeting, as did all the spectators, rather thrilling as we yelled our encouragement at our selected would-be champion. It certainly helped to dissipate our gloom.

Back to Chicksands again to find that I had a date to report to the Personnel Despatching Centre at Burtonwood on the outskirts of Warrington. I had time to get in some more leave and I took it. It would probably be three years before I would see Rosemary and Michael again, although there was just a slight chance of getting them out to Iraq in the event of being fortunate enough to be allocated a married quarter, but availability was very limited. We did all the things we needed to do, said our farewells, and, on the due date, started my return to Chicksands for the last time.

It was about mid-October when I left Chicksands for No. 5 PDC, Burtonwood. This station had been used by the USAAF as an aircraft maintenance base and most of it now served the RAF for the same purpose. It was mid-week when I arrived to find others also assembling there for the same draft, although none were already known to me. Accommodation was in Nissen huts, but they were very well maintained and scrupulously clean, with linoleum-covered floors polished to perfection. All sorts of Record Office and medical checks were carried out immediately. By the Friday we were told that we would be embarking at Liverpool for Basra the following Wednesday and would be required to parade on the prior Monday morning for the final Records Office checks. Until then we were free to go where we pleased but must be back in camp by 0800 on Monday. So what to do for the weekend? Someone came up with the great idea that there would be a great game of football at Liverpool on Saturday and five of us decided that was what we would do. I thoroughly enjoyed the experience, never having had the opportunity to see a major league game before. Liverpool was only a short distance, and the train took us there in very little time. As we approached Annefield, the location and name of the Liverpool Football Stadium, I was fascinated by the rows of closely packed houses with ships funnels and upper works towering above their rooftops. At last we arrived and found it impossible to get seats in the stands and would have to take our chance standing at ground level. We were, however, fortunate to get a stance at one of the four corners of the playing surface that was above ground level so that we were viewing the game with heads only slightly above the pitch. We watched the football stars of that time but the only one I can remember was the popular Bert Stubbins.

Monday morning came and we paraded for the final Records Office Check just to make sure they had the intended personnel for the particular draft. Before the check could start an aircraftman came out of the nearby office block and asked if there was a Flight Sergeant Jacobs present. I identified myself, wondering what I was about to be called upon to do. The aircraftman asked me to accompany him to the see the officer in charge. On being presented, I was told that I was to go to the Air Ministry the next day and report myself to Adastral House, Room Number *** for interview. On enquiring for the reason I was told that it was not stated in the authorising signal. I was to go to London by the first train and report to the designated location by 1330 hours. Arriving there at the appointed time I was seen immediately by an officer who introduced himself as an officer of the Equipment Branch. He asked me if I would like to consider a commission in that branch which was about to be reorganised and modernised, and that my service and experience were considered to be most suitable for the purpose. I pointed out to him that I had been involved in Intelligence Branch activities since late 1942 and was at the point of embarkation for Iraq imminently in that same connection. He assured me that he knew all about it and that I would be released from further intelligence duty. He also told me that the Intelligence Branch would progressively revert to civilian manning status. After asking a few questions of the kind that any senior NCO ought to know about the Equipment Branch function on a station, I did not hesitate to sign the consent form he placed before me. He then told me to return to Burtonwood, forget all about Iraq and await posting instructions that would be of a temporary nature until such time as I was instructed to report to the Officer Cadet Training Unit for the Initial Officer Training Course. This would be at the beginning of 1947 and, assuming successful appointment, would be followed by a course of training in the specialist functions of the Equipment Branch. I returned to No. 5 PDC and was assured the next day that I had been removed from the draft now embarked at Liverpool for Basra, and just to do as I pleased until further notice.

I sent Rosemary a telegram breaking the good news and announcing that I hoped to be home again soon for a spot more leave. I decided to spend a long weekend with my parents and, after getting routine clearance to do so, took a pleasant stroll to Warrington railway station. At the booking office I was pleased to be told that I would find a train for Manchester standing on the platform due to depart in a few minutes. Arriving at the platform, I was almost immediately aware of someone calling, "Hey! Bill." There were very few passengers, and I immediately recognised the head and shoulders of Harold Thompson waving at me from a compartment a little further along the train. I had not seen him, of course, since our parting at Heaton Park at the beginning of April. He was with his fiancée, and we had a wonderful little reunion. Harold was teaching at a school that was just outside the rear entrance of RAF Burtonwood on a pleasant thoroughfare appropriately called 'Lovely Lane.' I had noticed both features, so I knew where they were. Before leaving him in Manchester, we made an arrangement to meet a few days later. I met him again, as arranged, at the school closing time just as he was finishing a lesson and spent a few minutes answering a few questions to youngsters interested in RAF service. The National Service Scheme was in force by this time, and on attaining the age of eighteen years, all would become liable to serve in the armed forces for the prescribed minimum of two years. I found it a most interesting and enjoyable little session. Afterwards, we strolled to his home, where I met his parents, who welcomed me as though I was one of their own. Harold's fiancée was there also and we had enjoyed a most convivial meal and such a wonderful time afterwards. It was quite late when I was sent on my way, rejoicing in my lonely bed in the Nissen hut of which I was now the only occupant. My temporary posting came through in a few days, and I had my last meeting with Harold the night before I left Burtonwood. Subsequently, he married and took a house at 192 Lovely Lane and we exchanged letters for a number of years.

Not surprisingly, my posting was to Bletchley, on attachment pending transfer to Officer Cadet Training Unit RAF Cosford for Initial Officer Training Course on or about 1st January 1947. At Bletchley, they could, of course, keep me under quiet observation and gradually de-brief me out of the intelligence organisation. Bletchley Park in Buckinghamshire was the home of the wartime home of the cryptographic part of the intelligence organisation, now known for its part in the cracking of the German 'Enigma' machine ciphers. Long before the time of my posting this section housed in the large mansion house was closed down. The entire camp was strangely quiet and I never did get to the bottom of what was going on. Certainly there was a run-down in progress, but of obvious signals intelligence activity, I did not detect a trace. I was not really concerned, and I thought it best not to be curious about it. The station commander was the well-known Group Captain Evans-Evans. (Known generally as Evens Squared). He was a genial officer and showed great interest in me. I had no set duties but was placed under the Senior Equipment Officer but had complete freedom to do whatever pleased me during the normal service day. The mess was reasonably well organised, but my accommodation whilst more in keeping with intended peace standard, was rather dismal, and there was a constant shortage of solid fuel for the stove in my room, which was a cold and miserable place with the winter now well set in. I did not spend much more than sleeping time in it but sought the warmer places during the day.

Most of the personnel were in the wireless trades but seemed to be employed on several other duties quite unconnected with signals intelligence. Again my old friend from Cranwell days, Jack Hyde, was among them; we did seem to be following each other around. One of the activities that interested me particularly was the communication aspect of the Air Ministry Meteorological Office at Dunstable. Quite a number of the Bletchley operators were engaged in shift system working, at Dunstable, with the aircraft of the Meteorological Flight operating out of Ballykelly in Northern Ireland. The aircraft transmitted their weather observations direct to the Met Office at Dunstable. I found it most intriguing to get this information and then watch the forecasters interpret it directly. The weather maps formed the basis for the next day's national weather forecasts broadcast by the BBC throughout the day for the benefit of the many individuals and organizations to which it was often of vital interest.

I took a spot more of my accumulated leave and spent Christmas at home with Rosemary and Michael. I was back at Bletchley on the 30th of December to do my clearance routine before departure for OCTU on January 1st. New Year's Day was a normal working day for the RAF at that time, and I had a final meeting with Evans Squared before my departure. It was most informal back-slapping, welcome to the Club sort of stuff. I remember it was one of those cold and bright winter mornings of brilliant sunshine and everything covered with heavy frost. I bumped into Jack Hyde as I was doing the last clearance act at the bedding store at opening time.

CHAPTER XIX
OFFICER AND SPECIALIST TRAINING

I arrived at Cosford in the early afternoon in the same bright weather and saw the gigantic icicles hanging from the rooftop of the only two-storey building in the camp – Fulton Block – which contained the OCTU in its entirety for accommodation, messing, administrative and classroom needs. I arrived as a Flight Sergeant and, as my first action, was required to remove my rank badges to become, like all other members of the entry, just plain Mister. Our only distinguishing badge for the duration of our IOTC was to be the white band worn around our field service caps and ceremonial hats. Our working dress was to be combat clothing, Army pattern boots, gaiters, and freshly cleaned webbing belt with brasses shining; in fact, the standard working dress of the RAF Regiment from which all our instructors, commissioned and non-commissioned, were drawn. Even the OCTU commanding officer was the RAF Regiment.

After our initial kitting-out, we were taken to the station swimming pool, where we were instructed to strip, shower, get into our trunks, and then climb to the highest level of the diving stage and enter the pool by diving or jumping as we chose. For most of us, it was the highest entry ever into water. It was a case of do it or fail immediately. For the majority, it was taken with great hilarity, and we were permitted a little swim around as a reward for our effort. Afterwards, we were marched onto the parade ground for our first drill session under the stern but gentlemanly, Flight Sergeant Doherty, the unit senior disciplinarian in charge who was to be our guide and mentor. By the morning of the second day, there was a noticeable epidemic of common cold symptoms among us; everyone seemed to have a cold. No matter, we were taken out into the freezing weather, exercised by drill, marching, occasionally breaking into double marching, and generally put through a very energetic outdoor exercise routine. After lunch, we were shown the extensive battle course, where we would soon be required to demonstrate our qualities of leadership in the field. By the close of that day, which included an evening lecture period, we were ready for an early night, and, strangely enough, our colds had gone. Our days thereafter were a mixture of lectures and outdoor activity, all timed to perfection to keep us on our toes. The clatter of our hob-nailed boots attended our movement from one venue to another. It was quite amazing how quickly we got into the easy swing of things.

In no time at all, we had accumulated vast quantities of lecture notes, and a good swot session was an essential part of our evening activity that always included a lecture period after the evening meal. A certain indication of the energy we were using was the fact that we were always hungry. We had four meals a day, including tea, after the last afternoon period at 1630. The usual provision for this was plenty of bread that could be toasted and jam, to which many added whatever they were able to acquire from outside sources: meat pastes and other off-ration edibles that could be spread on bread. There was plenty to eat, and the three main meals were more than ample – we were just plain ravenous with the cumulative effect of each day's hard physical effort. We quickly reached the peak of our physical condition as the course of training, designed to test us in every possible way, sought our individual breaking points. The few who could not take it were soon weeded out and quietly disposed of.

Field training and leadership were perhaps the most testing. In turn, we were required to lead our section into battle situations that demanded instant decisions and action. I remember one particular action in which our most diminutive member was the chosen leader. Our line of patrol took us down a rather steep hillside into a valley where we found our war barred by a very deep mill stream about six yards in width. There was no visible way around or over it, and we came under enemy fire from a well-concealed position on the uphill slope on the far side of the stream. There was only one thing to do and that was to mount a frontal attack across the stream. Our section leader, a good natured Irishman, who we called Dinger Bell, gave the appropriate orders for the Bren Gun Section to provide covering fire as we went into the stream. Dinger immediately disappeared under the surface except for both hands clutching his rifle held aloft above the water. We clambered out of the stream and went straight into the frontal attack. After it was over our wet clothing began to freeze and was soon quite stiff with ice. There was great hilarity among us as we realised that Dinger, not much taller than five feet, had no doubt been deliberately selected to be the leader for this assault because the water would completely cover him. No matter. We just had to carry on with the next assault under a new leader. On another occasion, I inadvertently did myself a lot of good by assuming command when the chosen leader faltered at the critical moment of the developing situation. We were advancing over open ground when we came under fire from a cunningly concealed enemy position. The course of action seemed immediately clear to me as we came under withering fire and went to the ground, but the leader was obviously nonplussed and seemed unable to issue any order. I saw the problem and immediately called for rapid covering fire on the point from which the enemy fire was coming. This was a large hollow tree directly in front of us. To our left, there was a deep ditch with a line of bushes. Under our concentrated fire, I instructed two men to approach the hollow tree along the ditch and grenade the position. I then quickly repositioned the Bren Gun Section to give oblique covering fire from the left during the initial rush of our final frontal assault. After the action, the Regiment sergeant in charge quietly asked for my name and indicated that my initiative would be noted.

Our days were full of every conceivable item of knowledge contributing to Good Leadership, Discipline – though not of the bantering bullying type – Relationships with other rank personnel, Air Force Law, Administration, General Service Knowledge, Etiquette, Behaviour, (The image of the Service to the Public, and the importance of being seen to be a good representative) and, of course, an occasional talk by the Unit Padre on the importance of religion. Ability to address an assembled audience was tested by everyone being required to select three subjects for a talk. Quite unexpectedly the instructor, always an officer, would announce that someone would now give us a talk, the subject being randomly chosen by the instructor from the individual's selected three. Our working day was certainly full. We were up at 0600, and instruction started at 0800 for twelve hours a day, usually ending after an evening lecture at 2000 hours. We then had to prepare ourselves for tomorrow before collapsing, totally exhausted, into deep recuperative sleep.

Ten days before the course was due to end, those of us who were to be successfully graduated were assembled at a Friday evening session and given the news. This was done so that we could visit our chosen military tailors the next day to be measured for our uniforms and arrange the purchase of other items of officer clothing. The unfortunates were told of their failure individually and were quietly sent to a duty station. On graduation day, we had the usual parade and commissioning ceremony. We had already been given our course results, and I was pleased to find my name among three in the Distinguished Pass category. After the parade, we were free to proceed on seven days of commissioning leave, and I was delighted to find that I would have as travelling companion to Perth Robbie Cairns, who had to change there for his home in Brechin in Angus. It was the 27th February 1947. We had already had the first fitting of our uniforms at an evening visit a few days before. Final fitting was successful and it was early evening when we left our Wolverhampton tailor with our uniforms packed in our suitcases; we were prohibited from wearing them in the training locality. So we were still attired with the insignia of officer cadet as we started our rail journey to Scotland. It was a quiet, peaceful journey, and we had a compartment to ourselves in an un-crowded train. The next morning, we changed into our spanking new uniforms, and I said farewell to Robbie, with whom I would be reunited in a week's time at RAF Hereford for our Specialist Officer Equipment Course. After a further five hours or so, I arrived at Nairn as Pilot Officer W Jacobs RAF, much to the delight of my infant son, who seemed to be quite fascinated with my new hat and its shiny Badge of woven gilt wire worn by Royal Air Force officers since 1918.

The week passed all too quickly and I left home for RAF Hereford (also frequently referred to as Creden Hill, the topographical feature at the base of which the station was built). It had been snowing heavily and I stepped down from the bus at the camp gates into at least a foot of it. An airman escorted me from the guardroom to my accommodation, quite a distance in the newly fallen snow. I was dismayed to find that my sleeping quarters for the next three months were to be in other ranks type barrack hut; it was, however, furnished to officer standard, and the number to be accommodated was to be considerably less than the usual capacity. It was, in fact, quite comfortable and was soon filled by others from my Cosford entry. We had a number of batmen to provide for us and keep the place clean and tidy. We were a very happy company. The officers' mess was also a wooden structure but was comfortably furnished and provided with the facilities appropriate to officer standards. In fact, the entire encampment was built of wooden buildings.

Instruction started the next day, and we were soon immersed in the role of the Equipment Branch and our future place in it as specialist officers of that Branch of the Service. Any attempt to describe the course in detail would be of no value to any likely reader of these memoirs. Sufficient to say that it was most comprehensive in its scope, covering organization from the highest level of Director General of Equipment (DGE) down to the user level and all aspects of Provisioning from the industry. Final examinations took several days, and I was again most gratified to find myself among the leaders with a Credit Pass. We were called to Headquarters Maintenance Command for allocation to existing vacancies and I was delighted to be posted to an initial appointment in Scotland. It was to be RAF Errol located between Perth and Dundee, which was quite convenient for the main line railway link for Nairn. It just could not have been better for me.

CHAPTER XX
OFFICER SERVICE

Errol had been a wartime fighter base and was now serving as a Maintenance Unit (MU) of the Equipment Disposal Depot (EDD) category. Its function was to accept, store and dispose of, by sale, all equipment from redundant wartime stations in Scotland and Northern England. The officer staff was small, only eight of us, including the Commanding Officer who held the rank of Squadron Leader, the Chief Equipment Officer, and an Education Officer - both of Flight Lieutenant rank and three officers of the General Duties (Flying) Branch who had been allocated to equipment duties whilst awaiting release. These three and I were the only officers wearing flying brevets. The CEO and I were the only pre-war regulars. There were no locally engaged civilians and this fact alone provided the clue to the likely short-term duration of the station's post-war life. The non-commissioned ranks were predominantly National Service, among whom there was constant change. The officers were a small but happy band, with only four of us actually living in mess. We were comfortably accommodated with our own rooms in wooden huts of the long-term temporary type. The mess proper was, however, a large Nissen building, of which there were many, but it was well appointed and comfortable even to having a bar that was not manned on a full-time basis but usually the responsibility of one of the mess staff on duty.

Interesting activities for all ranks was a problem, but the CO had this well under control as together we tried hard to overcome its effects. I declared my interest in model flying and was given a free hand to organize a station club. I had no difficulty in getting this activity launched quickly as there was plenty of interest among the aircraftmen and corporals. One of the many unused Nissen huts was allocated to provide clubroom and building facilities, and we had an unused airfield all to ourselves. There was a Royal Navy base at Arbroath (HMS Falcon) and we were able to invite their club members to join us for model flying meetings at weekends. Cricket and football, always popular in season, was not a problem to organize with several Army units in the locality. During a cricket match with the Black Watch from their Perth barracks, I suffered the misfortune of a broken little finger on the left hand trying to take what seemed like an easy catch, but the ball went into the direct rays of the lowering sun and I was completely blinded at the crucial moment. On another occasion, still wearing my cricket boots and in a hurry to get dressed for dinner, I came an awful cropper as I stepped onto a slatted metal mat at the door of my hut and badly hurt my left knee that swelled to enormous size and needed medical attention for several days.

Despite the uncertainty of the station's future, I was quite happy. Rosemary was only an acceptable rail journey away, and getting an occasional long weekend was not a problem. I even had Rosemary and Michael down, and we spent a pleasant two weeks in a small hotel at nearby Inchture, where I could conveniently stay with them overnight. It was all very pleasant. However, it was not to last. A communication from the Air Ministry, addressed to the station for myself, informed me that I had been SELECTED for further specialist training and was to join No. 2 Movements Officers Course assembling at RAF Hereford on a date in July 1947. Traditionally, the Equipment Branch was responsible for the consignment of freight by land and sea. The movement of freight and personnel by air had always been the responsibility of the flying squadrons, who generally took care of their own needs within the squadron capacity or when instructed to assist other squadrons or ground units. (See Page 29 concerning Sgt Gaut at Catterick). It was in this recently embraced activity that I seemed most likely to be concerned because of my aircrew background.

So, back to Hereford for a further four weeks of training, which was to include the whole field of movement by land, sea, and air. It was a very interesting course that I found easy to assimilate. I revelled in the part that many seemed to find the most difficult as it touched on the more complicated mathematics used to determine an aircraft's initial weight and, more importantly, its centre of gravity (point of balance) balance at take-off and landing. Once again I had no difficulty in obtaining a Credit Pass.

Back at Errol I found myself hoping that I would now be left to settle down to a normal pattern of service life for a while. But it was not to be. At very short notice, I found myself posted to Air Booking Centre London, which turned out to be not quite what I had envisaged. I arrived there on a very hot afternoon in mid-August and, as I could not have managed my luggage on the underground railway system, had to take a taxi from Euston station to the unit location in St James Street off Piccadilly. The unit was housed most elegantly on the ground floor of a prestigious office block with an imposing entrance opening to an adequate lounge area for passengers to assemble for processing.

I was most impressed until, enquiring about where we lived, I was informed that it was up to individual officers to find their own accommodation. I was quite incredulous, where did one start to look for suitable accommodation that one could afford right here in the centre of London? Most were living with friends or relatives in the suburbs, then it was suggested that officers with my problem could stay at the Salvation Army Officers Leave

Club at Paddington but only on a short-term basis. Johnny Hayward, an officer known to me from OCTU, was, in fact, staying there. A quick telephone call to the club confirmed that I could stay there for two weeks, which initially solved the immediate problem. So in company with Johnny, I went to the club in Sussex Gardens, Paddington. It was not quite what one would have wished as an officers club being, to say the least, incomparable with that expected in RAF establishments. It was, however, clean and well-run by elderly ladies who were inclined to adopt a rather motherly and caring attitude. A single room was not possible, and one was required to share a room with someone else, perhaps as many as four.

We had an ample breakfast and an evening meal was available but had to be booked. The lunch meal was entirely up to ourselves, and we were not expected to be in the place between 1000 and 1600 hours. A bedtime beverage could be obtained in the kitchen at about 2200. The entrance door was kept locked and one had to ring the bell to get in. Last admission was at 2300 hours as the lady on duty was required to cook and serve the breakfast, and needed a good night's sleep. The maximum length of stay not exceeding fourteen days had, somehow, to be strictly enforced. There were no more than a dozen of us, all serving with Navy and Air Force elements in the city, and we seemed to be the regular guests, all having the same accommodation problem. We had to devise ways and means of breaking the duration of our stay and this could only be done by locating friends and prevailing upon them for an occasional night stopover. We had to do an occasional night duty stint that helped to break the continuity of our stay periods. It was a bit of a nuisance as it was clearly only paying lip service to some rule, probably a local licence rule authorising the existence of the place as a leave facility rather than a permanent accommodation feature. However, it was insisted on, but it did not seem to matter that we were, in fact, permanent residents, as long as we booked out for at least one night in fourteen. I made contact with Gordon Cairns, who was living with his wife at Ewell in Surrey, within easy commuting distance. He was working in the city as a Private Investigator. I also contacted an old school chum, Alf Mathews, who had a small Advertising Display business at Tooting Bec. These two contacts were able to offer an occasional night's shelter at weekends. Gradually I got the niggling little problems sorted out and tried to make the best of an unsatisfactory situation. The arrangement was not a good one, as only the bare necessities for board and lodging were provided. Although we had the use of an ironing room, personal laundry had to be taken care of by outside private arrangement. I believe the ladies were voluntary workers and, not surprisingly, had to limit their service to this useful and necessary facility according to their other personal considerations. Although far from comparable to life on an established RAF station, it served to provide the basic needs of the few who, like me, had no other alternative within the financial constraints of the time. We were in receipt of a supplementary London allowance, but even this addition to our junior officers' pay fell far short of the financial level needed to provide a reasonably comparable standard to that expected.

The work scene was good. Uniformed personnel were all officers except for the Unit Warrant Officer, who was responsible for the general duties requirement. The total complement of serving officers was seven, including the Unit CO, who was a Squadron Leader Lewis. Three flight lieutenants, one of whom – Alfie Smitz – was responsible for the currency exchange function, Bill Henry, awaiting release, and John Reddington hanging on, hoping for a permanent opportunity. Gilbert Brewer arrived from Hereford shortly after me; he, together with Johnny Hayward and me, three recently commissioned pilot officers, completed the total. All of us with the exception of Johnny and Gilbert, wore flying badges. There was also a retired Group Captain Staneley-Turner re-employed as a Civilian Substitution Officer in the post of Adjutant with the equivalent rank of flight lieutenant. Additionally, there were two junior Civil Servants, one male and one female, to look after the clerical side of things. We were a good company and got on very well, although Johnny was seen by all to be rather bumptious.

It was hardly a busy life. The RAF's Peacetime Air Transport Organisation was in the early stages of development. We had weekday schedules to Berlin and Warsaw operating out of Northolt using hastily acquired early post-war civil aircraft of the Vickers Viking type. These were very busy routes with a constant movement of Civil Service and Military personnel to and from these two locations in the immediate aftermath of the war. One of our frequent passengers was Mr Albert Pierpoint, the State Executioner who had succeeded his father in that role. We also had less frequent schedules contracted to civil operators flying out of Blackbushe using converted bomber aircraft, principally the Avro Lancaster, which – with a more capacious fuselage and renamed Avro York - filled the post-war manufacturing gap to good purpose. These schedules were designed to provide for the movement of priority passengers to the more distant eastern locations. Routine movement of personnel to these locations was to continue by troopship for many years.

The large reception area had elegant wooden counters on two sides. On one occasion, I was behind the counter close to the entrance door when in walked Lofty Fyfield, who, as a sergeant, had been a prominent instructor during my time at the Wireless Intelligence School at Newbold Revell. He was now a squadron leader. Recognising me immediately, he enquired what had happened to me to be still in the lowly rank of pilot officer. He told me that he remembered something about me and that I intended to specialise in German and Italian and should not have gone to the Burma Theatre. There had been an administrative error in switching me to Japanese. That is why I did not proceed to the overseas despatching centre until my request to see the commanding officer revealed the error to the Adjutant, who was believed to have been initially responsible for it. I was then disposed of hurriedly just in time to join 367 Wireless Unit, whose embarkation was imminent (Page 61). Thus, the mistake was complete and presumably went unnoticed until I finally got the matter brought to Air Ministry's attention early in 1945. This was obviously the reason for the, unfortunately frustrated, attempt to have me commissioned in the field whilst in Rangoon. It was also about this time that I met Johnny Crocket as I was walking up St. James Street towards Piccadilly (Page 44). He was then a wing commander at the Air Ministry. I had a great liking for him but regrettably was not to see him again. I believe he died quite young.

It was during this time that I learned from Rosemary that she was pregnant with our second child, expected about the end of the year. Whilst delighted at this news, I was aware of a degree of uncertainty about my future career in the RAF. We were still very much under the Emergency Powers Act and the terms of appointment to commissions were such that they could be terminated at short notice to satisfy the needs of the Service that were always the paramount consideration.

I was detached for a week to undergo further training at the recently established Air Transport Development Unit at Brize Norton in Oxfordshire. Here I was to be introduced to the deeper aerodynamic considerations of carrying loads in aircraft. On arrival, I met the Senior Instructor, who told me that he had been looking forward to my arrival as he had been told that I was knowledgeable in regard to aerodynamics. I was somewhat taken aback but immediately recognised the sort of thing that Johnny Hayward, who had recently done the course, was likely to say. I mentioned his name and was left in no further doubt.

This course was most interesting, and I entered into it enthusiastically but quietly. It was involved, and I soon realised that most were having problems getting to grips with the mathematics of it, although all seemed to grasp the importance of getting the centre of gravity in the right place. At that time weight and balance forms for aircraft by type had not been devised. Consequently, every single item loaded into an aircraft had to be weighed. Standard weights were used only for fuel, oil and water and the known basic weight of the particular aircraft. The fuselage of all load-carrying aircraft was divided into imaginary compartments, the centre point of which was calculated in terms of moment-arm length from a datum point at or in front of the aircraft's nose. It was, therefore, possible to calculate the effect that the weight of each compartment would have on the location of the basic centre of gravity located at the point at which the lifting surfaces developed maximum lifting force (the designed centre of pressure usually located at about thirty-three per cent of the mean chord of the wing). Understanding the Fore and aft effect is fairly simple but the precise location of the centre of gravity is not necessarily on the centre line of the aircraft floor but can be at a point above or to either side of it. Since the centre of pressure moves with any change in the angle of attack of the wing, it is important that the centre of gravity, which also moves with changes in flight attitude, should be within the narrow limits of the designed centre of pressure movement. These limits are usually in the order of only a few inches fore and aft of the ideal, allowing about eighteen inches into which the centre of gravity of the loaded aircraft must fall to ensure safety.

After a few introductory lectures, we were presented with an exercise to determine the weight and balance parameters of a bomber aircraft for conversion to the air transport role. For this, the aircraft was a Handley Page Halifax that had been stripped so that the fuselage space aft of the flight deck could be utilised for cargo carrying. Firstly, it was essential to calculate the basic, or empty, weight of the aircraft, and it was therefore necessary to weigh it. This was quite easy using specially designed weighing scales placed under the main wheels and tail wheel since the Halifax landing gear was so configured. From this point, we were each left with a set of formulae, some of which I was already familiar with, and told to take the rest of the day to complete the task of converting the aircraft to the air cargo role. It was late in the afternoon by the time I finished my calculations which occupied four foolscap sheets. Like the others, I had squatted uncomfortably on the hangar floor with my back propped against a wall and was relieved when the protracted task was finished. My calculations had produced a centre of gravity point well within the narrow centre of pressure limits for the Authorised All Up Weight of the aircraft for take-off and landing together with all the other information relating to aircraft and compartment weights. I knew, therefore, that my plan for the maximum compartment loading and the progressive calculations must have been correct. The next morning I was invited to see the Senior Instructor, who congratulated me on my result. Mine was, apparently, the only all-correct submission and was, in fact, the only one so far in the short history of the unit. For me, the most pleasing outcome was that Johnny Hayward was vindicated in his somewhat misplaced claim that I would never had made for myself or anyone else. I was never required to perform that task again, but found it useful in my general appreciation of the greater depth that went into the whole consideration of weight and balance problems.

During the early autumn of 1947, I was detached to Abingdon to assist with the first post-war Air Transport Exercise for which Abingdon was to be the forward main base. This was called Exercise Longstop and involved a large-scale airborne assault by the Parachute Brigade and all aspects of their subsequent air transport support. It was, from my point of view, a rather miserable effort throughout which I observed widespread disinterest. The cause was soon apparent in the fact that most of those involved were only concerned with getting back to civil life. The exercise main base was visited by Air Marshal, the Honourable Sir Ralph Cochrane, who was obviously concerned about the rather poor personnel state. During a discussion with the officers, he asked each individually about his future intentions, and I was amazed that the majority readily expressed the intention to leave the service. The general attitude seemed to be born of a complete weariness of what each had been forced into unwillingly and, of course, uncertainty of a future career. There were very few who had embraced the Service as a career on initial entry, mostly due to being obliged to enter under the terms of the National Service Act. I told the Air Marshal that, as a regular long-service entrant, my personal wish was to continue in the hope of appointment to a permanent commission. Whilst wishing me the best of good fortune, he briefly mentioned the associated difficulties in planning the future requirements of the Service at the time. Among the non-commissioned personnel, I found the attitude quite appalling, with the majority displaying little evidence of any wish to perform any duties for which their National Service training may have been directed. Their attitude seemed to be that as they were there against their will, they felt no obligation to make any effort.

I was to experience at closer range the effect of this tendency when, during the winter of 1947/48 I was detached for a few days to Germany to organise the return to the United Kingdom of No. 56 Squadron ground personnel and equipment. My point of departure for Lubeck was to be Abingdon where I was to collect a small number of qualified aircraftmen to assist me. It was bitterly cold as we emplaned the next morning. At Lubeck, although bright and sunny the cold was even more intense as I immediately set about weighing the passengers, baggage and cargo for the first four Dakota aircraft schedule to depart early the following morning. The only weighing scales that could be found were those used in the station sick quarters and they were calibrated in metric weights. So, all weights would have to be converted from kilos to pounds. None of my assistants were able to do this, and when I told them how to do it they seemed quite incapable of doing the simple sum. A technical senior NCO of 56 Squadron was close by and offered help that I gladly accepted while, with the aid of a wax pencil to temporarily mark the glass cover of the face, I quickly re-calibrated the scale in the sector of the average passenger weights. We soon had the queue moving quickly. By early evening, I had all the information needed to complete the passenger and cargo manifests, also the weight and balance sheets. The remainder should have been easy for the men from Abingdon. How mistaken I was when I reassembled the team after a break for the evening meal. Hopefully, I set each of them the task of completing a weight and balance form for the four aircraft scheduled to depart the next morning. All information needed was made available to them and the whole job should have been completed easily within an hour. Imagine my astonishment at the early realisation that they seemed not to have the least idea how to go about it. I had to complete the four documents myself, each involving long arithmetical multiplication and addition calculations in the order of hundreds of thousands of foot/pounds. I finished the job around midnight completely exhausted after a very long day and, disgustedly, dismissed the four useless individuals supplied by Abingdon.

I had a comfortable room in the officers' quarters but found the central heating rather fierce and had to open a window to the intensely cold outside air. The morning dawned frosty white for another cold though pleasantly sunny day. The station at Lubeck was built to the permanent requirements of the Luftwaffe and the facilities were to a very high modern standard. The officers' mess was well appointed, in fact, quite pleasantly different to our own. After an adequate breakfast, I found the aircraft parking area busily preparing for the departure of the 56 Squadron ground personnel. I soon had them assembled by their appointed aircraft into which we had already loaded and secured their baggage. I was somewhat heartened to discover that this simple task was within the capability of the Abingdon personnel, but only after I had given them precise instructions as to where the baggage was to be located in the only possible place in the loading plan which, since the Dakota was the aircraft to which they should have been most accustomed, should have been obvious to them. The four aircraft departed at their intended take-off time, and we were left with the small number of personnel and essential ground equipment forming the rear party. I quickly organised into a loading plan and had everything prepared so that only the basic weight details of the sweeper aircraft had to be added to the weight and balance form. This aircraft arrived from Abingdon by mid-afternoon and the task was completed before dark. That evening, I spent watching a film in a converted hangar, and it was nice to see the station personnel with their family members enjoying this facility; station cinemas were unusual at home but an essential entertainment facility in occupied Germany at this time. Afterwards I enjoyed a drink or two in the excellent mess. The next morning was simply a matter of tying down a few items of baggage and off we went on our return journey to Abingdon, where I lost no time in telling the Senior Air Movements Officer what I thought of the four aircraftmen he had loaned me. His attitude was simply that they were National Service airmen and as such, were regarded as useless anyway. He seemed to have no cognisance of the fact that their uselessness was in large part due to his failure to ensure that some local training would have assured at least a degree of usefulness and, perhaps, a great deal of personal satisfaction for themselves.

Shortly after returning from Germany and receiving the verbal congratulations of the Group Movements Officer, I thought it propitious to make a formal enquiry about the prospect of a Permanent Commission. The Unit CO, Squadron Leader Lewis, forwarded the letter to Group Headquarters, and I was surprised to be invited to attend for an informal interview. I had expected nothing more than a written response addressed to the unit. The Group Headquarters was at Bushey Park in the Greater London Area and the appointed morning miserably cold and wet. To make the day worse, I was sickened with influenza, which was rampant at the time. The interview was pleasant enough but there was nothing of encouragement in what I was told. Quite definitely, there was no chance of appointment to a permanent commission from within the Service at the time and there was no indication when it would be possible. The future manning requirement could not be determined until the post-war situation had settled down. No one had any future certainty except those already holding PCs. I was also told that many officers who had been regular senior NCOs before appointment to emergency commissions had been grantedd PCs hurriedly in order to ensure the retention of much needed experience, as many former senior NCOs could have left the Service in droves in a rush to secure civilian careers as soon as possible after the cessation of hostilities. The effect of this action was to be felt for many years. All that I could do was to stay in the hope of an extension that would be to complete a maximum of seven years of commissioned service. I left feeling rather disappointed and with no hope of a future long-term career in the service. I even contemplated the possibility of returning to the ranks where I would have the assurance of continuing my regular engagement to complete twenty-four years, taking me to the age of forty-two and a pension. I would also have the reasonable expectation of promotion to the rank of warrant officer at an early age and, perhaps, the opportunity of being appointed to a permanent commission when the opportunity was re-established. But that would have been a retrograde step that may not have worked as anticipated. I was certainly in a troubled state of mind about the course of the long-term career that I had initially embraced and which seemed to have taken an indeterminate change of course since my appointment to a commission.

It was early afternoon when I got back to central London and, as there was no reason to go back to SABC until the next morning, I decided to make my way to Baker Street where, close to Madam Tussauds Waxworks, a new entertainment feature had recently been opened. This was The Planetarium, where, seated comfortably in the auditorium, one could explore the heavens realistically projected overhead. Afterwards, with time still to spare, I found my thoughts dwelling on something that my mother-in-law had told me I must do whenever I had the chance. That was to visit the headquarters of the Mental & General Nursing Association, with which she had been involved for most of her working life, specialising in the mental aspect of the nursing profession. She was, at that time, in Torquay, where she had been for some time caring for a private patient at his home, where we had visited her several times since my return to the United Kingdom in 1946. She had often mentioned Mr Donaldson, the principal, and Miss Miriam, the secretary and general factotum, who carried out their work at the headquarters located in Hind Street. As this was no more than four hundred yards from where I was standing. I decided this was the best chance I was likely to get. So along, I went to Hind Street, a typical west-end thoroughfare of the Victorian era with terraced desirable residences on either hand. The door was opened by Miss Miriam, whose warm greeting and fussing made me feel like the returned prodigal son. I was ushered upstairs to meet Mr Donaldson, who was clearly delighted to see me. I had timed my arrival to coincide with the usual calling time coinciding, in polite society, with the time for afternoon tea, which appeared as if by magic under the hand of Miss Miriam. Mr Donaldson stayed on the premises during the working week and returned to his own home at Saffron Walden at weekends. He was a most genial host, and the three of us chatted about this and that for some time. Mr Donaldson seemed genuinely interested in my RAF career and on enquiring about my future intentions in that respect. I felt obliged to mention the happenings of that day and ventured the opinion that my future in the RAF was so indeterminate that I might have to abandon it and seek new pastures. I was aware of a great feeling of genuine warmth of the kind usually associated with family in this company, and I was most impressed with the obvious fact that my mother-in-law, for whom I had developed a great affectation, was held in such high regard in this most reputable organisation that she had served with distinction for such a long time. Private medicine and nursing were at that time a privilege of the very wealthy, and those chosen to reside and care for patients in their own homes had to meet a selection criteria designed to ensure the highest standards of personal integrity and professional ability.

By the next morning my influenza symptoms of the previous day had developed into nothing more than a nasty cold. Squadron Leader Lewis was disappointed to learn of the outcome of my visit to Group Headquarters, but seeing that I was suffering from a cold, suggested that I should purchase some aspirin and take to my bed for the weekend and see how I felt on Monday. So I called a convenient pharmacy on Piccadilly and went back to the club, where the kind ladies in charge moved me into the reserved room in the topmost part of the house where I would be isolated until I recovered. So I enjoyed a lazy weekend in bed and was looked after as well as I could have been in my own home. On Monday morning, I was feeling very much better, but the ladies thought I should take another two days particularly as the weather was very bad with a penetrating dense smoky fog for which the London winter was well known. It was certainly very gloomy, and I was glad to stay in bed and keep warm as, due to continuing fuel restrictions, space heating was still a problem. There was no central heating in my lonely little room, but the ladies had provided a small electric heater that was capable of raising the temperature by at least a few degrees.

Christmas 1947 came, and I spent the festive season on leave to be with Rosemary, who was in temporary residence with Alf Mathew's parents at Heywood, pending the arrival of our second child. I had made arrangements for her to be admitted to the private maternity unit of Bury Infirmary, where Douglas Ross was born on 3rd January 1948.

Alf and I travelled back to London together, and inevitably, our conversation got onto my own future intentions. He was working entirely on his own, producing, albeit not at the desired rate, high quality display model aircraft for the British Overseas Airways and British European Airways Corporations. They were of wooden construction in sycamore, mostly hand carved with the aid of simple electrically driven bench tools. Although his finished products were to the highest degree of perfection, his working conditions and equipment were so primitive that they would not have met the conditions of the Factories or the Health and Safety Acts. His workshop was a seriously dilapidated two-storey building in a secluded yard off the Balham High Road, quite close to the Tooting Bec underground railway station. The building was unheated and perishing cold in winter. He was plainly carrying on a business that certainly had potential but would never be profitable unless it could be expanded and modernised. He was looking for support and was, of course, familiar with my own modelling interest and capability. But I was not, at that time, in a position to indicate any future aspirations as I was bound to complete at least twelve months of commissioned service. Even then, my further retention was at the convenience of the Service. However, I told him that it was an interesting proposition which I would seriously consider, as the only thing in mind at that time was the possibility of getting into civil aviation.

The drab London winter, with its seemingly unending smoke-laden atmosphere, gradually came to an end. The working part of the days passed quickly enough but the evenings were rather boring as there was nothing for us to do at the hostel other than that which we were able to devise ourselves. The ladies in charge were well aware of our boredom and knew that we could not afford to spend much of our spare time taking in the films and theatre shows. There was no shortage of restaurants and public houses, but they were the most expensive luxuries and quite beyond our financial ability except for the occasional treat.

The 27th February 1948 marked the end of the obligatory twelve-month period that the terms of my commission required of me and as there was no indication of a compulsory relinquishment, I made a formal enquiry and was informed that I would be under no obligation to terminate my service in the foreseeable future, but if I wished, I could give a written undertaking to continue for periods of twelve months at a time. I was most unhappy about such an indefinite arrangement in terms of career prospect and, as the next move seemed to be a matter for personal decision, resolved that I would soon have to make that decision. I was aware of an increasingly nasty taste in my mouth at the growing uncertainty of my future. Uncertainty that could have been avoided had I not sought to progress to the higher level of commissioned service - what a price to pay for ambition!

My level of disenchantment only increased as 1948 moved into its beautiful spring, and I decided that my best move would be to seek early release. After a final attempt to gain the latest information in regard to the possibility of a permanent commission failed to produce any indication of change, I decided to quit at a date in June and sent in my formal request accordingly.

Gill Brewer had decided to quit at the same time as myself and together, we travelled from London to Wilmslow in Cheshire, where officers leaving the Service were processed out. I remember we had to stay for a night and decided to visit Blackpool, as the place at Wilmslow was anything but a hive of interesting activity. The weather was dreadful for the time of year. It was sometime in May, so we spent most of the evening visiting a few inviting-looking hotel bars along the promenade. Next morning, we were directed to the department, where we were issued with a complete civilian outfit with certain items to our individual choice. This was essential to everyone leaving the Service at that time as clothing was strictly rationed, and service personnel did not qualify for an issue of clothing coupons. The choice was rather limited when it came to taste in suits of clothing. The choice of a suit was really limited to two and, as I had no idea how long it might be before I would qualify for the coupons necessary for another suit, I chose what seemed to be the most sensible hard-wearing option: a serge suit in navy blue.

Gill and I were on our way by train to Manchester shortly after lunch. We were on a month of end-of-service leave and, after making a date for a final personal reunion in Manchester, went our separate ways to our home locations. I was reunited with Rosemary and Michael at the home of Alf Mathew's parents in Heywood by mid-afternoon. I had planned to spend half of my leave there, where I was close to my own parents, before leaving for London with Alf to get a closer look at the business I had decided to embrace for my career in civil life.

Chapter XXI
A FOOLS PARADISE

I was eager to get into the different ways of things and was glad when Alf came home for the weekend. We returned to London together on Monday, and I started the settling-in process at his flat, which is quite close to the work premises. I would soon have to look into the prospects of finding suitable rented accommodation for Rosemary and our two children. This I was to find extremely difficult. There was absolutely no possibility of an allocation of a house by the local housing authority, and it was soon apparent that my only hope was to purchase a property by taking out a mortgage that I doubted would be within my immediate financial means. However, on visiting a local estate agent, I was assured that a house purchase would be possible and it was simply a matter of waiting for a suitable property to come onto the market and that was likely to be sooner than later.

The work of making models to the advertising display standard was interesting but there were other things to be put in hand. I undertook the management of the financial and administrative aspects of the business. Alf was no accountant and the records were virtually non-existent. I visited a local firm of Chartered Accountants and asked them to act as appointed auditors for legal requirements and that my intended bookkeeping system was acceptable. Alf was conducting the financial aspects of the business through his personal bank account - that was overdrawn – so I went to see the bank manager and created an account for the business that we had decided to name Minavia Models (derived from Miniature Aviation). I arranged the transfer of my own account from my service bankers and negotiated an arrangement to start the business account, the manager being satisfied with my explanation that there would be an input from myself when my service gratuity was paid in, as it would be shortly. So the firm was put on a legal and more business-like footing, albeit with an overdraft, which was soon to become a standing feature.

Alf had a small apartment in a large Victorian terraced house. Actually, it was what would have been the servants' quarters occupying the topmost two rooms and a small kitchen in a back addition. It was adequate in size but sparsely furnished, lacking the degree of comfort to which I was accustomed. Our feeding arrangements were of the most

Spartan variety, and I soon began to feel that my usual standards were sadly depreciated. Perhaps it would not be too long before I would be able to have my own home. The end of my leave and, with it, my last day of paid service came about mid-June. My gratuity followed quickly and I instructed the bank to transfer an agreed sum to the Minavia Models account to formally buy myself in.

I was now beginning to feel like the proverbial fish out of water. However, I received a communication from the Air Ministry inviting me to consider accepting a commission in the Royal Air Force Volunteer Reserve Training Branch - RAFVR(T) that had been specially created to provide officers for training the cadets of the Air Training Corps to whom my experience would be invaluable. This was a part-time commitment, mainly one evening a week with the occasional weekend activity and an annual camp during the school's summer vacation period. There was no liability for active service and the commission could be terminated immediately by the simple submission of written notice on my part. The local Air Training Corps unit was within short walking distance, and I was expected when I made my first appearance in uniform and warmly greeted by the Squadron Commander, who was a local businessman without a Service background. Of the two other officers on the strength one was to become a good friend of many years. He was Sid Birchmore who had served during the war years as an Air Signaller, so we had something in common. But I was the only former regular and found myself regarded as the font of all RAF knowledge. I soon settled in and really looked forward to my weekly parade evenings and other cadet activities. At this time, the ATC was a pre-entry training organisation and was to remain so until the repeal of the National Service Act in 1960. Former ATC cadets were almost certain of being drafted into the RAFVR as their personal choice for the legal two-year stint. So, I regained a sense of still being a member of the RAF family, albeit an unpaid member.

The business also needed considerable attention on the working side of things where there was much that would not meet the conditions of the Factories Act. The electrically driven machinery, although of the simplest required for woodworking, had been made by Alf and lacked the essential safeguards for the protection of the operator. Spay painting of cellulose paints, an absolute necessity, was being done in the main work area as required instead of in a specially designed booth with an air extractor designed to discharge the toxic fume and solids through filters to the outside atmosphere. There were only the two of us, but it was obvious that we would have to employ additional hands if the business was to expand into profitability. But one thing became clear very quickly. The product of Alf's labours was being grossly undercharged, and it was obvious that he seemed not to have the slightest idea of relating time spent on creation to a realistic financial return to cover the pay and other overhead costs. Here lay the problem that was manifested in the bank overdraft. This problem led to a serious and somewhat heated discussion in which Alf pointed out that to apply my reasoning would not work as the customers, mainly the two national airlines, would cease to use models in their advertising displays purely on the grounds of cost-effectiveness. Whilst I appreciated his point of view I could not accept it as good manufacturing practise which in turn led to my belief that the venture could not become more than it was – a means of labouring for long hours for little more than an ordinary working wage. Thus began my personal dissatisfaction, but I had cast my dice and was determined to give it a fair trial.

The estate agent contacted me during July with the news that he now had a house on his books that looked like what I might be looking for. It was, in fact, almost directly opposite the house in which Alf had his flat. The only possible objection was that it was partly occupied, which would have the effect of lowering the asking price. The house was big enough to provide adequate space for my family in the top half. I had a look at it and decided that it was indeed adequate for my family needs and being part occupied was to be expected in the post-war London area. It would represent an additional income to help with the mortgage payment. So I decided to purchase and the agent lost no time in completing the purchase transaction with a reputable solicitor acting in regard to the legalities of ownership transfer. In no time at all, Rosemary and the two boys came down from Lancashire and life began to take on a new meaning again. Michael was now five years old and Ross still a babe of seven months. We soon settled in and made friendly overtures towards our tenants, who reciprocated in what seemed to be the normal manner. They had a daughter in her early teens who made a great fuss of Ross, but it soon became apparent that there was a serious estrangement between the husband and wife.

During the summer of 1949, we went to RAF Oakington in Cambridgeshire for our annual summer camp. This being regarded as a duty the officers were paid at the rate for their rank as compensation for the loss of occupational pay. We were accommodated under canvas, a great novelty for the youngsters, but feeding was in the station mess facilities, and the officers had full access to the Officer's Mess. Here, I met two old acquaintances: Alf Smitz, still a Flight Lieutenant but now settled into the recently developed post-war Air Traffic Control Branch. Also, Sqn Ldr Surtees, who had flown operationally with one of the 4 Group squadrons at the same time as myself and had served as an instructor with me at 19 OTU Kinloss. He was shot down during his second tour of operations and spent the last three years of the war in captivity. Surprised to learn of my reasons for leaving the regular force, he offered me advice and encouragement to apply for recall as access to permanent commissions would have to reopen soon to resolve the effects of lost personnel with pre-war training for long service careers, which was now becoming a serious problem again. The weather was good, and we enjoyed an excellent week away from the cares of post-war civilian life. I was reluctant to leave the familiar scene and experienced a yearning to return to it.

In an effort to expand the firm's customer base, I decided to put my RAF knowledge to good use by arranging a visit to the Air Ministry Recruiting Branch, which was likely to have a need for models to display in the many recruiting offices throughout the country. The timing of my visit could not have been more appropriate. There was immediate interest, and a need was indicated for a large number of models of the English Electric Canberra jet bomber that was entering service in large numbers. Costing was a seriously important matter when the requirement was presented to the Finance Branch and I was asked to supply a sample model made to our usual display standard. This we were able to do very quickly, but the cost, including the display stand and transit case, was considerably in excess of the cost allocation and we were requested to suggest a cheaper alternative. After some deliberation, we hit on the idea of producing the model in cast aluminium alloy. We had no difficulty in finding a foundry willing to produce sand castings for us at a reasonable cost and we were soon at work to produce the finished article. This required a degree of filing to prepare the surfaces for the initial coat of a heavily pigmented filler-type paint that required no more than ordinary rubbing down for the final coats of paint decoration. At this stage we also embraced the new technology of screen-printing by which we produced our own decorative decals on ready-gummed paper. We also introduced a simple photographic etching process by which we were able to produce sharp edged stencils for attachment to the printing screens and through which we could print precise decals. Our costing for the cast metal models was accepted, and we soon found ourselves with an Air Ministry contract that was to serve as a sound business base for some time. We took on an additional two employees who were both keen modellers and good at it. It seemed like we might at last be on the desired upward business curve.

About this time, we also began experimentation with large-scale display models involving moulding in Perspex, a clear plastic, through which a detailed view of the inside of an air-liners passenger cabin could be seen. Air travel as we know it today was at that time in its infancy and large passenger-carrying aircraft were only just beginning to emerge in early post-war Europe. The British Overseas Airways Corporation indicated an immediate interest and we produced a model of a Lockheed Constellation with its beautifully detailed interior in the Corporation's particular colour scheme, with passenger seats to exact scale and upholstery shade. To produce the tiny seats, we made a pattern in brass and used this to produce a number of quickly made moulds in a thermoplastic substance that set like rubber. From these, we were able to extract the pattern, leaving a perfect mould into which we poured Plaster Of Paris mixed with a chemical hardener. The resultant miniature seats were perfect and needed only to be painted - by hand of course. BOAC's Advertising Department were delighted and we soon had orders for a few more. This was modelling that required real artistic ability at which Alf excelled. He possessed a creative talent of the highest degree, but here again, we found ourselves having to virtually give them away in order to procure the orders. We were in fact in a situation that required us to accept what the customer was willing to pay, and although we had a vastly increased turnover, we were still not showing any profit but were working to keep abreast of the overdraft. Alf and I found it necessary to work unusually long hours and, not surprisingly, Rosemary, with two children to care for, was getting upset at my unending absences during the evenings and at weekends. This situation eventually led to words between Alf and myself and I made it quite clear to him that I had no intention of remaining a partner in an unprofitable business that was making such heavy demands in terms of work effort and undesirable domestic effect. I would be much better off in other employment. He pleaded with me not to break away as he felt certain that we could make the business profitable. Whilst remaining sceptical I decided to give it a little more time.

On the domestic scene, the relationship with our tenants was deteriorating. The husband and wife were obviously living separate lives, and the wife was bringing men into the house. There were drunken disturbances and other nocturnal activity of a most undesirable kind. When I spoke to the husband about it, his attitude was unexpectedly belligerent. He, more or less, told me that it was none of my business and, as long as the rent was paid, there was little I could do about it. So the unseemly behaviour of the wife and daughter continued much to our consternation and that of the next-door neighbours who were prominent members of the local Baptist church and had a daughter in her early teens. They were certainly concerned and sympathetic towards us. Rosemary and I discussed the matter with our solicitor who told us at length about the current attitude of the courts in regard to landlord/tenant relations. In the light of the present serious housing situation, the courts tended to be sympathetic towards the tenant and, whilst we were likely to lose the first case, we should nevertheless take the action since it seemed that we had a problem that was likely to persist. It did, and in due course, our first court action was heard. The husband and his estranged wife made the most atrocious but seemingly convincing denials and counter-allegations whilst pretending that their relationship was perfectly normal. They won the day, but our counsel told us that, in his opinion, the real sympathy of the judge was on our side and that in the event of further action, we would succeed. We were advised to keep a careful watch on their behaviour and take note of actual events, and to ensure, where possible, the corroboration of reputable witnesses. Their victory did nothing for us, but seemed to give them certain confidence of their supremacy in a home that they were obliged to share with the resident owner, a situation that they seemed to resent very much. In due course, beside the continuing unsavoury nocturnal behaviour, Rosemary lost her engagement ring and, after lengthy deliberation, concluded that it had been stolen. We informed the local police, who said they could not prosecute without positive evidence of theft but would circulate a description of the ring to all local jewellers and others to whom disposal might have been made. I also had reason to believe that our coal stock, kept in our part of the cellar in a separate - though easily accessible compartment – was being taken when their own allocated storeroom was, as it nearly always was, empty. But how could we prove the theft of coal, a precious commodity that was still on the wartime rationing scale, apart from catching them in the act. Eventually, the wife betrayed herself and gave us the essential evidence of theft. Rosemary thought that a large bed sheet was missing from our linen cupboard and was quite unable to understand how such an item could not be in the cupboard, on our own only double bed or in the laundry basket. To get into the back garden to use our clothes drying line we had to exercise right of access through the downstairs kitchen, which meant passing by the wife's bedroom next door to the kitchen. When passing by late one morning, the bedroom door was wide open and Rosemary saw a corner of her missing sheet hanging from the bed. All our bed linen was marked with our surname and there it was quite unmistakably. Rosemary came to see me at the workshop and together, we went to the nearby police station. They told us that they would send a detective to the house early next morning to catch the culprit in bed under our sheet. This they did and discovered that both the top and bottom sheets bore our name.

This case, prosecuted by the police, was heard in the local Magistrates Court. This time, her husband was not present. She was unable to offer any defence other than her marital situation had reduced her to financial despair and that she would have to throw herself on the mercy of the court. Besides producing the sheets, the police also mentioned our reporting the loss of the engagement ring. She was found guilty of the theft but the court was lenient in giving her only a warning. Her husband came to see me shortly after and I found his attitude somewhat changed. He was apologetic and sympathetic. He had decided to leave the house immediately but would ensure that the rent was paid for the remaining time his wife and daughter were in residence. I left him in no doubt that I had already instructed my solicitors to take action in the county court for eviction. I found myself feeling rather sorry for him as his own life must have been miserable for some time and, as he had mentioned an intention to seek a divorce, would now have a long wait before his marriage would be finally dissolved; divorce was a very lengthy business taking several years at that time. She stubbornly held out to the last until, but in due course, our case was heard.

The husband was the tenant named in the rental agreement and he was the person against whom the case was laid. He made no defence but admitted the whole sad story as it was revealed to the court by our prosecuting counsel. The eviction order was made, and they were given fourteen days to find alternative accommodation. Our counsel said to us after the hearing, "You must have had a dreadful time trying to bring up a young family on your own property during the past two years." He was certainly right. They departed quietly and we were glad to see the last of them as they had made our first real home together an unforgettable experience of the worst kind.

We had made great friends with Mary Mackintosh, a nursing sister at the local (Tooting Bec) hospital. She hailed from the Spey Valley and had known Rosemary's mother from their early training days in Inverness. She was a spinster for whom we had developed a great fondness and she, in turn, was very popular with the boys who knew her as Auntie Mary. We now had space available in the house and reorganised ourselves so that we occupied the greater part of it on the ground and first floors. Mary moved into the top-floor flat. It was a comfortable arrangement that was to work out very well for our remaining time in that house and for Mary until her eventual retirement and return to Scotland.

It was now late 1950 and there was no change in the working side of life. We had found no need to increase the size of the workforce beyond four and it was still necessary for Alf and me to work well into the evenings and at weekends. I saw no betterment of the situation and decided to terminate it. I wrote to the Air Ministry to enquire about the possibility of recall to the Active List. I received an acknowledgement with a promise of further information in due course. I heard nothing more until sometime in February 1951 when I was invited to present myself before a selection board at a date in March. So! If I was to be recalled, it was to be by selection and I realised immediately that I would be required to prove myself as good as, if not better, than other prospective candidates with or without previous service experience. I knew that I would have to be on my mettle, particularly as, at the age of thirty-one, I was dangerously close to the maximum age limit for entry, which was thirty-two.

The appointed day arrived and I found myself in good spirits as I entered the Air Ministry main building - Adastral House to which I was no stranger. I was in good time and shown to a waiting room in which there were already two or three others. By the reporting time stated, which I believe was 1000 hours, the party had grown to about twelve and we were shown what appeared to be a small classroom furnished with typical school desks. Here, we were to take the written part of the selection tests, of which there were several papers of a kind unfamiliar to myself. They were, no doubt, the very latest devices designed for diagnostic and attainment testing. I well remember feeling very keen, and determined. Although the tests were strange, I had no difficulty with them. They were no more than tests of intelligence, mental agility, comprehension and general knowledge. At the end of them I felt that I had completed that part of the selection procedure with success. There then followed several other tests requiring one to sit in isolation in a small cubicle confronted by a panel on which there was an array of knobs and switches. I put on the headphones as directed and waited for the disembodied voice to direct my actions. What followed seemed more appropriate to aircrew aptitude as I was told to look at images projected on a screen outside the cubicle. These tests, many of which were accompanied by flashing and coloured lights and strange noises, were obviously designed to test visual and aural perception. Again, I felt confident that I had passed through this stage with success. We were sent out to find some lunch with instructions to report back by 1400 hours.

There then followed other tests that I cannot now clearly remember and, after a short wait, I was summoned before the Selection Board, whose president was an Air Commodore. They were very interested in my motivation for recall and examined me closely in regard to my current occupation. I didn't miss the chance to tell them the name of my firm and mention that we had a long-standing Air Ministry contract for the production of aircraft display models for the Recruiting Branch. Here was something I knew they could check on if they felt the need to do so. The president seemed to be very interested in modelling, which he said reminded him of his own youth. An interesting dialog followed about the actual manufacturing processes and, when I mentioned that the models for the Recruiting Branch were, in fact, produced in cast aluminium alloy then painted and decorated in actual squadron colours he seemed genuinely fascinated. After a short wait I was directed to another building a short distance away, where I would find the Central Medical Board expecting me. Being sent for a medical board examination was usually a good sign that the preceding tests had been satisfactory. I was accompanied by one of the other candidates and, although both of us were some considerable time in the Central Medical Establishment, we did not see any of the others. I thought nothing of this at the time, being too preoccupied with my own jubilation. The other chap was a direct entry candidate, and we agreed to keep in touch and tell each other of events following our selection board. I did hear from him shortly after telling me that he decided not to proceed with entry anyway and had so advised the Air Ministry.

The waiting period was, for me, a long and agonising one and as the winter turned into spring, I seriously began to fear rejection. However, one fine afternoon, Rosemary, unusually, appeared at the workshop and whispered in my ear, "You are going back." I could hardly wait for the afternoon to pass so that I could get home and read the letter myself; I was quite elated. I was offered recall to a Seven Year Short Service Commission or completion of fifteen years commissioned service reckoning for Retired Pay, whichever was the greater. Whilst this was not a Permanent Commission it was the next best thing as Retired Pay, which was reckoned from the age of twenty-one, was a feature normally applicable only to permanent commissions; other short service commissions earning only a gratuitous payment. Since I had only a little over one year commissioned service to reckon, and I was now thirty-one, I was being offered a package that would place me favourably for selection to a permanent commission whenever the appointment competitions recommenced. So I had been treated very well really. I sent off my letter of acceptance without delay and soon received reporting instructions that also advised me that I was recalled to the higher rank of Flying Officer. I was to report in the first instance to the Air Ministry Adastral House to register certain personal details relating to pay, etc., issue of my identity document, and receive posting instructions.

CHAPTER XXII
RECALL TO ACTIVE LIST

Adastral House seemed very quiet when, dressed in uniform, I checked in at the appointed time and date in May 1951. There was the usual essential documentation for updating my personal records, and I had a very casual session with an officer in the postings section. I indicated my wish to remain as close to home as possible for the time being and was surprised to be offered the choice of Hornchurch in Essex, Biggin Hill in Kent, or Uxbridge in Middlesex. Whilst I would have preferred either of the two flying stations, I opted for Uxbridge as it was served by the London Metropolitan Railway and getting home to Tooting Bec would be easy and, if only in that respect, a good choice for a settling down period. After a small lunch in a quiet nearby pub, I had to return to the Air Ministry to collect my identity card. I also sought out the department dealing with appointments to permanent commissions to enquire about the future possibility and was delighted to discover that the annual competitions were about to recommence and I could apply immediately. I returned home to Rosemary and the boys late that afternoon, quite weary with a thumping headache; it had been a hectic day and I suppose my nervous system had been subjected to an unusual degree of tension. However, the next morning I was fine as I departed from home for a rather long journey by taxi, as I could not have managed my trunk on the underground railway, and arrived at RAF Uxbridge in time for lunch. I was back where I belonged.

RAF Uxbridge was in the Technical Training Command and was one of the oldest stations in the RAF. Also known as the RAF Depot, it was mellowed by time and custom. It always had a diverse role and was, perhaps, more aptly referred to as RAF Bullshit. Before the outbreak of World War Two all adult entrants to aircraftman service received their initial drill and disciplinary training here. It was also the Home Establishment for all personnel serving overseas. It had always been the odd job station of the RAF. The original dormitories in the airmen's barrack blocks had been converted to smaller rooms to provide the accommodation requirements for competitors in the first post-war Olympic Games held in London. It was, therefore, for many years, the only RAF station with this feature that eventually became the norm for all stations. Here also was a recently created unit known as the Recruits Advanced Drill Unit (RADU) soon to become The Queens Colour Squadron of the Royal Air Force. RAF involvement in State Occasions usually involved

Uxbridge, and I was soon to gain personal experience in this field. The station was located in the midst of a typical outer London township, with its main entrance gate on the high street part of the road to London proper. The Officers' Mess was a truly delightful place in which to reside and was the very model of restful rusticity. The entire mess facility was located in the greenest part of the camp with its buildings arranged in a square around an expansive lawn. I had a comfortable room furnished as a bedroom, sitting room and study that certainly became the favourite single officer accommodation of my personal RAF experience

The station was well provided with every recreational and sporting facility including a stadium and fully equipped gymnasium. It did not have a station cinema as there was a good one about four hundred yards from the main gate. I was immediately appointed Officer in charge of the Model Aircraft Club because I had stated this as one of my interests on my arrival form. The Station Commander was Group Captain R J A Ford, an officer of the old school, who I found very likeable. He informed me that I had been posted in a supernumerary capacity as the incumbent Barrack Officer, a civil servant of Higher Executive Officer rank (equivalent to junior officer RAF), had been seriously ill for quite a long time and, although not expected to return to duty, he could not be formally replaced without amendment to the station officer establishment; a move that would be opposed by the Civil Service particularly if taken whilst their officer was still alive and under retirement age. The Senior Equipment Officer (SEO) was Flight Lieutenant John Doherty, and being the only other officer of the Equipment Branch, I was his deputy. I was surprised that a station of this size and complexity had an Equipment Section in charge of an officer of junior rank. I was directly responsible to the SEO for the management of the large Barrack Stores, staffed entirely by local civilians all of whom had long service. The store ran like a well-oiled machine and was kept in immaculate condition under the Barrack Warden (a civilian rank of senior NCO status). As Barrack Officer My responsibility included the provision of furnishings to approved scales for all buildings and married quarters. There were also a large number of married quarters on the immediately adjacent RAF Hillingdon – location of the famous Headquarters No. 11 (Fighter) Group – that had recently been reduced to a care and maintenance basis for which Uxbridge was responsible. There was also an official residence at Hillingdon intended initially for the Air Officer Commanding 11 Group, now reallocated to the Air Ministry and shortly to be occupied by an Air Vice Marshal serving as a Vice Chief of Air Staff. The Station Commander had mentioned this to me as a responsibility of particular concern to him and for my own close attention.

Uxbridge was also home base for the RAF Central Band under its famous Director Wing Commander Paddy O'Donnell, whose deputy was Flight Lieutenant John Wallace, who was to become Director in his own time. There was also the RAF Hospital, Uxbridge, and the RAF Dental Centre. It will be seen, therefore, that Uxbridge was altogether a large undertaking in command and administration and certainly no sinecure for officers of the Equipment Branch. But I was happy to be here and quite at ease with the responsibilities of my appointment. It was to be a busy and interesting initial return to the Service life and I settled into it as though I had long experience of it.

The normal working week still included Saturday mornings, but officers were privileged to wear mufti for work on that day, so it was easy to get away without delay before or after lunch as one desired. It was nice to be able to get home for the weekends, and I really was delightfully content with life. I allowed myself to settle down and to get to know my fellow officers and to become known to them, I did so quite easily and naturally. There was, however, one personal consideration that concerned me as the coming year marked my thirty-second birthday, the deadline for consideration of appointment to a permanent commission. So in the late autumn, I submitted my application for recommendation. The Group Captain was delighted to add his recommendation and forward the application to Higher Authority.

The early winter of 1952 was to bring with it the sadness of the death of King George VI, plunging the station into a period of great activity with hurried preparations for the state funeral and the attendant ceremonial arrangements involving large numbers of RAF personnel for route-lining and the parade proper. Our main concern was the ceremonial equipment for the officers taking part, in particular, the local manufacture by our own station tailor of black armbands of the regulation size and crepe material. Each officer had to have a ceremonial sword and belt and, since these were high-cost, valuable and attractive items, had to be safeguarded by an escort whilst in transit by road from several locations. However, all was accomplished by the deadline, and we were relieved of the intense work and anxiety when the sad state occasion was over. Then, of course, we had the task of making sure all items on loan to the station were cleared to respective sources, ensuring that the swords, in particular, were returned to the sources from which they came. To accomplish this, we had devised a recording system that positively identified each sword with details of its source and the officer to whom it had been issued. We knew, of course, that the near future would bring a longer period of preparation for the coronation of HRH the Princess Elizabeth and we began to make our local preliminary planning for that occasion, which we were advised would not take place until the spring.

About this time, some faceless wonder at the Air Ministry decided that I should attend a long course of instruction in all aspects of storage and handling of Explosives, Fuels and Gases, a specialisation that I had no wish to add to my qualifications. The storage depots at which this particular specialisation was likely to be practised were, to say the least, miserable places. However, the Station Commander, learning of this, sent for me and indicated his concern at losing my services after such a short time. I assured him that I had no personal preference for the course and would be delighted to stay at Uxbridge. I was pleased when the posting notice was cancelled. John Doherty was posted and relieved by Flight Lieutenant John Freeman, with whom I formed a lasting friendship that was to continue throughout our service and in retirement until John's untimely death in the late nineteen nineties. Unfortunately he was not to remain at Uxbridge for more than a few weeks and was relieved by the first incumbent of a newly created post for a Squadron Leader in the SEO slot of the station establishment. Squadron Leader Eric Sankey was appointed as SEO and here I found an excellent immediate superior and another firm friend

A serious political situation arose in the early part of 1952 in the Aden Protectorate, if memory serves me right. This was serious enough for the Government to order the call-up of a special section of the RAF Reserve and I was attached temporarily to RAF Cardington, also a Technical Training Command station located near Bedford, to help with the tropical kitting-out arrangements. Cardington, famous for its role throughout the Lighter than Air phase of RAF history, was also still the home of the RAF Gas Factory, and also an initial Reception Depot with all that was essential to handle this kind of emergency. On arrival my immediate reaction was of being rather surplus to the requirement. However, the call-up was delayed and we had an early visit by a wing commander, Campbell, from the Command Headquarters Equipment Staff. Walking with him to the officers' mess, he said to me, "Your presence here seems to be rather a waste. What do you think?" I told him that I had done absolutely nothing since my arrival a few days ago and thought that the organisation of the station Equipment Section was quite adequate to deal with the issue of tropical kit to the reservists should the occasion arise. After lunch, the wing commander, in my presence, asked the station SEO, Squadron Leader Pashley, if I could be released. Pashley immediately agreed and said he had not personally made any request for additional help and assumed that my movement had been the result of an Air Ministry initiative executed through the Personnel Staff at Command HQ. The Wing Commander said that he would look into the matter as he felt my services would be of greater value back at Uxbridge in the developing situation relative to the forthcoming coronation. Sure enough, the very next morning, I was cleared by Air Ministry signal to return to Uxbridge that day. Eric Sankey was certainly glad to see me.

A few days later, I was summoned to appear before the Permanent Commission Selection Board to be held at HQ 22 Group. I was one of a very small number of candidates and was delighted when, after the initial rather gruelling experience of the board, I was instructed to wait for an interview by the Air Officer Commanding. This I assumed to be in my favour and found it a most pleasant, friendly end to a rather harrowing day that I knew had come to a successful conclusion. But I was to wait quite a while before hearing anything further.

Preparations for the Coronation were well advanced by the early spring of 1952 when, unexpectedly, the Civil Service incumbent Barrack Officer returned to duty, and I was immediately declared surplus to the establishment. Posting instructions followed quickly, and I was delighted to find that I was to be retained within the Command and posted internally to the Command Headquarters Unit, located at Brampton near Huntingdon, as Unit Equipment Officer. I felt most gratified at my selection as it was a good appointment for me at this stage of my career as I would be prominent to the Command Staff. I recognised the probable influence of that same wing commander who got me released from Cardington. Command Headquarters Units were responsible for the provision of Administration and Services to the Command Headquarters and its Staff, and I recognised the excellent opportunity it provided for me to show my personal qualities and specialist abilities.

The officer I was to relieve was about to depart for service overseas in the Middle East Air Force, and the time allocated for my take-over from him was adequate for the normal regulatory inspection to be carried out. My predecessor obviously enjoyed wide popularity. He was a Scot with a very English accent that, to my own northern ears, was unusual, sounding more acquired than genuine. Accepting responsibility for an Equipment Section requires the incoming officer to provide a certificate of discharge to the outgoing officer. The Regulations, allowing for the fact that a complete inspection is usually impossible, require only that the discharge should be provisional until such time as the officer taking over has been able to progressively complete a full inspection and stocktaking. During the obligatory basic checks I found nothing in the way of serious discrepancy, but I did note certain areas that would require my further early action for complete peace of mind. As there was no establishment for a Mechanical Transport Officer, I was automatically responsible for that undertaking that had most important overtones at a Command Headquarters where there was many staff cars, including, of course, that specifically provided for the Air Officer Commanding-in-Chief. My inspection here was, therefore, most thorough. I was impressed with the sergeant in charge of the MT Section and the drivers themselves, who, as one would expect, had been specially selected for prestigious

172

driving duties with officers on staff appointments. I found no reason that would prohibit my provisional acceptance of responsibility, but I had a rather uncomfortable feeling about the equipment set-up.

Having made myself known to the Command Equipment Staff under the Senior Equipment Staff Officer (SESO) Group Captain P J (Percy) Mote and his Wing Commanders George Hine and Jock Campbell (the one responsible for my rescue from Cardington), also the junior Equipment Staff Officers. I soon found myself left to my own devices. The Equipment Section was poorly housed in interconnected Nissen huts, but this was a normal consequence of the immediate post-war era.

The most important element, in my estimation, was the barrack stores that had to provide for a large complement of married quarters occupied by a good many senior staff officers. There was also a large measure of responsibility for the three official residences of the C-in-C, SASO and AOA. So, my initial attack was on the barrack store in the form of a complete stocktaking. The stock of blankets occupied a large amount of shelf space, and I noticed that the Barrack Warden seemed rather uneasy when I indicated my intention to do a full check. I had already assessed him as probably conscientious and reliable and. I found my provisional judgement of him quite justified when he immediately said to me, "You will find a considerable deficiency, Sir." Sure enough, there was, and it was of such financial value that it could not be written off under local power of write-off. I instructed the Barrack Warden not to say anything about it for the time being, particularly as he was directly implicated. We were dealing with a commodity for which there was a ready and profitable market in the local civil communities. I completed the stock check of the barrack stores and prepared the documentation relative to the blanket deficiency for presentation to the Unit CO, a Squadron Leader with whom I was not immediately impressed. At my initial meeting with him, he lost no time in telling me of the high regard he had for my predecessor, who had been a great tower of strength to him and hoped that I would be capable of matching him. I had already thought him to be somewhat out of place in his appointment, seemingly uneasy and inclined to obsequiousness. He was obviously disturbed with my discovery which he knew was of such enormity as could lead to a formal enquiry. He told me to leave it with him for the time being.

He came to see me the next day and revealed his true self to me. He was obviously concerned for himself and suggested that his career was at stake and my own also. I assured him that the only way the matter could be corrected locally was by recovering the missing blankets to the stock. There had been no falsification of the stock records to hide the deficiency and I was certainly not going to compound the matter by creating false documentation myself. I advised him to follow the correct procedure and forward the matter to Command for their action. They would probably convene a formal Board of Inquiry if they thought it likely to be fruitful, but more likely, a simple investigation would suffice. He took my advice, but he was clearly in a high state of mental turmoil. Sure enough I soon received a telephone call from Wing Commander Hine to say he was coming to see me. He duly arrived and after a short discussion we had a lengthy talk with the Barrack Warden and his storemen. We were left in no doubt that they were well aware of the increasing deficiency that was due to the previous Equipment Officer removing blankets without any covering documentation. They did not know what he had done with them. Our obvious conclusion was that by way of self gratification, he had given them to whoever asked for them with the intention of subsequently disposing of them by reducing them to produce – in this case, cleaning rags – which he had not got to the length of doing. The wing commander decided that there was no need for further investigation and that the matter should be concluded by write-off action. I took the opportunity to mention that I was rather unhappy about another matter that I thought needed the attention of the Higher Authority. I had examined the report of the last Command Staff Inspection and, as we were overdue for another, suggested that it would perhaps be a good time to implement this. He agreed and told me that he would probably come to do it himself. The Unit Commander was greatly relieved when I told him about the decision in regard to the blankets and I found him quite disabused about being deceived by my predecessor. He admitted this voluntarily and with great bitterness, but he did not know what was yet to come and I did nothing to forecast the likely outcome of the forthcoming Command Staff Inspection.

Formal notice of the inspection came and I did nothing in the way of preparation for it, having already decided that it should reflect the unsatisfactory state of affairs revealed by own inspection. My predecessor had clearly gone to unusual lengths to seek popularity and had been taken advantage of, whilst the results of slack management were to be found among the staff and the work of each department. I would have the task of clearing it up and I was by now determined that those in higher places should know the full extent of what lay before me. I was certainly not going to take any of the blame. He had been too dependent on the Warrant Officer with whom I was not impressed and would, in due course, have to put in his proper place. The Sergeant in charge of the cell responsible for the maintenance of the equipment accounting records was also due for a rude awakening. For the entirely civilian barrack stores staff, I had the greatest sympathy, but the uniformed personnel certainly needed smartening up. The overall standard of efficiency was well below that which I expected and there would have to be significant changes to avoid eventual adverse reflection on myself. A serious view was taken of misappropriation of

Service equipment that was, after all, the property of the Public for which the Equipment Branch had a specialist responsibility.

George Hine, with one of the junior Equipment Staff Officers, duly came to carry out the Command Staff Inspection. I had taken time to study the report of the last Air Ministry Audit and, although there was nothing recorded that pointed to serious failing, it fell short of being praiseworthy. I left them to get on with their inspection in the prescribed manner and it was not long before my attention was being drawn to those areas of particular concern to myself. The accounting records were seriously behind the normally accepted processing time, a suggestion of failure to expedite the return of completed transaction vouchers from inventory holders for final accounting action and lodgement. There were discrepancies in all the storage areas that were obviously due to the failure of stores personnel to keep abreast of the normal daily transactions – management failure in supervision at all levels. At that time, great emphasis was placed on the need for the salvage and timely disposal of saleable waste, some of which could be quite valuable representing considerable cash recovery to Public funds. Among these, the most troublesome category was waste paper, of which there was a tremendous accumulation. It was stored in a brick building located on the edge of an inactive quarry quite close to the station sewage farm. It was infested by a large colony of rats. This was the area of particular concern that I had mentioned to George Hine at the time of the missing blanket incident, although I had not disclosed the actual nature of my concern. He saw immediately the appalling and serious nature of the problem. The location was clearly inappropriate for the storage of waste paper, which was attractive to rats in that particular location. It had obviously been a long-standing matter requiring urgent action. George immediately went to see the Unit CO. This was something that the CO himself should have observed during his own routine station inspections. The Station Medical Officer was summoned together with the Clerk of Works and there was an on-site conference of all concerned. George authorised the immediate destruction by burning the entire stock of waste paper, and no more was to be accumulated until adequate storage facilities could be provided. The Unit CO was clearly worried, and this was reflected in his quite livid face. His misplaced trust in my predecessor was now firmly established and he was concerned for himself at a time close to his retirement from The Active List. I really felt sorry for him, but he had been too trusting and had been let down by him in whom his trust had been so sadly misplaced. On receiving the inspection report I went to see him to discuss the points needing action, but more to highlight the work required to recover the section to the required level of efficiency. The rat infestation had been put in hand immediately by the Medical Officer and the Clerk OF Works, and I had taken the necessary action to dispose of the undue accumulation of waste paper, which in itself was a difficult task during which I exercised a great deal of personal interest to ensure that the burning was properly controlled. The site was only just outside the boundary of the station proper and located, with the sewage farm, in the prevailing upwind direction, so there was little danger of causing offence to station personnel and there were no civilian properties close to the site on the downwind site. It took several days to complete the job. But as the storage area was the direct responsibility of the Equipment Officer he should have pursued the matter with the MO because of the serious danger to health. Noting again the depth of the CO's anguish, I was able only to comfort him by mentioning the certainty that officers of this type were usually detected at an early stage by the system and adversely reported upon in their periodic confidential reports when they would be formally warned and informed of the likely adverse effect on their careers. Little did I realise that I was to hear of this officer again before long.

Armed with the inspection report, I was now able to make my own dissatisfaction known to the warrant officer, who was, after all, the next in line below myself and to whom I had to delegate a degree of authority in the daily running of the section. He was inclined to the attitude that I should leave it entirely to him. But I quickly told him that the ultimate responsibility was mine and I would ensure that my responsibility was not denigrated by any of my subordinates of whatever rank. I made it quite plain that I was not satisfied with the inefficiency of the section, which itself was a measure of his unsatisfactory effort. He was clearly taken aback by my admonition that he seemed to think unjustified until I pointed out that he had quite obviously failed to discharge the trust placed in him by my predecessor. At that stage, he went off with his tail between his legs. He was nearing the end of his twenty-four years of service, and I judged him to be a rather lethargic individual and below the expected standard at that rank level. I immediately summoned the sergeant in charge of the Provisioning and Accounting cell and meted out the same treatment to him emphasising the importance of carefully monitoring the transaction registers to ensure that vouchers were processed through the stock records and inventories without delay. Meanwhile, I wanted urgent action to bring all the accounting records right up to date as the Air Ministry Annual Audit was due in August, only six to eight weeks away. I would be making frequent detailed random checks to ensure this was being done effectively. During the next few days, there was noticeable sullenness at supervisory levels but this soon cleared as the beneficial effect became apparent. They thought that I would pounce immediately on the incomplete entries in the voucher registers, whereas I decided to concentrate on completing my progressive check of stocks in the Technical, Clothing, and Barrack Groups. I then turned my full attention to the Equipment Provisioning and Accounting Section and gave them a bit of hell for their damned stupid approach to their problems. Instead of concentrating on the timely clearance of the more recent vouchers, they wasted much time and energy chasing the long overdue vouchers, thereby making little difference to the situation overall. However, a few days spent showing them how best to tackle the problem soon brought a better state of affairs although it was necessary finally to create certified true copies of vouchers that had apparently gone astray, most likely whilst in the custody of inventory holders.

However, I had other important things to consider. I had to get down to some serious study to prepare myself for the promotion examination for my next rank – Flight Lieutenant. This was a very stiff examination in five subjects. There were two Specialist Papers covering the whole very extensive spectrum of Equipment Branch work; there were also papers in Air Force Law, Administration and Organisation, also General Service Knowledge, the latter embracing the Army and Navy. This examination was intentionally the most difficult for all officers as the rank of flight lieutenant was the first gateway to the wider fields of responsibility in the senior rank part of the command structure. Preparation was mostly a personal matter, taking an estimated twelve months of intensive part-time study. It was unusual for officers to gain a full pass on their first attempt, but this was recognised by making it possible to obtain a partial pass in three subjects, provided a minimum overall percentage was attained in all five. The advice was to go for the partial pass, initially leaving two subjects to be taken again, usually Air Force Law and General Service Knowledge. I would have to commence study soon as I would be due for promotion in August 1944 on completion of four and a half years of commissioned service. Normally the time qualification was six years, but in my own case, because of my previous senior NCO service, I had the advantage of an eighteen-month time reduction. So, having obtained the necessary books from the education section where, I had a good friend in Norman Walder, the Education Officer. I enrolled for the examination due in the spring of 1953 and had the coming winter to prepare myself.

Sometime during July 1952, I was called to attend an award ceremony at the Command Headquarters where the Senior Officer in charge of Administration presented me with Her Majesty the Queen's Coronation Medal and certificate for my work at Uxbridge in connection with the preparations for the Coronation.

The weight of the corrective work necessary to bring the Equipment Section to the required standard and my responsibility for ensuring it was done did worry me somewhat, and I had quite a few sleepless nights. The appointment itself was a tough assignment for an officer of such junior rank, particularly in view of the many high-ranking officers one had to deal with. Because of the rank difference, it was very easy to depart from the regulatory limits when dealing with some of their requests and I found it a severe test of diplomacy when I had to point out that what they were asking was likely to have unhappy consequences for them and me. Generally, however, I found that the higher they were, the most understanding they were. I got on very well with most, and I obviously had the comforting support of Group Captain Percy Mote, the SESO who was also President of the Mess Committee (PMC) and had asked me to take over the running of the mess library, a task that kept me busy for half of the daily lunch break.

August 1952 brought the expected team of Air Ministry Auditors for the usual Monday to Friday working week. During my initial meeting with them I told them of the situation that had been revealed by my take-over checks and of the action taken to correct the shortcomings in the accounting registers and, of course, the serious deficiency in the blanket stock. All things they would have been able to see for themselves when examining the records. It was a good audit from my point of view, as my forthright initial talk led to a very searching check of all transactions during the audit period. The final outcome was a clear audit without observations other than praiseworthy comment for me. When I took them along finally to see the Camp Commandant, he was visibly relieved at the outcome and added his own comments about my predecessor and of the confidence that he had foolishly placed in him. The Command Equipment Officer was delighted, and I knew that I had gained a good friend in him. It would have been foolish to have done other than reveal the true state of affairs uncovered and to vindicate myself of any suggestion that the action taken was not done deliberately to ingratiate myself at the expense of my predecessor.

The prospect on the work scene was now brighter and the somewhat abashed warrant officer and senior NCO in charge of the accounting department were obviously now in no doubt that in me, they had an Equipment Officer who expected nothing but the very best from his subordinates and depended on them only for the professional support that was I obliged to give them and in return expect from them. Their changed attitude was obvious and a different working atmosphere was soon apparent.

I was recruited into a small but very active Scottish Country Dance Group that provided, for me at least, a very interesting activity within the mess society. There was a very accomplished local teacher, accredited by the Royal Scottish Country Dance Society, who ran a course of instruction for the Huntingdon Education Authority during the winter months and a few of us enrolled for her classes during the coming 1952/53 winter season. We made good progress and soon became so proficient that we were chosen to form a demonstration team of eight to perform before audiences at several venues throughout the county. We also received invitations to take part in the London meetings and competitions of the Society. I also became a member of the Huntingdon Caledonian Society comprised mostly of expatriate Scots farmers. I had good RAF friends in the Scottish Country Dance Group and a social activity that provided a very interesting diversion from my studies that occupied most of my winter evenings. Among these companions was Group Captain Jimmy Bruce, who hailed from Garve. Flying Officer Jimmy Caird from Perth, and the only two lady members, Mary Allan from Edinburgh, who was a civilian member of the Command Education Staff and Netta wife of Flying Officer Bunny Burness one of the Unit Administrative Staff.

I applied myself with determination to my planned course of study in preparation for the 1953 promotion exams and actually did a number of past examination papers supplied by Norman Walder so that I felt quite confident as the winter moved into spring and the examination date became the constant thought. The examinations for officers of the Technical Training Command were held at Halton. They called for a great deal of writing and were crammed into one very long day of concentrated mental effort. On completion of one paper, or the time allocated for it, it was essential to switch one's thinking exclusively to the subject of the next paper. In due course, the results were published, and I was pleasantly surprised and delighted to learn that I had a partial pass in four subjects, leaving me only with the General Service Knowledge subject, on which I had intentionally not devoted much effort, to retake at the next examinations in September 1953

I was allocated a married quarter, albeit of a sub-standard type, at the inactive station of Alconbury that had been vacated by the American Air Force and was on a care and maintenance basis, being the responsibility of RAF Brampton. There were no standard married quarters at this location where to ease the situation in regard to married quarters generally, the large bedded station sick quarters had been converted. The sick quarters consisted of a large Nissen building that had been converted into two MQs, of which I was allocated the larger. There were also two separate Nissen huts that provided another two MQs. Two caravans, the private property of two officers, were also parked on a convenient concrete area. One of these was the property of Squadron Leader Charles Harradence, a very popular officer who had a most attractive little daughter who they called Popsie. He and his wife became good friends. It was a small community consisting of a wing commander, two squadron leaders, a flight lieutenant, and myself, the most junior in the rank of flying officer. Good relations existed between all except one of the squadron leaders who was of the type that seemed unable to dwell at peace with anyone. No one liked him and he liked no one either. He was equally unpopular as a member of the Command Headquarters staff. However, he seemed determined to make my own family a particular target and this was seen as a rather obvious attempt to take unfair advantage of rank. But Rosemary left him in no doubt that although he was much more senior in rank to her husband, he had no rank advantage over her and she would not hesitate to report any unseemly behaviour in that respect. The other members of our little community applauded her action and I took the opportunity of mentioning the matter to the Camp Commandant, who assured me that he was well-known for his unfriendly behaviour. He had refused the offer of a standard MQ on the station, much to the relief of those who knew him and regarded him as a pariah to be cast out.

Shortly after moving into the Alconbury MQ, I received formal notification of my appointment to a Permanent Commission – a commission for life that is – which meant that I was guaranteed Active List Service to the lower retirement age of forty-nine, which applied to all officers of the specialist branches up to the rank of squadron leader. Things were looking up for me and I thought myself fortunate to have done so well in the two years since my recall. The letter notifying me of my appointment to a PC did mention that although I was over the age limit of thirty-two and my medical category was below that normally required, the Air Force Board had, nevertheless, decided to make the appointment. This was a good sign on two counts; firstly they had waived the age restriction in my favour (although I had been recommended before reaching the age of thirty-two), and secondly, the acceptance of my lowered medical category; whatever the cause of this it must have been attributed to Service and unlikely to affect my employment standard, or I would have been rejected. My medical documents recorded the same category that I had on initial appointment to a commission in 1947 and the Medical Officer could only enlighten me with the suggestion that something in my records, probably the serious nature of the bacillary dysentery attack in 1944, would have attracted attention. But not to give it further thought as my category was Fit Grade 1, and I was, therefore, liable to serve anywhere in the world.

With our occupation of the married quarter at Alconbury, we decided to rent out the property at Tooting Bec. There were many eager applicants and we had no difficulty in selecting a family without young children who apparently seemed maturely responsible and of good character and recommended by our estate agents. Their name was Henderson and the husband was of Scottish origin. The rent would be a welcome addition to my service income, which was less than junior officers of my rank really needed to comfortably meet the cost of living in the RAF community at that time. So, by the onset of the 1952 winter I was comfortably settled into a sub-standard married quarter with my Service and domestic situations in seemingly good order. The boys were happy with their local school, and our life generally had taken on an altogether different and pleasant prospect.

Our married quarter was the one that had the boiler house needed to ensure a constant supply of hot water to our small domestic complex, and we had to ensure that it was kept stoked with the solid fuel (coke) supplied from RAF socks. It was not a great responsibility, but a degree of care was necessary to safeguard against overheating that caused most

180

disturbing noisy vibrations, usually when all were taking their nocturnal slumbers. The furnace was located in its own room slightly below ground level and accessible only from outside and it was most unpleasant to have to go outdoors to attend to it in the dead of night, particularly in inclement weather. There was no shortage of domestic hot water, and we well remember one very amusing occasion when Mother-in-law came to stay with us for a while during the winter months. One very cold Saturday afternoon, she decided to take a bath; we had two of them in our extensive quarters. The water was very hot and produced a great deal of steam that lingered densely in the cold, confined space of the bathroom. After drying herself she reached for what she thought was her canister of talcum powder that she applied liberally to herself and then, much to her consternation, discovered that the canister she had used contained Ajax scouring powder. So she had to fill the bath again and take another dunking to remove the cause of her quickly developing discomfort.

Solid fuel stoves, except for the large lounge that had a large fireplace, heated the spacious rooms. We were quite comfortable but the stoves had to be kept going overnight to ensure a reasonable degree of warmth during the winter months as there was little insulation in the thin corrugation iron sheeting from which the Nissen buildings were constructed, although they were lined with panels of plasterboard that had no more than decorative value. So the winter passed quietly enough, although the snow was bothersome when it came and required a great deal of effort to clear from the unusually large areas, giving access to the individual quarters. The summer of 1953 was pleasant in our rural surroundings. Huntingdon and Cambridge were quite accessible and very nice places to visit at the weekends. We were happy with our situation; but things were not all that they should have been at our house in Tooting Bec. The Hendersons were falling into serious arrears with their rental payments, and I had to draw their attention to it. They made the usual excuses and promises until we received a telephone call from Mary Mackintosh suggesting that we had better come down as she had reason to suspect that our direct attention was necessary. So, as we had Mother-in-Law still in residence, we left the boys in her capable care and took a long weekend off to visit the scene and see for ourselves. Turning the corner into Louisville Road, we met Mary, who told us that she thought the Henderson's had done a moonlight flit. Sure enough, they weren't there. The premises were obviously vacated and in clean condition. They had left their television set that I immediately assumed was some sort of recompense for the considerable arrears of rent. But, we were not long there when the doorbell was rung by a man from a local TV hire firm who had called to collect the TV set. We reported the incident to the police who said they would go through the usual procedure for this type of thing but not to expect any positive result. We decided not to let the property again as I had already been warned that my next appointment would be overseas and, although seriously out of pocket as the direct result of this unfortunate experience, Rosemary would have to vacate our married quarter within the standard period of grace following my departure to wherever my overseas appointment was to be.

The Air Ministry Annual Audit came around once more and I was surprised to find the audit team the same as that of the previous year. Once again, the audit was clear. By this time, the Camp Commandant had been retired and replaced by a totally different successor, Sqn Ldr Graeme, who was ideally suited to the job. By August, Gp Capt Percy Mote was posted to HQMEAF on appointment as Command Movements Officer and was replaced at HQTTC by Gp Capt Tommy Head. Wg Cdr George Hine was also posted to HQMEAF on appointment to the HQ Equipment Staff. Before his departure, Percy Mote casually expressed the hope that I might join him at HQMEAF.

I didn't have long to wait for quite early in October, I was notified of posting to the Middle East Air Force for Movements Duties. My posting date was 3rd November 1953, and I was to proceed by civil air charter from Blackbushe as Officer in Charge, for the duration of the flight, of a contingent of airmen proceeding to the Canal Zone of Egypt.

CHAPTER XXIII
MIDDLE EAST COMMAND

My departure date arrived all too quickly and after completing the hand-over formalities with my successor, I left Rosemary and the boys in the married quarter at Alconbury. Mother-in-Law was still with them and would accompany them back to Tooting Bec when it was convenient to them within the three-month period of grace. I knew that they would be well taken care of and would want for nothing. I travelled to London by rail on 2nd November and reported, as directed, to the Assembly Centre at RAF Hendon, formerly Services Air Booking Centre London, and was pleased to find there two of the civilian staff that I had previously served with at SABC. I was off by coach to Blackbushe with the planeload of airmen early next morning, where I met the aircraft captain and his crew, who were pleased to welcome me, especially when I removed my greatcoat, and they saw that I was wearing a flying badge. We had a pleasant flight and arrived at RAF Fayid in the Canal Zone at dusk. After handing over the contingent to the Air Movements Authority, I was taken by road to the RAF Transit Camp at El Hamra, where my sleeping quarters were to be in the officers' section of the well-appointed tented area. Each tent, of adequate size, was pitched over its own short-walled area with a concrete floor a step below the level of the surrounding sand. The furnishing was to the usual single-officer standard, and the tented area was adjacent to the Officers' Mess proper. It was all quite civilised.

The next morning, I was taken to Headquarters Middle East Air Force located at RAF Abu Sueir, about half an hour's journey north. Here, I was warmly welcomed by Group Captain Percy Mote, the Command Movements Officer, and was pleased to meet again John Reddington, last seen at SABC London in 1948. He was now a Squadron Leader and was to be my immediate superior. Flight Lieutenant Colin Bettel and I were to be responsible for the movement by air and sea of all RAF and Civilian personnel and their families. Middle East Air Force was the largest overseas command of the RAF. Its area of responsibility was vast, taking in North Africa and the Eastern Mediterranean, Cyprus and the Levant including Iraq, The Aden Protectorate, South Arabia and the Persian Gulf, and East Africa as far south as Rhodesia's (now Zambia and Zimbabwe). Egypt was in a state of political turmoil following the deposition of the young playboy, King Fuad. Under the self-appointed president Gamal Abdul Nasser, there was a determination to rid Egypt of foreign influences, particularly the protectoral British, which, together with the French, held the principal interest in the Suez Canal that was Egypt's greatest single asset and, as the sea link between the Mediterranean and the Indian Ocean, was still of vital strategic importance to ourselves.

Whilst there was no armed insurrection, there was widespread civil disobedience, and it had become necessary to safeguard military installations by the erection of protective fences and to mount armed guards at night. Military personnel and their families were confined to their respective locations except for essential duty or travel. It was strictly forbidden to proceed outside the protected areas on foot and, when travelling on duty by military transport, were to do so only if accompanied by an escorting vehicle carrying at least one armed person besides the driver, who was also to be armed.

It was a difficult situation with attendant problems in the provision of adequate social activities, particularly for single and unaccompanied personnel. At Abu Sueir, we were fortunate to have a large station with an active airfield and the presence of the Administrative part of the Command Headquarters (the Operational part was at RAF Ismailia, which was also a large station with an active airfield adjoining the Army Depot at Moascar). Stations, therefore, had their own cinemas with frequent changes of top-rated films, club facilities, and sporting and other activities catering to every possible taste. There was no presence of Women's Royal Air Force personnel except for the occasional officer specially employed against the station establishment and UK Based civilians employed as schoolteachers. The married quarters were fully occupied, but it was, of course, not permitted to live off the station, and there was, therefore, a particularly difficult situation for married personnel who far outnumbered the married quarters available. A Command Headquarters always produced a majority of senior officers who, because of the points scoring system used for allocation, occupied most of the quarters. Not that the points scoring was anything but fair for everyone, but officers of the junior ranks were simply vastly outnumbered. Permitting officers to take their families privately into Cyprus overcame the problem to some extent. However, this, although an expensive option, was embraced by many junior officers as the only alternative to a lengthy separation from their families. Cyprus was not easily accessible as there were no civil air flights out of the Canal Zone, which was a Militarised Zone into which all British Armed Service elements had been withdrawn. The Service, therefore, had to make provision for its own needs. To this end, a weekly flight had been instituted utilising a Vickers Valetta aircraft of the ME Air Transport Force operating out of RAF Fayid at midday Friday and returning Sunday evening. It was ostensibly a training flight with the aircraft flying time recorded against the permitted training hours, but it was popularly known as The Passion Flight. The seats on these flights, as on all flights out of the Zone, were under the control of my own HQ

Departmental Staff, so I had to exercise scrupulous fairness in regard to my personal needs. Generally, I entrusted the allocation task to a junior NCO and ensured by frequent checks that the system was operated fairly for all and that a record was kept of all users to ensure that preference was not being given to particular individuals. The availability of seats were usually sufficient to permit officers with families in Cyprus to visit them every other weekend, which was generally regarded as fair in the difficult circumstances.

There was a model Aircraft Cub that needed an officer-in-charge and I got that job without asking. I soon had a model built of suitable size to take a small engine of the compression/ignition type that I had brought with me. Model flying was great on the wide expanse of the airfield, the surfaces of the runways being of hard packed gritty sand. The winter weather was ideal except for the occasional rainy day that was usually accompanied by wind. I also formed a Scottish Country Dance Group and was most fortunate to find an excellent pianist among the civilians of the Air Ministry Education Branch. I was quite amazed at his ability to play with absolute accuracy any piece of music that I placed before him. It was truly remarkable, and we were able to enjoy our dancing to the traditional tunes appropriate to each dance. Our weekly meetings, restricted to the winter months, of course, were most enjoyable.

Rosemary returned to our house in Tooting Bec in early 1944 and, on my instructions, put the sale of the house in the hands of the estate agents. She also contacted one of several shipping companies operating small merchant craft on routes through the Mediterranean on which there was limited passenger accommodation. She did not wish to fly, so I left it to her to make the necessary arrangements. Unfortunately, she was unable to obtain any positive indication of when the allocation of berths would be possible. There was no problem in obtaining suitable accommodation in Nicosia, so I let the matter ride until late March, by which time I had become impatient with the delay, as I had meanwhile received the offer of an excellent quite new bungalow ideally located among other families of officers known to me. It was too good to miss, and as it would become available early in April, I took a trip on the Passion Flight to check the offered bungalow that I found to be just the thing; no wife could have wished for anything better. So I told Rosemary to cancel her sea passage bid and take a regularly scheduled flight by British European Airways from London to Nicosia. This she reluctantly did, as it was her first air experience. As the day of her arrival was midweek, I got myself to Cyprus the day before by taking passage on a small vessel that was chartered by the RAF, under the control of the Command Movements Staff, to provide a regular freight service between Port Said, where we had an Embarkation Unit and Famugusta. There was very limited low-grade accommodation on board, but it was the only certain way to get to Cyprus midweek. It was evening when Rosemary and the boys landed at Nicosia, and we went directly to the small but well-appointed Averof hotel where the Cypriot owner, Freddie Photiades and his British wife Bobbie, had a preference for RAF officer guests and where I had stayed during my previous visit on the recommendation of fellow staff officers.

The April weather was perfect for new arrivals, and after breakfast the next morning, we took a taxi to our bungalow home located in the predominantly Turkish sector on quiet Tabac Dervish Street, a short walk behind the Ledra Hotel. The bungalow looked delightful with its red tiled roof and veranda around the front door accessed by a short flight of steps. It was cool and spacious and needed only the addition of a few items of furnishing that could easily be hired at reasonable rates; I had been warned that this was a usual necessity for anyone occupying rented accommodation in Cyprus. So this was our first task that was accomplished without difficulty. The electricity supply and telephone had to be transferred to our name, an account for Rosemary at the Nicosia Branch of Barclays Bank, and some other things to ensure the basic necessities. The British Military School, located nearby, accepted the boys, who soon made friends with other British children living in the vicinity. Altogether, it was an ideal location, and we moved into our new home after only four nights in the hotel. The officer's wives from adjacent properties were soon calling to make us welcome. I was, of course, well known to many of the officers who had reason to contact my department for their places on the Passion Flight. Too soon came the end of my two weeks, and I felt quite upset and anxious at having to leave Rosemary, but I did so with the assurance of help from the friendly neighbors, and that I would be back in two weeks' time.

Although a Command Movements Staff was functionally different from its related Command Equipment Staff, being of the same Specialist Branch, they were usually co-located. The Command Equipment Staff at HQMEAF Abu Sueir was in the same building. One day Wing Commander George Hine – previously known at HQTTC Brampton – came into my office to show me something that would be of interest to me. A team of his officers had recently carried out an annual staff inspection at one of the three staging post stations along the South Arabian coast leading to the Persian Gulf. At one of these was a large ration dump in the charge of the officer I had relieved at Brampton. They had discovered the same neglectful situation that I had to deal with at Brampton. Huge quantities of packed ration commodities had to be written off simply because they had not been issued progressively but left to become time-expired and, in many cases, with cans blown open at the seams and in an advanced stage of stinking putrefaction. The report hinted that the officer in charge seemed to be spending much of his time at the local desert races, a well-known pastime of the so-called Desert Princes. George, adding his comments to the report that had to be forwarded to the Air Ministry, said that he had knowledge of this officer in his previous appointment where similar neglect had resulted in considerable loss of Public Funds. Of course, I don't know what action was taken against him there and then. But I do know that the officer concerned was retired at the lower age limit and was not advanced beyond junior rank. It was justly so, and he was, perhaps fortunate, not to have been dealt with more rigorously by disciplinary rather than the administrative action which seems to have been the form taken. There had for some time been talk of relocating the Command Headquarters in Cyprus as part of the plan to return Egypt and its troublesome Canal Zone to the Egyptians. In fact the move of selected elements, mostly from Ismailia, had already started into hurriedly built temporary working accommodation at RAF Nicosia. This was to be a provisional arrangement until a new permanent headquarters could be built at Akrotiri, which would take a few years. The transfer of the administrative staff would take some considerable time to quit Abu Sueir completely, and the Command Movements Staff would be required to remain in-situ until all elements had been moved from the Canal Zone and would, therefore, be the last to leave. Being already in a suitable residence in Nicosia might have made my action seem unnecessary, but my own thinking was based on the desirability of getting my family out of a situation rather than a location. The matter of the future location of the Headquarters was not mentioned during my request for posting, more than likely because of uncertainty and the envisaged problems that would arise over a lengthy period of time in providing the essential temporary working accommodation at Nicosia and sufficient official quarters for married personnel. There was likely to be considerable inconvenience, in both working and social aspects, for a long time.

Air Ministry approval for my posting came early in November, with the 1st of December indicated as the official date of my take-over at RAF Idris in Libya's province of Tripolitania. I went across to Cyprus that weekend to break the news to Rosemary, who received it quietly. I did not enlighten her about my action in arranging the posting. I had already made the necessary arrangements for her travel from Cyprus to Egypt using the scheduled Medair service operated by Eagle Airways under an Air Ministry contract but under the local control of my own department. This would allow a few days at Abu Sueir during which friends had kindly offered to accommodate us in their married quarter. The Medair service had a scheduled flight out of Fayid that would take us to Idris on 1st December. There were things to do in Cyprus, however, particularly in regard to the house, and I managed to arrange most of these so that she was virtually free just to walk out of the place on the appointed date. I met the aircraft at Fayid in the dark of evening the boys being quite intrigued to see their father wearing a revolver at his hip and excitedly calling for me to let them have a look at it. I had a staff car waiting and they were even more excited at the site of the Sten Guns carried by the drivers of our own and escorting vehicles.

The political situation in Egypt had improved somewhat, and there were limited opportunities to visit selected locations in the Canal Zone but only by means of officially provided road transport arrangements with armed escorts during the journeys on the canal road systems. We had a pleasant break with my most hospitable friends, Sandy Powell and family, and managed to visit Port Said and the famous emporium of Simon Hartz. We also had the opportunity to have a look at Ismailia. It was, of course, strictly forbidden to leave the militarised zone to visit the usual places of interest such as Cairo, Alexandria ,the Pyramids, etc.

With a feeling of regret, I left Headquarters Middle East Air Force, where I knew I had registered a good score that would serve me well in the future. I would, of course, have preferred to continue for the intended duration of my appointment, but I was going to one where I would be the Senior Air Movements Officer at a station that was a major staging post on a mainline RAF air communication route. Here, I would have the opportunity to show again my ability to command and in the practical aspects of moving service personnel and dependants, as cargo by air; altogether a new challenge. We flew out of Fayid by way of Benina (Benghasi), El Adem (Tobruk), and Idris (Tripoli), where we arrived in the late afternoon of a beautiful North African winter day. Flight Lieutenant Eric Whitfield who had kindly undertaken the task of getting us into transit accommodation on the station until we had time to sort ourselves out, met us. He had sent me a signal message to inform me of this before I left Abu Sueir so although I had not met him before, it was quite like greeting an old friend. It was most kind of him, and I was grateful for the welcoming gesture that required him to be on hand after normal working hours.

We occupied two adjacent rooms in the Officers Transit Mess that were really intended for night stopping passengers. There was plenty to spare and no danger of our presence denying the accommodation to genuine passengers in transit. We had full use of the transit facilities for our meals, for which we had, of course, to pay the going rate, but it was extremely good value for money. RAF Idris was formerly a station of the Regia Aeronuatica known as Castel Benito. Built on permanent lines, it was of pleasant architecture with plenty of open spaces. It was not overly large but sufficiently compact to facilitate easy walking access to most places that personnel were likely to need access to. It was located in the pre-desert, some eighteen miles south of Tripoli, close to the small Arab village of Gasa Ben Gashir. There was no evidence of the original married officer's quarters, but the single officer's accommodation in the officer's mess area had been converted to provide adequately for those officers whose duties made it desirable for them to live at the station. As I was one of these, it was possible to get a firm indication of availability. In fact the next quarter to be vacated by an officer on his repatriation would be allocated to me, and it would be only a matter of two months or so. Meanwhile, it would be necessary to acquire private accommodation close to Tripoli, and, as there was a very large military garrison in the area, there was a facility that kept details of available private accommodation. Our search was, therefore, only a matter of a few days, certainly less than a week. There was a conveniently located bungalow in the village of Colina Verde, which, as the name suggests, was an Italian settlement. In fact, there were plenty of Italians remaining in Libya, no attempt having been made by the British occupying force to dispossess them from their legitimate properties. An elderly couple, Senor and Senora Vecchio, who lived in an adjoining addition, owned this particular property. They were original of peasant stock from the south of Italy who migrated under a Mussolini plan for the colonisation of his North African conquests in the 1930s. Senor Vecchio was employed as a gardener at RAF Idris and kept a very pleasant large garden at the front of his villa at Colina Verde. They were good to us, and we formed a very neighbourly relationship with them. There were several other RAF families in the village, and there was no need for loneliness. Tripoli was a pleasant place to visit and there was no problem in getting to it as most families had their own transport. One of my first actions was to visit a local Italian car sales company with whom I placed an order for a small Morris Minor car, which they promised me from their next batch shortly due from the United Kingdom.

Shortly before moving out of the transit accommodation at Idris, I discovered that my marital problem had accompanied us over the miles from Cyprus. Quite early one morning, I noticed Rosemary openly disposing of what looked like a piece of writing paper that had been torn into several pieces. She placed the pieces on a small pile of rubbish that the cleaners had swept from the rooms into a tidy little heap off the edge of the veranda. She was being taken that morning into Tripoli for the first time by one of the wives whilst I stayed behind to look after the boys. Shortly after moving to Colina Verde, the station commander asked me to represent the station at an annual conference of the Navy, Army, and Air Force Institutes to be held in Cyprus at RAF Nicosia as there were matters to be discussed touching on inadequacies in the Service Institute's families shop on the station.

So, off I went back to Cyprus again by the Medair service and stayed in the officer's mess at RAF Nicosia. The conference was of very short duration and, having made my intended contribution to the proceedings found myself free by about ten thirty.

I could not return to Idris until the next day. It was dusk when we landed, and Rosemary, with the two boys, was waiting for me. Gradually, life began to assume its normal pattern as I perforce went about the normal occasions of service life and its responsibilities.

Idris was a pleasant station with very hot and sometimes trying summer conditions, but winter was delightful and could be quite cold at night, particularly in the rainy months of December and January. We moved into our married quarter in February 1955 and were delighted with it. The officer's mess, married quarters, and single officer's quarters were compactly arranged around a central swimming pool, the whole being nicely secluded. The entire station had obviously been well planned, with much thought given to the provision of vegetation. The main roads were bordered with tall eucalyptus trees and there were well-tended gardens strategically placed in the areas of main use. The station headquarters was also a model of thoughtful planning, providing a conveniently direct and unobtrusive link to the airfield and its main technical work areas. The airfield itself provided for both military and civil use, with the air traffic control responsibility placed in the contractual hands of Airwork Limited, a United Kingdombased company with a global reputation. Civilian personnel of the Air Ministry Met Office staffed the meteorological office. The forecasters, being of officer grade, had honorary membership of the officer's mess but without entitlement to married quarters. They had to live off the station, and it was one of these, Ian Nixon, that we got to know whilst staying in Colina Verde; we became good friends with Ian and his wife and kept in touch with them until Ian's untimely death. We last saw them here in Nairn when they took lunch with us on their way from Orkney to Glasgow sometime towards the end of the 1970s.

The Station Commander was Wing Commander Peter Farr (brother of the well-known actor Derek). The only other officer of senior rank was Squadron Leader Peter Merriman, the Senior Administrative Officer. Officers in charge of the various sections were, like me, Flight Lieutenants whilst officers below them were Flying Officers and the occasional junior Flight Lieutenant. The establishment was small, but there were usually attachments from the United Kingdom; Tropical Trials of new aircraft by the Aircraft & Armament Experimental Establishment being a popular trial during the hot summer months. The isolated nature of the station made it essential to cater for all activities, and this, with the small number of established officers, produced a good many extraneous duties for them. There was enough interest in model aircraft to warrant a club and I soon had this activity up and going. I was in charge of the corporal's and aircraftmen's barrack blocks. The working accommodation for my Air Movements Section was conveniently located in the part of the Transit Hotel building, and I also had a hangar on the airfield perimeter just a short walk through the centre court of the station headquarters building.

There was plenty for married personnel who were accompanied by their families to see and do, provided they had the convenience of their own transport; otherwise, getting about was a problem. There were plenty of quiet beaches east and west along the lengthy coastline, and these afforded many pleasant picnic outings with the boys in the beautiful winter weather. There were the ancient Roman ruins at Sabratha and Leptis Magna, although the latter was a good run, needing an early start and late return. The troglodyte dwellings Jefran and Garian, situated on a prominent escarpment to our south, were fascinating places to visit, and the occupants made us very welcome. It was fascinating to see people living in well-made and comfortable dwellings below ground. They were surprisingly neat and clean and, whilst there was an obvious lack of modern toilet facilities, they seemed to enjoy a reasonable degree of simple comfort. They even had up-to-date radio receivers that seemed to be permanently active. The dwellings were hewn out of the sides of deep pits with steps cut out to facilitate safe access to the floor at the bottom. The whole thing, although seemingly of pre-historic origin, was amazingly modern and really quite civilised. The ruins at Sabratha amply illustrated the fact that many modern domestic facilities that we take so much for granted were invented long before our time and merely improved progressively to provide today's degree of sophistication that is not all that much more advanced than it was when first used more than two thousand years ago.

Tripoli itself was an attractive city of which the Italian colonists could feel justifiably proud. The Palazzo Royale, the official residence of King Idris, was a splendid edifice, as was the Cathedral. The Lungomare was a broad avenue with a tree-shaded promenade along the seafront. On the landward side of the avenue were located many fine residences, including that of the British Embassy and several fine hotels. Here also was the Bath Club, to which all serving officers had membership if they so desired. It was an excellent club offering good facilities and, although run very much on relaxed officers' mess lines, provided a welcome change of scene. Nearby, the USAAF had a large base facility known as Wheelus Field, where we were occasionally invited to social functions. By way of reciprocity, we also had guests from Wheelus at our own social functions at Idris.

After the end of the war, the British Government accepted the responsibility of providing a Caretaker Government for Libya. This was still in force during my time there. No attempt had been made to displace the Italians, most of whom were engaged in ordinary working pursuits, including many who were of peasant stock and happily involved with work on the land under a scheme for the colonisation of Libya known as 'Orientatsione Nel Deserto.' But the return of government to the Libyans was very much in process as one could see whenever it was necessary to visit government offices. The transfer of power seemed to be progressing quite peacefully and, if memory serves me correctly, was due to reach finality fifteen years after the initial setting-up of the process in 1945 and, therefore had another five years to run. Dissident elements were, however, discernable and there were early signs of moves to overthrow the Monarchy and to terminate British rule prematurely. Both Libyans and Italians were well disposed to ourselves, and we were respectfully treated wherever we went without restriction of movement. It was a most enjoyable and happy life. The summer months could be trying, particularly when the hot wind blew in from the Sahara. These winds, known in Tripolitania as the Ghibli and in other parts of North Africa as Hamzeen, were the natural phenomenon properly known as the Harmattan. As the heart of the desert became excessively hot in the early summer, the heat simply expanded outwards with considerable force towards the cooler north, bringing with it clouds of sand – sandstorms, in fact – the effect of which could be seen high in the sky as far as the north coast of the Mediterranean. The fine sand got everywhere as if we didn't have enough of it anyway. Windows had to be closed and shuttered; even so, it took days to clear the offending stuff from homes and workplaces. The winter came as a blessed relief with the sudden breaking of the heat during November, usually accompanied by torrential rain that filled the Wadis and created rivers where there had been dry gullies. The rains could cause havoc as many roads passed through the Wadis and became impassable, but usually for only short durations. Surprisingly, our water supply was not a problem, as there always seemed to be plenty of it in the deep artesian wells that had been carefully located and tapped during the initial survey of the location. Water was not usually a problem in those parts of North Africa that had been colonised by Europeans and equipped with modern pumping and plumbing systems. The electricity supply, whilst adequate for lighting and low consumption equipment did not extend to our domestic cooking needs. The married quarters had to depend on cooking on ovens heated by paraffin burners. These were quite efficient though slow, but woe betide those who did not keep the wicks of the burners adequately trimmed. Many attempts to produce roast meals were ruined due to smoke, and the messes that had to be cleaned up were unbelievable. I remember the classic story of one Arab servant who produced a roast joint that he had attempted to clean by washing it as he would have washed the dishes. A degree of space heating was necessary during the coldest winter months, and this also had to be provided by paraffin heaters that were quite efficient but only if kept scrupulously clean with carefully trimmed wicks. Each married quarter had a fireplace in the principal living room but as there was no solid fuel issue, it was for each occupant to arrange his own supply of wood or charcoal for burning, but cutting down trees was strictly forbidden.

One day during the delightful spring of 1955, I was doing my daily appraisal of forthcoming aircraft activity when I saw a familiar name from long ago. It was that of a Wing Commander Warne that I guessed had to be the Jimmy Warne whom I had known whilst with 102 Squadron at the beginning of the war. The signal message referred to the movement of a Scampton based Canberra squadron of which Jimmy was the CO. They had been on exercise at some location further east – Aden I think – and were transiting Idris on their way home and would be night-stopping. On the day of their arrival, I telephoned the Station Commander to tell him of my personal interest in this movement, and he said he would like to be on hand to see their arrival. It was well into the afternoon of a beautiful spring day perfumed by the scent of the wild Jonquils growing on the airfield that the entire squadron streamed onto the runway at immaculately timed intervals and were lined up with equal precision on their designated apron by our ground marshallers. I had told the Line Chief to point Wing Commander Warne to the spot where I would be waiting with the Station Commander and after divesting himself of his flying clothing, Jimmy came over in our direction and immediately raised his hand, pointing to me in recognition. We hadn't seen each other since 1942 at Kinloss – thirteen years previously. We laid on a quiet little greeting session in the station officer's mess after dinner that evening, and I enjoyed a pleasantly sober reunion with Jimmy. Some forty years later, there was to be a most unusual and quite amazing continuation of our Service relationship. My first grandson Blair, My son Michael's first-born child, that is, had spent most of his early years in Scotland and, whilst visiting his younger brother in Devon, met Roxanne, who he later married and brought to live in Inverness. One day Roxanne was using our hall telephone to have a chat with her maternal grandmother when she asked if I had ever met a Jimmy Warne during my RAF service. It transpired that Jimmy, who had died in 1992, was her mother's father, and her grandmother (Joan), with whom she was talking, was living at her home in Holmbury St Mary, Surrey ,where she had shared with Jimmy since his retirement from the RAF, as Group Captain, in 1971? It was truly amazing that such an unlikely thing could happen in the circumstances. It is, however, sad that it had to be accompanied by Jimmy's prior death. I often think how wonderful it would have been for us to have been able to share the delight of our joint relationship as great-grandfathers of Dulcie Rose, our lovely little girl who, as I write this, is just past her third birthday. The hand of God certainly does move in a most mysterious way.

During the winter of 1955/56, Peter Farr returned to Home Establishment on repatriation and was replaced by Wing Commander Bowen, who came from RAF Eastleigh at Nairobi in Kenya. Rumour had it that he had been transferred following a mutiny that had received a great deal of adverse publicity in the United Kingdom media. Not surprisingly, he was received at Idris with a large measure of reserve and was not immediately popular. He certainly was a much different personality than Peter Farr and did not enjoy the immediate confidence of his subordinates. His wife, however, was seen to be actively involved immediately with the theatrical group, of which Rosemary was a member of the production team. Inez Bowen was a very good actress who played the lead part in the station's excellent production of 'The Best Years of Their Lives' that had been very popular on the West End stage with Joyce Grenfell in the lead. The Idris production was likewise an immediate success, and there were calls from the Army Garrisons in the Tripoli area for the production to be staged at their locations. This, of course, entailed a great deal of organisation, particularly for the transportation of the cast and the stage properties. The use of Service transport facilities was permitted but only on recovery of costs charged at the recreational rate, which meant that the drama club, an entirely voluntary body, would be faced with a sizeable bill for something that would earn them nothing, as this sort of entertainment, was expected to be provided without cost. This brought Rosemary into conflict with Squadron Leader Peter Merriman, the Senior Administration Officer with whom I enjoyed excellent working relations. We also had a close social relationship with him and his wife, Winn. Peter, being a most conscientious administrator, was naturally reluctant to cook the books, as it were, by authorising the use of transport for a reason other than that which was proper and for which the cost should be recovered to the Public. This consideration does not attend to the thoughts of those who are not financially responsible for improper authorisation of equipment provided by the Public. I cannot remember how the problem was finally resolved, but I do remember the outrage and indignation of Rosemary and some of the other ladies of the Drama Group. The obvious way was to ask those who wanted the facility to agree to pay the transport costs from their own Non-Public funding arrangements which, I suppose, was the method finally resorted to. However, 'The Best Years of Their Lives' did a complete tour of the Army locations in the Tripoli garrison by invitation and earned the Drama Group of RAF Idris wide and well-deserved acclaim. It called for a great deal of organisational skill and effort on the part of those engaged in the physical aspects of production ,particularly, the adaptation of the stage properties to the stages at the different locations. Time was, of course, another problem that called for personnel involved to be released from their ordinary duties, as it was not always possible to carry out the work involved during the off-duty time because of distance and transport considerations.

The schooling of children of junior school age was in the capable hands of Miss Lorna Booth, a UK based civilian of the RAF Education Branch, assisted by suitably qualified volunteers selected from among the wives of serving personnel. Pupils of senior school age had to attend the Garrison School at Medicine on the outskirts of Tripoli which involved a sixteen-mile journey by service transport that for most seemed to be a daily event that was more of an adventure than a trial in the heat of summer and the flooded wadis during the winter rains. The summer vacation was, of course, very lengthy, covering the hottest months of July and August.

Boredom was a constant problem for the junior non-commissioned ranks despite the excellent provision of recreational and sporting facilities. It was surprising to find so many who seemed totally apathetic to their situation, some making little personnel effort to use the facilities available to them. There were a good many National Service personnel, and it was among these that the problems of boredom were greatest. They seemed not to be interested in anything except doing their time and getting back home. From the personnel management point of view, National Servicemen were more of a liability than an asset in a situation that provided at most establishments a worrying degree of under-manning that had to be tolerated besides the apathy of the unwilling conscripts. The real cause of boredom for single non-commissioned personnel was, of course, the lack of female company, which could not be fully compensated by the provision of other recreational facilities. We were the only RAF station in the Tripoli area and although the Army presence was considerable, there were no young unmarried girls because children over the age of eighteen were not permitted to accompany their parents on overseas postings at Public Expense. There were no Women's Service personnel on the bases and the cultural differences meant that there were none of the usual leisure places at which young people gather. An attempt was made to organise a social evening with dancing to which the daughters of the USAAF personnel at Wheelus Field were invited but as they had to be chaperoned by an appropriate number of mothers and we had to ensure an equally appropriate parental presence, it was a dismal failure as far as the young members from both bases were concerned. It was tried only once during my time, and the idea was written-off as an expensive failure.

My own life, by the very nature of my professional responsibilities, was full and included many unusual occurrences that provided lengthy diversions at odd times. I remember one unusual situation that caused me the lose a night's sleep because of having to mount a search for missing dogs. I had received notification by a signal of a load of hunting dogs (of the Beagle breed) that were being flown out of the UK to RAF Habbaniya in Iraq. The flight was a scheduled freight service with a night-stop at Indris could we please make suitable arrangements for the dogs' overnight stay. Now, the carriage of livestock of any kind is prohibited in RAF aircraft, so someone at a high level had done a bit of spadework to get the regulations waived in order to build-up an expensive hunt facility at Habbaniya. However, a load of dogs duly arrived, each one in an adequate flight kennel. I had made arrangements for them to be taken over by the station police and kept in a large outdoor cage adjacent to the guardroom. It was, of course, intended for such accommodation but not used, as we did not have police dogs at the station. However, at an unearthly hour of the night my bedside telephone rang; it was the CO to tell me that I had better get my pants on as the dogs had escaped by burrowing under the compound wire. I organised a search using as many personnel and vehicles as I could muster. The station and the airfield perimeter were combed using the vehicle headlights but to no avail in the darkness. At first light, the search was continued, but by this time the dogs could have been miles away into the wide expanse of the desert where there were many of their wilder relatives. Eventually, tired and hungry, I had to call it off and get back to base to instruct the aircraft captain to depart on schedule with the only dog that had failed at the escape and evasion attempt. I sent a signal to all concerned explaining what had happened, without any hint of concern or apology, I might add, and heard nothing more of it than I expected. This was typically a case of an attempt to evade the regulations going sadly wrong for reasons to which no blame could be attributed. It was an expensive lesson for someone at Habbaniya, and the escaped dogs were no doubt readily assimilated into one of the many desert Pariah Packs to improve their kind by the in- breeding of quality stock.

My tour of duty with the Middle East Air Force was marred only by the personal happenings of my private life that, thankfully, I was able to contain and deal with by my own initiative, but only because of my fortunate appointment on the Headquarters Staff. Otherwise it was a good tour that probably did not contribute as much to my career possibilities as might have been if the tour had followed its original plan without disruption.

The day before our departure I had not received any intimation of my UK appointment but had to report to Air Ministry London anyway. That evening, I had arranged a small farewell drinks session in the bar of the Bath Club. The CO came in and told me that my posting details had been received that very day, and I was posted to RAF Kinloss as a Families Agent. While the location was what I had indicated as my personal choice the appointment as Families Agent was disappointing. Although it was related to the duties of the Equipment Branch it was a new type of appointment that, in my own opinion, was more appropriate to the Administration Branch. It was said to be experimental for a period to decide which branch would eventually become responsible for the function. The party went on into the early hours of our departure day, and after a very brief sleep, we were on our way to the Tripoli docks. Our baggage was packed into the small car like bricks and mortar leaving only just enough space on the rear seat for Michael and Ross. With the help of contacts in the Customs Department, our car was loaded without delay, and we were on board in good order. We were rather anxious as there had been signs of political trouble brewing in Egypt that had spread into Libya, where there was some trouble caused by Libyan dissidents threatening the Italian Embassy at the time of our embarkation. It was rather tense, and we were glad when we moved out of the harbour. It transpired that only a week later the situation was so bad that all families were moved out of private accommodation and into the station for safety. This was shortly followed by the evacuation of all family members to the United Kingdom. The real cause of the trouble was the issue of the Suez Canal which soon developed into a minor war involving our own Armed Forces to protect our interest in the canal. I decided to spend some of my ex-overseas leave of twenty eight days travelling home at private expense as the chance of getting space to ship the car in any of our UK bound aircraft was very remote. We planned sea passage from Tripoli to Naples in the SS Argentina on one of its Sunday sailings in early August 1956. Thence by road with night stops at Cassino, Civitavecchia, Viareggio, Turin, Amberieu-en-Bujey, Paris, and Boulogne.

It was quite early in the morning when we left Tripoli, and we were in Malta before midday to be met by our old friend Bunny Burness, who we had first met at Brampton. He was waiting for us with a rowing boat at our berth in Valletta harbour and soon had us ashore to meet Netta and their children, with whom we spent a most enjoyable day. We had to be back on board by early evening for dinner and an overnight journey to our next port of call, which was Syracuse on the island of Sicily where we arrived very early next morning. We were on our way again before breakfast, heading through the Straits of Messina with Mount Etna plainly visible with its eternal plume of smoke on our port side. Out into the beautiful Bay of Naples, passing Sorrento and other well-known resorts, and into the harbour at Naples by mid-morning. Here, whilst waiting for our car to be swung ashore, we witnessed the tearful reunion of a long separated Italian family from Libya returning to their homeland; it was very emotional and quite touching. We went through the customs formalities with commendable speed and were directed to the state tourist office, where we picked up various travel documents and vouchers that enabled us to buy petrol at special tourist rates. Everything seemed to be going to plan with unexpected ease. I had, of course, taken advice to join the Touring Club Italiano, which had provided me with route details into France to supplement the route information supplied by our own Automobile Association, of which I was also a member. In no time at all we were on our way to have lunch in the shadow of Mount Vesuvius and had plenty of time for a leisurely tour of the fascinating ruins at Pompeii.

CHAPTER XXIV
NAPLES TO NAIRN

A short journey took us to Cassino, where, in leisurely fashion, we found our first Italian night-stop hotel before sundown. Our departure from Cassino the next morning was planned to be early as the hotel did not provide anything more than a light refreshment of a cup of coffee. As this was insufficient for the first meal of a lengthy journey, we took provisions on board for breakfast and lunch before leaving the small, attractive town. We had no problems buying bread rolls, butter, the most delicious ham, and milk. We stopped on the road at the foot of Monte Cassino, where, in a convenient area, we had a picnic breakfast that included a brew of tea made to our own specification using a little primus stove that I had purchased before leaving Tripoli. Regrettably, we were unable to visit the famous monastery at the peak of Monte Cassino as it had been declared unsafe for sightseers due to heavy structural damage inflicted by the Allies, who had to engage in a lengthy and bloody battle to clear this stubbornly defended German position that dominated their advance northwards. With satisfied appetites we were soon on the way again for our next planned stop at Viareggio on the west coast. We diverted a little distance from our main route to take in the sight of the famous marble quarries at Carrara, where we had no difficulty in picking up from the ground a few small souvenir pieces that we still have.

We found Viareggio, a pleasant seaside resort that was very busy at this time of high summer. We had no problem with accommodation at our intended hotel on the seafront. Here again, we had to make our own provision for a picnic breakfast, but there was no problem in doing so, and we were soon on our planned route for Rome, where we intended to have a leisurely look around the Vatican. The weather was very hot and Rome was sweltering in the heat as we entered Saint Peter's Square with its majestic fountain. We noticed that the space around the fountain was crammed with cars taking the benefit of the peripheral spray to cool down. Our own small car was certainly like a furnace on wheels, so we did likewise whilst we wandered around the sights, which took longer than we had intended so that we were somewhat behind schedule as we left for Turin. We soon realised our error as we still had a long way to go and some difficult terrain to cover and although we found our intended hotel with a little help from the friendly locals, it was well after dark when we arrived with two tired boys. However, rooms were available, and after a good supper, we were pleased to get to our beds.

The next stage of our homeward journey was to take us through the Mont Cenis Pass with beautiful mountain scenery all the way into France. I was most impressed with the efficiency of the Italian provision of facilities for motorists and particularly with the services of the Touring Club Italiano. The mountain section of the route was hard going for all cars, and it was necessary to stop occasionally to let engines cool down. There was ample provision for this, and I was surprised at one such stop to find a small wooden building at the roadside belonging to the Touring Club Italiano where members could obtain any assistance required, including more petrol vouchers for cheap fuel. It was a truly wonderful section of our route with its breathtaking scenes of mountains and lakes. We descended through the lower slopes of the Massive and into France, where the first place of any note was Chambery. From here, it was but a short journey to Amberieau-en-Bujay, where we drove straight to our hotel with the seeming ease of those who knew the place well.

We entered the hotel and felt that we were in the very centre of the local community. The entrance door led directly into a bar where a small gathering of locals was enjoying a convivial drink at the end of another working day. It seemed so friendly and welcoming as we were recognised as visitors to be made a fuss of by the proprietor and his wife busily working behind the bar. We were shown to our comfortable rooms in the upper part of the building and invited to freshen up and return to the bar, which was quite extensive and also served as the dining room. Here we were seated at a table already laid for us and, without much ado about the choice of menu were served with a very substantial meal that included a large dish of what we now call French Fries, much to the approval of the boys. We were glad to get to our cosy beds in the friendly atmosphere of this small and simple establishment. Amberieau is very picturesque with its backdrop of high mountain terrain. Its streets were, not surprisingly, steep in places, but it was clearly an attraction for passing motorists, particularly for those who had made the journey out of Italy. It was a place that we found difficult to leave, such was its effect on us and I remember it with a kind of longing to return. So we tarried for quite a while as I thought we should have no difficulty in making our next stop, which was Paris, by that evening.

We soon left the mountains behind us and got onto the main route- National Route No. 6 – I think. We now experienced a build-up of traffic in both directions, but we were not unduly bothered by it, although it did seem to have a slowing effect on our progress. We were crossing a wide river spanned by a low bridge where we came to a lengthy halt. Looking at the open topped car stopped alongside us going in the opposite direction, I recognised a familiar face. Rosemary must have thought me crazy as I called out, "Hi, Eddie, where the heck are you going?" It was Flight Lieutenant Eddie Wiles who was at the Officer Cadet Training Unit with me. I had seen him a few times staging through Idris, and I knew that by some means, he had succeeded in getting himself transferred back to flying duties and was flying with Transport Command as a Hastings Captain. He was now the Transport Command Liaison Officer at Orange, a French Air Force Base at which we had an agreement for staging facilities. He and his wife were returning to Orange after a spot on UK leave. I never saw him again after that most unusual brief meeting on a bridge in France.

We were still well south of the Foret de Fontainebleau, and I realised that we could not make Paris before dark. But I had allowed a whole day in excess of our estimated journey time in case of unforeseen emergency, so we decided to make another stop before dark. I cannot now remember the precise location, but we found a most inviting small hotel that had the name La Diligence just south of the forest. I also remember that the name of the proprietor was Ernest Rousseau. Strange that I should remember that, but it seemed as though we were expected, or perhaps hoped for, as we were the only guests in his spotless premises. The next morning, we had a leisurely journey through the forest and entered Paris in the middle of the afternoon. I felt confident that I knew my way as I drove into the Place De La Republique and stopped outside the Hotel Moderne, where I had stayed for a weekend break in February 1940 whilst held on the ground at Villeneuve by atrocious weather conditions for almost three weeks waiting for a break to carry out a leaflet dropping operation on Vienna. Our intended night stop was the recommended one that was located in a side street off Grande Boulevard, but unfortunately, we had to go right to the top and around the Etoille in order to get onto the right side of the road to make the turnoff. The traffic was rather terrifying, with three lanes in either direction, but we made it and arrived outside the rather nondescript address. I was not impressed but the weather was turning nasty with a high wind and threatening rain, so we decided to make it do. The place was clean enough, and the rooms reasonably furnished, but it was no more than a sleeping facility, and we would have to take our meals elsewhere. Still, this was no problem, except that we had to go out in the now wild and windy weather to find a place for an evening meal. As it happened, this was very easy as there was a convenient self-help restaurant just along the boulevard where we had a decent meal in pleasant surroundings. But when writing the account of our journey for the benefit of those at RAF Idris, I mentioned this accommodation address as below standard, particularly for families.

Before leaving the city the next morning, we purchased sufficient supplies for breakfast and lunch and set forth on the last leg of our journey to the Channel port of Bologne, where our hotel accommodation and cross-channel passage had been booked by arrangement with the Automobile Association. These were the only bookings made in advance, but all had gone according to plan, and we had made all-night stops at the intended places and hotels with the exception of our stop before Fontainebleau that had been allowed for in the plan. So far, we have been fortunate. The weather was dull and stormy as we got closer to the Channel, and it was rather cold for August. However we arrived at Bologne by early evening and had no difficulty in finding our hotel, which was conveniently close to the ferry departure point. The hotel was excellent, and our embarkation next morning went without incident. Customs at Folkestone was easy, although our car number plates in Arabic and English (LTB 802) did attract attention and, of course, it was necessary to register the vehicle as being the first entry into the UK; all went smoothly as we explained that we were RAF repatriates. Folkestone was Rosemary's birthplace on 15th June 1917. Her father, Donald John Morrison, was a member of the famous Princess Patricia's Light Infantry Regiment of Canada. He was originally from Kiltarlity, close to Inverness, and had immigrated to Canada some years before the 1914-1918 war. His regimental depot in the UK was at Shornecliff, Folkestone, where Rosemary's mother was living in married accommodation. We had no reason to linger and started our journey to London immediately as I had to report to the Air Ministry to confirm my arrival and verify my appointment in the Home Establishment.

We visited Mary Mackintosh, who was still living in our old home at 92 Louisville Road, Tooting Bec, and had arranged a night's accommodation for us. We went into the city the next morning, and I reported to the Air Ministry at Adastral House. Entering the waiting room, the only occupant was a very attractive young lady who immediately jumped up and threw her arms around my neck with a delighted "Hello Bill, where the heck have you come from?" She was, in fact, Jeannine, a French girl who had spent much of her younger days in Egypt, where her father was concerned with the Suez Canal administration. She had lived with her parents in Ismailia but worked at HQMEAF Abu Sueir as a secretary where she had met and married Flight Lieutenant Oscar Armstrong, a fellow member of the Command Movements Staff. This is where I first met her. Oscar was also reporting on arrival in the UK. He arrived in the waiting room having done the necessary and I was called immediately to do likewise. I registered my displeasure at being appointed to the Families Agent post but was told that it was for a trial period only, pending a final decision as to which Branch, Equipment, or Administration would be responsible for the function that was to become a permanent feature at all major stations. The consensus of opinion seemed to be that it would become an administrative responsibility. However, the location at Kinloss suited me and was my request posting, and that was a major consideration; I certainly had no qualms about my ability to do whatever the job entailed. Oscar and Jeanine were still in the waiting room when I returned, and we had a cup of coffee together before going our separate ways.

Our next stop was my parent's home at Heywood where we were expected to spend a few days. This gave us the much-needed opportunity to sort ourselves out after our long time spent on the roads of Italy and France and, of course, to tackle a rather formidable pile of personal laundry. The time passed quickly, and we had to be on our way to Nairn and the new experience of road travel by private car through the Highlands by a road system that was still a long way from that enjoyed by motorists of today with its motorway systems. Our route had been planned by the Automobile Association and was designed to avoid dense traffic areas that involved wide detours with consequent added mileage. This was undoubtedly the most trying and tiring part of our entire journey home, the worst part being that it took us through the populous parts of Central Scotland. I cannot now remember where we made our planned night-stop, but it was somewhere in the gap between Glasgow and Edinburgh. The worst of the route was yet to come as we proceeded northward from Perth through the Highlands with the winding road never ending as it seemingly followed each contour with wearying monotony. However, the weather was quite good, and we eventually arrived at the sleepy highland town of Aviemore with only the final forty miles of familiar territory before us. So we arrived in Nairn late in the evening, hungry, tired, and grubby, to be met by friends and family not seen for over three years. It was the end of an epic journey for those days and we look back on it with a feeling of accomplishment. Our journey over the UK section from Folkestone was about half as long as the journey from Naples to Bologne. The whole route had been covered in eleven days of motoring, something of a marathon for those days particularly for a small car not built for touring in comfort.

CHAPTER XXV
COASTAL COMMAND - THE COLD WAR

September 1956 was to mark the beginning of what was to become the most trying and testing period of my entire RAF career. It was also a most difficult time for the RAF, which was soon to be faced with the onerous task of guarding our maritime frontiers against the threat of communism posed by Russia. This period was to become known politically as the Cold War, in which the RAF Coastal Command was to play a prominent role with inadequate operational facilities and equipment. Kinloss, providing the pivotal location, needed extensive modernisation of its operational and supporting facilities, and I was, without realising it at the time, right at the heart of the politically determined situation that was to continue for many years.

I was the first incumbent in my appointment as Families Agent, and I found myself a prominent member of the Station Headquarters Staff. My basic function was responsibility for the occupation of married quarters and liaison with the Equipment and Works Services Staff for the comfort of the occupants. Several secondary duties were also required of me, including families' welfare in the entirety with, among other minor functions, the title of Officer in Charge of the Station Pig Farm, although, thank goodness, I had the services of a hired manager who was the local Veterinary Surgeon, and a labourer to do the real work involved. The pig farm provided a ready means of disposing of waste food from the messes and, by breeding and selling, earned a good income to supplement the provision of the Station Welfare Facilities. The job was anything but boring, as there was a large element of married personnel on the station that was soon to increase in strength with an extensive building programme to provide for the increasing need for facilities. I was soon in no doubt about the appointment of a Families Agent, soon to become formally known as Families Officer, but I maintained my reservations about these new appointments being filled by officers of the Equipment Branch as the only relationship with the responsibility of that branch lay in the furnishing of married quarters and the administration of the occupation and vacation procedures, known as Marching In and Marching Out. Otherwise, the job was patently one for the Administration Branch. My presence in what was regarded by the Command Equipment Staff, as an unusual appointment for an equipper was not overlooked on the occasions of staff inspections when I was always visited and left in no doubt that such employment was regarded as inappropriate and seen as gross misemployment. I kept a good relationship with the Station Senior Equipment Officer who was of like mind. Otherwise, I was quite happy with the work and its undoubted importance and found it rewarding knowing that my performance was greatly appreciated by the Station Commander and his senior administrative officers; the Officer Commanding the Admin Wing and the Senior Administration Officer. I felt that I enjoyed a large measure of popularity and was happy in the knowledge that I was registering a good score; I would not do otherwise than give my very best whatever was required of me. However, I was aware of the likelihood of becoming typed outside of what I believed was my intended role, and this caused me some concern.

The station had changed only in minor respects since I last saw it in 1942. The station headquarters still occupied the extensive wooden buildings adjacent to the main entrance. The officers' mess and single officers' accommodation were exactly the same. The sergeants' mess was now in a permanent building situated much too close to the technical area and would obviously have to be relocated as the station developed. On the airfield, the only apparent change was the addition of runways, whilst the workshops area adjacent to the hangars now included a purpose built electronics section. The old wooden buildings were, however, still to be seen on every hand. No. 45 Maintenance Unit – the lodger unit of Maintenance command – was still in occupation of the only permanent pre-war working accommodation. The winter of 1956/57 was as cold as it could be, and the problems associated with solid fuel heating unchanged. It was generally uncomfortable in offices on arrival, as the fires had only been lit just before the start of the working day. The wooden buildings were poorly insulated and did not retain any heat overnight.

The main function of the station was to provide for the Operational Training of Maritime Aircrew Personnel which; end the unit on the station was No. 256 Operational Conversion Unit equipped with American Neptune aircraft provided under the Mutual Aid Defence Programme arranged between the United States and United Kingdom Governments. There was a resident operational squadron of Avro Shackleton Mark II aircraft. This aircraft, a development of the wartime Lancaster design, was the standard operational aircraft for the Command that had other bases at St Mawgan and St Eval in Cornwall, Ballykelly in Northern Ireland, and, also in Northern Ireland, the Joint Anti-Submarine School at Limavady. There were squadrons overseas located at Gibraltar and Malta.

So life continued at Kinloss with relative ease for me as I found the work of Families Officer busy and interesting enough but unchallenging for a Specialist Branch officer. The spring of 1957 started a period of change for the Command and Kinloss particularly. No. 45 Maintenance Unit was disbanded, and its permanently built accommodation was handed over to Kinloss for use as Station Headquarters and technical functions. I was allocated an office in the new SHQ but I was to occupy it for only a very short time. Fortuitously, for me, at least, an officer-manning problem occurred in the Equipment Section. The Deputy Senior Equipment Officer had some sort of a personal problem that required him to be moved, perhaps prematurely retired – I cannot now remember - but he could not be replaced immediately, and the post could not be left unmanned indefinitely in view of the operational needs of the station. Now I was targeted, and after a short discussion to finally confirm my own wishes and the necessary manipulation by Command with the Air Ministry, I found myself re-appointed as Deputy SEO, much to the disappointment of the Station Commander, Group Captain JMN Pike, who had seemingly tried hard to retain me as Families Officer. However, an officer of the Administrative Branch was quickly found to fill that post, and shortly thereafter, all these posts were confirmed for that Branch.

I immediately found myself in the deep end. The Lease-Lend Neptune aircraft were to be returned to America. A new Training Unit, to be known as the Maritime Operational Training Unit, was formed, absorbing the Operational Conversion Unit at Kinloss and a sister OCU at St Eval. No. 120 Squadron of Shackleton was transferred from Ballykelly. All this produced a considerable increase in the station's workload with a proportional effect on my newly acquired responsibilities as Officer in charge of Equipment Provisioning and Accounting, the main responsibility of my function as Deputy SEO. The Avro Shackleton was getting rather long in the tooth, and there was much discussion of replacing it, but whilst the aircraft industry had a ready plan to offer the Air Ministry a suitably modified aircraft in the guise of the Shackleton Mark III incorporating all the latest gizmos, the economic situation simply could not afford it, and so it was decided to purchase enough Shackleton Mark IIIs to equip two new squadrons, and to launch a Modification and Reconditioning Programme to convert the existing Mark IIs to the same standard. The work entailed by all this in the light of the demands made on the Command by the increasing intensity of the political situation was, to say the least, extremely burdensome, and I was to feel the weight of the additional work imposed on the Equipment Section.

In addition to the technical aspects, there was to be a building programme to create new messing and station institute facilities for the junior ranks, a new officers mess, and more married quarters for officers and airmen. The eventual furnishing requirement for these new buildings itself provided an additional workload of considerable size involving the creation and administration of contracts for all kinds of work to be carried out, including the laying of floor coverings, manufacture of loose covers for chairs and settees, manufacture of curtains, etc. There was to be no increase in the size of the equipment staff to cope with this extra workload. The officer strength was three, including myself, with the largest element of the section's total strength to cope with the core activity of provisioning and accounting for the technical, clothing, barrack, and contractual work. One officer junior to me was responsible for the physical aspects of receipt, storage, and issue of equipment of technical and clothing items, whilst the barrack warden with a small civilian staff took care of the domestic requirements. All this, of course, was superimposed on the routine running of the Section on which the personnel establishment was determined. It can hardly be mentioned that the work pressure was immediately felt at the very beginning as the preparatory work was instituted. It was envisaged that the building work would be completed by 1960, with the exception of the Shackleton Modernisation and Reconditioning Programme, which would be ongoing for some considerable time beyond the completion of the building programme.

There was an almost immediate effect on the station's overall strength as personnel were transferred within the Command to create the new Maritime Operational Training Unit and settle in the relocated No. 120 Squadron. That part of the task seemed to be done with remarkable ease, the main effect being felt in the officer's and sergeant's messes where the accommodation soon began to bulge at the seems. The effect was considerably increased when the instructional courses commenced and numbers were increased by the addition of the student element. Many more married personnel had to seek accommodation off the station and the nearby towns, particularly Forres and Nairn, had population increases with consequent growth in the overall economy of the area. The Air Ministry Works Department did a wonderful job of planning the extension of the station boundaries, the additional buildings being erected to modern standards on vacant ground without loss or disruption of existing accommodation. So, at the time of my departure from the station on 1st July 1960 only the new officer's mess remained to be occupied after an official opening ceremony by Her Majesty The Queen.

On the technical side, things were somewhat different as there was a large element of dependence on industry over which we had no direct control. However, things had gone reasonably well as far as the aircraft modernisation work that had to be done on the station. All aircraft had to be progressively returned to industry for modernisation work to be done to extend the structural integrity of wing main spars etc., but the installation of additional operational equipment had to be done on the station, and my own responsibilities lay in the timely provision of a whole new range of electronic and avionic equipment. My early technical background came in very useful in my appreciation of this equipment that included many modern developments of earlier applications of radio and radar techniques with new names like Blue Satin, Green Silk, Autolycus, Sonobouys, and many more devices, the names of which are now beyond easy recall. It was soon being said that the Maritime Shackleton was fast becoming a Christmas tree with all the equipment being hung on it. Certainly, the internal spaces were being crowded with gear. Of course the all-important operational function had to be maintained as the modernisation work proceeded. An aircraft on the ground because of some technical unserviceability was a serious matter, and we were plagued by many shortages of older items that were still needed as the industry was switching to the manufacture of newer versions. In this respect, the Air Ministry Provisioning Branches that dealt directly with industry were having problems in estimating continuing needs. One particularly troublesome item that I can never forget was the absolutely essential Engine Driven Generator that supplied the aircraft's electrical system. At any time, there were more aircraft on the ground (AOG) for this item than any other. Despite our efforts at the station level, this particular provisioning problem with the Shackleton EDG was not resolved during my time there. I am sure this single item caused more correspondence to be generated than any other, as all that the Air Ministry seemed to be capable of was repetitious calls for unserviceable generators to be returned for repair more timeously; they never got the message that larger stocks were required due to their initial under-provision

I had spent rather more than three of my four years at Kinloss on the Shackleton Modernisation and Reconditioning Programme, together with the improvements that were necessary to equip the station for its revised task. The pressure of the work had been quite relentless and had left its mark on my general health and well-being. I knew that I had enjoyed great favour at the Command Staff level and, perhaps, should not have been surprised to find myself posted to the Command Staff Headquarters at Northwood, Middlesex, for Equipment Staff Duties with effect from 1st July 1960. I was sorry that I could not stay for the formal opening of the new Officers Mess by the Queen, but my presence at Northwood had to be taken prior consideration. Friends already there had kindly made provisional arrangements for a nice property to be available for us to move into. So arrival and settling-in were easy. As usual, the central part of this very large headquarters was a rambling mansion house that served as offices for the Commander-in-Chief and his immediate staff. It was also the location of the Officers' Mess. All other staff elements were housed in a collection of wooden buildings built on sloping ground in a seemingly unending line, each hut being joined by a continuous corridor that was said to be the longest in the RAF. However, despite its length, it provided essential cover in adverse weather conditions for the unending traffic that it had to carry. The Senior Equipment Staff Officer was Wing Commander Sydney Swain (known to his subordinates as Sinister Syd because of his be-spectacled and rather unfriendly appearance). I soon had him typified as one who believed that all work should be delegated to his subordinates, even that which called for his own signature. I hated this practice as it was frequently returned for modification of wording, which he seemed unable to do himself. My immediate superior was a Squadron Leader, BVM (Brian) Birch, who was the most senior officer of that rank in the entire RAF Active List. His seniority was such that it should have been obvious to him that he was not going to be advanced further, particularly as he was now on his penultimate appointment before retirement at the age of forty-nine. His appointment was Equipment 2, and mine was EQ2a. EQ2b was a warrant officer who had the comfortable task of recording the movement of Shackleton aero engines and power plants. Together, we formed the staff responsible for all technical equipment. The other two elements of the Equipment Staff were EQ1-Sqn Ldr Charles Laing with Flt Lt Phil Filbey, responsible for equipment administration and accounting, clothing, and barracks. EQ3 dealt with explosives, fuels, and gases under Sqn Ldr Arthur Lloyd. There was a small movement requirement that was taken care of by Flt Lt George McElroy. We had an office staff of three locally engaged civilian ladies who were kept very busy with unending typing and office duties.

My in-tray was always high enough to provide an effective screen between my desk and my office door. Of course, I had the advantage of familiarity with those at the sharp-end and was never at a loss for remedies to the unending problems that arose on the troublesome operational scene at the station level. Birch knew this and lost no opportunity to capitalise on it. Occasionally, there were very weighty staff papers to be written, and it was by these that I soon came to the particular attention of the Air Officer in charge of Administration (AOA), Air Commodore WIC (Bill) Innis, who had asked at my arrival interview about my operational flying stint and was delighted to discover that we had both flown with No.4 Group at the same time. The AOA made a practice of reading all staff papers dealing with policy matters, and one of mine caused him to note it as a model of excellence, being one of the best of his experience. He instructed his senior personnel staff officer to compile a report on me and used it in an attempt to advantage my career prospects by bringing it to the Air Ministry attention. It earned me a Laudatory Report that did eventually have some effect, I suppose, on my future promotion but not to the full effect that was intended. Although he tried hard, it was difficult for Birch to hide his true feelings in this matter and I felt, thereafter, a degree of animosity towards me. He was the type to whom personal advancement was the main consideration, and he tried noticeably by every possible device to enhance that consideration. Despite his sickeningly obvious, and sometimes flamboyant, efforts to achieve the next promotion, he failed and was eventually retired, a very disappointed officer who no doubt thought he had been badly done by.

About twelve months before leaving Kinloss, I responded to an Air Ministry invitation to officers who would be willing to serve with Commonwealth and Foreign air forces on secondment for exchange postings. I had indicated a preference for the Royal Malaysian Air Force, then in the process of formation. Receiving no immediate reply, I thought no more of it. Now I found myself being offered secondment to the Lebanese Air Force for a period of twelve months to be followed by two years of service in Malta to complete the normal overseas tour of three years in the Middle East. This news was broken to me by Syd of the sinister visage himself. He advised me to decline, claiming that as the Lebanese Air Force was a foreign force, I would be reported on by an authority that was unlikely to be as advantageous to my future career as my present appointment would be. I could see that he really wanted to avoid unnecessary turbulence in his own staff, particularly E2, but I had no reason to doubt that staying where I was would be to my ultimate benefit, so I declined the Air Ministry offer.

Also, about the time of my departure from Kinloss advice had been circulated of the introduction of a New Career Structure for officers appointed to permanent commissions. The general effect was that officers would be retained until reaching the normal maximum retiring age of fifty-five, irrespective of their rank. Those selected would be advised personally and given the opportunity to accept or decline. The scheme also introduced a lower retiring age to be called the thirty eight/sixteen point which meant that PC officers would be reviewed as they were approaching their thirty eighth birthday , provided that they had served at least sixteen years reckoning from the age of twenty-one, they would be compulsorily retired unless assimilated to the new scheme Not surprisingly, this raised a great deal of anxiety for PC officers who, like myself, having passed the thirty eight/sixteen point would be retired at their previous retiring age of forty-nine up to the rank of squadron leader unless they were assimilated to the new structure. However, my personal fears were allayed when I received my offer of assimilation in the middle of 1961. Brian Birch had not received his offer and was noticeably upset about it as it became obvious that the selection process was being done in alphabetical order by branch. That there was a selection criteria was obvious, but we did not know what it was, although it undoubtedly had some bearing on age and advancement prospects, the latter always having been pre-determined to a large degree. My own belief was that we all had an allotted niche into which we had been, at least provisionally, slotted early in our commissioned service. PC officers had a reasonable expectancy of reaching the senior ranks, that is to say, the ranks between flight lieutenant and air commodore being the ranks of squadron leader, wing commander, and group captain. I now had a reasonable expectation of further advancement but many PC officers did not make it for reasons that they were never to know. I had no illusions about this preferring to let matters take their own course whilst I continued conscientiously to give of my best. Despite an initial large redundancy in 1957 that did much to clear a badly clogged system and open up promotion it made only a marginal improvement, and promotion was still very slow. In my branch, the average time for promotion from flight lieutenant to squadron leader for the majority was ten to twelve years, and there was nothing automatic about it as promotion above Flt Lt was done strictly by twice yearly selections of the Air Ministry Promotions Board to fill the requirements of the existing establishment. There was no time qualification for promotion above flight lieutenant.

Sinister Syd was posted and replaced by Wing Commander ED Hills, a more affable officer who was later promoted in a post to Group Captain, illustrating the increased responsibility of the appointment. At the Command Staff Equipment level there was no reduction of workload but rather a noticeable increase occasioned by the additional number of stations, including Gibraltar, to be overseen. All stations were required to report details of Aircraft on Ground to my office, where part of my overall responsibility was to progress the supply of any item of equipment responsible for each AOG reported. To this end an AOG State Board occupied a large area of one of my office walls. There was. Of course, a noticeable number of aircraft in the AOG category at any time due to the inability of the holding maintenance unit to supply the problematical Engine Driven Generator. I was constantly in touch with the Air Ministry Provisioning Branch regarding this item, but they would not accept my word that the only answer was to take special contractual action to increase the basic stock level. They remained convinced that the real problem lay with the stations not returning unserviceable items for repair promptly. I did a lot of work for myself by initiating a special study of each station's demands for this item, which, because of the supply situation, they were unable to hold in local stock. My eventual report showed quite clearly that the real trouble lay in the repair contractor's inability to return them to the stock holding depot quickly enough. But the problem was not solved during my time on the staff. The operational requirement in the politically intense Cold War situation produced a working atmosphere that was, to say the least, traumatic at Command and station levels of equipment and technical responsibility. It was said that officers of the Equipment Branch were the most likely to suffer ill health due to heart attacks and duodenal ulcers, as I was soon to discover for myself.

By the beginning of 1962, I was feeling the stress effects of undue work effort over the past five years with a marked deterioration in general well being. The spring brought some hope of relief with a warning from the Air Ministry that I was becoming due for another tour of overseas duty, and in due course, I was informed that I was appointed to RAF Luqa, Malta, in June for Movements Duties. I was delighted, but Birch was clearly unhappy about his forthcoming loss. On the day before my departure for Malta, my intray was piled as high as ever, and Birch gave me no respite, particularly as a relieving officer had not yet been indicated for me. At 1600 hours that day, I still had to complete my clearance action from Northwood which involved visiting several sections of the station that required notification of my departure. Birch, in a most surly manner, said to me, "Where are **you** going?" I told him that I had yet to complete the clearance procedure and had less than an hour to do it before the various sections closed for the day, and, as he knew, I was departing the next morning before routine duty time. I also had to spend an hour or so out of the office that morning to hand-over my married quarter, which we would, of course, finally vacate on departure the next morning. I suppose he thought that I would at least clear my in tray before leaving but that would have been impossible even by working throughout the night. On my hurried return, I took the tray of files with my office keys and deposited them on his desk with an apology for being unable to accomplish the impossible but assuring him that what was left of today's arising and not of immediate concern. I must confess that I felt a degree of pity for him being left without a replacement for me, but I was leaving at the instance of Higher Authority, and there was nothing I could do about it. I finally took my leave of him at about 1730 and went home to my married quarter to complete the arrangements for my departure with Rosemary and Ross at 0800 hours the next morning. (Michael had entered the Army under the Junior Leaders Training Scheme in 1958, on completion of which he was nominated for service with his choice of regiment, The Queen's Own Cameron Highlanders. At the time of our departure from Northwood, he was in Singapore with his regiment based at Seletar, soon to be involved with the Sultanate of Brunei campaign).

We left Northwood according to plan and travelled by the Metropolitan railway to Central London, arriving at the Forces Reception Centre with a little time to spare before being entrained for Swindon and thence by coach to our departure airfield at RAF Lyneham in Wiltshire.

CHAPTER XXVI
MALTA

We arrived at Luqa late in the afternoon and, after meeting Squadron Leader Jack Hone, the Senior Air Movements Officer, spent our first night in the Officers Transit Mess.

The next morning, with relief, I saw my car in the customs pound at the RAF Air Movements Section and set the customs release action in motion. On the Sunday before my departure from Northwood, I had taken the car to RAF Abingdon, from where George McElroy had arranged for space to be made available in a scheduled transport aircraft for conveyance to Malta. George was a most helpful friend who escorted me to Abingdon in his own car and then took me back to Northwood.

The next and most important person to be contacted was the Families Officer, who assured me that I would have no difficulty in finding suitable accommodation and recommended that I should confine my search to Sliema, where he could provide me with a number of addresses to start with. Meanwhile, he had arranged for us to stay in a small hotel in Sliema, at which there was an official arrangement for newly arrived officers and their families to stay temporarily, and he would arrange for us to be transported there that day. There were many things to be done, principally to get the car out of customs first. To this end I went along to the civil part of Luqa, which was a joint-user airfield used also as Malta's Civil Airport. I introduced myself to Mr Francis Galea, the Chief Customs Officer of whom I was to see a great deal in the following three years. We soon had our wheels in motion and, by that evening, were comfortably housed in our temporary hotel, the Plevna, in Sliema. As the families officer had assured us that officially hired married accommodation, currently nearing completion, would be available, we decided not to spend too much time searching for a private place to live. We were fortunate to find one of the suggested addresses ideally suitable for our needs at Britannia Flats, which is conveniently located on the seafront at Sliema. We moved in and had ourselves sorted out in no time at all. Ross was enrolled at his new school, which, as the services schools in Malta were a Royal Navy responsibility, was the RN Senior School at Tal Handaq and a most elegant establishment it was. However, Ross was not disappointed to discover that his enrolment was just in time for the commencement of the long summer vacation, so he would have plenty of time to adjust and make friends in the RAF community before really getting down to the serious matter of his continuing education.

It was early June with the weather trying to settle into the heat of summer. It was that time of year when the Higher Authority (Air Headquarters Malta) had difficulty in deciding the date on which the change from winter to summer dress should be made. The earliest date was the beginning of the working week of our arrival, but they had decided that it would be better for everyone if the change was postponed for a week. But, as was usually the case, they didn't make the right guess, so everyone sweltered in-home service dress for a few days longer than necessary. The weather was wonderful when we got into tropical dress, but the temperature was rising rapidly, as it does in those parts, and by the beginning of July, the long, hot summer lay before us, but we were comfortably settled and happy with our domestic situation. We had been allocated our future home, which was in a block of up-market flats at Guardamangia situated on high ground above Msida Creek. We went to see it, but it would still be a few weeks before we would be able to move in. Meanwhile, we had our first visitor from the United Kingdom and were delighted to have an old friend from Nairn, Miss Margaret Main, a schoolteacher and a most welcome and delightful guest who was to assist us with the move into our new home on the ground floor of the eight flat building of four levels named Parioli Flats. It was large and airy with a small enclosed garden at the rear whilst its three bedrooms gave us all the accommodation we were likely to need. Winter heating was to be by the usual and most convenient method of paraffin heaters that were fine if kept clean and in good working order. Cooking and hot water were provided by bottled gas.

The only disappointment lay in the pattern of my employment, which was, regrettably to be as a Duty Air Movements Officer working the routine shift system. I was now forty-two years of age and had been desk-bound for over ten years. I did not take to it easily; in fact I did not take to it at all. The disruption of normal eating and sleepy habits soon had a telling effect on my general well-being. The stress effects that I had first experienced at HQ Coastal Command began to manifest themselves in the form of abdominal trouble, usually a feeling of intense hunger long before the next meal was due, and I found it necessary to allay this with a snack. Tiredness was a great problem, and the long night shift was usually very busy as aircraft had to be loaded and generally prepared for departure at an early hour. Whilst not directly engaged in the physical aspects of loading, load planning and the calculations relating to weight and balance were my direct responsibility as Duty Air Movements Officer besides the general management of the shift and its duty personnel. Luqa was a very busy terminal and staging post combined, and there was always plenty of air transport activity. After a night shift, I was completely exhausted both physically and mentally and soon began to easily lose my normal composure with frequent bouts of irritability. I went to see the Medical Officer, who told me immediately that my very pose on entering his consulting room was that of a person suffering the effects of a duodenal ulcer. So he arranged for me to see a specialist at The Royal Naval Hospital at Bighi. The Navy was responsible for hospital services in Malta. Sure enough, I was diagnosed as expected when the surgeon stabbed the precise abdominal spot with his forefinger. I was admitted shortly thereafter to start the process of strict dieting as the cure preferred to surgery. I was in the hospital for three weeks and then discharged with instructions for a continuing strict diet and normal routine feeding.

Jack Hone was a good Senior Air Movements Officer, but I found myself somewhat critical of his employment of his officers. He seemed to be more concerned with safeguarding against the disruptive effects of change with the consequence that experience was not being used to the greatest benefit in the overall running of the section. My own employment as a Duty Air Movements Officer was, in my own opinion, a serious misplacement of my rank, seniority, and experience, particularly as two much younger officers of lower rank and/or seniority were employed in management posts at a higher level. Shortly after my arrival, I was pleased to be joined by Flight Lieutenant Norman Myers. He was the officer I relieved at Idris back in December 1954, but I did not meet him, as he was required back in the UK before I could get to Idris. However, he arrived at Luqa on a Saturday and came to get a quiet look at the Air Movements Section on a Sunday when I was doing the day shift. So, as his visit coincided with the quiet late morning part of the shift, I was able to take him along to the mess, where we had a good talk about the unusual management situation. Norman was somewhat older than me and was also senior to me in the rank of Flt Lt. Of course, I didn't know what Jack's plan was for Norman but as he was replacing a much junior officer about to depart, I warned him of the likelihood of his being placed in the shift pattern, as in my own case, whilst there were two much younger and junior officers in the two higher management day slots. He agreed that the whole situation seemed to be quite ludicrous and would not tolerate it. Although Norman was a fellow member of the equipment branch, he had somehow been employed continuously on movement duties, and his experience in that activity was, therefore, profound. He was also a pre-war regular then at the age of forty-nine with six years to go to retirement. He had a very sensitive approach to seniority and was not the type to brook any disregard for it. I was pleased to see him displace the younger officer of lower rank who was effectively occupying the desk that was that of the deputy SAMO. On my return to duty after discharge from hospital, Jack told me that there would be no more shift work for me as he had suffered the effects of a duodenal ulcer himself and knew the importance of regular eating and sleeping habits. But I thought it more likely that there had been a mention of it in the medical staff report that would have been passed to him. So I displaced the younger and much junior officer in charge of the department known as Passengers, Mail and Cargo (PMC), which meant that I was responsible for the organisation of these three essential operational activities. I was, in fact, the controller and planner of space and payload utilisation in all aircraft and, as such, was the director of the activities of the shifts in regard to the work to be carried out. Norman and I were the only two flight lieutenants and probably more senior than any other flight lieutenants likely to be posted in. Now, the situation was as it should be with the experience in the right places. We ran the section like clockwork and left Jack to arrange his retirement, which was to be in Australia. His wife was Maltese, and Australia was a favourite choice for Maltese émigrés. I think Jack had been more concerned with personal rather than personnel considerations. Alan Gillham, who, like me was formally aircrew, shortly replaced him without any organisational change but with an obviously better appreciation of the employment of personnel as intended by the station establishment document appropriate to the Air Movements Section. Alan sensibly discussed this with Norman and me after consulting the master establishment document held in the station central registry. He also verified that we were posted in to fill the established flight lieutenant posts, as distinct from the juniors held against posts designated for the five officers established for the Duty Air Movements Officer slots. Alan was not long experienced in the air movements field but was appreciative of the experience available to him and did not hesitate to consult us when necessary. We had a good understanding and worked well together.

The lower rank personnel were mostly locally engaged airmen of RAF Malta whose employment was restricted to the island or the Libyan stations in the provinces of Cyrenaica and Tripolitania. There were quite a large number of locally engaged civilians, most of whom also had another job, a feature that was necessary to support the local economy. There was no unemployment, and they were, generally speaking, very good workers. All my own department staff members were civilians employed as clerks and I found them conscientious and meticulous in the matter of documentation that was such an essential feature of the work. There was only a small element of RAF airmen in posts designed to provide experience. An RAF Malta Flight Sergeant filled the top Senior NCO post, later to become Warrant Officer, and a thoroughly good senior NCO he was. There was a Maltese sergeant and corporal on each shift, and the whole system seemed to work well. However, there was a tendency of corruption among the locals and it was necessary to be constantly vigilant. The officers and sergeants mess at the three Libyan RAF stations, Benina, El Adem, and Idris purchased their supplies of alcoholic drink, cigarettes, and tobacco from Maltese merchants who had legitimate arrangements with the Malta Customs Authority who were themselves most vigilant in seeing that consignments delivered to my department for shipment were consigned and shipped as intended, and a customs officer was usually present at each aircraft departure to carry out a check. However, despite these safeguards, we did have a serious infringement of the customs regulations that resulted in one of our Maltese corporals being sentenced to a lengthy spell in prison and ignominious discharge from the Service. He was involved with others in North Africa in a scheme to ship booze from Malta by the usual legal customs procedure and then have them sent back as other air cargo. I never did discover who tipped off the customs, but one of their officers was present when a particular scheduled flight returned to Luqa and carried out a detailed examination of the load. Our own corporal was the only airman of RAF Luqa involved, and the officers of the Air Movements Section felt so badly let down by a junior member who had been held in such high regard and absolute trust. It was a foolish thing to do, as the manner in which it had to be done could not have passed without being noticed by others. The movement of booze was a one-way business from Malta to North Africa only, and a familiar-looking consignment on a returning flight could easily have been suspected by a crew quartermaster apart from having been noticed by other shift personnel of the loading team at the point of origin. The risk factor was so high that it was difficult to understand how he expected to get away with it. We never did discover how the customs were alerted but my own feeling was that the supplying merchant was perhaps suspicious of an unusual feature of the manner in which the particular consignment was ordered and paid for. I think it was an isolated attempt that went disastrously wrong for those involved, and the corporal paid the price that should have been shared with others.

During November 1962, following my spell in the hospital, Rosemary and I took the opportunity to revisit RAF Idris and Tripoli. We spent a week at the Del Mehari Hotel situated at the eastern end of the Lungomare (promenade) and had a most enjoyable time. We hired a car and visited all our previous haunts with several visits to Idris, where we had friends, including Colin Betel, with whom I shared the personnel movement responsibility whilst on the staff at HQMEAF in 1953/54. Colin was doing the job of Senior Air Movements Officer that I had done in 1955/56 on posting from HQMEAF. Things at Idris seemed unchanged, and our batman Abd N'Oor was still serving the occupants of the married quarter that we had occupied. He welcomed us with a great show of affection and thought that we were returning for another tour of duty. In the city, however we noticed a great change of attitude to the British presence, which had been largely replaced by the Americans who were involved in prospecting for oil deep into the southern desert province known as the Gefarha. By this time the administration had been completely returned to local government that, to say the least, seemed rather unstable. Certainly, as past caretakers, the British were not popular with the indigenous citizens of Tripoli. There were still a few Italians in civil employment, one of whom I was pleased to see in his familiar job with the auto-dealers from whom we hired the car. There were a few others at Idris, one of whom, Carlo, was still running the bars in the Transit Mess and recognised me immediately. I was, however, concerned at his changed facial appearance, which was decidedly that of a man with little time remaining. Our week passed quickly, and when the time came for us to return to Malta, there was only one free seat available on the aircraft. So, as Rosemary had to get back to resume her motherly responsibilities that had been kindly taken on by a friend, she took the seat, and I was glad to stay in transit for another few days to wait for the next flight. I quite enjoyed my enforced stay which was amply covered by my intended period of leave.

Our life in Malta was good, with a social aspect that was almost impossible to keep up with. We made many friendships in both service and civilian communities, many of whom have withstood the test of time. We revisited Malta for a month's vacation during March/April 1984 and stayed at The Plevna Hotel, which was run by the Tabone family, whom we had known from our first arrival in Malta in 1962 when we stayed there for our first few days. Lisbet, the daughter of service friends Sqn Ldr Bill Naples and his wife Jenny, had married Peter Tabone, son of the owners, in 1965, and we were guests at their wedding. So we felt quite at home.

We enjoyed our tour in Malta. Quite a number found it boring, but they must have been extremely unimaginative as, apart from being architecturally photogenic, it has a fascinatingly rich history, which is amply reflected in its ancient architecture and geological remains. I retain a great love for Malta and its people and was sad to leave when my tour of duty came to an end in the summer of 1955. I had to extend the tour by two months to allow Ross to sit his General Certificate of Education examinations, which he accomplished successfully. I was initially advised that my next appointment was to be at the Air Ministry Harrogate for duty with the Directorate of Equipment (A). Another staff appointment, although at the Highest Level, did nothing to please me and I did, in fact, seriously consider premature retirement and started to examine the civilian alternatives. However, my dilemma was quickly resolved by a cancellation of the appointment and notification of promotion that amply illustrates how two departments, that which deals with putting arses on seats, do not always know what is being planned by that which deals with selection for appointments at senior rank level. In my own case, the action now being taken illustrates why I was posted from equipment staff duties at Headquarters Coastal Command, where I could not be immediately replaced, and sent to movements duties in Malta. Without knowing it I was being prepared for the next stage in my career plan. I was posted to RAF Abingdon, then in Berkshire, for duties connected with Mobile Air Movements, an entirely new and challenging appointment, as I was soon to appreciate.

CHAPTER XXVII
SENIOR OFFICER

I had been a flight lieutenant for eleven years and had made senior officer rank in advance of most of my contemporaries, many of whom never did make it. For myself, I felt that it would be the zenith of my career, but I experienced a marked degree of satisfaction in having been found suitable for advancement to senior rank level. Many will not understand that this includes the three ranks: squadron leader, wing commander, and group captain. The ranks below the senior level are Junior Officers, and the ranks above the senior level are Air Officers. The same rule applies to equivalent ranks in the other two services. We left Malta in August 1965, and I had to be in my new post by a date in September after twenty-eight days of ex-overseas leave.

Abingdon had already informed me that I would be allocated a married quarter shortly after arrival, but it may, as a temporary expedient, be inappropriate to rank. A senior officer's suite would, in the meantime, be available for me in the officers' mess. Whilst I was delighted with the domestic arrangements I was to find total disenchantment with the work scene. I had been given no more than an indication that my appointment was to be in connection with Mobile Air Movements, but in what respects, I had not the slightest knowledge. My posting was to fill a newly created post in the establishment of RAF Abingdon. The station, therefore assumed that I was to take charge of the small Mobile Element of the Air Movements Squadron already in existence on the station. What seemed unusual was that the squadron already had an officer commanding the squadron leader rank. It was apparently required that I should assume command of the mobile element and run it as a separate entity, although the station establishment document clearly showed it as an adjunct to the stations' Air Movements Squadron. Strange indeed, and the incumbent officer commanding, Alec Yates, although no wiser, was delighted to surrender responsibility for the mobile aspects. He had, in fact, delegated one of his flight lieutenants to look after the day-to-day running of what was shown in the establishment document as 'THE MAMS TEAM'. The Flt Lt so delegated was experienced and capable and obviously enjoyed the favor of the Station Commander, Group Captain GLP Martin, who I had met briefly whilst he was on leave in Malta shortly before my own departure. He knew at that time that I had been promoted to fill the newly created establishment vacancy at his station. The Flt Lt had been expecting to be promoted to fill it and said so, but he should have known that such was seldom done as it was regarded by Air Ministry as poor practice in peacetime. The Station Commander had clearly been thinking on similar lines and I soon judged that there was an unusual relationship that might prove detrimental to myself. There was an unmistakeable resentment on the part of the Flt Lt himself who seemingly was of the type who never lost the opportunity for ingratiation with superiors in influential positions. As time passed, my own assessment of him was that he had been somewhat overrated in his overall performance and was, to say the least, inclined to be obsequious. As he was my most senior Flt Lt, I was obliged to make him my Executive Officer and Deputy, but I knew that I would have to proceed with caution.

At that time, the main base in the Transport Command organisation was Abingdon, where the principal air transport units were located. These included the Air Movements Training School (AMTS), the Air Transport Development Unit (ATDU), of which the Air Movements Development Unit (AMDU) was an adjunct, and the No 1 Parachute Training School. There were also two air transport squadrons one of which was equipped with the heavy Beverly-type aircraft and the other with the recently introduced light and most versatile Andover. The Mobile Air Movements element of the station Air Movements Squadron was required to support the work of the ATDU when called upon to do so. It was a very busy station, and the so-called Movements Team, which in fact consisted of four teams, each comprised of a junior officer, two senior NCOs, a corporal, and two aircraftmen, was seldom at the base for more than a few days. Tasking of the Mobile Air Movements element was done directly by HQ Transport Command for work connected with Strategic Air Transport, whilst the responsibility for tasking with the Tactical Air Transport element lay with HQ No 38 Group. Duplication was seldom a problem and I was able to deal quite amicably with both taskmasters and usually found myself in daily contact with the superior Command Authority. My four teams were in constant demand for work at overseas locations to provide essential air transport facilities where none existed. This work needed special qualities of improvisation and extemporisation, for which I was required to provide the necessary training without a unit-training element for personnel who were seldom at the base. Mostly it was something that seemed to have developed by the differing needs of each assignment, but it was something that would have to be done at unit level in the interest of uniformity and overall efficiency. It was already quite clear to me that this small Mobile Air Transport element needed expansion, but I also recognised the need to proceed with studied caution.

On arrival, I found the Team occupying two dismal rooms in the corner of the Air Movements Squadron hangar, looking for the entire world to see as an inconsequential nuisance. I felt gravely offended to have been promoted to command such a bloody apparent ragtag and bobtail outfit and, at the same time a fit of rising anger at the obvious need to improve the overall appearance of my newly acquired command. I made a quiet nuisance of myself in the Station Headquarters, where the necessary action would have to be taken to provide more appropriate quarters for my needs as I saw them. I lost no opportunity to point out the deficiencies to visiting Command Air Movements staff or when I visited Command Headquarters as I was frequently required to do. There appeared to be little or no concern on the part of the station administration, and all the Command Staff seemed to be able to do was recommend that I keep plugging away at the station who, had to deal with an accommodation situation that was already bulging at the seems.

My personal accommodation in the mess was excellent consisting of two rooms to pre-war standard. Abingdon was one of the older stations, mellowed by time and reminiscent of happier days. How it became so prominent as an air transport base was always a mystery to me as a more obvious location would have been Lyneham in Wiltshire, which was more adjacent to the Army territory concentrated on the Salisbury Plain. The RAF air transport responsibility was, after all, mainly concerned with the deployment of the Army, and we already had an air transport base there that had been developing since the war years and was now the home of our strategic squadrons engaged in the air transport of passengers to overseas locations. In the fullness of time, Lyneham took the place of Abingdon and, to this day, is the home base of the Mobile Air Movements element.

I was allocated a temporary married quarter, albeit of junior officer type, and Rosemary joined me with Ross about three weeks after my arrival. We occupied a quarter appropriate to senior rank in the early summer of 1967. Ross was determined that he was not going to continue his education by returning to normal schooling. He wanted to start working despite the parental wish to advance his education to the higher levels, which he was qualified to do. However he did agree to undertake part-time education at the local evening institute. He found himself a job at a chicken farm but soon reacted to the dirty and smelly task of cleaning the chicken's quarters. His personal smell soon took on that of his working environment. He quickly tired of it and was taken on at the local brewery, where he came to the notice of the managing director, who, being most impressed, offered the possibility of a career prospect, but he would have to progress through the entire brewing processes with which he would have to develop a high degree of experience and proficiency. This included the need for absolute hygiene in all the processing stages, and young Ross soon came home smelling like a brewery. But this was not what he wanted to do anyway. His ambition lay in a flying career, and he wanted to gain entry to the RAF. The best he could hope for initially with his educational qualifications was an initial entry to a short-service commission for twelve years with the prospect of competitive selection for appointment to a permanent commission. I warned him that he was likely to be rejected on the grounds of immaturity and should wait for two years until he was twenty. However, he presented himself for selection at the Officer and Aircrew Selection Centre and went through the entire five-day selection programme, a good indication of the Boards' interest, but was not accepted, almost certainly on the grounds of immaturity. He was advised to present himself again in two years' time. He was unwilling to wait and thought he would like to get into civil aviation, so I made contact with Eagle Airways, with whom I had been involved during my time in Middle East Command in connection with the Medair contract that was performed by the company for several years. I arranged for him to have a selection interview and was delighted when he came out with the news that he had been selected.

I was barely settled into my new surroundings when I received an operation order, committing myself with one team to an exercise in the Libyan Desert, where we still held a large slice of real estate. Three teams were to remain at base with my deputy to look after other tasks. I was to be reinforced at El Adem by an officer detached from RAF Idris. It was not to be a major exercise itself but rather a preliminary to exercises planned to make good use of our desert stations in the short time remaining before political obligations required us to vacate them. The object of this particular action was to support the Royal Engineers in the reclamation of a desert airstrip known as Got El Afrag, or just plain Afrag, a small oasis some sixty miles south of El Adem, which was itself situated a few miles into the pre-desert south of Tobruk.

We were to position ourselves at Luqa, our main base in Malta, whilst the Royal Engineers positioned themselves at the site of the airstrip. Their heavy equipment was to be airdropped from our large Beverly transport aircraft direct from UK bases and we, of course, would be required to recover it using the same aircraft that would then be able to make better use of the re-graded strip. We had a pleasant few days in Malta and were summoned to El Adem, where we found quite a buzz of activity. Of course, the heavy drop had not gone quite as smoothly as was expected, and there was apparently a most essential piece of equipment - Blaw-Knox grader – that had come to grief. A replacement for it would be dropped in, and we were to recover the unserviceable item without delay using the airdrop aircraft that would be positioned at El Adem after the drop. There was another rather hectic activity that required a continuing presence at El Adem, and I was, therefore, unable to send my only team into the desert at this time. So I decided that the only thing to do was to go out myself with Flying Officer Kit Ayres, my reinforcement from Idris, and we would do the job ourselves. A commendable gesture that turned out to involve a lengthier task than expected. The Beverley flew us to the site, where we found a lonesome Lieutenant Colonel of Engineers who seemed to be the only Army person there. The damaged grader was nearby ,having suffered a cracked back axle due to one of the parachutes attached to each corner of its supporting platform not deploying properly. We had no difficulty in positioning the grader at the rear of the Beverley for loading by winching it up the ramp and into the capacious belly using the on-board winching equipment. But the winch, driven by the aircraft electrical system, wasn't bloody well working, was it? Nothing for it but to do it the hard way with much toil, tears, and sweat, using the emergency hand-operated 'Tirfor' winch by which the grader would have been pulled up the ramp inch by inch, taking a dreadfully long time. However, we got the winch rigged and set about the wearisome task. The grader was of considerable length and weight, and our oscillating arm movements on the operating lever seemed to be having only the slightest effect. It was about mid-morning when we started, and by mid-day, only the front wheels were halfway up the ramp, and we were already quite exhausted and soaked in our own filthy sweat. After a rest for a mug of tea and some food from a small field kitchen facility we set to again and finally had the wretched thing in the correct position. We did the necessary documentation and summoned the crew. The shadows were lengthening as we got airborne for El Adem, leaving the Engineer and his few men to complete the reinstatement of the strip, which he assured me would not take them more than a few days. Kit and I were glad to be back in the comparative comfort of RAF El Adem where we were able to take a much-needed shower and a decent evening meal in the mess. The exercise soon came to its intended conclusion and we had no difficulty in recovering the engineer's equipment to the UK. Kit and I are still in touch, and we see each other occasionally when he and his wife Maureen visit us on their trips to Scotland during the summer months when they like to motor from their home in Stow-on-The Wold to spend a vacation at Spean Bridge. We often talk of our wearisome encounter in the Libyan Desert with the Blaw-Knox grader and the unfortunate Beverley with its unserviceable winching system that caused us so much fatigue.

In early December 1965, I was instructed to hold my MAMS Team on standby for possible deployment to East Africa, where serious political trouble was brewing in Southern Rhodesia. Northern Rhodesia had already attained its planned independence from British Rule to become Zambia. The Government of neighbouring Southern Rhodesia under its Prime Minister Ian Smith was, however bitterly resisting the intention of the United Kingdom government to similarly declare it independent under the rule of a black majority. The situation looked very grave as the air transport route was activated, and two of my teams were provisionally pre-positioned at one of our North African stations. I was to remain at base with the two remaining teams and administrative cell to deal with other tasks and await further developments. The United Kingdom Prime Minister Harold Wilson was busy with prolonged negotiations that kept him out of London for conferences, some with Ian Smith, held aboard one of the Royal Navy ships at Gibraltar, where he was located for a seemingly lengthy spell. The stalemate situation extended over Christmas 1965, and we were reactivated early in January 1966 and deployed shortly after the Rhodesian Prime Minister issued a Unilateral Declaration of Independence. The Royal Navy immediately blockaded the Beira Strait, effectively denying sea access to both Southern Rhodesia and Zambia. The object was to compel Prime Minister Smith to accept the UK government's terms for home rule on the basis of government by the black majority. The blockade meant, however, that Zambia would also be deprived of essential supplies of petroleum products that had to come in through Beira and on to Zambia by the railroad system that passed through Southern Rhodesia. It was necessary, therefore, to inaugurate a 'Zambia Fuel Lift' using the Britannia aircraft of Transport Command and the Beverleys based in the Aden Protectorate. Additional support by civil cargo aircraft under contractual arrangement was essential. Initially, the entire operation was to be from Dar es Salaam on the coast of Tanzania, with the destination airfields at Ndola and Lusaka, respectively, serving northern and southern Zambia.

My two teams were now split between the three locations, and essential reinforcement by air movement personnel drawn randomly from Cyprus and Aden was necessary. Political problems soon attended the presence of British military personnel and aircraft at Dar es Salaam, compelling President Julius Nyreri, to request our withdrawal. A rapid redeployment of the military aircraft and personnel from Dar es Salaam to the civil airport at Embakasi (Nairobi) was negotiated with the government of Kenya, and personnel were accommodated at nearby RAF Eastleigh. The civil aircraft were permitted to continue operating out of Dar es Salaam without RAF assistance. I was ordered by my masters at Transport Command to proceed to East Africa to carry out a reconnaissance of the three active locations and return with a detailed report. Of particular concern was the need to use the recently introduced Britannia aircraft in the heavy freight role, as it was feared that their floors would be damaged by the action of loading/unloading the forty-gallon barrels used to contain the petroleum products. The aircraft was designed to carry freight on lightweight metal pallets slid into position on rails and locked at pre-determined load positions. This system had to be dispensed with because of weight and payload considerations, particularly as it was necessary for the aircraft to carry sufficient fuel for the return journeys from both Zambian airfields to Embakasi. The round-trip fuel requirement for the Britannia was approximately the same weight as the fuel carried as cargo. It was a very costly exercise, and in the logistics sense we had to cram in as many barrels as could be accommodated within the space and weight limitation. As for the Britannia floors, the best we could do was to protect them by laying down sheets of plywood cut to the suitable size. This proved to be adequate and enabled the barrels to be rolled into their loading positions quite easily, and a system was soon devised whereby sixteen barrels could be nested at each loading station and secured by a chain necklace that was, in turn, secured to the floor attachments. It was necessary to hire local native labour at all locations to assist with the heavy work involved in handling the oil barrels, the greater number being required at Embakasi, where the fuel had to be received and loaded overnight to the four aircraft employed ready for departure to Ndola and Lusaka early the next morning. The task at both destinations was unloading supervision, with only occasional backloading of operational equipment being returned to United Kingdom maintenance depots. We had No. 30 Squadron equipped with the Javelin fighter (one of 38 Group's two tactical fighter units) in position at Ndola to provide tactical air support if required. A fairly large staff with an Air Officer Commanding exercised overall control of the operation with headquarters comfortably located in school premises in Lusaka. Here, I was comfortably accommodated in a shared room for the seven nights of my stay. There was not a specialist member of staff with total responsibility for Air Transport aspects of the operation, and this, I thought, was an omission that should be considered.

Returning to base, my first task was to visit Command Headquarters and make my report. The obvious inadequacy of the command's inability to mount an operation of this size with its present Mobile Air Movements organisation was the salient consideration. Wing Commander Brian de Burton, Command Movements Officer, assured me that he already discussed this with the Director of Movements at the Air Ministry, as it had been necessary to reject much of the continuing demand to support other Army and Air Force activities. I suggested that immediate action should be instituted for an increase in the size of the MAMS Team by at least four teams to ensure adequate scope to reinforce and rotate personnel already deployed for the Fuel Lift and maintain adequate cover for additional tasking. On the political front, there was a strong suggestion that The Zambia Fuel Lift would develop into a log-term requirement that may even prove the need to increase the MAMS involvement. He assured me that the need to increase the MAMS capability was under active consideration at the highest level and suggested that I should now take the opportunity to prepare a case for an increase in the establishment. This would have to originate at RAF Abingdon, as it was that station's establishment that would be affected. I suggested that I should prepare a paper for immediate submission to the Establishment Committee for an additional nine teams.

Back at Abingdon, I discussed the matter with OC Admin Wing and ensured that he was thoroughly acquainted with the plan. He told me that a Station Establishment Review was expected during April and that now would be a good time to prepare my case for the expansion of the MAMS Team. I set about the task immediately in full consultation with Headquarters Transport Command. The paper was of some considerable size and highlighted the full extent of the present deficiencies including also the need for a small training element and technical support cell. The paper was received enthusiastically at Command Headquarters, where I was assured of Command Staff support on the appointed day and time of my forthcoming ordeal. The purpose of the Establishment Committee is to ensure that stations and units can efficiently discharge their intended function with economic manpower utilisation. Economies were always sought and one always approached these routine reviews with a measure of fear that there was more likely to be reductions than increases.

Meanwhile, however, there were other things that required my attention away from the base. I had not been back from my initial reconnaissance for more than four weeks when a telephone call from the Command Movements Officer indicated an urgent need for me to return to East Africa where my presence was required, but would I attend Command HQ for a detailed briefing. The Group Movements Officer (whom I shall call Sqn Ldr Ron) had been at Embakasi since shortly after my return and was to be relieved to serve as my stand-in at Abingdon until such time as I could be replaced at Embakasi. There were several other matters that were of concern particularly expensive damage being caused to aircraft and associated equipment. I got the impression that there was some dissatisfaction with the management of the air movement personnel, although nothing specifically was said in this respect. However, off I went, somewhat reluctant to leave things in other hands. But he couldn't go far wrong with only two teams and reduced tasking to manage, and I was, after all, going to where the real action was being taken by my actively engaged teams, which was my proper place in the present situation.

Arriving there by the weekly rotation aircraft out of Lyneham on Fridays, I immediately took over the task, and Ron returned by the same flight. I found that whilst the fuel lift was proceeding satisfactorily there were problems that needed very tactful handling. I flew down to Lusaka where I was quickly made aware of the operational problems that were seemingly due to air transportation shortcomings. The squadron of Javelin fighters at Ndola was practically grounded in its entirety for lack of spares from UK sources, and I would make this my first priority. What the hell had been going on?

Ron had casually mentioned that the Chief Customs Officer was uncooperative and a difficult person to deal with. So, this was my first port of call on getting back to Embakasi. I made myself known to the officer on duty at the customs post and requested an urgent audience with the chief. I was shown into a rather large office and told to take a seat, one of several, placed some distance from a desk at which the chief – a white Rhodesian - was busily writing. Eventually, he looked up and said rather sarcastically, "So! Someone else to fight with". I responded with, " Not at all. I am not here to fight with anyone but merely to ensure that the task of supplying fuel to Zambia, which has the full support of your President Jomo Kenyatta, is not impaired due to aircraft grounded by the lack of essential operational equipment probably impounded at Embakasi." I could see that I had disarmed him and realised that my predecessor, who was inclined to offend with his authoritarian manner, had promoted the hostility of his most important contact in the airport authority. The chief invited me to go directly to the cargo shed and contact the supervisor who would be expecting me. There, a large, smiling indigenous Rhodesian was awaiting my arrival. He escorted me to a caged area containing a very large accumulation of unmistakable RAF airfreight packing cases sufficient to make up more than one load for a Britannia. The packing cases, several of very large proportion, were labelled IOR (Immediate Operational Requirement) or AOG (Aircraft on Ground) and had obviously been lying there for unusually lengthy periods of time. I could easily have lost my temper at this discovery but that would only exacerbate the already strained relationship. I restrained myself and made polite, friendly overtures to this amiable black Rhodesian who invited me to come to see him at any time. I arranged clearance of the total accumulation and told him that I would relieve him of it later in the day as soon as I could arrange transportation. The next morning the lift into Ndola went short of much of the intended daily load of oil but received instead all of the urgently needed aircraft spares. I shortly received a signal from the Air Officer Commanding the Operation addressed to Headquarters Transport Command and Headquarters British Forces Aden, with a copy to me, advising them of the noticeable effect in the expeditious movement of urgently needed airfreight since my take over at Embakasi. I made a daily visit to the customs shed thereafter. I also asked Operation HQ to ensure that the UK Maintenance Units despatching priority air freight to Embakasi for onward movement copy their despatch signal to me. There were no further complaints about delays in the onward movement of air cargo from Embakasi.

Shortly after this, I had a visit by Wing Commander Bill Carr, the Senior Movements Officer at HQ BF Aden, whose interest had no doubt been roused by the signal of appreciation from The Operational HQ at Lusaka. I left him in no doubt about the undesirable state of things that I had found at Lusaka and the corrective work that would be needed to bring about the necessary organisational changes that I had in mind to improve things and safeguard against further damage to the aircraft floors and pallets etc. I left him in no doubt that I would need a lot of support from RAF Eastleigh particularly in the way of temporary, though somewhat costly, works service assistance.

The cause of damage to the aircraft floors was immediately obvious. Although plywood floor coverings were preventing contact damage by the oil barrels, the dirt being carried into the aircraft on the barrels was a primary factor of the problem. Moreover, nothing had been done as the task developed to correct the undesirable effects as they became obvious. The rainy season had started, and the dirt being taken into the aircraft was produced by clinging mud that covered the open ground to a depth of about three inches. This mud acted like a water barrier to the dry ground underneath and was easily lifted in large clods by anything that touched it. Consequently, it collected on the barrels as a thick coating as they were rolled onto the pallets that were, in turn, not only damaged by the barrels but also by the tines of the forklift trucks as they were forcibly driven between the underside of the pallets and the muddy ground. The pallets, designed for use as part of the aircraft load-carrying system by a firm called 'Trianco,' cost £1200 each and were simply not intended for this kind of use. They were, in fact, being used to move a load of as many as sixteen barrels by the forklift trucks to the platform lift at the aircraft loading door. The barrels were then lifted to door level and rolled by hand into the intended load position on the plywood floor covering, nested, and secured. The barrel storage area and its surrounds were completely covered by the mud that was rapidly being extended onto the extremities of the aircraft parking area. These expensive pallets had been sent from the aircraft base at RAF Lyneham fitted to the initial four aircraft as role equipment that had been envisaged as a requirement before it became apparent that the weight of it was seriously detrimental to the payload consideration, apart from the likelihood of the pallet life being drastically shortened by damage that would be caused by the barrels. The pallets were made of Duralumin, somewhat thinner than the aircraft floor and would have needed similar protection by plywood or other means. The rails into which the pallets were conveniently slid with little physical effort had to be fitted to the aircraft. These had been removed from the aircraft, the pallets being retained in use as the only means available to ease the task of conveying the barrels to the aircraft for loading. I could do nothing immediately but continue this deplorable practice until I was able to devise a more suitable and cheaper alternative to be locally manufactured. It would also be necessary to devise a system that would make it easier to load the barrels onto pallets for conveyance to the aircraft.

I drew up a rough outline plan of my proposed method and took it along to the Station Commander at RAF Eastleigh and explained that it would entail a good deal of work for the Air Ministry Works Department. He immediately called the Station Engineer by telephone and arranged for me to see him, which I did. I convened an on-site meeting for the next day. I had made prior contact with the airport manager and obtained his clearance to use a corner of the aircraft parking area adjacent to our allotted operation area for the deposit and storage of the incoming barrels from Mombassa. This would ensure that the barrels did not have to touch the ground surface and the vehicles could be kept off the mud thereby eliminating the spread of mud onto the aircraft parking area. He gave his approval for the plan and, with splendid cooperation from Works Services, in no time at all, we had wooden pallets made that were strong enough to take the weight of sixteen barrels. These were laid on short walls built of brick with space underneath to facilitate easy insertion of the forklift tines. This made it possible to pre-load four pallets, each with sixteen barrels, from a narrow gauge rail system that extended from the barrel storage area and rose gently to a position immediately behind and at the same height as the pallet loading bays. The use of the forklift trucks was minimised it now being necessary only to convey the loaded pallets to the aircraft, where they were placed onto the Freight-Lift Platform that was then raised to the level of the aircraft-loading door, the barrels rolled off and into the load position on the protecting plywood floor. The whole plan was implemented expeditiously and was a complete success, much to the acclaim of all personnel. It all seemed so ridiculously simple; the time and labour saved were immediately obvious. The entire system could be quickly filled to capacity with little physical effort and was always kept so that a load for one aircraft was always ready and could be loaded as soon as the plan for the next day's flights was confirmed and aircraft cleared for loading. Whilst the first aircraft was being loaded the next load was being prepared ready for conveyance without delay to the second aircraft. The loading of all four aircraft was now usually possible before nightfall, leaving only the simple task of documentation and final checks to be done by the night shift. Moreover, it was now possible to keep the aircraft and the tarmac clean, much to the delight of Wing Commander Tom Kennedy (later to become Air Chief Marshal), one of the Britannia Squadron Commanders from Lyneham doing a spell as RAF Detachment Commander at Lusaka.

Our location was now becoming a place of interest that seemed to be attracting an increasing number of visitors from within the Fuel Lift Organisation at Lusaka, British Forces Aden Command, and the United Kingdom. The President of Zambia, Kenneth Kaunda, arrived quietly by civil aircraft, without our knowledge, for talks with the President of Kenya. We were requested through local UK Diplomatic Sources to provide a return air passage to Lusaka for him. No problem, but he was a VIP as far as Tom Kennedy and myself were concerned and we did not have the facilities to convert our aircraft to that status. A quick signal to Transport Command shifted our responsibility, and we were instructed to isolate the most forward section of an aircraft from the load, which meant the loss of a number of barrels, fit a partition together with a table and seat, and explain to the President that it was the best we could do for him in the circumstances. We even managed to borrow a long strip of red carpet from the airport manager. On the afternoon of his departure, we had the aircraft parked on the civil part of the apron opposite the terminal building, where the departing guest was seen off by Jomo Kenyatta and his retinue. He was brought to the aircraft by one of the ground hostesses and Tom introduced himself and me. Our inability to provide the usual facilities was explained and was very politely brushed aside giving us the impression that he was grateful for the free ride home.

The Lyneham Station Commander was also a welcome visitor. For the purpose of this narrative, I shall call him Group Captain Freddie. His visit coincided with a matter affecting the accommodation of the Lyneham crews, who were required to vacate their hotel on the outskirts of Nairobi. They had enjoyed a private bar facility in the outdoor swimming pool area and decided to have a bar stock clearance party to which Freddie, Tom, and I were invited. It was a lively, if short duration, occasion that ended quite early in the evening. Freddie suggested that we should sample the cuisine of one of the Japanese restaurants in Nairobi. So off we went and found a nice looking place on Nairobi's main Kenyatta Avenue. We were the only customers. We had a very nice meal accompanied by several carafes of hot Sake. I still have one of the carafes that we were invited to take away as keepsakes. After the meal Freddie wanted to go along to the EL Sombrero nightclub that he had heard so much about from his crews. This place was located on a well-lit side street off the main thoroughfare. The clientele, all RAF, were pouring in as we arrived. The entrance was a small, plain door and a long, narrow stair with, about halfway up, a small hole in the wall where one was required to sign the admission register. Of course, the register did not contain one genuinely British name, but every well-known historical, film, and traditional story personality was to be found as visiting guests on that night. We soon found ourselves in a large bar room filled with familiar faces. It was noticeably bereft of furnishing. A young, attractive woman escorted by two males entered the room from a door at the rear. Immediately, the aircrew personnel turned in her direction with a unified shout, "Get 'em off." With her escorts, she passed through the room and the crews seemed to know, from previous visits no doubt, that the show was about to start. We three senior officers went into the room where the show was to be and sat down at a table on the edge of the room. It, too, was very sparsely furnished but had a fenced-off area, which was obviously the place where the performance was to be staged. Amidst roars of applause, the now scantily clad young woman appeared and started her dance routine. "Get 'em off," roared the delighted audience as she cavorted around the coral. Freddie got up from the table and went off, presumably to chat with the crews. Tom and I sat with a bottle of beer feeling like a couple of gooseberries. We became even more embarrassed when we realised that Freddie was inside the coral dancing around with only a woman in the place whilst she was trying to cover her embarrassment with a totally inadequate fur stole or something like that. Freddie had his dance to the delight of his Lyneham crews, and it marked the end of the short performance that had been long enough for Tom and me. We departed from the scene, Tom with Freddie in his car and me in mine. The next morning at Embakasi, an unknown Flight Lieutenant entered my office with a "Good morning, Sir, I'm Officer-in-Charge of the RAF Police Section at Eastleigh. Last night, your staff car was seen parked adjacent to the EL Sombrero, which is out of bounds. I am sure my face registered complete surprise when I replied, "Is it?" he then said, "Well, Sir, since yours was not the only staff car there, you were obviously in company with Group Captain Freddie and Wing Commander Kennedy, so on this occasion, we shall have a good laugh and forget all about it." I tried to join, somewhat sickly no doubt, in his mirthful laughter as he saluted and left.

I then went to look for Tom who told me that he had also been visited. When we later met Freddie, he said that the station commander had contacted him that morning at Eastleigh. He jokingly suggested that we should never talk about the incident north of the equator. I had never heard of the El Sombrero, let alone the fact that it was out of bounds, and I don't suppose the other detachment personnel had either. It was no doubt the subject of a local standing order but there had been some failure on the part of the Eastleigh administration in not bringing it to the attention of temporarily attached personnel. As a place of entertainment, it was miserable as was the entertainment itself, but I imagine that it had been placed out of bounds as a possible security risk.

The Fuel Lift was now well underway and coming to the attention of a wider field of interest, with Embakasi the nucleus of its operational activity. We kept the lift going nicely with four aircraft on station providing two flights each day into Lusaka and Ndola. Every Friday, we received a replacement aircraft from Lyneham and sent one back for routine maintenance. These also served to rotate personnel and provide a standing weekly scheduled service between the three detached locations and the home base. The detachment personnel were now contented. None were required to serve more than three months as, by a Records Office order, anyone doing so would have to be credited with an official tour of duty overseas that would play havoc with the routine selection for overseas liability. As for my own personnel, they, too, were rotated to comply with the same ruling, and it was never necessary for me to deploy more than the three teams initially tasked. The Transport Command Movements Officer had asked me to make a photographic record of the activities at Embakasi for the command archives, and this I had done progressively during this detachment period that I now began to consider near its end as I was at a loss to see the need for further improvements at this juncture. (A duplicate set of these slides is retained in my personal collection). Not surprisingly, Brian de Burton was thinking that I had been away long enough, and as it was now spring and summer fast approaching, thoughts were turning to other demands for UKMAMS support and particularly to the planning of the traditional autumn exercise, the main annual event usually mounted during September and lasting for four about weeks.

A relief for me at Embakasi was provided from within the Home Establishment and I was given a generous period of a week to hand over the task to him. He was Sqn Ldr Jack Ellis, an experienced air-mover to whom I warmed immediately and felt happy to pass the job on to him, having no doubts whatever about his suitability for the task. He had served at Eastleigh previously and had a daughter married to a Tom Rowe, the son of long-term British residents of Nairobi, so Jack, now a widower, was quite delighted with his three-month detachment. Jack kindly invited me to accompany him into Nairobi on Saturday after his arrival. What a pleasant day we spent with the young couple and Tom's parents.

We went to Lake Naivasha to see the famous flamingos, then onto a vantage point at the eastern end of the Rift Valley where we were able to see this mighty work of nature as it disappeared into the misty vastness of its westerly course, a truly awesome sight. At this viewpoint I was also quite fascinated by a small church that had been built by Italian prisoners of war during World War II. The decorative interior artwork was truly astounding in its magnificence and lovingly well-preserved. It was a truly wonderful day that ended with a happy evening in the hospitality of Tom's parents in their comfortable, typically British bungalow. Apart from this day, I had not had the time or opportunity for local sightseeing except for one occasion when I went for a Sunday excursion to the nature reserve at the invitation of the NAAFI Regional Manager who stayed in the officers' mess at Eastleigh. That was quite a memorable day during which I was able to take a few good camera shots that are still among my collection of photographic slides. Of course, we were not permitted to get out of the car inside the reserve because of the obvious dangers.

I arrived back at Lyneham by the weekly scheduled flight and was met, on a miserable wet April Saturday morning, by one of my drivers from Abingdon and taken home where Rosemary was eagerly awaiting my return.

Ron was still at Abingdon but had been replaced at Headquarters No. 38 Group. He was to remain at Abingdon in a supernumerary capacity until the Air Ministry could arrange a posting. Thank goodness his stay was of short duration, as he did not enjoy popularity seemingly due to his unfortunate aloof manner. Of more immediate concern was the news that the Establishment Committee was to visit the station the next week, and I had better get myself into top gear for my forthcoming ordeal.

When the day of my ordeal came, I was scheduled for an early afternoon slot in the committee's programme. Command had sent down Sqn Ldr Ken Lee, with whom I had an excellent rapport. He arrived in the morning, and we had plenty of time to discuss my plan. On being summoned to the presence, I was well aware that the usual approach would be to question the need for the present establishment. I was able to go straight into the counter-attack, which I did with the confidence of absolute conviction, and I was pleased to see the immediate effect on the faces of the members. I was, of course, examined at great length and soon gathered the impression that they were convinced of my argument. Operational effectiveness was discussed at some length. Ken Lee was asked for the Command opinion, which was fully in support of my own, and OC Admin Wing took in the whole proceedings with obvious relish. The Establishment Team congratulated me on the manner in which I had handled the lengthy request and said that they would recommend the increase in light of the operational nature and increasing workload of the MAMS team.

Following this day's work, I discussed the matter of accommodation with OC Admin Wing (Wg Cdr Ron Churcher) and suggested that an empty building last used by the Parachute Training School had apparently been abandoned after the school's initial training requirement (practice jumps from tethered balloons) had been transferred to Weston On The green. I assured him that it would adequately suit the immediate needs of the larger MAMS team now envisaged and he agreed that I could have it. I lost no time in vacating the two dismal rooms that did absolutely nothing but suggest that the occupants had been ignominiously consigned to total obscurity. The building was located on the far side of the airfield adjacent to the inactive bomb dump. It suited my requirements admirably and provided ample office accommodation together with a large operations room that would also serve as the general office for my Executive Officer and the Administrative Staff. A large Crew Room, a separate room for the officers, and offices for the Training Warrant Officer and myself. It had toilet facilities and heating by thermostatically controlled electric heaters. It could hardly have been better if I had planned it myself.

Things now started to develop quickly. Ron, who had been held supernumerary was posted to RAF Abingdon as OC Station Air Movements Squadron, but his stay was short-lived ,and he was eventually replaced by Squadron Leader Mick Spaul. My flight lieutenant was posted to Malta, but the first I knew of it was when he entered my new office accompanied by the Station Commander, who conveyed the news and asked me what I thought of it. I was rather surprised at the manner of this unusual occurrence since it was clear that I had been bypassed in regard to the posting notification. The question also seemed unusual, as the CO was aware that I was well acquainted with Malta. I answered simply that I thought Malta was among the better places to serve an overseas tour of duty. But it soon became obvious that the purpose of the visit was occasioned by a large measure of disappointment that the posting was not being made on promotion, and that was the reason for the involvement of the Station Commander with whom he sought favour. The CO later rang me to discuss a recommendation for the award of the MBE and whether I would take the appropriate action to write it. I was not at all pleased but had to make an attempt, which I did not find easy as I thought this sort of thing quite abhorrent. However, I did it, and he left in July for a UK location on promotion to Acting Squadron Leader. So there had been some string pulling somewhere to get the overseas posting changed. I later learned that he did not get the MBE but was awarded a 'Laudatory Commendation' as had happened to me whilst at HQ Coastal Command. As a replacement for him was not immediately forthcoming, I had to make some internal changes to provide a temporary Executive Officer. I selected Flying Officer Ted Worsley, the oldest of the team leaders whom I had recommended for appointment to a permanent commission, to which he was eventually appointed. I had to wait until January 1967 for a Flight Lieutenant designated for the post of Executive Officer.

The formal amendment to the RAF Abingdon establishment followed quickly, and I was delighted to find that my requests had been met in full with provision for a Warrant Officer in the training role and a technical senior NCO for the maintenance of equipment. Now, this was a significant increase from four to nine teams with a total establishment of Eleven Officers, One WO, Nineteen Senior NCOs, Nine Junior NCOs, and Nineteen aircraftmen. Still a little on the small side as regards personnel, but it brought great satisfaction for me.

Shortly after this confirmation, I was delighted, and somewhat astonished, to receive, on the first day of May 1966, a signal addressed to me personally from the Director Of Movements RAF congratulating me on the elevation of my unit to Squadron Status with the title 'United Kingdom Mobile Air Movements Squadron'. This meant that we were no longer part of the RAF Abingdon establishment being dependant only for the provision of her supporting services but totally independent in the operational sense and could be relocated as required. The truth of my personal situation now became clear, although it had not been mentioned. In fact, I am certain that it was not known below the Air Ministry level that in the overall reorganisation plan, MAMS was planned to become a Specialist Operational Squadron of Transport Command. I believe that it happened somewhat prematurely because of the effect of the Zambia Fuel Lift but had otherwise intentionally been kept secret, as it would obviously have been. My only clue lay in my unusual appointment to a squadron leader post to head such a small element in a station section that already had a squadron leader as section head. I had, in fact, been selected to become the first officer of the Equipment Branch to be appointed to form and command an operational squadron; in fact, the only operational appointment to which an officer of the branch could be appointed. The realisation brought a feeling of great elation.

CHAPTER XXVIII
OPERATIONAL SQUADRON COMMANDER

It was now being confidently forecast at the Command level that as the plan to run down the overseas Commands progressed, the newly created squadron would be increased in size to meet the greater dependence of the remaining overseas locations for reinforcement from the United Kingdom. There were, of course, many in high places that doubted it would last; how wrong they were to be. The new establishment was almost immediately overborne by an increase of four teams for the duration of the Zambia Fuel Lift. So, I now had an overall establishment of thirteen teams and a great deal of organisational work on my hands.

I set to work immediately to wean the new squadron from the station to which it no longer belonged. I had an oak panel made from a discarded dining table doing much of the wood finishing myself at home. This was to display the names of successive Squadron Commanders in gilt. For the first name, myself, I hired a professional sign writer in Oxford to do the work at my personal expense, hoping that it would set the future example. There was sufficient space to name at least a further eleven successive squadron commanders. I had a flagpole made in the station workshops to standard size and pattern and got the Station Works Services to create a suitable site for it adjacent to the squadron headquarters building. I was now entitled to fly my personal rank pennant at the masthead whenever I was on the base, and this was done immediately.

I felt that it was desirable to have a squadron badge, but I knew that this would not be possible until the squadron had been established for at least five years. However, I wrote to the Chester Herald King of Arms, who is also Inspector of RAF Badges. I had a telephone call from Chester Herald himself, and what a pleasant and helpful person he was. Most eager to help, he advised me that the only way to legally acquire a squadron badge was to seek the Transport Command Commander-in-Chief's authority to utilise the central motif of the Command Crest with my Squadron Title in the surrounding regulation circlet. He would then have the official drawing of the crest prepared and the necessary authority for its use issued. All of this took surprisingly little time, and I was then able to agree on a design for a suitable squadron crested tie and a Christmas card for members of the squadron to use to mark the first Christmas of the unit's new status. The effect on personnel was quite noticeable, but I was only too well aware of the many other things still to be accomplished to improve their lot compared with that of the aircrew personnel with whom they were required to operate. There were matters touching on increments to basic pay, particularly for lengthy periods spent at overseas locations.

The annual exercises for the autumn of 1966 were to be held within the United Kingdom. An unexpected departure from the usual overseas deployment that required movement by air and sea to the exercise areas in the Middle East where we still had extensive standing facilities with none of our bases as yet disposed of. However, this time, the centre piece of the exercise required us to concentrate our efforts on the deployment and support of the Second Parachute Regiment from a main location in Yorkshire to an air-landed assault against enemy forces concentrated in the south of England. The main assault was to be on the Salisbury Plain and there were supporting elements to be mounted from locations in Scotland and East Anglia involving the tactical transport aircraft of No. 38 Group. It was to be quite a big exercise with many unusual aspects for UKMAMS. In my own Operation Order, I placed myself with my main element at Leconfield in East Yorkshire, from where the main airborne assaults were to be mounted, with smaller elements at the other locations to liaise with the Army Royal Corps of Transport in the loading of troops, vehicles and other equipment.

Now, there was only one of me, and no one, myself included, had foreseen the need to provide a deputy. The initial work in the Positioning Phase of the exercise was such that my constant presence was required throughout the first forty-eight hours after arrival at Leconfield. Consequently, not having slept for those forty-eight hours, I was very tired when, at about midnight on the eve of the Operational Phase, I found it possible to retire to my tent for a few hours much-needed sleep. All the necessary preparations had been made for the emplacement of the various Chalks to the eighteen 'Hastings' aircraft lined up with great precision on the perimeter track of the airfield. Everything, including vehicles, had been loaded, and aircraft identification numbers had been given to the Chalk Commanders so that all they had to do was march in to their allotted aircraft location and board under the supervision of my personnel and the quartermasters of the aircraft crews. Chalk One in the first aircraft and Chalk Eighteen in the aircraft at the other end of the line. I departed, leaving the officer of the night duty team with instructions that I was to be wakened an hour before the scheduled time of emplacement of the assault troops. Accordingly, on the edge of a very dewy dawn, I was aroused after a good six hours of sleep and reluctantly climbed out of my sleeping bag. A quick wash in the cold water poured from my canvas bucket into my canvas field washbasin soon revived me. Thank goodness I had the presence of mind before retiring to put a mess tin of water on top of my turned-down Tilley Lamp to provide for a pleasant hot water shave. In no time at all, I was in the ruins of what had once been a substantial farm building now doing good service as a temporary officer's mess. The duty cook plied me with a hot mug of tea and a most welcome bacon sandwich in the field kitchen that also provided a warm spot in the chill of early dawn.

A quick journey in my Landover vehicle soon took me to the scene of the developing action. I arrived at the flight line just ahead of the first Chalk of troops, confidently believing this would be Chalk No.1. Alighting from the vehicle, I could see that the Chalk Commander was looking for the aircraft tail number that had been given to him and immediately realised that things were going wrong from the start. I intercepted the young officer while still on the march and said to him, "If you are Chalk No.1, your aircraft is the first in line; march on the way you are going until you come to it." "But I am Chalk No.6, Sir." "Well then," said I, "Your aircraft is sixth in the line from that end. Halt your chalk at your aircraft and await instructions to emplane. Where is Chalk No.1, by the way?" "Don't know, sir; we were told to proceed to the aircraft as soon as our chalks were complete." "Well, you should have moved from your assembly area to the flight line in the order of your chalk numbers." The following confusion was quite unimaginable as the various chalks sought to locate their aircraft by its tail number, that was, of course, the number of its position in the line. The Army Liaison Officer of the Royal Corps of Transport was now on the scene and I gave him the benefit of my annoyance that such a simple procedure with which one would expect Parachute Brigade personnel to be well acquainted. However, bigger trouble was brewing for me as leaving the liaison officer to sort the chalks out into the required order as they appeared, I turned to my own very flustered looking Duty Officer who said to me, "Sir, I think you had better come to the Chalk No.1 aircraft where Colonel Farrar-Hockley is jumping up and down demanding that his command vehicle be transferred to No.2. Arriving at the aircraft post-haste, now amidst the deafening crescendo of increasing noise as the aircraft was starting engines at due timing, I discovered the very irate Regimental Commander doing just as my duty officer as said. The problem was that the aircraft had a slight fault on one of its four engines. It was a common occurrence known as 'Mag drop' which meant that the secondary magneto for that engine was not delivering a constant electrical charge to the spark plugs. I tried to calm down the Colonel and got hold of the line chief, who confirmed the problem and added his assurance that it would probably be rectified before the due time for the aircraft to taxi out for takeoff. I explained to the colonel that if I acceded to his request to transfer his vehicle, it would cause a delay of at least twenty minutes because of the work involved in positioning and repositioning the loading ramp alternately to get both vehicles onto the ground to affect their transfer. He should, of course, have made a contingency plan against this happening by duplicating the second chalk to include a vehicle similarly equipped as his command vehicle in No.1, all if it was the radio installation that was of primary concern, the vehicle in No.2 was similarly equipped so why not simply transfer himself and the whole chalk to the No.2 aircraft which I would gladly arrange to depart as No.1. But no way was I going to upset the entire plan by doing as he wished. I advised him to give the engine chaps a little time as this was not an unusual problem for aircraft kept in the open overnight; probably nothing more than a slight dampness that they would soon locate and rectify. Sure enough, thank goodness, the engine mechanics soon had the problem resolved, and the recalcitrant engine burst into life and we got the thumbs-up signal from the cockpit as the instruments registered a normal situation. I invited the colonel to board, and the aircraft started to roll exactly at the due time, followed nose to tail by No.2 et seq., and the whole stream of eighteen was airborne as scheduled at thirty-second intervals. Peace and quiet replaced the intense noise generated by the aircraft, each with four engines, at least six of them being run up at the same time. But the quiet respite was to be of short duration as, almost immediately, we entered the Tactical Phase of the exercise.

Other elements were to be deployed to the imaginary troublesome locations using the Armstrong Whitworth 'Argosy' aircraft only recently brought into service as the Command's Tactical Transport. This aircraft was something of a noisy beast that introduced a new noise produced by its four turboprop engines. It had a twin-boom arrangement to carry the tail unit that, together with its own particular noise, soon earned it the sobriquet 'Whistling Wheelbarrow.' It had excellent facilities for loading from the tail end, but great care was necessary when loading with the use of fork-lift trucks as it was easy to lose sight of the tailplane as the forks were raised to the height of the aircraft floor for insertion of the item to be loaded. The lesson was soon learned as I had an early case of damage to a tailplane to deal with despite prior warning to all concerned. It never happened again during my time in command.

The elements now to be deployed were the supporting arms with their equipment that included specialised vehicles, light weaponry including Wombats and Mobats, ammunition, and all manner of paraphernalia peculiar to modern warfare. This phase of the exercise went on with sustained effort as the need for reinforcement and replacement dictated. We were kept busy night and day until the exercise ran its intended course over a period of two weeks or so. It was designed, among other things, to test the ability of No. 38 Group's new aircraft, and it surely did so. We then had to deal with the Recovery Phase, which took another few days as each location was cleared of all items of equipment that had to be recovered by air. There was some need for haste as we had been warned that the Zambia Fuel Lift was to be brought to an abrupt end for political reasons, mostly financial, I understand, as the lift had been in place for almost twelve months by this time. I was instructed by Command Headquarters to recover all my exercise elements to base as soon as practicable against the likely need to deploy additional personnel to the Fuel Lift locations.

Returning to base myself with the final element from Leconfield, my first interest was to discuss with Command the situation at the Zambia Fuel Lift locations. The withdrawal had already commenced but the UKMAMS teams would, as was always the case, be the last out. There was little to recover in the way of equipment that could not be conveniently lifted out by our own aircraft resources. Personnel and equipment located at Lusaka and Ndola had already been cleared, and the personnel to Embakasi, where the greatest physical effort would be required. The withdrawal would be completed in just a few more days, and it would be unnecessary to deploy more assistance. The Squadron Operations Record for the Zambia Fuel Lift, which began on 29th December 1965 and came to an end on the 7th November 1966, shows that, in additional to the fuel lifted, we handled over the period: 37,546 passengers.167 tonnes of baggage.15, 531 tonnes of freight. Total additional weight: 15,725 tonnes.

With the collapse of the Fuel Lift it was necessary to give some thought to the likely action by the Establishments Committee to amend the unit establishment by deletion of the four teams overborne for the duration of the fuel lift. As the action to acquire these additional four teams had not been of my own volition, I thought it proper that any case for their permanent retention should be a matter for the Command Staff. It was agreed that a strong case would be needed to accomplish this but would I submit my own thoughts on the matter to reinforce a case that they would be willing to submit. This I agreed to do and said immediately that the case should be based on the inability of Command and 38 Group to meet the tasking requests being made upon them for UKMAMS support, plus the effect on my personnel of the excessive workload prior to the addition of the unit establishment being overborne. The personnel aspects were no problem for me, and I was able to make a strong case based purely on morale factors, particularly on married personnel who were frequently called upon at short notice to proceed overseas in support of all manner of requests for assistance to be provided at locations where necessary facilities were not available. Command did their part and I was pleasantly surprised to find the proposals accepted without condition. This I suspect, was mainly due to a predetermined plan for the envisaged eventual size of the unit that I had been selected to form and command, the whole process having been somewhat accelerated by the Zambia Fuel Lift.

The pattern of the new unit's existence in the general scheme of things soon became manifest. There was no apparent reduction in the workload but it was now possible for personnel to take their annual leave entitlement in full and to be compensated by time off in lieu for any public holidays missed due to tasking needs. On the financial side of things, my argument for the award of crew pay to bring UKMAMS personnel more in line with the flying personnel could not be granted on the grounds that crew pay was, in fact, qualification pay. However, UKMAMS personnel were to be granted all other financial benefits applicable to aircraft crews in terms of allowances at the rates applicable for the overseas locations visited, where they were to enjoy the same facilities as the crews in terms of accommodation and messing. Working clothing was also a matter that I had to represent as that generally available was quite unsatisfactory for the proper protection of UKMAMS personnel who were required to work in all climatic conditions. The Army was responsible for the design and provision of all uniform clothing requirements, and I was eventually required to undertake a visit to the Army Clothing Development Centre at Colchester, where I was enthusiastically received and given splendid cooperation. It was possible to redesign the existing patterns of protective clothing to more acceptable garments that would ideally satisfy not only the UKMAMS requirement but also be acceptable for general usage, thereby satisfying the need for economy. Arctic clothing was a particular problem; the hands, being vulnerable in sub-zero conditions, required effective insulation when handling and adjusting load restraint equipment. I had already had one case of severe injury to the hand of one airman who lost the skin from the palm of a hand when he foolishly, and despite instructions not to do so, removed his glove to make an essential adjustment to a load restraint. Arctic clothing was very expensive, but a satisfactory solution did not seem possible to avoid the high wastage rate of arctic gloves caused by the need to use them for a purpose for which they were not designed. The high wastage rate and cost involved would have to be accepted until an alternative could be found.

The normal pattern of tasking continued to the maximum capacity of the squadron. We had a very large slice of territory to cover. Besides the United Kingdom and Europe, we had Iceland, Canada, the USA, the whole of the African continent, The Mediterranean, Aden and the Arabian Gulf, the Bahamas, and Honduras and contingency plans for wherever there were British subjects and British interests. There was no wastage, and all personnel were kept busy with interesting diversions to many parts of the world, which they were seldom able to enjoy to the same degree as the tourist. Neither were they allowed to stagnate at home. I was occasionally able to task myself with an occasional visit to an overseas location as a means of personal familiarisation with the more frequent task locations and an opportunity to unobtrusively observe personnel performance. There was always activity in the overseas locations. The management of the squadron, however, kept me fully occupied at the base, and I was, seemingly, always on the go with visits to Command, Group, and all manner of places in the UK, RAF, and Army, in connection with the planning of forthcoming activities, reorganisation and so on. There was no end to the UKMAMS involvement in the realm of Air Transport Support and Logistics, which was the very heart of our existence

So, 1966 had been quite a year in the developing history of UKMAMS. We had entered the year as a somewhat insignificant adjunct of four teams of the RAF Abingdon Station Air Movements Section and came to its close as a fully-fledged and tested Specialist Squadron with its own establishment of thirteen teams and a sizeable headquarters element. 1967 was to see further consolidation.

The first half of 1967 produced nothing more than the usual round of tasking activity that continued to take the teams to the many and usual UK and overseas locations. This, however, was carried out against the growing pattern of events in the Middle East and Nigeria. By the beginning of June we were required to cancel many scheduled tasks and hold seven teams at seventy-two hours readiness for deployment to the trouble spots.

Squadron Leader Ron who had been held supernumerary to the unit establishment, was posted during January to relieve Alec Yates as Station Senior Air Movements Officer RAF Abingdon. He was not in the post very long before being relieved by Squadron Leader Mick Spaul. My new designated Executive Officer arrived in the form of Flight Lieutenant Robert (Jock) McKay, a former Flight Engineer who was well-known within Transport Command. A pre-war regular entered as a technical tradesman and was selected for flying duties; he was later commissioned. He was a no-nonsense person who, having lost his flying category on medical grounds, was quite happy to serve out his remaining time in his own preference of Air Movements duties within the Equipment Branch. Quite happy with his lot in life, he was noted for his gravelly voice and was a prolific smoker who liked a large measure of good malt. He was, in my opinion, excellent value for money, and I liked him a lot. Unfortunately, he died shortly after his retirement from the Service, but I have maintained contact with his wife, Doris, who still resides close to Abingdon.

In February, I decided that I was due for a well-earned break. I thought that I should task myself to visit a location frequently visited by my teams when the rotation of Honduras (now Belise) Garrison came around at three monthly intervals. The location was Nassau in the Bahamas, where, on this occasion, we were to position 43 Royal Marine Commando for an exercise that was given the name 'Winter Sun'. On the return flight I arranged to take in another exercise that was taking place in Canada with the main location at Winnipeg, which was also a scheduled night stop on the route home from Nassau. I found the Bahamas delightful, if rather expensive, so expensive that it was quite impossible to enjoy the delights of our daily subsistence allowance of ten US dollars. No wonder it is appropriately called a millionaire's paradise. With our daily allowance, it was possible to buy only a decent steak, without trimmings, for the evening meal. The hotel at which we stayed under a contractual arrangement had to devise a special low-cost menu to provide three meals a day for the ten-dollar allowance. If one stuck to the special menu, there was nothing more interesting than the basic need for sufficiency. It was expensive enough for the officers to provide attractive additions, but for others, it was quite impossible. Beer was so expensive as to be almost out of reach. The cost problem seemed to be due to the fact that the islands were little more than attractive places, with the means for enjoying life having to be imported from America. The wealth that the islands attracted was to be seen in the harbour at Nassau, which was jammed with the yachts and cruisers of the very rich. Here, too, in a separate section of the harbour, were many private aircraft of the amphibious kind, and at the nearby airport, the parked private land planes were mostly capable of carrying several passengers in luxury. It was difficult not to feel envious. I think I stayed there for three nights in excellent hotel accommodation, but the real pleasure was in the delightful island scenery, the clear water of the hotel's private strip of beach and the warmth of the climate.

On the day of our departure we left the commandos to get on with their exercise and, wearing tropical kit, headed north across the cotton fields of the Southern United States. It seemed no time at all before we crossed the northern snow line and into the Canadian Prairies. At this point, we changed into a home dress. The snow was so deep that the treetops looked like young saplings poking through it. Landing at Winnipeg, the aircraft disappeared behind a wall of snow on either hand, with lateral vision completely denied. I emerged looking like an Eskimo in a sealskin parka and gloves to be met by my own personnel similarly attired. They were in their usual high spirits. The Canadian Air Force officers offered to show me something about downtown Winnipeg's nightlife, but after feeling rather weary after a long day, I politely declined and found my way to my room in the bachelor officer's quarters. I was rather surprised that after mounting several steps to get into the building, I then had to descend as many to the ground floor, where I found my allotted room with its more than ample size. Finding it uncomfortably hot, I tried to turn down the heater a bit, but the control handle just kept going round and round and was obviously broken. So I opened the double-glazed window and touched the snow that was barely below the level of the sill.

By this time, I was bathed in sweat, so I got undressed and had a shower. Returning to the bedroom, I found it somewhat cooler, but as it was a still night with a very frosty-looking full moon, I left the window open and slept soundly for about ten hours. Breakfast was a very substantial meal, and shortly thereafter, we were airborne for our last leg to Lyneham and home. In my report on this short visit to the Bahamas, I went to great lengths to highlight the inadequacy of the daily subsistence allowance. The administrative arrangements were the responsibility of the Senior Naval Officer West Indies (known by the abbreviation SNOWI), who was located in Barbados. He, of course, was tied by the Ministry Of Defence's financial limitations and simply could not do any better than the contractual arrangements already in place. It was a most unsatisfactory arrangement that never seemed to get better, and we just had to live with it.

I was having a spot of trouble with pain in both legs due to varicose veins and was admitted to RAF Hospital Wroughton on the 17th of July for surgery. I was discharged from the hospital on the 28th of July and granted fourteen days of sick leave. I found for some time that after sitting for any appreciable length, my knees got so stiff that it took a few seconds to straighten them to the fully erect position.

By mid-August, I had two teams deployed to locations in the Salisbury Plain area for rehearsals in connection with an exercise designated 'Unison 67'. This was designed to demonstrate to selected officers of Group Captain to Air Marshal (and Civil Servants of equivalent rank) battlefield techniques using the tactical helicopters of No.38 Group. The location for the initial enplanement was to be the Royal Military Academy at Sandhurst with the officers themselves, a total of 116, being emplaned in a stream of 12 Wessex Helicopters timed at approximately thirty-second intervals. I was to personally supervise the activity at Sandhurst, assisted by a team of four specially selected young female officers who were to be rehearsed and briefed by myself. As I was still unable to drive, I had to be driven to Sandhurst where, on arrival at the entrance steps to the Academy, a young officer dashed down to open the car door, which, of course, he did with an accompanying salute that was the very model of the Academy standard. On alighting, I found myself in the ridiculous situation of having to return his salute, still trying desperately to straighten myself to a fully upright position. The four specially selected young ladies were there to meet me; what a wonderful selection job had been done. They were absolutely the most gorgeous young female officers I had ever seen, and I was quite astounded that they were almost identical in shape and size, like four peas from the same pod. They were all recently commissioned in the most junior rank of Pilot Officer and, of course, obviously delighted at their selection. I went through a form of rehearsal with them and emphasised the need for a no-nonsense approach to the senior ranking officials they would be required to lead out to the helicopter enplanement point and see them safely on board. I would ensure that the passengers themselves understood the need for their own unhesitating movement and strict compliance as essential to the success of the operation. And I would be right there with them throughout to see that there was no nonsense with rank etc. The day for the exercise proper was the 29th of August. It was dull, and I arrived at the Academy quite early as the 116 officers and civilians of equivalent rank were to be briefed at some length on the use of tactical helicopters in battlefield conditions. I sought out the Group Captain responsible for this briefing and suggested that I might address the officers myself whilst they were being briefed, but he assured me that he would impress upon them the need for their absolute cooperation with my small staff of female assistants. The enplanement point was a spot just beyond the far edge of the parade ground, about two hundred yards from the Academy steps, and it was most important that the point should not be overcrowded. It was, therefore, essential that the only passengers at the spot should be those intended for the helicopter on the ground; timing was an important safety factor. As the passengers came down the steps I was immediately visible to them wearing on my left arm the red Movements Officer Brassard with its RAF eagle and crown badge. I had no problems in quickly grouping them into parties of fourteen as they arrived at the foot of the steps, talking to them all the while. By the time the first aircraft was about to land, I had the first four groups ready and gave the go-ahead signal for the first group to move off. I knew that I had eight minutes to complete the loading and despatch of all twelve aircraft, and the success of the operation depended greatly on my own control and timing. So I had one eye on the loading point and the other on the assembling passengers all the time. I kept up a polite chatter throughout and even found time to say a special few words to Air Marshal Sir Augustus (Gus) Walker, whose one-armed figure was well known, and I was able to mention that, like himself, I was also a former flyer of No. 4 Group in the early war years. He was in his usual easy, jocular mood and very talkative. He seemed to be the only Air Marshal among a mostly civilian gathering, most of whom were civil servants of equal rank to Group Captain. There were very few uniforms. It all went off splendidly with clockwork precision well within the eight minutes allowed. Their first destination was a location on the Salisbury Plain designated 'Round C,' where one of my teams was waiting to receive them and later move them on by the same means to their final exercise location at RAF Boscombe Down, where another team waited to deplane them and disperse them to their final Ministry of Defence destinations.

The main exercise for 1967 was to be designed to test the forces of the North Atlantic Treaty Organisation in Europe. It was to be held at locations in Germany with RAF Geilenkirchen as the theatre's Main Base, where I was to position my HQ Element with five teams. The exercise was named 'Overdale,' and it was an intense activity over a period of four weeks with most of the action concentrated in that rugged area of Germany known as The Eiffel. Quite early in September, I positioned myself at Geilenkirchen with one team for the Activation Phase and set-up my HQ in a hangar on the edge of a large aircraft-parking apron. Our accommodation was good using the station messing facilities that had been extended by the use of suitably large marquees to accommodate the greatly inflated number to be catered for. It was pleasant enough on the personal side of things, although the sleeping accommodation was somewhat overcrowded. A considerable amount of the Army's heavy field equipment, tanks, etc., had been transported from the UK by the Logistics Landing Ships operated by the Royal Fleet Auxiliary, and as the activation phase progressed, I was joined, as planned, by a further five teams to cope with the personnel and equipment that was flown in by our most recently acquired C130 'Hercules' transport aircraft that were to become the mainstay of the RAF logistics organisation. The army Air Corps was obviously to be a main feature of this exercise, judging by the number of their small tactical helicopters (Sioux and Lynx) that we had to unload. Sadly the exercise was to claim one of them and its two-man crew in an accident with an overhead cable during the exercise proper somewhere in the Eiffel. We had to repatriate the victims in one of our returning aircraft; one of those sad things we had to take in our stride.

It was all go with never a moment to spare in an exercise of considerable intensity that surely tested to the limit the ability of the NATO forces in the European Theatre of Operations. By the end of it, I had fifty-four of my personnel engaged, and, as was usually the case, we were the last to leave the Theatre Main Base on the final day of the Recovery Phase.

To end a very active 1967, we were to become involved, during November, in one of the most troublesome of our Middle East areas – The Arabian Gulf and the Aden Protectorate. The families having already been evacuated, we were now required to finally evacuate the Protectorate where Army units, principally the Black Watch under its notorious commander Lieutenant Colonel Mitchell (known as 'Mad Mitch'), were engaged in what was to be a fighting withdrawal from the Radfan where they were in constant action against dissident forces. The Aden part of it was to be taken care of by the resident Air Movements Section at RAF Khormaksar (Aden), whilst UKMAMS would look after the final movement to the United Kingdom from RAF Muharraq (Bahrain) in the Arabian Gulf. On the day of the evacuation of the last of the Black Watch from Aden, I thought that the Station Commander (Group Captain Bill Lamb), who I had previously known in Malta, might wish to be on hand to welcome 'Mad Mitch' himself who was to be on board the last aircraft out. The aircraft parking area at Muharraq was very expansive, and aircraft were usually parked a considerable distance from the buildings in which passengers were processed. For the purposes of the Aden Evacuation, an entire hangar was specially allocated as a reception area. Unfortunately, the Stn Cdr was not on hand at the time of the aircraft's arrival, but I thought it was propitious to be on hand myself. Sure enough, the first person out was Mitch himself, who was, of course, outranked by the Stn Cdr, on whose behalf I offered apologies. I accompanied him myself on the long walk to the reception area and chatted with him amiably enough, but on arriving at the hangar, I could see that he was expecting a reception committee and was most disappointed to find that there was to be no publicity for him at this location; not even the Stn Cdr at the time of our arrival. Bill arrived a few minutes later and, after effecting the usual introductions, I withdrew, having many other things to do. But I could see that Mitch was not pleased. He was that type of flamboyant individual who was clearly trying to make a name for himself.

244

In doing so, he soon offended high places and decided, for some reason, to curtail his army career.

During my stay at Muharraq I well remember an occasion when I was perforce kept out on the parking apron for some reason to do with a particularly unusual load. Darkness had fallen, and I was still wearing only a shirt and shorts. On leaving the aircraft, I was immediately aware of the intense cold, and by the time I had walked quickly to my appointed office, I was uncontrollably trembling with its intensity. Of course, it was November, during which the cold of the winter seemed to strike with a suddenness that took one completely by surprise. This was such an occasion.

During 1967, Group Captain Martin handed over command of RAF Abingdon to Group Captain Adams, whose stay was unusually short. Group Captain Norman Hoad, in turn, relieved him before the end of that year. Shortly after assuming command, Norman invited all the senior officers and their wives to attend an evening meeting in the Officers' Mess, where he broke the news that RAF Abingdon had been selected as the venue for the Official Fiftieth Anniversary Celebrations of the founding of the RAF on 1st April 1918. However, mainly due to weather considerations, the appointed day for the celebrations would be in June 1968, and all senior officers with their wives would be required to play a significant part in the preparations for this important event that would be attended by members of the Royal Family and a whole host of VIPs (Very Important Persons). There would have to be rehearsals at which we would be selected to play the role of these VIPs, including at least two rehearsals for the formal banquet to ensure that the mess staff had attained the standard of meticulous etiquette demanded for this Royal Occasion. Of course, the cost of providing the menu would not be charged to us but would represent two free meals and a never-to-be-forgotten experience. The station would, of course, celebrate the anniversary properly on the first of April, but this would be a matter for the station itself to arrange without outside influences. 1968 was going to be a very busy year.

The squadron continued to develop under the influence of demanding operational tasking, which was designed to practise the techniques that attended to the needs of highly mobile forces capable of rapid reaction. UKMAMS was rapidly becoming a vital factor in the implementation of these developments, and noticeable changes were soon to be found in the Army units as closer contact and inter-service cooperation became inevitable. All Army units initially progressively underwent training in air mobility by UKMAMS. They were instructed in the loading and tie-down of their own equipment and, after that, required to provide loading and lashing teams to work under UKMAMS guidance whenever they were moved by air in RAF transport aircraft.

On the Abingdon scene, the preparations for the fiftieth anniversary celebrations began to take place quickly under the direction of Group Captain Norman Hoad who rapidly gained popularity by dint of his personality and enthusiastic example. Rosemary and I were to take on the mantle of Air Chief Marshal Sir John and Lady Whitworth-Jones for all the rehearsals, whilst my fellow senior officers assumed the roles of the many other VIPs who were to receive the Royal Invitation to attend the great function. The flying and static displays involved a tremendous amount of work, particularly the provision of aircraft for the static display, which was designed to portray the history and development of the flying service from its formation in 1912. At the same time, the Royal Air Force Museum was to be formed by the creation of a trust with its main location at the oldest RAF Establishment at Hendon, where some of the old flying school features were to be preserved within the proposed design of the new creation. Finding the aircraft for the Anniversary Static Display and eventual display in the museum was, as one can imagine, a task of tremendous proportion. Since the RAF is not in the business of writing its own history and creating a museum as a charge against public funding, initial costs were to be provided by a loan arrangement and assistance from RAF stations within the existing provision. At Abingdon, we were tasked with the restoration of two Avro 504 series aircraft, also a Hawker Hind, latter gifted by the Royal Afghan Air Force, required one a my UKMAMS teams to fly to Kabul in January 1986 to load it into an Argosy transport aircraft and accompany it to Abingdon for restoration. My collection of photographs includes these exhibits with pictures of the Hind before and after restoration, as I was particularly interested in this type in which I had done some of my pre-war training. It had a Lewis machine gun fitted in the rear cockpit, but the magazines supplied were of the forty-seven-round type normally used on the ground version of the gun. These could not be fitted to the airborne weapon that was designed to take the larger ninety-seven-round magazines, and I was quick to point out this error. All of the aircraft were restored to flying standard, but for obvious reasons, flying them was strictly forbidden. I can say, however, that the engine testing on one of the Avros was seen to include some rather fast taxiing that lifted the tail skid and wheels off the ground. Temporary accommodation and workshop facilities for the completed exhibits were provided at RAF Henlow in Bedfordshire, where the beginning of a civilian museum staff was also created.

All stations celebrated the 50th Anniversary of the founding of the Royal Air Force on the appropriate date, which, of course, was the first of April 1968. The dawning of this day found Rosemary and me on leave in Nairn. I was, of course, expected to attend the formal dinner to be held in the Officers' Mess at my home station, RAF Abingdon. So, at a ridiculously early hour, we were up and soon on the way to the Inverness airport at Dalcross for the first flight to London. It seemed appropriate to be airborne at about twenty thousand feet as we took a leisurely breakfast on that beautiful sunny morning. We were back at base before lunch, and after a spell in my Squadron Headquarters, I was soon up to scratch with the latest developments. Dinner that evening provided an initial opportunity to rehearse the mess staff for the Official Celebrations to be staged by the station in June. Of course, we were not treated to the actual banquet intended for the big day, but our usual monthly Dining In Night dinner had a few more additions than usual, all at our own expense, you may be sure. It was a good night, what I remember of it. The RAF was fifty years of age and I had served thirty-one years of it.

This additional work required for the Official Celebration in June went on against the normal tasking background for 1968 that also included the major annual exercise to be held again using the North African desert locations.

The Main Exercise for 1968 was scheduled to take place in April. It was to take me back to Malta and North Africa, where we had ample opportunity to test the capability of the Argosy and the more recently introduced Andover in desert conditions. Initially named 'Parula' and then renamed 'Crayon,' the exercise was an interesting experience for everyone. The activation required me with one team to position at RAF Luqa, with which I was, of course, very familiar, on the 16th of April. I was joined the next day by three more teams from Abingdon. This phase was designed to include an initial assault by airdropped troops of the 16 Parachute Brigade, followed by an airdrop of heavy equipment required by the Royal Engineers to ensure the surface maintenance of the Afrag airstrip (reinstated in late 1965) that would be extensively used throughout the entire duration of the exercise and also to position the Airhead Agencies of 38 Group. There was little for us to do in Malta, which served as the Theatre Main Base but really as a staging facility for aircraft that had been loaded initially at UK stations. We were mostly concerned with the receipt of the aircraft, checking the loads and final preparations for despatch at the appointed hour for the actual drop. On the 25th of April, I deployed two of my teams to the airhead at Got El Afrag to receive the 38 Group Agencies and the main body of the 16 Para Brigade. I was to reposition myself on 28th April with the remainder of the detachment at RAF El Adem to ensure that facilities were in place to expeditiously unload the Argosies and turn them around to re-position at the Forward Area Main Base at RAF El Adem. After the Desert Airhead was firmly established, I was to manage the air transport needs of the exercise as it developed, leaving two teams to handle things at the Afrag strip. When the Tactical Phase started, the two teams at Afrag were required to work at high pressure in difficult conditions, and I found it necessary to rotate them at frequent intervals, not only to ensure that all gained experience in this type of environment but also to provide adequate rest as a safeguard against fatigue.

The engineers had done a great job at Afrag, which was not so much an oasis but a well. There was no vegetation and no pool. But the engineers had provided an adequate water supply that included a much-appreciated shower facility built of stout timbers supporting a forty-gallon drum to provide a good head of water. A topographical feature of the location was a low escarpment on the southern edge of the site. The shower facility, together with other domestic requirements, tents etc., were grouped on the active northern side of the escarpment in what was the obvious place for them. The small encampment with its shower facility was a very busy spot, particularly during the early morning and evening. The clouds of dust that attended the frequently concentrated arrival and departure of aircraft aggravated working conditions. The graders were frequently required to clear the strip of loose sand that seemed to be always present and there was quite a high verge of it on both edges of the strip. Towards the end of the Tactical Phase of the exercise, I visited the airhead, flying in and out by one of the Argosy aircraft whose pilots had been instructed to practise low flying along the route in both directions. The day following my last visit was one of great tragedy, causing the loss of seven lives: three RAF and four Army. An Argosy had taken off from the strip in the direction of the escarpment over which it flew to disappear to the south. However, it soon reappeared low over the escarpment, still descending to its intended low-level flight to El Adem. Its starboard wingtip caught the top of the shower causing the aircraft to roll and crash alongside the strip with the loss of all on board. Besides the four Army passengers, the aircraft was loaded with two Landrover vehicles and their trailers. We then had the sad task of repatriating the seven casualties by a specially arranged Argosy flight. The initiation of the Recovery Phase started whilst the Tactical Phase was still in progress, a severe test of the capability of my five teams. We were glad to return to our UK base at Abingdon. Despite its sad ending, this was a most useful exercise that was put to good effect in the training of all concerned in the desert conditions of North Africa that would very shortly be no longer available to us. It was, in fact, my own last visit to Libya.

After completing my exercise report, I decided that a short break was necessary and, with Rosemary, took a few days to leave to visit as yet-unseen places in North Wales. We made our base at the attractive small town of Betws-y-Coed in a quiet hotel and, from there, visited the well-known coastal resort locations.

The Official Celebration of the formation of the Royal Air Force was scheduled to take place at RAF Abingdon on 6th June 1968. This was to include a static display of many historic aircraft types, many of which had been painstakingly rebuilt at numerous RAF Stations and were now the property of the developing RAF Museum. Others had been borrowed from aircraft collections principally the Shuttleworth Trust. The static display was truly magnificent, and I treasure several slide photographs in the photographic collection. There was also a static exhibition of equipment that had been tastefully created in the station's largest hangar that had been purpose-built for the servicing of the Short 'Belfast,' our latest heavy-lift aircraft that was actually based at nearby RAF Brize Norton.

Many of the early aircraft types flew at the beginning of the flying display that went off in grand style attended by beautiful summer weather. Of course, the events of the day had been well rehearsed, with those of us selected to play the parts of the VIP Guests going through the intended routine for the actual day. As I have mentioned already, these rehearsals included two for the early evening banquet, which, although intended to practice the mess staff, actually provided the Dramatis Personae with two magnificent free meals. The whole day was a tremendous success and a wonderful experience for those selected to attend by invitation only. There were adequate feeding arrangements for all officers and their guests in marquees, but the formal banquet in the officers' mess was for the official VIP Guests only, and the public rooms of the mess were out of bounds to resident officers for that day until HM The Queen, HM The Queen Mother and other Royal Personages had departed during the early part of the evening. Special feeding arrangements were made for the resident officers during the short period of dispossession from their homes. Of course, there was a real humdinger of an impromptu party in the mess after it was all over, and the mess was back to normal by breakfast the next day.

We still had plenty of exercise activity to deal with during 1968 to test, among other things, the capability of the new aircraft recently introduced to Transport Command, principally the Lockheed C130 'Hercules' that was scheduled to become the centrepiece of the strategic element. The Ministry Of Defence (Air) sponsored an exercise appropriately named 'Carter Patterson' to practice Airhead Loading/Unloading techniques. It was to be a joint exercise involving the tactical elements of No.38 Group and the Army 3rd Division at the inactive airfield at Keevil, for which I was to provide five teams operating directly under my own direction. Scheduled to take place in July, this exercise again called for concentrated effort, with aircraft arriving and departing at short intervals carrying every possible type of load and requiring loading and unloading to be carried out with engines running. The noise of many aircraft on the ground at the same time, all with engines at idling speed, is quite beyond description. Little wonder that subjection to such intense noise causes hearing problems in later life. It was about this time that I was visited, informally and without prior notice, by a senior officer of the RAF Medical Authority who wished to address all available personnel on the serious view being taken of this problem. All personnel exposed to high-intensity noise were to be issued with earplugs, initial supplies of which would soon be available through station medical officers. Many years later, when well into final retirement, I was awarded a disability pension for a twenty per cent loss of my own hearing. The 'Hercules' was a particularly noisy beast but an excellent aircraft which, as I write this some thirty-five years later (2003), remains in service, though somewhat modified, in the same air transport role as was intended for it - the mainstay of the RAF air transport element - still based at Lyneham.

There was nothing that required my direct personal involvement away from the base during the later part of 1968, except, of course, the ordinary demands of organisation and administration. However, there was ample activity to keep the teams fully occupied, as the Squadron Operational Record Book shows. The traditional autumn exercises were not held this year, as there were plans afoot for a winter exercise early in 1969 in which I was to become involved before it was formally announced. Early in January 1969, I joined staff officers from HQ Transport Command in the reconnaissance for Exercise 'Bold Adventure,' which was to be held in February/March in Denmark and North Western Germany. This reconnaissance, which was necessary because of strange locations, took me to the Royal Danish Air Force base at Skrydstrup, which was to be the theatre's main base, and to the German Air Force base at Schleswig-Holstein which was to be the Forward Area Main Base. We stayed a night in a hotel in Skrydstrup close to the RDAF Base and took in Schleswig-Holstein on our homeward route the next day.

Exercise 'Bold Adventure' was mounted on 19th February 1969 when I deployed with my HQ Element to RDAF Skrydstrup, where I was joined the next day by six of my teams from Abingdon to complete the air movements organisation prior to the commencement of the positioning phase. This was a NATO exercise in which tactical elements of 38 Group with 24 Brigade were required to reinforce NATO in the area of the Baltic approaches. On the 8th of March, we redeployed the whole of 24 Brigade to Schleswig-Holstein, and on that same day, two teams drawn from the Middle East Air Force reinforced us. The need for this reinforcement illustrates the occasional inadequacy of UKMAMS even with its thirteen teams, to meet the demands of the tasking requirement. This was a tough exercise for everyone, providing valuable experience in the severe cold of winter in the Baltic region. It was to be my last major exercise with UKMAMS. I had been informed beforehand of my next appointment, which was to be in Singapore.

I realise that I have written at great length about my UKMAMS appointment. Because I was the founder and first commanding officer of this specialist squadron, I suppose it was considered of the utmost importance that its intended formation within the overall establishment should have been fully accomplished. There was, of course, much more to it than I have subscribed to by writing of my own participation in the major exercise and other events of my time with the unit. This is simply because there were so many other things going on all the time that I could not possibly have been directly involved in personally other than by my overall responsibility for the direction and administration of these unit activities. There was constant activity of minor proportions all of which is recorded in the squadron Operations Record (Form 540) that would require a tremendous amount of space and which I cannot remember in detail. Life with UKMAMS was very demanding, particularly for married personnel with families. There were those set in authority above me only too willing to exert influence in various ways. Some forwarded the idea of creating an elite unit of specially selected personnel. This I knew to be contrary to opinion at the Ministry level because of the difficulties in applying selection criteria. My counter was to ensure a selection system based on ordinary levels of achievement with specialist training within the squadron organisation. This was the accepted method, which I believe is still in being. What did arise out of this was a guarantee that the Records Office would protect the unit interest by safeguarding personnel against the effects of turbulence arising from the movement of all but that essential to career advancement or paramount exigencies of the Service.

I was to be posted during June accompanied by Rosemary who was delighted at a posting she had always dreamed of. It was, of course, quite obviously to be my last overseas posting and from my own point of view, it was a good one to which the Appointments Committee had to give a large measure of consideration in view of its Joint-Service nature. It was a prestigious appointment being the command of the Services Air Booking Centre, Singapore. The unit, lodged at RAF Changi, was not an Air Force Unit, neither was it Navy or Army. It was all three, being what is known as a Defence Establishment, placed directly under the Ministry Of Defence with a personnel establishment drawn from all three services to agreed proportions that were not interchangeable.

CHAPTER XXIX
FAR EAST COMMAND

We left the United Kingdom to a terrific send-off from my UKMAMS officers as we emplaned in one of our latest VC10 aircraft now doing long-range trooping out of Brize Norton where No. 10 Squadron operated them. The route to the Far East included an outward-bound refuelling stop at Muharraq, and I had warned Rosemary to be prepared for a climatic change that she would find devastating if wearing the clothing in which she had left the UK. As we passed through the aircraft door into the pitch-black midnight of the Arabian Gulf, the heat was like a blast from a furnace. But she was well prepared and went straight to the ladies' room, where she had a refreshing wash and changed into the lighter clothing that she had been able to pack into her hand luggage. She was the envy of the other wives who were not similarly prepared. Our next scheduled stop was at RAF Gan in the Gilbert Islands of the Indian Ocean. Here, we had breakfast in the brilliant sunshine of early morning, the heat being mitigated by the pleasant sea breezes and the blue ocean on either hand. It was truly a schoolboy dream of Treasure Island. Lunch was served on board, and soon, on our starboard side, flying east more or less along the equator, we saw the northern tip of jungle-clad Sumatra. Our arrival in Singapore was to be at the international civil airport of Payar Lebar as our intended destination of RAF Changi was temporarily out of use because of work to the runways. Sqn Ldr Mike Banks, to whom I was successor, met us. We were to be temporarily accommodated in the Good Earth Guest House, which sounded much grander than it turned out to be, but it had the basic essentials and we had been assured that our stay was unlikely to be more than a few days.

The availability of a married quarter was forecast as being in the order of a few months, but there were plenty of suitable houses that had been taken over as official hirings, and there was an immediate prospect of one being allocated to me. Sure enough one was offered to me at short order in the Toh Estate that was situated alongside the officers' married quarters only a few minutes drive from the station proper. It was nicely situated on a raised site and in an area that was occupied predominantly occupied by fellow officers of similar rank some of whom I already knew. Transport was no problem as there was a proliferation of cheap taxis running an unending service on the nearby main route between Changi and Singapore City. We were quite happy, and we had our dog 'Nicky' who had been flown out privately but had to spend a short quarantine period in an approved kennel facility. She just about went crazy with delight when I went to collect her and take her home to Rosemary, who was equally delighted to have her back. We soon found ourselves an Alma who turned out to be quite an excellent housekeeper and a good cook to bargain.

On the work side, things seemed to be quite satisfactory, if somewhat unusual, in an organisation consisting of all three services. There were also a good many locally engaged civilians, among whom were a few wives of RAF personnel. But all seemed to be well integrated into a happy though very busy work scene. In the Far East Command structure, the unit was directly under the Commander-in-Chief Far East Command (CINCFE), who was the only authority that could act directly with the Ministry Of Defence to vary the conditions of the Unit Policy Statement. In this way, the unit was protected against any attempt to exert authority by the respective individual Navy, Army or RAF Commanders in the Far East Theatre. The unit was responsible for the effective control of the movement by air of all forces personnel (Service and Civilian) and their families, as well as cargo, out and through Singapore. There was no responsibility for the physical aspects of passenger and cargo handling, which was the responsibility of the Air Movements Squadron at RAF Changi. We were a lodger unit on RAF Changi, which obliged them to provide accommodation, messing and administration for the RAF element. Similar arrangements were also in place with the Navy and Army authorities for personnel of respective elements. On the disciplinary side of things, I had full powers over the Army and RAF, but because of differences with the Naval Discipline Act, I was required to refer any naval disciplinary matters to the Commander Far East Fleet.

The unit also had a small office at the Singapore International Airport. We did, in fact, have quite a number of arrivals and departures by civil aircraft particularly high-ranking civil servants of the Navy and Army departments. It was also necessary to arrange bookings for personnel on civil flights to destinations not served by the RAF. This called for the allocation of two Army officers who were established against this requirement, whilst the Navy requirement was catered for by two non-commissioned officers in the rank of Petty Officer. It all worked splendidly, and this small-detached portion of my command was never a problem except for a local RAF Air Movements administrative matter for which I was unwittingly the responsible trigger the day after I arrived in Singapore. It happened during my initial meeting at HQ Far East Air Force with the Command Movements Officer Group Captain Ridsdale, who I had previously met at the MOD (RAF) in London. He asked, "Who met you, Bill?" Somewhat taken aback, I simply replied, gesturing towards Mike, "Mike did." He then said, "No, I didn't mean that but rather, who met the aircraft? Was it met by an RAF Air Movements Officer?" To which I was obliged to say truthfully that the aircraft seemed to have been met by an Army Lieutenant who introduced himself as one of the SABC officers located at the civil airport. He then asked me what my opinion was in regard to RAF passenger transport aircraft being met by officers of the Army Royal Corps Of Transport. What he was getting at now began to dawn on me. I said that it seemed to be contrary to what I understood to be the Official Joint-Service Policy, which placed full responsibility for the provision and operation of Air Trooping arrangements on the RAF and required that the supervision of passenger enplanement and deplanement was ordinarily to be under the supervision of a qualified RAF Air Movements Officer. He seemed quite satisfied and steered the conversation onto the responsibilities of my new appointment, which I already knew had nothing to do with passengers and cargo beyond the allocation to available resources and the timely issue of calling forward instructions. Responsibility for the loading/unloading of RAF Transport Aircraft at Singapore locations was the responsibility of the RAF Changi Air Movements Squadron. The SABC officers at Singapore International Airport were there to ensure that personnel arriving by civil flights or departing on flights booked by SABC were offered the same assistance appropriate to travel in RAF aircraft. I heard no more of this matter for some little time when it transpired that the Duty Air Movements Officers at RAF Changi, contrary to instructions issued specifically by the Command Air Movements Officer, had themselves been arranging with the Army SABC officers at Payar Lebar to relieve them of their responsibilities for the RAF VC10 aircraft using the civil airport during the RAF Changi closure period. Of course, the chap who took the flak for this was Wing Commander John Maguire, who commanded the Changi Air Movements Squadron. My predecessor, Mike Banks, should also have ensured that the SABC Army officers at the civil airport were not involved. The conversation with the Command Movements Officer on my arrival was, of course, carefully staged to ensure that Mike and I knew that the complicity between the duty officers of Changi and the SABC detachment had not escaped attention.

The RN element was the smallest, with Lieutenant Commander Richard De Courcy-Hughes and three petty officers, including the two at Payer Lebar. The Army element was the largest with Major Jim Card with the two officers at Payer Lebar and quite a few non-commissioned personnel, none below the rank of corporal, with the main body at the Changi head office. The RAF element comprised myself with a Flight Lieutenant who, together with the Lt Cdr and major, were the three air movement controllers for their respective services. The Flt Lt was, however, my only authorised deputy, and irrespective of the rank, consideration took over command in my absence. This seemingly unusual arrangement was necessary because of the inter-service policy that required the Commanding Officer to be a qualified air movements officer of the RAF. The two senior officers of the RN and Army were subordinate to me in the command structure. The arrangement worked very well, and I had nothing but the most affable relationship with these two fellow senior officers of equivalent rank. In fact, the inter-service relationship between all ranks was splendid, and I did not once have to deal with any breach of discipline. I also had an air movement qualified Unit Warrant Officer of the RAF who acted as Chief Clerk to the rather large element of locally engaged civilians, which included a few wives of RAF personnel. The cargo section was in the capable hands of a Flight Sergeant. A small front desk section under an RAF corporal carried out civil air bookings. The entire organisation worked splendidly and I had no occasion to vary it.

At the time of my arrival I expected my tour of duty to be about eighteen months as the Government of the day had declared an intention to run down the Singapore Command to extinction by the end of 1970. However, the political party in power was defeated by the General Election, and the intention was modified at the request of the Singapore Government, which was concerned about the effect on the economy of the colony, which was dependent to a large extent on the employment of a significant part of the local population. Additionally it would be necessary to progressively form indigenous naval, military and air forces with United Kingdom advice and assistance.

My responsibilities brought me into contact with the other naval and military establishments, and apart from my own duty visits' Rosemary and I soon found ourselves invited to many social occasions that required the exercise of alcohol restraint, particularly if one had to drive home. A most hospitable civilian host was Philip Coleclough, an expatriate Yorkshireman, who was the manager of Anglo-French Travel, a company with whom SABC had a long-standing arrangement for civil travel bookings. He and his wife, Kay, had a well-appointed home in Singapore's top residential area where one could always be sure to meet the most interesting fellow guests, usually business people passing through Singapore. Philip was in Singapore prior to the outbreak of war with the Japanese and, being a member of the local militia, was taken prisoner and incarcerated in the notorious Changi prison. The civil airlines, mainly Malaya Singapore Airlines and Cathay Pacific Airlines, were also regular hosts, as well as the Australian QANTAS, whose Singapore representative suggested that I might like to consider premature retirement from the RAF to take up a job with them in Geneva that he thought would be right up my street. Mr Lee, the local manager for Cathay Pacific, was a charming person to do business with and an equally likeable host at his company social occasions. His chief executive was an unusually large Japanese who I fondly remember. Named Peter Yueda, he too was in Singapore before it fell to the Japanese in 1942, after which he was soon conscripted into the Air Force and flew the Zero Fighter in the Burma theatre. He returned to his job in Singapore after the cessation of hostilities and seemed to have no genuine desire to return to his native land. I was also to have an unexpected reunion with Leonard Cheshire who had a cousin resident in Singapore. Her husband was also in the city before the coming of the Japanese and had been incarcerated in Changi Prison for the duration. Post-war, he became head of the Army Kinema Corporation (AKC). There was a Cheshire Children's Home close by our eventual married quarter where Rosemary joined other wives in doing voluntary work. Leonard was visiting the home and the RAF Changi Broadcasting System decided to devise a little programme about him. As I had served with him in the early part of the war, I was invited to go along with the recording team to his cousin's home, where the interview was to take place. Following this, I was asked by his cousin if I could arrange for a consignment of toys to be flown into Hong Kong, which I was glad to do. We subsequently received an invitation to dinner, which turned out to be a very pleasant occasion. Our social life was very full, so much so that it was occasionally necessary to decline invitations in the interest of health and the need for rest.

During November 1969, I thought it would be nice to revisit Hong Kong and take Rosemary for a change of scene and, as the Hong Kong winter began at that time, it would be a pleasant change from the constant heat and humidity of Singapore. So, I arranged Indulgence passages for us on a scheduled VC10 flight. Hong Kong was a popular destination, and as there was always a long list of spare seats, I had to take care that I was not seen to be taking unfair advantage of my position as OC SABC. So, I submitted our travel application in good time to ensure that it was genuinely at the top of the list by the intended travel date. The booking arrangements for the use of capacity out of Hong Kong were the responsibility of a small Joint-Service Authority located at RAF Kai Tak, where I knew the personalities involved, including the Army member, Major Larry Egerton, who was serving at HQ Middle East Land Forces (MELF) whilst I was with HQ Middle East Air Force (MEAF), so there was unlikely to be any problem getting back to Singapore. Indulgence travel was strictly on a fill-up basis and was therefore not without a degree of disappointment, sometimes with serious consequences, particularly if one was obliged to pay the cost of travel by civil flight because of time consideration. We stayed at a small, comfortable hotel off Nathan Road in Kowloon and enjoyed a good week taking in the sights. Hong Kong had changed only in that it had expanded upwards since I had last seen it in 1945. There were people from Nairn that Rosemary knew from her younger days and we had no difficulty in contacting them and were made most welcome in their homes. One, formerly Joan Ralph, and her husband, Magnus Williamson later returned to Nairn after we had retired to Nairn ourselves. Sadly, Joan died long before her time, and Magnus departed in due course also somewhat prematurely.

During February 1970, I was allocated a married quarter appropriate to rank on the Lloyd-Lees Estate adjoining the Toh Estate. So, the distance was negligible, and the move was accomplished easily in one day. The married quarter was, of course, much more comfortable than the hiring and better furnished. Servants' quarters were attached, and full maintenance facilities were carried out routinely through the station organisation. It was altogether very pleasant, being spacious and airy and well equipped with large ceiling fans to keep the air moving. Air-conditioning was not a luxury provided in service married quarters. We were very comfortable with plenty of natural green surroundings that served to mitigate the heat and glare of the tropical day, each one being very much the same and without seasonal change. Additional heat was never needed and extra clothing, a light woollen sweater, for warmth in the evenings only on those rare occasions when the rain was prolonged to such an extent that unusual cooling resulted. But this was very rare.

At a very early date in 1970, Group Captain Mike Dyer arrived to take over the appointment of Command Movements Officer FEAF. I had not previously met him and did not anticipate the close bond that was to develop between us, as he was not responsible in the overall Command sense for my unit other than being my immediate RAF Specialist superior. I did, however, find myself quickly becoming an outside member of his headquarters staff to whom he frequently confided his trust. I believe he recognised the value of my experience on which he came to depend to some considerable extent.

It was, I think, towards the end of February 1970 that Mike called me on the telephone to ask me to attend a meeting in his office to act in an advisory capacity on a matter that had just arisen. He could not discuss it over the telephone because of its nature and security rating. On arrival I was given a copy of a Headquarters Transport Command Operation Order dealing with a forthcoming major exercise that had been given the Malay name of 'Bersatu Padu.' This exercise was tabled as a South East Asia Treaty Organisation (SEATO) Exercise that was to be staged in Singapore, and the southernmost part of the Malay Peninsular was cast in the familiar setting of a small country in which there was a serious political threat by a dissident body in a state of armed insurrection. The main purpose of the exercise, which was not mentioned in the order, was obviously to test the ability of UK-based forces to reinforce the area of the present Far East Command if required to do so after the planned transfer of responsibility at the beginning of November 1971. The unusual length of the supply route from the UK was the only unusual feature of this otherwise unusual exercise setting. The overall control of air movements would, of course, be in the hands of the mobile elements of HQ Transport Command and HQ No 38 Group. The only Singapore element involved was RAF Changi, which was to be the exercise theatre's main base as though it would have become the actual theatre's main base in the envisaged exercise scene. RAF Changi was, therefore, required to make its existing facilities available and would be suitably reinforced by the mobile elements of RAF Transport Command and Headquarters No.38 Group in both strategic and tactical aspects. I offered my opinion that there were no unusual air movements aspects for them to worry about and assured them that RAF Changi Air Movements Squadron would experience only the

257

minor inconvenience of being reinforced by UKMAMS, who would assume full responsibility for the additional organisational and physical workload placed upon them by the exercise requirements. Mike's two staff officers and OC Changi Air Movements Squadron were present at the meeting. One of the staff officers was a recently arrived Squadron Leader, Ernie Stanton of the Royal Australian Air Force, who was on an exchange appointment and with whom I was to have almost daily contact in his staff function, which was on the operational side of air movements known as MOV Ops. Ernie, a little under my own age, was a regular officer in the RAAF and had flown during the war with Bomber Command in the United Kingdom.

The opening phase of the exercise was timed to take place during April with the positioning of the 19th Infantry Brigade from the United Kingdom together with No. 72 Squadron of 38 Group with its tactical 'Wessex' helicopters. A UKMAMS detachment of two teams would also be positioned to take care of this sizeable lift into RAF Changi, which would require specialised unloading of the RAF helicopters from the long-range transport aircraft and, of course, supervise unloading the numerous aircraft bringing in the army personnel and equipment, assisted by army personnel travelling with each load to supply a degree of manual labour. The arrival would be well-timed to avoid undue build-up at Changi and facilitate rapid disposal of personnel and equipment to pre-determined locations as planned by the army organisation. The helicopters would remain at Changi, as arranged by HQ 38 Group, until required for the tactical aspects of the exercise proper that would shortly follow. It all seemed very straightforward to my well-practised thinking on these almost daily matters that attended my former role as OC UKMAMS.

Shortly after this meeting, Ernie and I, together with Rosemary and Jenny, were attending an evening function in the city and were being driven by Ernie in his own car. Ernie and I were talking about this when he casually mentioned SABC having an involvement in the control aspects of the forthcoming exercise. Not wishing to discuss such a classified matter with the wives in easy earshot and being somewhat taken off guard, I simply said that I didn't think that would be possible. Nothing further was said at that juncture. Some days later, he again casually mentioned the matter at a similarly inappropriate moment. A few days before the Positioning Phase of the exercise was due to commence, he came to see me unannounced at a time when I was heavily engaged with a difficult UK passenger load that had to be tactfully rearranged due to the withdrawal of passenger seats by MOD (RAF) for some priority need. I was without my deputy at the time and was handling his control duties besides my own command responsibility and working in the very busy controller room. Ernie mentioned that he had come at the suggestion of Mike Dyer to discuss the SABC role in exercise Bersatu Padu. I immediately felt the anger rising and told him that SABC did not have a role in it, nor was HQ FEAF in any position to create such a role. I suspected that he was not aware of the invariable policy role for SABC, and I was surprised at Mike Dyer's action. I left him for a minute while I went to my administration office and got the unit policy file. Opening it at the Policy Statement, which I placed before him, I told him that I was surprised at the need for me to have to point this out to members of the Headquarters Staff, as they should be familiar with the policies of all units for which they had any measure of responsibility. I also told him that one of the main reasons for the role of SABC Singapore being so protected was that, although the unit was under RAF command because of its specialist function, it was not an established unit within the Far East Air Force but a Defence Establishment of the Ministry Of Defence within the establishment of the Far East Command. There were members of the Royal Navy and the Army directly under my command, but over whom only CinC Far East had the superior command responsibility? I suggested that he should go back to HQ FEAF and ensure that C Mov O was fully aware that he would have to get approval from MOD through CinC FE if he wanted to vary the role of SABC and involve it in Exercise Bersatu Padu. If he was seriously contemplating this action, would he please discuss the matter further with me as I would certainly oppose the action on the grounds of an unacceptable and unnecessary workload for which the unit was not established? In any case, there was absolutely no need for any local control as this would be the responsibility of the exercise control elements and, as far as control of air movements was concerned, this would be adequately provided by UKMAMS, whose commanding officer would be the lead figure by the time the Tactical Phase of the exercise was mounted, and for the Recovery Phase. There was no need for HQ FEAF to exercise any control that could easily be seen as interference with the conduct of the SEATO exercise. My SABC responsibility would simply be to ensure that maximum use was made of any payload offered to SABC by MOD (RAF) in the returning aircraft. This was likely to be minimal. I heard no more of the matter, but I suppose I ought to have felt flattered that Mike sought some comfort in having me in control of the air movements aspect. I was to experience more of his faith in me and high regard for my experience before long.

However, in the brief spell between the arrival of the main body of the UKMAMS element and the Tactical Phase I was able to meet again with some of the officers who had served under me during my command of the unit at Abingdon. As always, on these occasions, they had precious little time for socialising, but I did manage to arrange a time when it was possible for several of them to make an evening visit to my married quarter and reduce my stock of beer and other booze. They were soon dispersed to locations in the southern end of the Malay Peninsular, where they were deployed until the recovery phase that extended into June. This big exercise employed personnel from the five nations that would be affected if the need should arise to reinforce the Far East theatre after the planned withdrawal of United Kingdom forces.

We were able to make two leave visits to the highlands of central Malaysia. The first was later in 1970 to a delightful hill resort called Fraser's Hill, where there were several spacious bungalows, each owned by one of the larger business concerns as a leave facility for their personnel. There was a small Royal Navy training facility at this location and a bungalow known as the Admiralty Bungalow, to which my Royal Navy member of staff steered me. There was no problem in making the arrangement that, of course, involved a little cost but excellent value. We undertook the journey in our own car, which was something of an old banger (a fifteen-year-old MG Magnette). It was amazing how the Singaporeans were able to prolong the lives of cars; they were so good at it. However, we arrived as planned at Seremban, where the main roads of the Malay Peninsular intersect. Here we had booked our night-stop accommodation in the Government Bungalow that provided adequate though somewhat basic accommodation and restaurant facilities. Journey Planning had failed to offer any alternative to this recommended facility. The location was pleasant enough, and we spent a comfortable night finding it necessary to use a blanket for comforting warmth. The next morning, we were awakened by the Muezzin (the call to prayer), which I had heard many times during my travels in the Muslim parts of the world, but for the first time here by a public address system that could be heard well beyond the boundaries of this small town. The mosque from which it emanated was located on the far side of a large lake that separated it from the bungalow. It was so loud that we found it rather startling. Certainly, it was the most effective alarm system for an early awakening.

After an ample breakfast, we continued our northward journey by passing the sprawl of Kuala Lumpur and onto the gradually rising and scenic country at the foot of the Malaysian Highlands. We made our last fuel stop and shortly passed through the lower gateway that controlled the long final one-way section of the roadway to Fraser's Hill station. We had timed our arrival at this point to coincide with the opening time which ensured that there would be no problem with passing traffic on the narrow road. We were slowed down somewhat by a large lorry carrying a load of teak logs that looked anything but safe so we kept behind it at a reasonable distance until we came to a wider section at which the driver courteously waved us on. We passed the spot where, some years previously, during a troublesome communist uprising, a British Governor had been ambushed and taken from his car and hacked to death whilst his wife and children looked on. We arrived at Bukit Fraser about mid-afternoon and soon found the Admiralty Bungalow on a pleasant hillock at the end of an approach road shared with its neighbour that was owned by the Shell Oil Company if my memory serves me right. We had a wonderful view of pine-clad hills stretching into limitless distance. It was all very pleasant with delightful many-hued plants among which the largest geraniums ever seen bloomed in abundance. A Chinese family who were most welcoming staffed the well-appointed bungalow. Our bedroom with adjoining bath and toilet facilities provided an excellent degree of comfort, and we settled in to enjoy a good break in the relaxing atmosphere of this delightful hill station. At dinner that evening, we met our four fellow guests who, strangely enough, were all RAF from Singapore, among whom was one I recognised from my youth training days at Cranwell. He was Group Captain Maskell, called Dan after the well-known tennis champion of pre-war days. I was to be in touch with him frequently after; my appointment at OC SABC Singapore made me a desirable contact to be remembered by many who met me socially. The evenings were pleasant, with after-dinner chat sessions in the small sitting room with a good log fire burning in the spacious fireplace. A fairly large colony of swifts had taken over much of the roof space and was inclined to be noisy at inconvenient times, but as there was nothing we could do about them, we tried to put up with them, but they were very early risers with large families to feed, an activity that seemingly never stopped.

It was truly a quiet and relaxing location with a delightful climate that I call eternal summer. What a pleasant change from the constant humidity of the lower levels here, mitigated by altitude and a deliciously clean atmosphere. The central feature was a nine-hole golf course surrounded by a road from which shot spurs provided access to the bungalows. At the entrance to the station was a large building that served as the Administrative Centre and also housed a small Natural History Museum where one could identify the many indigenous nocturnal flying insects that could be menacingly large, such as the Stag Beetles, of which I have a specimen in my collection from that place which also includes several butterflies that colonised a charming clearing with a high waterfall and a pool of cool sparkling water.

All too soon, our two weeks came to an end, and the resident housekeepers asked us if we would take their son with us as far as Kuala Lumpur, where he went to school and stayed with relatives during the school terms. After delivering him to the required address, we proceeded to Seremban, but instead of making that our night stop, we decided to divert to the coastal route where, at Port Dickson, we found much better accommodation in very well-appointed seaside chalets that were air-conditioned and beautifully furnished to a high degree of comfort with modern en-suite facilities. The dining room was open to the beach with a stretch of beautiful white sand. We quite fell in love with it and were sorry to depart the next morning.

From here, we found our return route to Johore much more interesting than the main highway that we had taken for our outward journey. It's not such a fast road, but so much more picturesque and quite fascinating. Much narrower, taking us via Malacca, Muar and Kota Batu through seemingly endless rubber plantations with tall trees on either hand providing welcome shade to mitigate the heat and glare of the day. Through villages with houses on stilts from which smiling women and children waved to us in greeting as we passed. Eventually, crossing the Johore causeway and through the Singapore customs and passport control, arriving safely home to our RAF Changi bungalow by late afternoon, our Alma Ah Sim making a fuss of us with the much-needed cup of tea. Our fifteen-year-old MG Magnette had completed a difficult round trip and had performed in a completely trouble-free manner, with fuel and oil consumption appropriate to an engine of much lower mileage. We liked Fraser's Hill (Bukit Fraser). It was such a blessed relief from the unrelenting heat and humidity of Singapore and other lower-level locations in the region. We promised ourselves a further visit to the Malayan Highlands if future circumstances were to permit.

One of my three Royal Corps Of Transport Officers was Captain Norman Ward, who, together with another captain, shared the Army work at the Payar Lebar civil airport. Together with his wife Joyce, Norman occupied one of the married quarters at Selarang Barracks, which was still tentatively held by the British Army and adjoined RAF Changi. They had a son who had recently graduated from university and had become involved in Voluntary Service Overseas that had brought him into South East Asia where he was, at the time, backpacking in Thailand. Quite early one evening I received a telephone call in my married quarters from a senior member of the British Consulate in Singapore. He advised me that he had received information from the British Embassy in Bangkok that two young British men had been admitted to a hospital at Songkhla after being seriously injured in an attack whilst sleeping on one of the local beaches. One of these was named Ward whose father was believed to be a Captain Ward of the Royal Corps of Transport serving under my command. He explained that it had taken him quite some time to locate an army officer serving with a unit under RAF command. So, having found him, all he could do now was to leave the matter in my hands.

There was no point in panicking the Wards at this point as they would be unable to do anything themselves. On this particular evening I was Duty Protocol Officer for RAF Changi, a duty that was performed by all Wing Commanders and Squadron Leaders on the base. It was a duty that came around about every six weeks and ensured that anyone of equal or higher rank to the Station Commander arriving, departing or passing through RAF Changi by air was accorded the appropriate treatment and hospitality. I never had one of these duties that did not require me to represent the Station Commander at the hospitality suite located adjacent to the passenger handling area. Shortly after receiving the message from the Consulate, I had to go to the airfield to act on behalf of the Commanding Officer and attend to such a passenger passing through from the United Kingdom, a duty that would take about an hour and give me time to think about a rescue plan for young Mr Ward lying seriously injured at Songkhla in Thailand. I met the special passenger and settled him into the VIP Suite with the usual alcoholic hospitality. Fortunately he was one of those who thought that I might have other duties to perform and politely suggested that he was quite happy to relax quietly with his drink until called to rejoin his onward flight. So I excused myself and told him that I did have a rather serious matter to attend to and that I would leave him with the duty barman in attendance should he require another drink and that I would be back to see him before his departure. I then went off to find a large-scale map that would enable me to calculate distances between locations and make a plan. Songkhla is on the east coast of Thailand, and we had no facilities in that country that I could call on. The only place within reasonable distance was Butterworth on the west coast of the Malay Peninsular, a straight-line distance of about 120 miles, where there was a Royal Australian Air Force presence occupying what until quite recently had been RAF Butterworth. So I made a telephone call and spoke to the RAAF Duty Operations Officer who was of equal rank to myself. He was most cooperative and assured me that he would act immediately to arrange for an aero-medical evacuation and to leave the matter in his hands. He would keep me informed on my married quarter's telephone. So, after seeing my VIP charge safely and happily back onto his aircraft, I went home to await developments.

At a very early hour the next morning, my telephone rang, and I was given the good news that Ward Junior had been safely evacuated to the RAAF hospital at Butterworth, where, after a few days, he would be fit enough to be transferred to our own RAF Changi Hospital. Unfortunately, his companion was found dead on the beach. What had happened apparently was that the two young men had decided to spend their last night in Thailand on the beach at Songkhla in their two-man tent. Three young Thai males approached them, and as they seemed well-disposed, they enjoyed a friendly evening with them until it was time to sleep. However, sometime later, the three young Thais returned and set about the two Brits with heavy pieces of timber. Leaving them senseless, they then robbed them of their attractive possessions and left them. Ward eventually came around and staggered off to find help. Both were taken to the local hospital, where Ward's companion was found to be dead on arrival. I decided not to take any further action until a more reasonable hour, as there seemed to be no point in disturbing Norman and his wife and creating a state of anxiety before the normal start of their day. So I waited until I was up and ready for breakfast and then rang Ward's married quarter at nearby Selarang and acquainted Norman with the details of his son's unfortunate last night in Thailand. I advised him to be prepared for the next move, which was to get Joyce, or both of them, to Butterworth as soon as I

263

could arrange for an aircraft to take them there. This was unlikely to take very long after I got to my office in a few minutes' time, depending, of course, on the availability of resources. I would call them again as soon as I had it laid on.

A few minutes later I was in my office waiting for the short time pass when I knew the Command Movements Officer would be to be in his office. Sure enough, Mike was on the line when I rang and soon outlined the sad account of young Ward's misfortune and the obvious anguish of his parents and whether he would lend his weight to the need for an aircraft to take one or both of them to Butterworth. No trouble; in a matter of minutes, I had the authorisation. I rang Norman and told him to stand by for a departure time, which I expected to have soon. They had decided that only Joyce would go as there seemed little point in both of them going as Joyce would be able to telephone Norman and keep him posted as to their son's progress for the length of time it was necessary for her to stay. I thought them right in their decision and immediately spoke to the FEAF Communications Squadron, who confirmed that they had received Command authority and asked what time I would like the aircraft to depart. I gave what I thought would be a suitable time of 1100 hours and that I would have Mrs Ward at Changi Air Movements in ample time. After confirming to Norman, I made a call to Butterworth Operations and asked them to arrange for Mrs Ward to be met and conveyed to the hospital, where I understood it would be possible to stay until her son's condition was such that she could return home with an easy mind. I collected her at their Selerang married quarter and took her to the waiting aircraft at Changi. She was home again in a few days, travelling by rail from Kuala Lumpur to Singapore; her son was eventually transferred to RAF Changi Hospital, where he completed his recovery. I contacted the Consulate in Singapore to inform them of the latest developments since their call to me last evening, and they informed me that they had received word from the British Embassy in Bangkok that the three Thai youths had been arrested and appropriately charged with offences, including murder that would almost certainly bring the death penalty. I later met the RAAF Squadron Leader who had been so helpful to me on my first contact. I arranged a return indulgence flight for him to spend a few days in Hong Kong. It was the least I could do to repay his willing assistance.

Ward's son gradually recovered from his serious head injuries and eventually returned to his Voluntary Service Overseas Work whilst the work of SABC Singapore went on without noticeable effect. I had been in Singapore for twelve months or so, and it was June 1970, time for the publication of the Queen's Birthday Honours List, which was always displayed on the mess notice board. Looking at this particular list, I was astonished to see the names of three UKMAMS personnel – my own successor, Jock MacKay's successor as his deputy and the training warrant officer who had served under me. Here, we have a typical illustration of the unfairness of the Honours and Awards System. With the exception of the warrant officer the other two had been in their posts for no more than twelve months and had clearly reaped the benefit of the efforts of those who had gone before them. From the time of its elevation to squadron status, it had occurred to me that the dubious matter of recommendations for these awards, so far as I was personally concerned, was no longer a matter for the station administration since we were no longer part of the station establishment. I had several times broached this matter verbally during my visits to Command Headquarters. I had, of course, made my own recommendations when required to do so by the twice-yearly memorandum calling for recommendations, but the only person who could do it for me was my immediate superior, the Command Movements Officer. There had been two during my time and I suppose neither of them thought they had known me long enough to make a recommendation. However, it seems odd in view of the fact that a further change of C Mov O had taken place only two or three weeks before my departure, that the awards resulted from action by him, as in the general scheme of things, he simply would not have had the time or opportunity. What had happened seemingly is that Group Captain Bill Carr, the C Mov O who had left on promotion to Air Commodore to become the Director Of Movements RAF, had used some influence at the Ministry level to ensure that the squadron received some much overdue recognition for the work it had done during his time has C Mov O. Unfortunately he overlooked the fact that some who had been responsible for it had been moved on. The result was that the awards were made to the Squadron Commander, his Deputy and the Warrant Officer rather than those who had earned them. So, the MBEs were actually awarded to those in post. As our American cousins might say, "That's the way the cookie crumbles," but in this case the matter was apparently viewed with some disgust at Abingdon and throughout the RAF Movements organisation generally. I received several personal indications of this from movements' personalities in the Far East Command, including the Command Staff. I must confess to being somewhat put out by the unfairness of the awards, which I blamed directly on Bill Carr.

I continued to enjoy the work and responsibilities of my Defence Establishment appointment, and things went along smoothly, with only the occasional disruptive incident, usually caused by a simple act of omission or commission by a member of my staff. Generally, however, things went along quite smoothly. Our social life was always hectic with unending invitations to this and that part of the Singapore Base Movements Organisation and many other functions Naval, Military and Air Force. Rosemary had become involved with the Singapore Cheshire Home located quite close to us and, together with the other members of the station ladies group supporting the Home; she made periodic visits to the staff and the children in their care. In due course, Leonard Cheshire himself made one of his periodic visits to the homes founded by his own Charitable

Organisation, and it was on the occasion of such a visit during September 1970 that I had the opportunity of a short reunion with him. Rosemary was also a volunteer member of Changi Broadcasting, a purely local station entertainment facility which, using a cable network, supplied audio entertainment to a wide station audience. She had a regular music request programme and thoroughly enjoyed doing it. Now Leonard Cheshire's visit just happened to coincide with the annual 1970 Battle Of Britain celebrations, and Changi Broadcasting thought they would feature him in a special programme to mark the occasion. Of course, Rosemary mentioned that I had flown with the same squadron as him early in the war, and I was therefore invited to join the recording team for the session that was to take place at his cousin's home in Singapore City.

Leonard Cheshire had changed a great deal since I last saw him in 1940. Of course, thirty years and the dreadful effects of tuberculosis that he had suffered as the result of the demands that he had willingly accepted during the war had taken their toll on his general health. In the unremitting heat and humidity of Singapore, I was surprised to see that he was wearing a red flannel vest. He was, however, his lucid self and was quite dismissive of the adulation directed towards him, particularly in connection with his record of wartime operational escapades, freely admitting that he had enjoyed an undeservedly charmed life and had sought glory throughout a wartime experience that amounted to a hundred operational missions which was what earned him the final accolade of the award of the Victoria Cross.

His cousin later contacted me at my office and asked if I could help to get a consignment of toys to Hong Kong, a request I could hardly refuse and which was duly carried out without any great effort on my part other than that of acting in the capacity of the controlling influence. Rosemary and I received an invitation to dinner after Leonard had returned to the United Kingdom and enjoyed a most enjoyable social occasion. His cousin, I thought, rather toffee-nosed, particularly when she declined acceptance of our return invitation, but her husband, whom I have already mentioned, who was in the local Singapore defence Volunteers and taken prisoner by the Japanese, had spent most of the war in the dreaded Changi Prison. He was a most friendly individual who, after the war, had returned to his work with the Army Kinema Corporation and was still actively serving in it. I found him a most affable individual.

At RAF Changi, there was an RNZAF detachment of 47 Squadron. This detachment of four Bristol Freighter aircraft was engaged in a standing commitment undertaken by the New Zealand Government to supply certain essential commodities to South Vietnam, involved in war with the communist self-declared state of North Vietnam. The control of payload in these aircraft was placed in the hands of SABC Singapore on the understanding, of course, that the Vietnamese commitment took priority. But who would want to go to

Vietnam anyway? However, one of these Bristol Freighter aircraft was scheduled to be returned to the squadron's main base in New Zealand routinely every month for servicing and major maintenance work and to be replaced by a newly serviced aircraft. This monthly flight to the Antipodes was routed through Bali in the Lesser Sunda islands that stretch from the south of Sumatra rather like a necklace. These islands were in the communist state of Indonesia normally out of bounds for British Service personnel. The staging time at Bali was kept to the minimum required for refuelling. However, one day, towards the end of February 1971, Mike Dyer, the FEAF Command Movements Officer, rang me to ask what I thought of the idea of a long weekend in Bali using the RNZAF aircraft to fly there and back. I reminded him of the travel restriction and that we would have to get special approval from the Ministry Of Defence (RAF), which he understood and would have a word with the Command Security Officer. So with a provisional outline plan for Mike, Squadron Leader David Gamble of RAF Changi, myself and our wives to make an indulgence passage on the next routine flight to New Zealand over the first weekend of March 1971, we gave the necessary personal details to the Command Security Officer who said he would place the matter before his masters at MOD.

I was pleasantly surprised when, only a few days later, the authority for us to go was received. The authority was more of a guide for the Command Security Officer who was to ensure that we were adequately briefed in regard to certain things that we should avoid during our stay. We were all officers of senior rank and positively vetted (security cleared for access to information essential to the performance of our particular service roles). It was really an exercise in common sense and service knowledge. I arranged with 47 Squadron for the passengers to be available for a departure time of midnight on the night of Thursday/Friday, 4th/5th March. The flight was scheduled so that the crew would have the Saturday and Sunday clear with their families, leaving their New Zealand base early Monday for their return to Changi with refuelling stops in Australia and Bali. They were due in Bali late afternoon, with arrival at Changi at about midnight. The Bristol Freighter – more popularly called The Frightener – was a cavernous twin-engine freight carrier offering no comfort for passengers. However, basic seats sufficient for our number had been fitted, and we had a reasonably comfortable flight to Bali, where we arrived at about seven on Friday morning. We, passengers, were escorted to the terminal building where our passports were examined, after which we were taken to a large, sparsely furnished room by two armed guards who positioned themselves one at each of the two doors. We thought it best to quietly await developments.

After what seemed an interminable length of time without any exchange between the guards and ourselves, we began to feel a degree of concern. They knew by our passports, which they had so far retained, that we were British and employed in Government service.

No doubt they were very curious about three passengers in civilian attire, with their wives, arriving in an aircraft of the RNZAF. Mike's wife, Trudy, was of Dutch origin, and her parents had been residents for many years in the former Dutch East Indies Colonies. Mike thought that if she was to speak to the guards in Dutch and tell them of her family connections it might just evoke some action. So Trudy did just that, and the effect was immediate. The guard to whom she had spoken went out and returned quickly with a man who, by his very manner, was obviously a minor official but plainly the person in charge at the moment. He was smilingly pleasant and, though unable to converse in English, got on very well with Trudy's Dutch. In no time at all, our passports were returned to us (we still have them showing our date of entry as 5th March 1971 and exit on 8th March). They courteously summoned two motorbike rickshaws, and we clattered off to our hotel in the island capital, Denpasar.

We had chosen the Hotel Denpasar, on Trudy's suggestion I think, as being the only place suitable for Europeans at a reasonable cost. We learned later that a Hilton Group hotel was, in fact, under construction on what seemed to be an extensive tourist development, but that was for the future. Our chosen hotel was located in a prominent position on the main route into the capital. It was typical of those dating back to the turn of the century, being entirely without modern conveniences. The central building was spacious and airy, being as open to the atmosphere as design considerations would allow. High ceilings with electric fans ensured adequate movement of air for personal comfort in the prevailing conditions of heat and humidity. The sleeping accommodation was very basic and quite obviously unchanged since its initial creation. The rooms were large enough for two beds that offered an acceptable degree of comfort but were otherwise sparsely furnished and designed only for sleeping and, of course, personal ablution in the adjoining bathroom that I find difficult to describe in simple terms. The bathroom itself was large enough, but the bath was indeed of the very earliest time being nothing more than a bricks and cement structure of sufficient depth to accommodate a seat, also of brick and cement. A tap provided the essential water that was, as you will have already guessed, without any heat other than that imparted by the ambient temperature. It was acceptable for a short stay but my own experience of personal hygiene requirements in this kind of tropical climatic condition illustrates the essential need for a daily bath in water sufficiently heated to ensure that the pores are opened to ensure adequate cleaning. The water was, I suppose, naturally warm enough for comfort, and no one seriously complained about it being otherwise. Water released from the bath simply ran along a channel in the floor to disappear somewhere outside. All very simple and only a little more sophisticated than any primitive native bathing place in that part of the world.

Bali was to remind me very much of my travels in British India. The principal religion is Hindu and places of worship formed a predominant feature of the towns and countryside. The highways and byways, too had something redolent of southern India, the dwelling places and mud-brick walls, the freely wandering water buffalo, chickens and waterfowl. Perhaps more green and lush on the higher ground than India. The island was made by volcanic action, now long extinct, with two central peaks, the lower slopes having interesting man-made terraces that were fed by ingeniously designed water channels to provide the irrigation essential for growing rice and other vegetable crops, the whole providing a really magnificent prospect for the eye to behold.

Hindu culture was to be found on every hand. For the tourists, surprisingly quite numerous, the main entertainment was based on Hindu folklore featuring, principally, The Ramayana, which I had learned in India. The story is surprisingly similar to that of The Young Prince and the Young Princess in Tales of the Arabian Nights, although of considerable length, requiring one to visit numerous places, by day and night, to see enactments of the seemingly unending story. Performances are usually adjacent to temples using the expansive courtyards with thoughtfully provided head cover and seating in spectator enclosures. Whichever venue one chooses to visit for a particular performance, one can be assured of a most colourful and spectacular experience, always attended by the tremendous ear-shattering noise of the Barong, which, if memory serves me rightly is, I think, the name given to the percussion orchestras comprised of many drums and gongs. There is some tourist literature about the Ramayana in my retained artefacts.

Attempts to provide Western food were woefully miserable, and, most essential to any good British subject, a good cuppa tea seemed totally out of reach as they had no fresh milk, using instead the antiquated substitute of the condensed canned variety. In Singapore, we had supplies of powdered milk from Australia, which, properly diluted with cold water, provided an excellent substitute for the real thing.

Mike suggested that for our last evening meal, we should try roast-sucking pig, a local delicacy. This we had to order in advance at breakfast time. The roast piglet produced expressions of regret from the ladies, and although the meat was very tender and well marinated with herbs, I found it not particularly flavoursome to my taste. The next morning, we all suffered looseness of the bowel and had to spend an unusually long time within easy reach of the toilet facility to ensure that complete evacuation had taken place.

We made for ourselves a full daily schedule so that we could gain the maximum benefit during our short stay. On one day, we went on a tour of the island taking in an early morning scene in a recommended location where one could witness a country market in full swing. This we found to be an experience that amply illustrated the gentility and friendly, welcoming nature of the country folk. Everywhere, there were colourful parasols, their symbol of shelter from the elements. There was much evidence of the strength of their religious belief in their deities to whom their morning sacrifices, usually in the form of artistically arranged fruit and flowers, were offered. From this convenient point, our driver took us to the highest mountain level accessible by car, from where we climbed to the top to see the extinct volcanic crater with a very deeply dark-looking lake of considerable area. We found the entire scene reminiscent of our familiar Scottish Highlands, although more softly clad in the lush vegetation. Here, with due reverence, we passed through a cemetery of many man-made platforms supported on stout poles where, from this highest point, the dead were laid to rest so that their souls might more easily rise to heaven.

On our last morning, after recovering sufficiently from the visceral effects of our last evening meal, we went into the city by means of the noisy but prolific motorbike rickshaws in search of souvenirs in the shape of carvings in teak wood for which Bali is famous. We had no problem other than being spoiled for choice; the products of our search are displayed among the ornamental adornments of our home.

Somehow, in this tight schedule, we managed to visit the beach scene at Sanur, where there was ample evidence of those who sought escape from the normal demands of a life of gainful employment into the preferred alternative of a close relationship with the welcoming arms of Morpheus. They seemed quite happy with their chosen lot and, as far as I was able to determine, were living in a sort of commune comprised of a small area of purpose-built beach huts. This particular beach location, with high breakers of the Indian Ocean pounding the beach, was noted for the surf. I found myself somewhat deterred by the strong undertow that seemed intent on keeping me underwater. I found a certain reluctance to throw myself repeatedly at the advancing wall of the sea as many others were doing, with obvious great enjoyment.

We were required to be at the airport for an early evening departure. We found the replacement 'Frightener' waiting for us on the apron, and after the usual departure checks our passports were stamped, and we enplaned for our return flight to Singapore. This was to be an uncomfortable experience attended by the misery of intense cold. The main cabin heating system was unserviceable, so there was insufficient heating to the rear of the empty cargo area where our seats were located. At our particular flight level, the night temperature was a good thirty degrees below that to which we were acclimatised, and we had no means compensating for the difference by the use of additional heavy clothing. At the farthest point forward, the main heating duct below the flight deck was glowing a dull red, and we spent the long journey paying frequent visits to its locality to stand close to its comforting warmth. We were glad to thaw out in the familiar feel of the Singapore night at RAF Changi with its constant heat and humidity and our beds in the comfort of our married quarter bungalows.

Shortly after our return from Bali, I was pleasantly surprised to have the unexpected pleasure of being host to Air Marshal Sir Roderick Carr, then long retired but who had been the Air Officer Commanding No.4 Group with which I had flown with 102 Squadron. Sir Roderick was passing through Singapore and staying the night with the Station Commander, Group Captain Dan Honley, who was to be a guest at one of our own house parties that evening. He rang to ask if he could bring Sir Roderick along with him. I told Dan that we would be delighted to have him along and mentioned, of course, my former wartime connection with the Group he had commanded for such a long time.

Not surprisingly, in my conversation with Sir Roderick, I mentioned my time with No.4 Group and my recent brief reunion with Leonard Cheshire, who flew with 102 Squadron during my time. This led to a lengthy discourse about the difficult time Cheshire had given him when he was Air Officer Commanding No. 4 Group. Cheshire had been taken off operational flying after completing three tours and somewhat in excess of eighty missions, some of which had been of his own devising whilst with No.5 Group under its AOC Air Vice Marshal Ralph Cochrane and designed to demonstrate that night target marking could be done more precisely, and more effectively, than the methods developed by No.8 Group Pathfinders. For this he had been provided with an unarmed de Havilland 'Mosquito' aircraft in which he had done some extremely dangerous low-level (practically rooftop) marking at night. He had been promoted to Group Captain and given command of one of the No.4 Group stations. He came to see Roderick at Heslington Hall, York, especially to request a return to operational squadron duties for which he would gladly surrender his Group Captain status and revert to his previous rank of Wing Commander. Roderick was, of course, absolutely astonished at such a request, which he saw as bordering on refusal to carry out a duty to which he had been appointed after special selection that he should have recognised, as it was intended, as a mark of distinction.

Furthermore, he pointed out that he had already done far more operational missions than could reasonably be expected of him or anyone else and that he had been more than just plain lucky to have survived. Cheshire was, however, adamant to the point of exasperation until finally, Roderick agreed to discuss his request with the AOC-in-C Sir Arthur Harris. Seemingly, Cheshire had learned that Wing Commander Willie Tait was about to be posted from 617 Squadron (Dambusters) and coveted appointment to the command of this prestigious squadron made famous under its first CO, Guy Gibson. Roderick was firm in his condemnation of Cheshire who foolishly sought glory beyond the normal personal consideration of survival. Cheshire did, in fact, get his wish, and Roderick thought that Butch Harris had decided that granting Cheshire's request would best serve the needs of the Service. As it happened, 617 was not called upon to do any further operational tasks as demanding as the Ruhr Dams for which it was initially created. I am sure Sir Roderick enjoyed our party and the company attending it. We had intentionally arranged it to coincide with Ross' visit for a stay of three or four weeks, which he was able to arrange with his employers at that time, if memory serves me right, Middle East Airlines.

Rosemary and I had not had a break from the heat and humidity of Singapore since our visit to Fraser's Hill in 1970, and I thought it appropriate that we should make a second visit to the central highlands of the Malay peninsular before we got too far into 1971. In the normal process of my daily round of duties, which included contact with many and varied personalities, I had come into contact with the officer commanding the Army Training and Leave establishment at Cameron Highlands. He had previously contacted me by telephone regarding an application he had made for indulgence passages for himself, his wife and daughter to Hong Kong for a leave visit. I had, of course, interested myself in it and was pleased to meet them when they called at SABC whilst in transit on their return to Cameron Highlands. The major, whose name I cannot remember, told me that his Cameron Highlands establishment was now almost totally inactive as a training centre and was becoming more like a holiday resort. He had been advised that it was to remain open against the possibility of it being required for unforeseen accommodation requirements in the event of any situation likely to arise during the final stages of the rundown of the Singapore Base. I was not to hesitate to contact him personally if I should feel inclined to use the facilities there for a spot of leave. On making enquiries through the RAF Changi administration I was delighted to discover that an arrangement had already been made whereby limited numbers of RAF personnel and families could use the Army facility for leave visits. So, I passed my application through the normal channels and was pleased to receive an early confirmation of the dates I had indicated. As this was regarded as an official leave scheme, I could claim entitlement to travel at public expense for the whole journey by road and rail. All I had to do was pay for the additional comfort of sleeping accommodation on the rail part of the journey between Singapore and Kuala Lumpur, which entailed only a visit to the Singapore railway station to make the necessary booking arrangements.

What a delightful experience this was for both of us. We travelled in air-conditioned comfort and enjoyed a good night's sleep to be awakened with tea and biscuits in good time to shower and dress before arriving at Kuala Lumpur, where in the pleasant station dining room, we were able to take a leisurely breakfast before continuing our the rail part of our journey to Tapah Road where a vehicle awaited us for the final stretch by mountain road with the usual hair raising bends affording views of terrifying deep chasms. Rosemary and two other ladies at the party were glad to reach the top with its pleasant surroundings.

We were quickly shown to our bungalow that was large enough to accommodate three families, one including two delightful children – a boy and a girl not yet of school age. Local women who took care of everything, including the preparation of meals, staffed the house. It was truly wonderful to be in the clean mountain air and enjoy the warming comfort of a solid fuel fire in the evenings and sleep without the sound of a ceiling fan whirring around. The scene was very much the same as Fraser's Hill, with a nine-hole golf course as the central feature, but this one was somewhat larger with a small clubhouse. The whole complex of Cameron Highlands was more like a resort that was patronised by holidaymakers who were obviously civilians, but not in large numbers. It was, in fact, very sparsely populated, and we had the rather exclusive feeling of having the whole place to ourselves. I do not recollect any occasion of seeing others using the golf course at the same time as the four officers in our party. There was very little to do during the day other than play golf and take frequent walks around the location that provided such a pleasant walking prospect. The whole two weeks were really an ideal opportunity for complete relaxation that passed too quickly. Rosemary and I had lunch one day with the camp commandant, his wife and his teenage daughter. Their official married quarter was a bungalow not far from, and similar to, that which we occupied. They were very comfortable, and I envied him for what I saw as a most desirable appointment by comparison with those of us who had to suffer the heat and humidity and all who attended a tour of duty in the more demanding climatic condition of the lower levels of the Malay and Singapore topography to which we had to return reluctantly.

Our return journey to Singapore was as pleasant as the outbound journey. Back to Tapah Road, but this time downhill all the way. Past the occasional primitive homes of the Malay jungle dwellers dressed in little but a loincloth, each male carrying a long blowpipe usually pointed upwards towards their favourite delicacy of a small monkey. Our train to Kuala Lumpur afforded us the luxury of a whole carriage that was pleasantly furnished as a lounge and, of course, air-conditioned. A nice dinner in the station restaurant at KL and then into our sleeping berths on the night train for Singapore, where we arrived at an early hour. Transport was waiting to take us to Changi, and our good Ah Sim welcomed us back to our bungalow and fussed around with breakfast.

Things seemed to be going too well with the planned rundown of the Singapore Base and I found myself somewhat uneasy that the inevitable snarl-up was about to happen at any time. I gave my controllers a hard time for a while and made a few discreet telephone calls myself to commanders of the principal units to ensure that the plan was proceeding as intended. I found no backlogs of applications for movement to the UK. As 1971 progressed, so movement of personnel from the UK decreased noticeably as units were progressively disbanded. There was, however, a dangerous trickle of free riders between the UK and Hong Kong, and I saw a serious problem developing here with indulgence passengers finding themselves stranded in Singapore and having to pay their fare for civil flights to the UK, something that they were required to do in the event of seats not being available in RAF aircraft. I thought it propitious to highlight any tendency of this happening and sent a signal to all concerned at MOD (RAF) and the UK departure stations to emphasise this concern. Hopefully it had some effect as we had no serious problems as indulgence traffic from the UK was noticeably reduced as the rundown proceeded. Our own base personnel were, however, keen to seize last-minute opportunities to visit Hong Kong and no problems arose on that sector of the main route. The rundown of the Far East Command was intended to be accomplished by utilisation of resources within the established pattern of scheduled flights as should have been easily possible, and I had no occasion at any time to request additional resources that I knew would place an unacceptable strain on the capability of the long-range air transport squadrons. There was no under-utilisation as it was usually possible to call forward personnel and dependents, with ample warning notice, within the date bands requested by their individual units.

As the summer months of 1971 passed, the number of service personnel at all Singapore locations diminished quite noticeably. The round of social activities, however, seemed to maintain the usual exhausting pace as persons and units about to close held their farewell parties. I agreed that SABC should hold their farewell party as an evening barbecue but leave it as late as possible as we would not be losing any of our personnel until the last few days.

During September, the Chief of Air Staff made his valedictory visit to his most far-flung overseas command. For this occasion, all officers, not on essential duty wherever located, were summoned to attend the FEAF Headquarters Mess, Fairy Point RAF Changi, at the close of a working day. Here, we were told about the reduced size of the RAF and the rundown of the Far East Command, which was all rather old stuff for many of the assembled. The Air Chief also took the opportunity to criticize the younger element for the sadly deteriorating traditional standards, particularly for the misuse of RAF terminology and the preservation of standards both viewed with great concern in high places. He illustrated this point by quoting the now quite common use of the expression 'On the squadron'. How can one possibly be on the squadron? Another was the increasing use of the non-existent term 'aircraftsman' and 'aircraftsmen'. This was, to me a matter that was sadly in need of corrective action if standards were to be preserved. But I felt that the words fell mostly on deaf ears as deterioration in traditional practices, particularly in the social sphere, continued to what those of my vintage now consider quite appalling. I recently acquired a book touching on a bit of RAF history of which I had been a part. The author, a serving officer well known to me, had used the term aircraftsmen at considerable length. I took the opportunity to write and congratulate him on his excellent work but pointed out the serious misuse of the term aircraftsmen that I had attributed to the ignorant civilian publishers. In his reply, he told me that I was not the only one to point this out to him, but in today's RAF, whilst it is well known that the correct term is aircraftmen, the common preference was for aircraftsmen. How can one possibly correct this sort of thing when senior officers responsible for command at the squadron level now condone the practice of it? How can there be aircraftmen when the root word for both singular and plural aspects is aircraft? My own feeling is that this sort of sloppiness is due entirely to serious omissions in the basic training of personnel and failure on the part of officers and NCOs at all levels in the command structure.

It was about this time that I had a telephone call from Mike Dyer, the FEAF Command Movements Officer, asking me to come and see him as soon as I could. I did so almost immediately and found him studiously engaged in his office. He handed me a form that I immediately recognised as an Officer Annual Confidential Report (Form 1369). I was somewhat taken aback as he was under no obligation to show me his report on me unless it was in any way adverse. My superior authority as Officer Commanding SABC Singapore, a Defence Establishment, was the CinC Far East Command, whose staff did not have an RAF CMovO, so my immediate RAF Specialist Branch superior was the FEAF CMovO who was responsible for reporting on the specialist operational aspect of my appointment. I need have had no misgivings, for the report was couched in the most glowing terms, and he simply wanted me to know of his high regard for me, something of which I had never been in any doubt. I was most gratified by his report of my suitability for promotion, of which he said that I was eminently suitable; in fact, he amplified it by adding that he was firmly of the opinion that there had been some detriment to the Service in that my qualities had been far from fully exploited. I thanked him for his glowing report but said something about it being hardly likely to influence my remaining career, which was now in its last four years and that officers appointed to permanent commissions went out of the normal promotion zone for the previous three years of their service. Nevertheless, that is what he thought, and he was not going to fail me by not saying it at his reporting point in my career.

Next on the list of official things to be done was the final Trooping of the Far East Air Force Colours before their return to the United Kingdom for Laying Up in the RAF Church of Saint Clement Danes, London. This was to be a sunset ceremony at RAF Changi on the main aircraft parking area, timed to take place about ten days before the 1st of November whilst there were still sufficient personnel available to make a turnout of reasonable size. It was an emotional event for many of the older officers present, and I felt quite moved by it. It was, after all, the end of the largest of the overseas commands of the RAF in which we had served for most of our adult years. We were witnessing a major event

275

in the planned reduction of the RAF we had grown to love, and we hated to see it being progressively dismantled; however safe our positions in it may have seemed at that time. I was with the senior officers grouped on the right flank of the parade, and an officer next to me, of similar vintage to myself, said softly in a voice charged with emotion, "I think we have seen the best of the RAF, Bill." I said something by way of agreement, but on later reflection thought that it would be a sad thing for anyone who had dedicated himself to a working life of service with any of the armed forces to find himself, at the end, unable to say that he had seen the best of its years. I remember that I made mention of this in my own address at my farewell dining-out night at RAF Church Fenton in 1973. A copy of that address is included in the appropriate place in these memoirs.

By September, the small ANZUK (Australia, New Zealand, UK) Force that would assume interim responsibility until the Singapore Government could safely accept it began to form at its pre-determined location at RAF Tengah, soon to be handed over to the Singapore Armed Forces. The Air Movements Member contacted me to arrange an early initial meeting at SABC. He seemed to be a carefully chosen young officer of seniority and experience appropriate to the task. Not surprisingly, he asked me where my next appointment was to be and when I told him that I was posted to RAF Church Fenton as OC Supply and Movements Squadron, he surprised me with the news that he had recently married the daughter of Group Captain Bill Able who commanded that station. He intended to bring his new bride out to Singapore as soon as the married quarter requirements for the ANZUK personnel were settled with SAF. I was to have frequent contact with him during the last few weeks of the life of Far East Command.

We held our unit farewell barbecue while it was still possible to use the site and its facilities set aside for that purpose. It was a very enjoyable and quite unforgettable occasion. There was a beer mug in Selangor pewter suitably inscribed with personal and unit names, which I presented to each member; afterwards, Major Jim Card presented mine, which is still among my household effects.

The RAF Changi population was, by this time, noticeably thinning as its supported elements were finally closed down. It was sad when, about mid-October, the various messes were closed, and the remaining personnel transferred to the Changi Creek Hotel for their last few days. My own unit started its rundown during the last week or so until, by the 31st of October, only the warrant officer and I remained in the otherwise totally empty and scrupulously clean premises. We closed the place at the usual time of 1600 hours that afternoon and planned to reopen for the last time at 0900 the next morning to meet the representative of the Singapore Armed Forces to hand over the premises as planned. He was there and had in his possession the master copy of the inventory. The warrant officer was the responsible holder of the unit inventory and held the unit copy. Checking took surprisingly little time, and there were no discrepancies between the two copies. The appropriate receipt documents were exchanged, thereby relieving the warrant officer, and I counter-signed both as commanding officer to validate the transaction and formally close SABC Singapore and my appointment as its last commanding officer. I took my leave from the warrant officer who would be flying back to the UK that evening. As we parted I looked around me and realised that the usually busy scene was deserted except for the departing man from SAF, the warrant officer and I. I got into my car and left the station by the route to the main gate. I saw hardly a soul until I approached the gate, where there was still a little activity at the NAAFI families shop. The Station Headquarters area was quite deserted, all offices having closed with the last essential functions moved to a temporary final location at Changi Creek. I decided to see what was going on in the nearby Changi village. It seemed to be unchanged as remaining personnel and family members went cheerfully about their final tasks before their own departure. The scene at Changi Creek Hotel was rather busy, with obvious signs of disrupted routines among those uprooted from their usual places of work.

I returned to my married quarter on the Lloyd-Lees estate and realised for the first time that there were very few residents left. We no longer had next-door neighbours on either hand, our nearest being some distance away. Those of us who were required to remain in the post were permitted to stay in our married quarters, and there was no sign of haste on the part of SAF to acquire them. We had parted with our dog Nicky about two weeks before the final closure date. She had been sent home to the UK privately. She was met at London Airport by Ross, who, being a working member of the airport community, was permitted by the Public Health Officials to have a short reunion with her before she was taken away to her quarantine kennels in Yorkshire, selected by ourselves as closest to our own next UK appointment station at Church Fenton. Ross informed us that Nicky just about went crazy with delight as she was released from her made-to-measure RSPCA air transit case. He was able to spend a little time with her in the compound before the vehicle from the Yorkshire kennels arrived to take her away for her six-month quarantine period. We were going to miss her very much.

We now had two weeks to go before our own planned return flight and I had nothing to do other than be on hand in my married quarter to respond to any enquiries by the ANZUK Force that would be notified to me by telephone. So relax and enjoy the remaining time. The thinned-down Changi Air Movements Squadron was still in place now under the executive officer Squadron Leader Richard Mighall, and I had arranged for the ANZUK Air Movements Member to leave messages with him in the event of my not being at home; there was no requirement for me to be immediately in contact so long as the Changi air movements section was functional. In the event, all went according to plan, which demonstrated how well SABC had played its part in arranging flights for all those who had to remain after the 1ˢᵗ of November. I was to remain until the night departure flight on the 15th but was to attend a final handover conference scheduled for the morning of the 14ᵗʰ of November at the former Naval Base at Nee Soon. We had several last-minute purchases to make that would take us into the city. I had the good fortune of being able to dispose of our faithful MG Magnette to a member of the ANZUK Force, who was glad to get it at the price I had paid for it. So we had no car of our own, but that was hardly a problem as we were close to the main road into the city with cheap taxis available at the raise of the hand.

It was a Saturday when I said a sad farewell to our old MG Magnette. But we were not to be long without an independent means of conveyance. I had a telephone call from our most genial Philip Coleclough asking us to attend one of his evening house parties that he knew would probably be our last. I had to express my regrets due to the transport problem that could not be resolved by taxis on the particular route to his home. Nothing daunted, Philip said that he would arrange transport for us, just be ready at 1900 hours, and transport would be there for us. As usual, we had the most enjoyable evening spent with other guests, mostly members of large international concerns en-passage through Singapore and dependent, no doubt, on his own Anglo-French Travel enterprise. At the end of a delightful party, Philip was bundling us into his car to be driven home by his syce when he said that he would call us early next day to arrange for a vehicle to be placed at our convenience until our final departure from Changi. Sure enough, whilst we were at breakfast the next day, we had the promised call from him, and shortly after that, two cars arrived at the gate, one for us and the other to take its driver back to base. We had at our disposal a prestigious air-conditioned black 'Jaguar' the model produced by the Daimler Corporation. We did, of course, feel quite overwhelmed by Philip's spontaneous generosity; he was that kind of individual, particularly in his dealings with those he served. It made a great difference to the enjoyment of our last ten days in Singapore and meant that we were able to make the very most of them.

We did all the things we wanted to do: our last visits to Singapore's very attractive shopping emporiums to make last-minute purchases of small items that could easily be packed into our accompanied baggage. We came home in the late afternoons quite ready to put our feet up for the evening and watch the TV programmes on our portable receiver that was small enough to be packed into its case and included as an accompanied item. Our usual places of entertainment in and around the RAF Changi complex, the Officers' Club, which was our usual retreat for an evening meal and dancing to the quiet relaxation of a small orchestra, was no longer available to us. However, somehow, it didn't seem to matter, and we still had our devoted Ah Sim to cater for our every need for food and home comfort that, at least, continued to our last moment in the bungalow that had been our home for the previous two years.

On the morning of the 14th of November, I put on my tropical working dress for the last time and set out on my final duty to attend the meeting of the officers of the ANZUK Force to ensure that there were no matters requiring my final advice. The venue, for some reason I cannot recall, was to be at the former Naval Base at Nee Soon. I intentionally chose the route that would give me access by the main entrance that was quite close to the Johore causeway as I was unsure of the exact location of the building in which the meeting was to be held. On arrival at the main gate, I was completely surprised to find it wide open with not a soul in sight. So through I went into the wide well, kept grounds and immaculate lawns of this prestigious former Royal Navy establishment. I saw not a single person until I was well into the area that I knew as the most likely for my meeting and there I saw a few cars parked outside what must surely be the intended venue. I entered the building and immediately knew that it was the obvious conference centre dedicated to that purpose for all time. There seemed to be nothing more at one end, the end through which I entered, but a spacious reception hall beyond which, through diaphanous curtains gently swaying in the breeze, could be seen the long conference table with officers in various styles of dress, assembling. The other end of the long room looked out onto the Straits of Johore clearly visible through similar diaphanous curtains. Overhead ceiling fans kept the air moving and the whole scene was one of well-ordered efficiency, but not a single naval figure anywhere to be seen. The base had, of course, been handed over to SAF, who were apparently only too willing to permit their new partners to use the premises that were apparently more suitable to the occasion than the ANZUK quarters at the former RAF Tengah. I was immediately recognised by the RAF Air Movements member, who came forward to greet me and introduce me to the Royal New Zealand wing commander who was to preside at the meeting. It seemed that I was the only RAF officer present from the previous administration, and as the meeting was to deal with future issues, the president thought it proper that I should be the first on the agenda so that I could get away and tend to other personal matters in the last few hours remaining to me. There was a discussion on the run-down so far, and I was able to assure them that not only had it gone entirely as planned but that the very few essential personnel required to remain to the very end were all satisfactorily allocated to the remaining UK flights and that there were no foreseeable problems except of course any that might arise due to sickness or accident, in which case there could be a need for repatriation by civil aircraft. The few remaining personnel in the Changi Creek Hotel would proceed to the Air Movements section after handing over the hotel premises to SAF. They would then join the air movement personnel, who would also have handed over their premises to SAF, ready for enplanement in the last scheduled aircraft. A few final questions and information readily tendered by myself brought my part of the meeting to its end. I was warmly congratulated for SABC's part in the successful withdrawal programme after which I took my leave of the assembled company with a great feeling of regret. I shall never forget that meeting in that most pleasant conference room in its tranquil location.

I decided to leave the base by its rear exit that led directly into Nee Soon village, which, like Changi village, was on Ministry Of Defence ground. It seemed unchanged but nothing like as busy as it usually was only a short time ago. The shop premises were known officially as Encroachments for which a small ground rental was charged, the buildings being the responsibility of the respective ground tenants. In the case of Changi, the village also included a small area of married quarters for the locally engaged supplementary personnel of the Service Police Section and other essential civilian support personnel. I imagined that these would mostly be required to continue in the employment of SAF once it became firmly established. I drove back to Changi in a quiet relaxed mood but feeling rather sorry that I was taking my last look at scenes that had become so familiar and would, perhaps, never see again.

On our last morning, we went to take our last look at Changi village, where Rosemary had set her heart on a particular gold bracelet, the purchase of which I found would be possible from our remaining local funds. I had intentionally kept it as a final surprise, and she was, of course, delighted to take possession of it. She has worn it every day since and it always looks as attractive as it did then.

Our last day was drawing to its close when, in the late afternoon, Philip Coleclough came as intended to take tea with us and convey us to the Changi terminal building. He had his syce with him who drove the car, that we had so much enjoyed the use of, back to Philip's home. Ah Sim served our last tea with her usual care and attention to detail and then cleaned up, ready to finally vacate the bungalow with us. We had to leave her standing outside, as she had to wait for her husband to collect her and her belongings to take her home to Yan Kit village, just a short distance away. I can see her rather sad face as we took our final leave of her; she had been a good servant to us. Richard Mighall had kindly arranged to relieve us of our accompanied baggage, so we had nothing to carry other than what we would take on board with us. We were able to proceed straight to the VIP facility that was at our disposal, and we were able to enjoy a last quiet farewell drink with our most generous friend, Philip. All too soon, the time came for us to board the aircraft, and after a fond farewell to Philip, we were driven out and boarded as the last passengers. We took off with the sun setting on Singapore as we flew westward only sixty miles or so north of the equator that we would cross on our first leg to Gan, one of the Gilbert Islands group, about sixty miles south of the equator. As we were chasing and regaining some of the passing day, we arrived at Gan, where the same sun was just dipping below the horizon of the Indian Ocean. After a pleasant evening meal whilst the aircraft was being refuelled, we went again, now on the long northwest leg that would take us across Arabia to Cyprus, where we arrived with the dawning of the 16th of November 1971. Here, Sqn Ldr A E L (Alf) Wigley was the air movement boss who was well known to me. But it was a little too early for him so I left a little courtesy message for him with one of his duty staff. The final leg of our homeward journey took us over southern Europe and soon we were crossing the Alps, already clad with their covering of new snow that was to remind us of the probable nature of arrival in the UK during November.

Chapter XXX
Home Again

Actually, when we arrived at Brize Norton about mid-morning, it was not too cold, although I spotted several personnel wearing their greatcoats. We were soon into the warm interior of the reception area. Rosemary was wearing her fur coat that she had carried on board, and I had changed into warmer slacks and a sweater during our stop in Cyprus.

I shall always remember Rosemary's indignation at being asked by the customs official if she had the receipt for the purchase of her mink coat, which he obviously thought had been recently acquired overseas. It had not, but had, in fact, been bought in Nairn, and I had thoughtfully decided to take the receipt, which I had kept for insurance reasons, with us on leaving the UK. So I was able to satisfy the customs enquiry. All other items of our baggage were passed through without question, including our portable TV set and radio, but the gleam of gold on Rosemary's wrist seemed, thankfully, to go unnoticed. We had friends at Brize Norton who knew we were arriving at this time. They were Ina and Drew Shaw, and Ina was there to meet us and take us to their married quarter, where we could change into suitable clothing for our rail journey to London, where we were to have a short stay with him at Slough. Unfortunately, Drew, who was a Britannia captain, was away from base on some routine transport flight, but Ina kindly took care of our every need. We were soon at the mercy of the British Rail transport system, and on the way to Slough where we were met by Ross, who took us to the flat which he shared with two friends also working in the London Airport complex. Before leaving Brize Norton I had used the RAF system to contact Church Fenton and have a chat with OC Admin Wing about the married quarter situation. Whilst a quarter was not immediately available for me, he did not anticipate any great delay. He advised that I should consider arriving on the due date with Rosemary and, if necessary stay in a hotel in nearby Tadcaster until I got sorted out with a quarter or other private accommodation. It wasn't looking too bad.

I had arranged the purchase of a new car through the NAAFI car purchase system, and it was to be available from the Ford sales facility at their main Dagenham factory. So, on the appointed day, in company with Ross, I set out by the London Metropolitan Railway to collect our gleaming new Ford Cortina GXL model. By the time we got back to Slough, it was late in the afternoon as dusk was falling on a rather cold but dry scene that possibly heralded a frosty night. Rosemary was anxious to start for Hereford, where Michael and his wife were living with their son, Blair, then about nineteen months old. They had been there about twelve months after Michael, who was serving with No.22 SAS, had taken his discharge from his initial Army engagement. I was rather disinclined to start the journey at night in a strange new car, knowing that we could not possibly complete it by a reasonable hour and would almost certainly have to stay somewhere on an unfamiliar route. However, she was insistent and off we went, much to Ross's relief, I think, as we were rather an inconvenience in the somewhat overcrowded flat. Thankfully, the weather that night turned out to be quite kind, and we made the distance to Ross-on-Wye before midnight and found a comfortable hotel. We were within easy reach of Michael's place at Holm Lacy, a pleasant village on the river a few miles outside Hereford. Here, we met for the first time our firstborn grandson, Blair, who was a very loveable wee chap, still a bit wobbly on the legs and already with a vocabulary of considerable length with many easily recognisable words.

After a pleasant few days, the time came for us to start our journey to the northern locations that we were also obliged to visit. Firstly, to Heywood where my mother was living in a small sheltered housing complex where she had a comfortable flat with her own entrance and independent facilities with many familiar items of domestic furniture transferred from her marital home. She seemed to be reasonably happy, particularly at the thought that Church Fenton was within easy distance, and she would, therefore, be seeing us quite regularly once we got ourselves settled. Of course, we were able to enjoy several visits to my sister Irene and family, who were quite close on the outskirts of Rochdale, Irene in the village of Norden, her eldest son, Peter and family who had the village post office at Whitworth, aunt Betty and her husband Arthur at Smallbridge, all within easy distance and providing an interesting family programme for a short duration, during which we stayed with Irene and Colin at Norden and saw quite a bit of Rochdale, a town that I had always had a liking for. I remember that John Bettjeman when he was Poet Laureate, had been enthused by the architecture of the majestic town hall and had waxed lyrical at considerable length about it.

But our journeying was far from complete, and we had to head further north to where our hearts really dwelt, in the highlands of Scotland. It was now December, and the real winter weather was setting in. The main highway route was not as it is now and many stretches could provide considerable anxiety at that time of year. But we had a new car with an excellent heating system and knew that we could make the distance to Nairn with a one-night stop and a bit of luck. The first hurdle was to get over the high point of the route over the notorious Shap Fell in winter. From there, the remaining route through the Lake District to Carlisle was easy enough and I had planned our first night stop in the vicinity of Carlisle. We made it in good time and stayed at a small hotel conveniently located close to the main road. The next morning, we made an early start, knowing that our route through the Scottish Central Belt between Glasgow and Edinburgh was likely to provide serious problems of the navigational kind.

We were not exactly strangers to the route, but one needed to have more than casual experience of the route through Central Scotland. In fact, one could hardly call it a through route as it passed through a good many townships, of which one was really required to have a good knowledge of the streets and roads. Not at all like today when the route through is a modern fast motorway system. However, after many mistakes we thankfully found our way to Perth and the home stretch to the north. This, I always referred to as The Agony Stretch meandered wearily through the mountainous terrain that somehow seemed unending. Wearily, we made Aviemore, which at that time was not the resort location it has since become. But at least we were now on our final forty miles to Nairn, where we arrived tired and weary but thankful to be there all the same.

CHAPTER XXXI
TERMINAL APPOINTMENT

After spending the remaining time of our leave with relatives and friends in Nairn, we were eager to take a look at our new location close to the Yorkshire town of Tadcaster, situated about halfway between Leeds and York. My date to be in the post was sometime during the first week of January 1972, and we timed our arrival at Tadcaster for the early afternoon of the previous day. We had decided to take the A9 route to Edinburgh with a night stop thereabouts, and thence via the A1 road system through Newcastle and York. We arrived at Tadcaster shortly after lunch and found our intended hotel on the main road through the town. Altogether, a rather dismal scene on a dull early January day, with an all-pervading smell of stale beer from the brewery, provided the main source of the local economy. The hotel, though obviously the best in town, was somewhat uninspiring and much in need of a good facelift. However, it was the best we could do, and with some misgivings, we booked a room that I seriously doubted would be much of a comfort for Rosemary during my daily absences. But we left our bags and went off to RAF Church Fenton which we found to be a typical station of the late 1930s expansion era.

I went immediately to the station headquarters and made myself known to the Officer Commanding Admin Wing (Wg Cdr Barry Atkinson) who summoned the Senior Admin Officer from a nearby office to provide the latest forecast about the married quarter possibilities. There was not one available immediately but he did mention that the quarter that I would occupy would be available within a few weeks. In fact the officer, whose family were still in occupation, had been posted a few weeks ago and was hoping to be allocated a quarter at his new station any time now. So hang on in Tadcaster at the hotel or try to get more suitable accommodation for a short stay. They then put a call through to the Officer Commanding the Supply Squadron and asked him to come to SHQ to meet me. He was Sqn Ldr Peter Tacon, whose brother Bill I had known and had frequent contact with in his post as OC Middle East Transport Force during my time at HQMEAF. I mentioned that I had my wife in the car, and Peter suggested that we should go to the mess and have tea in the Ladies' Room, which we did.

Peter was Australian and had transferred to the RAF after the war. Bill, his older brother, had recently retired and was back in Australia, and Peter had another tour to do before his own retirement from the active list. In my last annual confidential report, I had indicated my wish for a terminal appointment in the north of Scotland with a preference for Kinloss or Lossiemouth. Unfortunately, the farthest north that was available at the time was Church Fenton, but due consideration would be given to my request, bearing in mind that I still had more than three years to serve to my retirement at the age of fifty-five. I was quite happy with Church Fenton, really, and delighted to be back to the equipment aspect of my specialisation. Church Fenton was a busy station whose principal unit was No.2 Flying Training School. Other smaller units included the Royal Navy Elementary Flying Training School, the Yorkshire Universities Air Squadron and No.9 Air Experience Flight. All these units used the de Havilland Chipmunk primary trainer aircraft, of which there were fifty-two on charge, so keeping that little lot of ageing aircraft up to scratch was going to be quite a responsibility. There was a large officer population, mostly officers under flying instruction who were accommodated in their own student officers' mess, of which I was to be President of their Mess Committee.

Whilst we were pleasantly whiling away the time with tea and chat, I had a telephone call from Barry Atkinson, who had suddenly realised that, as a temporary expedient, it would be possible for the senior officer suite that I would be entitled to occupy if I decided to live in a mess myself would otherwise be empty. So why not put in an extra bed in the bedroom and accommodate Rosemary, who would have the privacy of the suite lounge to retire to during the day? She would also have the closer company of the other wives resident in the officer's married quarters adjacent to the mess. It sounded like an excellent idea to me, provided there was no objection from the other officers living in the mess; after all, the mess was their home. Barry assured me nothing like that was foreseen, providing Rosemary kept out of the public rooms other than the ladies' room. She would be with me during meal times anyway and at other times when ladies were normally permitted in the other public rooms. So I made a telephone call to the hotel to cancel our room reservation, which the management was most understanding. So we had better go back to Tadcaster to collect our bags.

Arriving at the car parked in front of the mess, I discovered that I had stupidly left the keys in the dash and locked the door using the door lock buttons. Furthermore, Rosemary had left her handbag, containing the spare keys, in the car. So, the only thing I could do was to summon help from the local office of the Automobile Association, of which I was a member. "Oh certainly, sir," said the man at the other end of the line. "It happens all the time; we will soon have you up and running again." I was quite surprised to see the familiar car of the AA at the front of the mess and its driver with the biggest bunch of keys imaginable. But not one of them was designed to fit my car. So, the man from the AA was compelled to resort to the most useful tool in his toolbox – a piece of stiff wire. He bent this way and that and formed a suitable loop on what was to be its business end. Then came the problem of getting the wire through the door seal without damage and probing until, at long last, on the very edge of the dark, he managed to get the loop over the door lock button and release it. The whole operation took what seemed to me to be a very long time, which I spent with the man offering as much encouragement as I could in my state of serious doubt. So off we went to Tadcaster and collected our baggage from the hotel, offering our further apologies for any inconvenience to them which they assured us was no inconvenience at all.

We immediately occupied the two-room suite that I would have occupied myself had I opted to stay in single officer quarters, except that the bedroom now had two single beds whilst the sitting room, though unaffected as regards furnishings, was a private place to which Rosemary was able to retire and feel that she was not intruding onto the preserves of the resident officers. Of course, she could use the ladies' room to entertain other ladies at appropriate times. But she would be given lots of attention by the mess staff, particularly the female staff, who would see that she was well taken care of and protected against any unlikely trespass into the male resident preserves. It was a very happy arrangement that saved me a great deal of expense and inconvenience.

So, the next morning, I started the routine procedure of arriving at my new station, where I was to be the Officer Commanding the Supply and Movements Squadron. I had my first formal introduction to the Station Commander, Group Captain Bill Able who immediately referred to my having met his son-in-law with the ANZUK Force in Singapore. I felt an instinctive liking to this tall, slim and obviously fit commanding officer; clearly, of the no-nonsense type, I was soon to be impressed by his example of the level of behaviour he expected from his station officers. He went to some length to confide in me regarding punitive action he had taken against a certain young officer, whom I shall call Chris, and with whom I would have close contact in the discharge of one of the very important secondary duties that would bring me into close contact with the student officers for whom there was a recognised special responsibility for ensuring the inculcation of high behavioural standards in all aspects of service life, but with particular regard to social standards. Apparently the officer in question, a married officer living on the station with his wife and child, had disgraced himself by improper behaviour with the wife of an airman. By way of punishment, as an alternative to the normal obligatory administrative action that would have ended the officer's career, he had banned him from all station social activity, including the use of the station officer's mess. There was no limit to the length of the ban, which would be determined when Bill was satisfied that it had served its purpose to the best effect on the young officer's future career. Shortly after that, I had to make contact with this young officer who held the rank of flying officer (lieutenant). With whom I was to have almost daily contact in my capacity as president of the No. 2 (Student) Officers' Mess. I found this officer to be most excellent in the discharge of his professional responsibilities and the management of the personnel under him. He did not seek to hide his misdemeanour from me but wisely and correctly assumed that the group captain had acquainted me. He did not attempt to minimise the seriousness of his departure from accepted standards, and I sensed in him a measure of genuine contrition. I made it clear to him that I was only concerned with his performance in matters affecting my responsibility as Mess President and would judge him as I found him and make my reports on him accordingly, leaving him in no doubt that he would find my own standards at least as exacting as those of the station commander. He had the very responsible job of station catering officer that affected all the station messes, but my interest lay only with that part of his station responsibilities that affected the student officers' mess. I shortly met his wife, Felicity, who was trying bravely to carry on a normal social life with the other wives under the dreadful imposition of her husband's widely known but seldom mentioned social restrictions. She was, I thought, a most charming person, and I found myself wondering how he could have subjected her to such disgrace. It would have been much worse had Bill Able gone to the extreme length that could easily have reached the public and caused a scandal which, in those days, would have resulted in the termination of his commission as the only means of demonstrating the service attitude to marital misbehaviour and protecting itself against disrepute. I kept a very close eye on the student officers' mess and insisted that Chris should take the dinner at the monthly dining-in night at which I had to restrict his attendance to the dinner only. The Station Commander invariably attended this function, which I was, of course, obliged to attend myself, thereby having two dining-in nights each month. Throughout my time at Church Fenton, I never had any cause to complain about the standard of the menu or the performance of service by the kitchen staff. I made sure that the student elected mess committee included a messing member who knew what was required to keep the members happy with the menu and standard of service and deportment by the mess staff.

I started the professional take-over of the Supply Squadron with my initial familiarisation with the station during my third day, the Wednesday after my arrival. By the Friday, I had it pretty well tied up and was satisfied that I was assuming command of a well-run squadron. On Friday afternoon, I had just returned to the mess to join Rosemary for tea when I was summoned to the telephone to take a call from OC Admin. Wing, Barry Atkinson. He told me that the Command Movements Officer of Strike Command, Group Captain Mike Dyer, had requested that my services be made available to Strike Command for a short time in connection with a political issue that had arisen, probably necessitating the evacuation of families from Malta. This was the sort of thing that Mike was likely to do: put the matter in the reliable hands of those he knew and trusted. All most gratifying to me, of course, but somewhat insensitive in regard to other personal and station considerations. Bill Able was not pleased about it, but as there was no hurry for me to complete my take-over from Peter Tacon, who had time to spare before reporting for his next appointment, he had been unable to object, as the matter had already been provisionally agreed at the top level. Would I, therefore, contact Mike Dyer directly and proceed from there?

I found Mike Dyer still in his office, although it was now well after the normal end of the working day. After the usual niceties, he explained that the political situation in Malta had occurred at a most difficult time when he was unable to provide, from resources immediately available to him, a suitably qualified and desirable senior officer to deal with a problem that was likely to arise involving families of RAF personnel evacuated in civil aircraft to civil destination airports. The airport to which civilian personnel and families resident in Scotland would be evacuated was Prestwick. RAF Transport Command had recently been amalgamated into Strike Command. It was the last of the operational commands to be absorbed into the intended single-command operational organisation within the United Kingdom. So, things at HQSC High Wycombe were somewhat chaotic. Church Fenton was now in the recently formed Training Command, an amalgamation of the former Flying Training and Technical Training Commands with headquarters at Brampton that I knew so well from my previous appointment to HQTTC back in 1952. My specialist superior at the new HQ Training Command was the Senior Supply Officer, Group Captain Philip Renkin, with whom I had previously served at RAF Kinloss. The request for my services on this occasion had obviously been cleverly devised and accomplished by Mike Dyer, and I saw no point in trying to evade the issue, which I suppose was a compliment to myself made with some impact on my present appointment superiors at both Church Fenton and its Command Headquarters. Mike thought that action before the coming Monday was unlikely and would I arrange to be at Prestwick by 0800 hours that day, and be ready to move beforehand in the event of a call to do so from the Strike Command Duty Staff Officer. I hurriedly made arrangements for a staff car and driver to be placed at my convenience to meet that requirement and hoped that I might be left in peace to enjoy my first weekend at Church Fenton with Rosemary. My departure, to ensure arrival at Prestwick by 0800 hours on the coming Monday, would have to be at the most unsocial hour of midnight on Sunday anyway.

We arrived at the Prestwick terminal building at the dawn of a dreich November day. There was no sign of any activity at this early hour and not a soul to be found in the vicinity of the British Overseas Airways Corporation section of the reception area, or elsewhere for that matter. I managed to find an unlocked door behind the long row of reception desks and came upon an office labelled 'Duty Officer' with the holder of that title inside, asleep at the desk. I was apparently expected by the BOAC Station Manager, who would not be on hand until 0900 hours, would meanwhile make my way to the premises of the resident RAF unit, of which I had not previously been informed. However, it was quite close to the terminal, and I got my driver to deposit me there and arranged for him to get breakfast at RAF's expense at the airport before starting his return journey to Church Fenton. The RAF duty officer was a member of a small unit that had the task of maintaining radar surveillance of the North West Approaches to the United Kingdom with the object of ensuring that unwelcome foreign aircraft did not gain entry to our airspace. These approaches formed an extremely busy channel by which aircraft entered and left the country legally with prior notification of the flight-planning system. The RAF unit operated alongside the Ministry Of Civil Aviation Sector Control Unit that monitored and controlled civil aircraft movements. The two control rooms were directly connected, but the RAF controller was able to see all aircraft on his wall-mounted display immediately the uni-directional radar scanner detected them. The civil controllers got their information by radio contact with the aircraft. The Prestwick Airport Air Traffic Control Centre was a separate local control entity.

It was a busy enough scene, even at this early hour, with numerous civil controllers in a very spacious room adjacent to the comparatively minuscule room occupied by the RAF. My own quiet observations of the civil control arrangement left me, finally, in no doubt that it had already been overtaken by a continuously increasing demand that was still some way from reaching its maximum and would soon need to be considerably extended and modernised. The RAF unit was, however, commanded by a wing commander who I would meet a little later, an indication of its operational responsibility and importance. Meanwhile, the duty officer directed me to a toilet facility where I had a much-welcome wash and shaved before going down to the airport terminal to get breakfast under a contractual arrangement with the airport in a small dining space close to the main restaurant.

Now feeling a little more human, I thought it proper to go along and make myself known to the BOAC Station Manager, who was a Mr Morrison. Whilst in conversation with him I noticed a lone individual working at a desk on what looked like an aircraft Weight and Balance Sheet. The young man looked familiar and I had the feeling that I knew him. Sure enough, he was one of my former UKMAMS corporals who returned to civil life and worked with BOAC at Prestwick, conveniently located at his home. I was able to add my personal recommendations of his excellence in both work and character to those already formed by his BOAC superior.

Returning to the unit location, I now found the whole place buzzing with peak activity under the full cover of the day staff. I met the unit commander, who was almost due for retirement. We were soon on the friendliest terms, and we spent quite a long time talking about the sort of things old stagers usually talk about. I put a call through to Mike Dyer at Strike Command, who told me that the balloon had not yet gone up, and they were in a state of suspense, waiting for it to happen. Meanwhile, they would inform me through the RAF Surveillance Unit as soon as they had news of anything about to happen that would affect me and Mike mentioned his personal comfort in having me there. Later in the day, the Unit CO told me that arrangements had been made for me to stay at the Caledonian Hotel in Ayr, where I was to settle the bill personally and claim costs at the standard service rates that I knew to be usually quite adequate. Transport would be available for me to bring me into Prestwick and take me back at the usual working times and otherwise on demand as necessary. The unit was manned continually and the duty officer would call me if needed out of ordinary working hours and provide transport for me. There was a facility that was referred to as The Officers' Mess that offered no more than a quiet place where one could relax in a modicum of comfort and have a cup of tea or coffee with biscuits. It was a small residential house set among others that had been acquired to provide a facility for visiting staff officers to hold discussions in a relaxed atmosphere and where they could wait in comfort until the time for their departure. It did not provide accommodation or meals, but there was a resident locally engaged civilian, Batman, who was responsible for keeping the place in good order. I was invited to make use of this facility but seldom did so, preferring instead to watch the activity in the RAF Control Room, to which no one ever displayed any objection. I found it very interesting to watch the sharp beams of light flashing across the wall display as aircraft were detected and immediately recognised. Still, there was always concern on the rare occasions when recognition was delayed, usually due to some simple human omission. Still, very swift action could be summoned to intercept any unexplained presence that could not be identified within the short time permitted.

One day, I was walking along the main internal corridor when, at a corner, I bumped into an old RAF friend. He was Flight Lieutenant Ted Pike, now retired and working as a controller in the Civil Aviation Authority Sector Control. Ted, initially a Bomber Command wartime navigator, had spent time as a POW after being shot down. He was transferred to maritime flying with Coastal Command after the war, and we had become close friends during time spent at the same maritime locations, principally Kinloss, HQCC and Malta. He was living within easy commuting distance with his wife, Violet and was quite happily resettled into civilian life.

I had friends in the Prestwick area staying in their long-time home at Alloway, the birthplace of Scotland's most celebrated poet, Robert Burns. They were Alastair and Barbara MacDougall. Barbara was a Nairn girl whose parents, George and Isa Ellen, had been close friends for many years, so much so that our own children always knew them as

Uncle George and Auntie Isa. Alastair was a successful businessman and father of two daughters and a son; a very happy family who made me welcome in their home where I spent two evenings that would otherwise have been very lonely. As it happened, the situation in Malta produced only one evacuation to Scotland. During the entire working week that I spent at the location, I had to deal only with the arrival of one young RAF wife and child aboard a BOAC-scheduled flight. It involved no more than being on hand to meet her and assure her of an RAF presence and interest. She had already been furnished with a travel warrant to get her to her final destination by rail. There was really no work in it for me worth mentioning other than being on hand to meet her as the first passenger to alight, which I had arranged, and ensuring the availability of transport to convey her to the local railway station from which there were frequent trains to the main destinations. I received a phone call from Mike Dyer late on Thursday afternoon telling me that the panic was over and that I could stand down immediately. It had been a rather long week during which I was grossly under-employed, but it could have been different. The size of the Malta establishment had diminished since my own time there, and it was fortuitous that there was only one family unit to be evacuated to Scotland. But I was left with the thought that there had been ample time at the beginning for a simple census to be taken to determine an exact requirement by UK destination. I left Ayr by an early morning train on Friday and was home to Rosemary at Church Fenton by late afternoon, having been picked up at Leeds railway station by a pre-arranged staff car.

The next Monday, Peter and I resumed our handover/take-over checks, all of which went very smoothly. I found nothing of an adverse nature and signed the temporary release document for Peter with an easy mind. The squadron leader whose married quarter was to be allocated to me arrived during this same week with the news that he had been allocated a quarter at his new station and would be moving his wife and family during the next week. He invited me to bring Rosemary along to see the quarter he was about to vacate, which, apart from the obvious fact that it was long overdue for redecoration, was of the type appropriate to rank. We were delighted with the manner in which things were working out for us. We agreed to purchase from him an electrical night-storage heater that he had installed privately in the hallway as an absolute winter necessity. We took over the quarter during the next week and moved in immediately. The need for redecoration was something that irritated us for several months due to financial constraints at this late time of the RAF financial year, and we had to wait until April 1972 brought in the new financial year and available funding.

I was quite happy with my new appointment and carried out the remaining take-over checks progressively and found all in good order. There was an area, always worth special attention, where some improvement seemed to be necessary. This I found, as expected, in the accounting section where a not unusual fault had been mentioned in the previous annual audit reports regarding transaction vouchers not being cleared timeously. I decided that this would be my particular area of improvement. The RAF computerised equipment accounting system was being progressively built up, and the Training Command stations were to be the first stations to be embraced by it. It was ten years (1962) since I attended the Computer Appreciation Course at Hendon Technical College and I still had the course notes, not that I was able to find much in them that now seemed applicable. However, I was summoned to attend a one-day seminar at RAF Linton-on-Ouse, the station selected for the Group; this was quite handy for me. Arriving at the appointed location, I was pleased to find that the officer conducting the seminar was none other than an old acquaintance, Group Captain John Ireton, with whom I had had close contact when I was doing staff duties at HQMEAF whilst he, then a squadron leader, commanded that air movements squadron at the MEAF main base at Fayid in The Central Canal Zone of Egypt. It was a very pleasant experience during which the need for accounting records to be accurate and right up-to-date was emphasised at great length, particularly as one of the main objectives was to ensure that the global location of assets could be immediately determined.

The computer centre was nearing completion at RAF Hendon, where it had been commissioned amid great acclaim not only within the RAF but also by many of the larger trading organisations in the United Kingdom. The initial station system for daily inputs to the computer centre was simplicity itself requiring only an itemised transaction input at a pre-determined time of day for each station. For this purpose, a basic terminal was installed in each station's equipment accounting section with a dedicated communication link, available only at the programmed time, to the computer. Meanwhile, the established station equipment accounting records were to be maintained as usual. I took a great personal interest in this new computer accounting system, of which I fully understood the need for input accuracy and continuously impressed it on my accounting personnel.

To drive home the importance of transaction accuracy, a Training Command annual competition was instituted in which the station with the highest degree of accuracy above a pre-determined qualifying level would be awarded a certificate of merit. For the initial year of operation, the only certificate that could be awarded was the Silver Certificate, which was an essential prerequisite for the subsequent award of the Gold Certificate, but only if the desired standard was achieved in the second successive year. I was absolutely delighted to receive for my supply squadron the Silver Certificate for the first year, 1972. Imagine my feeling of total elation on receiving the news that we had done it again for the second successive year in 1973 when I was invited to the Command Headquarters at Brampton for an official ceremony and presentation by the Air Officer in charge of

Administration (AOA), of the Gold Certificate Award, and to be guest of honour at a formal luncheon to be attended by all the senior equipment officers of the stations in the command. On taking over at Church Fenton, I had spotted the weak spot. My concentration on it, although perhaps not fully appreciated by those under my command, was paying rich dividends that were now well reflected by all who worked in the accounting section to achieve the highest standard. My action was well rewarded and actually received a mention in the local newspaper. Photographs of this event at Brampton will be found in my personal effects. It may be of some interest to invite attention to the number of Supply Branch officers in the group photograph wearing flying badges.

I was enjoying my time at Church Fenton and, although the local town of Tadcaster was rather disappointing, the cities of Leeds and York, on either hand, amply made up for it. Social life at the station was good, and I relished the activity of the flying training scene. I suppose my heart was really very much inclined to the flying side of Air Force life whilst understanding the importance and absolute necessity of those engaged in the other supporting professional and specialist endeavours. There was an angling club in which I became quite active but I am bound to say that quiet water angling was, for me at least, not to be compared with the fast water fishing of Scotland. I took part in the RAF Angling Championships in the summer of 1972, held on the mighty River Trent at a location somewhere in the north midlands. The river was wide, very deep and still navigable at this location. The winner was obviously one who had been there before and had been able to make an intelligent reading of the water and knew what was needed to win, but the one and and-a-half pounds of minnows that brought him the winner's trophy could hardly be called a good days fishing. I remember catching fish of that size with a bent pin on the end of a length of cotton thread when I was a small boy. There were more interesting places to fish in the Church Fenton area; even the local River Swale could produce a good range of freshwater fish, whilst a few sizeable lakes could almost certainly guarantee the loss of end tackle to lively Pike.

I was able to follow my interest in model aviation, but this was seldom more than an occasional and lonely session in the summer evenings and at weekends when the airfield was clear of other activities. There was very little local interest in this sport/hobby and surprisingly little throughout the entire Training Command at that time. I found this very disappointing and difficult to understand particularly after the enthusiasm during my time in Singapore. I can say unhesitatingly that throughout the whole of my service I found greater interest and derived more enjoyment from it at my overseas locations. I suppose the reason is to be found in the differences in climate and the availability of other kinds of entertainment and social life generally. It is, of course, an activity that I always found to be attended by fluctuating interest. Perhaps Church Fenton was in a trough of low interest during my time there.

Great things were being planned for the future, and I was warned that I would shortly find myself involved in preparations for the supply support of the Multi-Engine Test Pilots School (METPS) that was to be relocated at Church Fenton during 1973 after being re-equipped with the new Scottish Aviation Jetstream. It was also intended to re-equip the existing resident units with the Scottish Aviation Bulldog and dispose of the Chipmunks that had given such sterling service since the end of WW2. But they were now seriously out of date and in need of replacement by a modern type more suited to the ab initio training of pilots intended for final training on the jet aircraft now being operated at No.1 FTS at Linton-on-Ouse. So, there was a busy time in prospect for me. What of it? The Royal Air Force was always ready to meet the challenge of changing circumstances, delays in doing so being due only to the attitude of our political masters to the cost involved.

The 1st of July, 1972, brought the half-yearly Officers Promotion List. I was not listed, nor was I expecting to be. The salient feature of the list was its ever-decreasing size as the reductions in overall strength became more apparent. For the Supply Branch, there were, if memory serves me right, only four promotions to wing commander. They were all officers younger than me and junior in rank. Now, I knew for sure that there was no further prospect of promotion for me as permanent officers were automatically removed from the promotion zone on reaching their last three years of service prior to retirement. I was due for retirement on 3rd July 1975 – my fifty-fifth birthday. It was a sad fact, but I found consolation in the knowledge that I was high on the shortlist, being well-qualified, experienced and highly recommended. I knew, too that the promotion board had to ensure that officers had to be promoted to ensure future progress to higher rank. I had had a good career but had reached the age/rank point at which there was no longer any future gain to the service by my further advancement. There were many of my peers with much greater rank seniority who, no doubt, found reason to feel bitterly disappointed at being excluded from the last few years' promotion lists, but I never felt that in the reducing strength of the RAF, I could make the next higher rank, so I felt no bitterness but rather great satisfaction in my overall achievement that had, after all, been outstanding bearing in mind that my initial prospect was advancement through the non-commissioned ranks to Warrant Officer that most of my entry had not attained anyway. The ball was now in my court, and I had to play it in my best future interest. I could stay and enjoy the guarantee of continued employment to the normal upper retirement age of fifty-five or seek the Air Force Board's approval to be retired voluntarily at my own request at an agreed date; the exigencies of the Service, of course, always being paramount. Permanent officers were encouraged to seek opportunities for what was called a short second career. There was a penalty for those who were permitted to retire before reaching normal retirement age that resulted in a reduction of retired pay by one thirty-fourth for each year of service before the age of fifty-five. However this penalty was not applied to any officer who was permitted to retire in his last five years. Of course, the years lost were not reckonable for the award of final retired pay.

I decided to take my time and not make any rash move that might have caused regret. I had played the game and tried to live my service life as the service had desired its professional officers to live it in the best interest of the service. I had occupied available married quarters and played my part as a fully integrated member of the various station communities, unlike many who were at this time choosing to live off base in order to get themselves into the house purchase market, which was all very well for them but not for the service. They also ran the risk of being penalised to the extent of being required to pay the rental for a quarter that was empty as a result of their refusal to occupy it. Quarters were, after all, provided to a pre-determined level related to the stations married establishment and an empty quarter was seen as a financial loss to the Public. What I had done towards my future need for a home on my retirement was to initiate a mortgage arrangement with a building society that would serve me well when eventually needed. So, I was quite happy to carry on and take a quiet look at what the future might hold for me. My thinking was directed to the field of civil aviation, and over the months, I wrote to several airlines and airports to test the employment opportunities. They were not good, and I quickly got the clear message that I was seriously overqualified for entry at my age and experience level. No doubt, it was thought that those who had progressed through their own organisations to the senior levels might feel threatened by experience. I got the feeling that I might have stood a better chance had I been non-commissioned rather than of senior commissioned rank.

I tried hard to carry on without my thinking being clouded by the dreadful prospect of unemployment at the age of fifty-five. Something would turn up, and I still had time to think about it and make plans. I still had a lot to do for the service that I loved, and I would carry on regarding that as something to which, as always, I would give my best to the very end. Retirement from the Active List was, after all, something that eventually came to all officers holding permanent commissions; I would still be in the RAF but simply transferred to the Retired List of Permanent Officers and liable to recall if so required in the event of an emergency. As regards a future home and livelihood, my own provision, together with terminal benefits and subsequent retirement pay, would ensure that we didn't starve.

By the autumn of 1972, I had made the provisional arrangements for the receipt of the station's holdings of special-to-type equipment required for the two new aircraft types planned to re-equip the station sometime, yet to be announced, during the coming year.

There would be no problem regarding storage space. However, I had some reservations about the height of the main plane store in regard to the Jetstream wing, of which we still did not have full details in terms of size and whether it was to be supplied in components of a size that could be stored in existing space. Eventually, these details were provided to reveal that we would have adequate space in the event of having to provide temporary storage for the parts of a Jetstream wing. I also had some misgivings about the capacity of the bulk fuel installation in which there was only one tank for AVTUR (Aviation Turbine) fuel. In the absence of information on which to assess the requirement, I brought it to the attention of Command, who would give some thought to the matter at their level, where a decision to increase the station capacity would have to be made, and funding sought for an expensive works service installation.

Towards the end of 1972, news from Nairn was delivered by the local newspaper, 'The Nairnshire Telegraph,' to which we had always kept a postal subscription, carried information relating to the development of a North Sea Oil Project taking place right on our intended doorstep. An American company called McDermott had already set up an office in Inverness. This was going to be a big boost to the local economy that envisaged a work force in excess of one thousand when fully developed. The main work site was to be built on the carse land just outside Nairn in the form of an expansive oil rig construction yard with a deep water facility for the barges on which the rigs could be loaded to transport them to their intended North Sea location. It was then sometime in December, and I wrote immediately to the office address in Station Square Inverness. Imagine my complete surprise when, well into an evening shortly thereafter, I received a telephone call, through the station switchboard, to my married quarter made by a Mr Frank Abercrombie, the McDermott personnel manager. It seems that I was the first applicant for employment in my particular professional line, and they were most interested. He would like to meet me as soon as possible and sought to arrange a meeting at the earliest date. When was I likely to be next in Nairn? I was able to tell him that I would be in Nairn over the coming Christmas and Hogmanay and he suggested that I should contact him then to arrange a meeting. I did, of course, explain that it would take a little time to arrange my retirement from active duty, which I thought might take about six months. "Excellent," said he; "that will be just about the time that we are likely to be able to offer you employment."

Shortly after Hogmanay, I contacted Frank Abercrombie again, and he immediately said that he would like to meet me for lunch in Nairn the next day and I could suggest a suitable location. We met at the time and place I had indicated and I found him a very likeable individual, the type that one could warm to immediately. After a pleasant lunch, which he insisted was to be on his expense account, he invited me to attend a meeting of a small number of potential employees that he had planned to take place later that week at

297

the job site that was still in the early stage of development. At this time, he made no positive indication of an offer of employment but seemed more concerned that I should be fully aware of what the company was all about. So, on a very cold and beautiful morning in early January 1973, I drove from Nairn to the site that was being created on a spit of land protruding into the inner Moray Firth about two miles west of Nairn that was, for convenience, to be known by the name of Ardersier, a village a little further to the west. The approach, from the Nairn – Ardersier road to the site proper, was of some considerable length and, at this stage, very rough, whilst the site itself was little more than a vast area of sand that was in a state of tremendous upheaval with a couple of large excavator vehicles shifting it around in seemingly total disorder. There was a large crane in the process of assembly, a caravan and some sort of a structure in the process of construction from pipes of various sizes. We were immediately introduced to the site manager, an American called Tex Johnson. The first thing was to be invited into the caravan where a local chap called Paul Munn from Ardersier, Texs' chief clerk and man of all means, already had the appropriate number of paper cups laid out and the boiling water ready to be poured onto the coffee.

Milk was, of course, of the powdered variety, but the hot brew was most welcome on this very cold, bright morning. It was a very friendly meeting at which Tex and Frank appraised the half dozen or so of those assembled with what the now desolate area of sand would look like in a very short time as it took on its planned shape and appearance. There was talk of the pipe mill, the assembly area, the office block and many other features that would be necessary to complete what was obviously to be a vast undertaking, the like of which was likely to be outwith the comprehension of most of the local population many of whom would, obviously become involved. Tex was the only American present, all the others, including Frank, being of Scottish origin with some from the heavy industrial central belt. The major engineering trades seemed to be represented whilst I was the only one in the supply and logistics field of endeavour. I had the feeling that I was being introduced to something that was to offer an exciting challenge. None of those few present had yet been offered positive employment, but I was to meet them all again very soon. I later had the chance to speak to Frank alone and reminded him of the time factor that was a major consideration for me in the matter of being able to accept any offer of employment that might be forthcoming. He told me that he was not yet in a position to give any positive indication, and it was really up to me. He suggested that I should start the ball rolling as soon as possible and keep him informed of progress. I left him with no doubt that I was interested and would certainly consider an offer in my own professional line. Although without positive indication, I decided that I would start the premature voluntary retirement procedure immediately upon my return from leave.

As soon as it was reasonably possible to do so after my return to Church Fenton, I contacted Barry Atkinson and told him of my intention to seek the permission of the Air Force Board for Premature Voluntary Retirement at my own request. He thought that he had better tell the group captain immediately and we went into the adjoining office to tell Bill Able of my intention. Bill was most interested in my account of what had transpired throughout my leave and said, "Why don't we get this sort of thing happening down here in England?" I made it quite plain that while I did not have a confirmed offer of employment at the moment, the opportunity was too good to ignore. The prospect was right on the doorstep of my intended retirement location, and it was up to me to take the initial steps to secure it. He could not, of course, oppose my request unless he considered that there were strong reasons that my premature retirement might be seriously disadvantageous to the best interest of the service, a matter that would be the paramount consideration for the Air Force Board anyway. He said that he would forward my request with his favourable comment regarding the suitability of the employment opportunity for an officer seeking a second career opportunity on retirement from a retained permanent commission. He did, of course, have to give appropriate consideration to the suitability of the intended employment in regard to anything that might bring the service into disrepute. So, I set about compiling my request to the Air Force Board and indicated a carefully calculated exit date that would ensure that I had a complete final year of service to reckon for my retired pay. Incomplete years were not reckonable. I calculated that the 15th of June 1973 would be the ideal exit date in all respects as far as I could possibly see at that juncture. It gave the service sufficient time to revise the senior officer-manning requirement. For myself, I also had to bear in mind that prior to the proposed exit date, I would also have twenty-eight days of rehabilitation leave during which I could attend any of the many courses held under service sponsorship or spend the time with a future employer, plus a final twenty-eight days terminal leave all on full pay.

I was surprised at the rapidity with which the application was acknowledged and the relative documentation forwarded for administrative action. The Air Secretary's Department agreed on the 15th of June as my exit date and gave me clearance to proceed. I informed Frank Abercrombie by letter immediately, and he asked me to indicate, in due course, a short period during which I could present myself for a final interview at the Inverness office. The Ministry Of Defence's action was surprisingly impressive. I had a letter expressing regret that the final arrangements in regard to my replacement at Church Fenton could not be made due to manning considerations in a manner that would facilitate my rehabilitation and terminal leave periods being continuous. My replacement would not be possible earlier than fourteen days prior to my final leave, and I would, therefore, have to remain in post for the handover to my successor and final clearance on the date of commencement of my leave. So I knew what I had to plan for in good time to make the necessary arrangements, so I thought. But what about a home of our own to retire to? Well, that should not be much of a problem. So I arranged for a week's leave in March, during which I hoped that we would be able to tie up the matter of employment and future accommodation.

The winter of 1972/73 passed very quickly for me. I had a good many things to attend to besides personal considerations regarding my immediate future. I still had a very busy command responsibility to discharge, and this took no cognisance of personal matters. There were still the routine Staff Inspections and Audits to take in my stride. I took the planned leave in March, and Rosemary and I went off to Nairn by road to put our final plan into operation. I reported to the McDermott Scotland new headquarters offices, now on Old Edinburgh Road Inverness, for the official employment selection interview. I now found that Frank had an assistant who was inclined to be somewhat officious and went to considerable lengths about my suitability and qualifications for the position of Purchasing Officer. Clearly he had not the remotest idea of what was entailed in my RAF responsibility as a specialist officer of the Supply Branch. So I had to enlighten him somewhat and offered to provide a Curriculum Vitae if he so desired. He conceded that it was unnecessary in my case. Frank asked me to go along to see Jim Cromer, who was to be the American Head of the Purchasing Department, and to ensure that I attempted to fully explain what my RAF duties entailed. There seemed to be some uncertainty that Supply meant something to do with the provision of food. However, I met Jim Cromer and found him in some doubt about my suitability. But I thought this was probably intentional rather than born of ignorance. He said that his father had been a professional officer in the US Army and was absolutely useless on return to civil life. I tried to assure him that I had no intention of being so considered myself. I left with a feeling of some doubt, but the die was struck, and I had to put the matter of accommodation in place.

Rosemary was not having much success with house hunting. There were only three properties on the Nairn housing market, and these did not fit our envisaged needs, being hopelessly below our standard. We had indicated our needs to the two main solicitors in the town and were prepared to return to Church Fenton with an unaccomplished mission. However, on the day before our departure Rosemary got news of a property that was about to come onto the market. Fortunately, she knew the lady into whose hands the disposal of her late sister's property had passed. We were able to view it immediately and, whilst it was not exactly what we were looking for, decided that in the difficult circumstances, it was the best we could hope for at the time. So we indicated an interest and got an assurance of first refusal. We set off on our return to Church Fenton the next day, feeling somewhat relieved.

After a few days, I received a letter from Frank Abercrombie confirming an offer of employment as a Purchasing Officer at a salary which, together with my retired pay, would assure an income that would permit us to live in the manner to which we were accustomed. My start date was to be the 1st of June, which suited me ideally. Now I had the Air Secretary's permission to retire from active duty on the 15th of June, a job to go to but no roof over my head. Providentially, the housing matter also moved along quite quickly. However, we had to do a bit of bargaining with the solicitor handling the deal, who was obviously trying to squeeze as much as possible out of us for the purchase. However, we got the final figure sorted and after tying things up with the building society, the house was ours. We knew that it needed a lot of work doing to it. Rewiring was an absolute essential as was the installation of a background heating system, and then complete decoration inside and out. It was going to be difficult to get all this work done in our absence and I saw that the best way was to arrange for the bulk of the work to be done during my rehabilitation period that I had arranged to spend with my future employer. Jim Cromer seemed quite delighted with the arrangement. So with that plan firmly in mind, I was able to go about my normal RAF duties with a reasonably contented mind.

At the beginning of April I received news from Command Headquarters that my squadron was to be honoured by the very first award of the Gold Certificate of Merit for the best input to the Central Computer for the second consecutive year. I was to attend the award ceremony at Brampton and be a guest of honour at the formal luncheon (See page 248). Apart from my intense delight and satisfaction at the receipt of this wonderful news, my visit to Brampton would also serve to enable me to take my formal leave of the AOA, the SESO (Philip Renkin) and several other staff personalities whom I had known for many years at various previous locations. Seated on the right hand of the AOA, our conversation never lagged for a moment. The photographs of this occasion show many officers of the Supply Branch wearing flying badges. The AOA himself will be seen as a former air observer, so we had lots to talk about, particularly pre-war and operational wartime flying experiences. It was a truly wonderful occasion so near the end of a long career that concluded with a final note of professional achievement; making an occasion never to be forgotten. The wartime airfield at Elvington, though long inactive and unmanned, was still designated an Emergency Landing Ground for which RAF Church Fenton was responsible for care and maintenance. Selected student pilots who had progressed to the solo stage also used it occasionally to ease congestion at Church Fenton. I made my final visit to Elvington, now the home of the Yorkshire Air Museum, by air in a Chipmunk aircraft of No.2 FTS, which was to be my last flight as a serving officer. I have visited the museum several times since it was inaugurated as a civilian venture by enthusiastic local volunteers who, over the years with commendable effort and resource, have produced not only a museum but a museum in a well-restored former wartime RAF station, all of which they can feel justly proud.

My dining out was a feature of the monthly mess dinner night for April, and this followed the customary pattern of having one's virtues extolled by the Station Commander, who was well-plied with details of service and accomplishments, particularly as they might have affected the Service generally or the Station in particular. Bill Able was most complimentary in mentioning my war service and the fact that I had done my first operational mission during the second night of the war and the last to command the SABC Singapore at the closure of the Far East Command. In regard to Church Fenton, he said, "He took over a good supply squadron and improved it; such is the mettle of this officer." He then went on to elaborate on the importance of computerisation in the supply organisation and my success in putting Church Fenton in the lead position at the time of its introduction. One was expected to make a suitable response, and mine was based on acknowledging the assistance of capable personnel in a basically sound organisation that was there to start with. In regard to service, I mentioned that my first posting had been to a Yorkshire station, and it seemed fitting that my last posting should be at a station in the great Air Force county of Yorkshire. I also placed great emphasis on my feelings at the end of a long service career and illustrated it with a mention of my emotional feelings at the final parade to mark the closure of the Far East Air Force. I said that it would be a sad thing for anyone to look back on his years spent in the Service and not be able to say that he had seen the best of its days. (See Page 234 regarding the final parade of the Far East Air Force Colours).

Rosemary and I had our farewell party in the officers' mess just a few days before we left to start my twenty eight days rehabilitation leave to be spent with Jim Cromer at McDermott's Inverness office. My final act the day before my departure was to hand over the presidency of the Student Officers' Mess. As for the Supply Squadron, it would, as was usual during my absence, be the responsibility of the more senior of my two junior officers. So, off we went to Nairn to start the adventure of our return to civil life. It was not easy at first as we had a house with nothing in it and had to put up for a few days with a lady who ran a very comfortable bed and breakfast facility, which she kindly extended to include an evening meal. Rosemary soon had our own house furnished with the bare essentials and I got the electrical rewiring job underway, including the installation of an electrical background heating system that was the most convenient option.

Initially, we found ourselves living among the most unimaginable mess of plaster and broken brick. Thank goodness we had many friends who came to our rescue in many ways. I really do not know what we would have done without them; they were kindness itself with their gestures of willing help with household items such as essential bedroom curtains.

Still, I found a great deal of satisfaction in returning to our new home at the end of each day although wondering if there would ever be any noticeable difference in the scene of complete chaos. On the work side, I found that Jim was already up to the armpits in purchasing activity, and I had to learn the ropes quickly. It was mostly a case of getting what was needed by the most expedient means, but there was some reluctance to understand that it would take a little time to develop local businesses to the standard to which McDermott was obviously used back in the US. Jim had already been in touch with prominent local suppliers of various hardware and tools, but seemed unable to appreciate the capital outlay problems that faced them in expanding their businesses to accommodate the wider need of the developing off-shore enterprise.

Obviously, there was a tremendous attraction for the larger business organisations in the south. We had a constant stream of representatives of companies located in the central belt seeking business. Many of these businesses were to extend their interests by building premises on the industrial sites that were to develop quickly close to Inverness and its environs. We rapidly built up a supply base for the innumerable items of equipment that were required on an almost daily basis, but there was nowhere to store it. Storage was not a responsibility of the purchasing department, although my own thinking was that it should be. So, we had to accept a hand-to-mouth type of existence, which was not in keeping with my idea of an efficient and cost-effective organisation. But it was clear that things were not going to be done the British way. Economy and cost-effectiveness seemed strangely of little consequence against the background of immediacy. The job site at Ardersier was changing rapidly as the various buildings began to appear, and the workforce increased with the increasing capability of the site. It was all quite exciting, and I felt the satisfaction of being in at the beginning of what was to become a huge economic development that was to have a marked effect on the economy and the character of northeast Scotland. However, many were decidedly against the industrial development of an area traditionally dependent on agriculture and tourism. My rehabilitation leave passed quickly, and I had to get back to Church Fenton to prepare for the arrival of my relief.

I motored down and arrived comfortably in the early evening in time for dinner. It was a Saturday, and I had telephoned my junior the day before, asking him to ensure that the mess staff left a cold meal for me in the event of my being late. Living in a mess for my last two weeks of active list service did seem rather strange after my time spent with Rosemary in married quarters, only a short walk away. My relief was due to report the following Monday week, and I would be free to start my terminal leave as planned after duty on the 16th of May to meet the agreed exit date of the 15th of June.

There was little for me to do during these last two weeks as careful pre-planning had ensured that everything was, as it should always be, in good order. My relief arrived on the due date, and I had him, settled in comfortably in single quarters in the mess. The handover procedure started with a familiarisation tour of the station and introductions to prominent personalities. The requirements of the Supply Organisation Regulations were covered progressively, and I was relieved of my command responsibility when, on the day before my due departure, we went to see the Station Commander to formally tender the required release certificate. At lunchtime that day, there was a pre-lunch gathering of the squadron and section heads in the mess, where I was presented with an inscribed tankard from the officers of the Administrative Wing. A pleasant lunch, and I was free to depart the next day at my leisure. Ross wanted to come up from London to spend the last night with me and I arranged accommodation for him in the single officer quarters adjacent to my own. We had dinner together that evening and spent the time after having a quiet drink in the bar.

After breakfast the next morning, I went through the final stage of clearance from the station, and we then departed together in our two cars for a short visit to my mother at Heywood. Here, we found Grandma in a new location where the sheltered accommodation, although providing her with a degree of independence, offered the additional facility of constant attendance by a resident warden and his wife. She was comfortable, quite happy to be in a familiar locality and I had the comforting thought that she was in safe hands. Ross stayed for a little while and then departed for London whilst I stayed in the relative's room in the small sheltered complex that was right opposite the Sunday school and Church of my childhood where, from my infant days, I spent many happy hours. The next morning, I called the bakery shop of my sister and brother-in-law to take my leave of them. It was a very busy scene, and I left with more than ample food for my journey home to Nairn, where I arrived in the early evening. I was home to our own home where I wanted to be. I now had fourteen days to spend there getting things into final order, if such a thing is possible, before taking up my post as a purchasing officer with McDermott Scotland on the 1st of June.

CHAPTER XXXII
THE SECOND (SHORT) CAREER

I called Jim Cromer to tell him that I was home and would be with him on my intended start date and gathered that he would be very pleased to see me. But I had lots to do. There was still much to be done in the house. The electrical heating installation was just about complete, and the decorators would be able to make an early start after the place had been thoroughly cleaned, which they would see to. Soon, the place smelt of new paint, and Rosemary had decided on the carpets whilst the curtains would take a little time to make by a local firm in whose hands we left the entire matter of furnishing; I wanted nothing to do with it until the time for payment came. By the 1st of June, it was more like home when I joined Jim Cromer only four weeks after leaving him, but the difference in the workload was immediately obvious to me.

A second new member had joined a few days earlier, and we shared a separate office. He was Donald Morrison with whom I got on very well. Much younger than myself, I thought he was likely to be an impressive performer with an ambitious approach to the work in which he was not well experienced but quick on the uptake. I was back on the scene only a few days when Jim told me that I was to set up an office on the job site at Ardersier as a preliminary to the move of the department at some future date, but not likely for a few months. Meanwhile, he wanted me to operate by myself alongside H.J Roget, the newly appointed American Site Manager, with a desk in his office caravan, to ensure immediate action on all urgent equipment requirements. This was to be a very tough number indeed. In no time at all, I was more than busily engaged with a continuous demand for all manner of things that had to be located and purchased, and all were absolutely top priority urgent in a system that simply could not be controlled by the imposition of any system that would determine what was and what was not urgent. No one wanted anything to do with such a thing. Just get every damned thing at once, and don't ask questions. The idea was that demands for non-urgent items should be passed to Inverness for action, and I soon had to devise my own system of determining what was urgent and what could be conveniently passed up. Of course, the system was thought to be greatly inadequate by the section heads on the site, and it was clear that it would not be improved until the entire purchasing department was adequately staffed and located on the site. This was the situation in which I found myself on the 15th of June, 1973, my last day of service on the Active List of RAF Officers and transferred to the Retired List.

I feel, particularly in view of the seemingly sad level to which general service knowledge within the RAF seems to have deteriorated at present (2003), to add at this stage a short explanation of what the term 'Retirement' is intended to mean in the British Armed Services. All officers, no matter what type of commission they hold, be it regular or reserve, are listed in the Active List. This listing is done so that members of the Public and civil organisations can check the veracity of those claiming to be officers. The RAF lists are published, usually during August each year, by the Stationery Office and can be purchased by anyone. Regular officers are those holding Permanent Commissions and any type of Short Service Commission. Short Service Officers, on completion of their period of service, have their commissions relinquished by announcement in the RAF Section of the London Gazette.

On the other hand, officers appointed to Permanent Commissions retain their commissions and rank for life and, at the retirement age appropriate to their rank and branch, are transferred to the Retired List. So, 'Retirement' in service terminology is intended to refer to the latter category of professional officers who form the officer nucleus of the regular establishment. Short Service officers are usually paid a lump sum gratuity on completion of their period of service. But officers retired from permanent commissions receive Retired Pay for their remaining life and are usually liable for recall to Active List service until reaching the age of sixty. Retired Pay is normally based on the half-pay concept for a maximum length of thirty-four years of service reckoning from the age of twenty-one to the normal upper Active List age limit of fifty-five.

I continued my lone vigil type of operation until the autumn by which time a large wooden building had been built to temporarily accommodate the essential site elements until the permanent headquarters building became available in the spring of 1974. The winter of 1973/74 was unpleasantly cold in the inadequately heated wooden building in which I shared a small room with a young assistant buyer who certainly made the ever-increasing workload easier to deal with. That winter was a particularly memorable one with the prospect of a very small and very cold office to greet one first thing in the morning. Thankfully, we had the means of heating the space rapidly but there was no way in which the building could be safely left overnight with its electric radiators left on. But we got through it whilst the Inverness element of the purchasing department was built up to a more effective strength. By May of 1974 we were able to occupy the splendidly more acceptable working conditions of the permanent office two-storey office block prominently located at the entrance to the site. Here, the working accommodation and facilities were, in every respect, to a very high standard, giving the most favourable appearance to all who visited it and a feeling of pride and satisfaction to those who had to work in it.

I felt myself very much a part of the developing work scene, and being the kind of person I just happened to be, I took the ball as it was passed to me and found myself working harder than I had initially intended. All I really needed was a nice little job to help pay off the mortgage on my first home after my long RAF service, but I got more than intended. On the 2nd of August, 1976, I suffered a heart attack that hospitalised me in intensive care for three weeks and kept me out of action for a total period of seventeen weeks. I still take daily medication for the resulting condition for the rest of my life, but it is well-contained and no trouble as long as I don't seriously exert myself. But life was not the same after that, and I decided at the age of fifty-eight to leave McDermott, Scotland, in July 1978. The work pressure at that time was no less than it had ever been and I was aware that I had been working at a high pace under constant stress of such magnitude that I was much too old to carry. It was a matter of common sense to get out of it, but I felt that I had to continue in some sort of productive occupation until I reached my intended final retirement from working life at the age of sixty.

Chapter XXXIII
Final Venture

During the winter of 1977/78, Michael had made the acquaintance of Lord Cawdor, whose Nairnshire estate was, to say the least, vast. In fact, the land now occupied by the McDermott fabrication yard was acquired from the estate. Lord Cawdor, through the estate, was providing a cautious degree of initial assistance to Michael in the development of an industrial waste disposal enterprise. It was plain that Michael was having some difficulty in keeping his one-man operation viable and really had to search the countryside for such work as was within the limited capability of the means available to him. This capability was mainly limited to emptying the septic tanks of the numerous farms. Having gone through the emotional upset of a divorce pursued by himself, he was living a lone existence in a small farmhouse owned by the estate whilst his five-year-old son, Blair, who had just started school, stayed with Rosemary and me. It was a rather upsetting time and we felt a great deal of parental concern for Michael in his unfortunate situation; he was plainly struggling. He obviously needed some support, and I undertook the accounting and bookkeeping side of things for him on a purely voluntary basis. It was at this stage that Michael suggested that I should come along with him to an evening meeting with Lord Cawdor at the castle. This I did and we had a lengthy discussion at the end of which Lord Cawdor agreed with Michael's observation that expansion of the business would not be possible without the introduction of a dedicated tank vehicle with an integral pumping facility. This was agreed, and funding of £15,000 was made available as an estate investment. This was the state of affairs during the summer of 1978 when, after leaving Mc Dermott Scotland, I decided to join Michael, initially without pay.

My own financial situation was now of some concern in view of the loss, albeit voluntary, of a steady salary to support my RAF retired pay whilst I still had the non-reducing monthly mortgage to discharge. But I found myself able to do so but only after cashing in all my realisable assets and, as I had no intention of taking a mortgage liability into final retirement, enforced or voluntary when it came, I decided that the discharge of the mortgage there and then was a matter of essential immediate necessity. My five-year spell with McDermott had made that possible. Since I had left on medical advice and had written proof of that, I was not unduly concerned about immediate further employment as I was assured of a degree of state assistance whilst unemployed. But I had no intention of being seen to be in any way dependent on the support of a benevolent social system. Michael was courageously trying to establish himself in a new and very difficult field of business endeavour that could not possibly succeed without an initial high capital investment to provide the essential plant and machinery. I was unable to make any subscription to the financial provision, but as I had no other object in view, I decided to give Michael whatever support I was capable of in the matter of financial control and general business administration about which Michael had appraised Lord Cawdor.

Joining him at the time I did was quite fortuitous as, unexpectedly, Lord Cawdor had apparently decided to insinuate a person of his own choosing into the business. He was a young man of the type then becoming popularly known as 'Whiz Kids.' He was from the London scene and clearly enjoyed the Cawdor favour. No intimation had been given in regard to the nature of this young man's casual appearances. I soon got the feeling that he was a spy instructed to quietly observe and report directly to Lord Cawdor with a view to eventually assuming a similar role to that which I had voluntarily undertaken. None of this had been directly intimated, but I suspected the move was an indication of Cawdor's well-placed doubt about Michael's inability to manage other than the practical aspects of running the show and probably felt his financial interest threatened by my own action. However, he had not said so directly. I saw the move as distinctly disadvantageous to Michael's future interests. The matter required very tactful handling, and for my part, I merely treated the newly insinuated personality politely, never giving any indication of work being needed on his part, not that he gave any indication for work to be allocated to him. He seemed to be at a loss and rather unsure of himself and awkward in my company although he did nothing to offend. The whole experience was rather strange, and really the only meeting with him that stays clearly in my mind is of one occasion when I bumped into him one morning in Nairn High Street. On this occasion, his topic of conversation was to impart the idea of the great time he was looking forward to on his forthcoming weekend visit to London and the sexual prowess that he was about to display to the satisfaction of the young ladies of his acquaintance. This clearly illustrates my personal assessment of him. He finally departed as quietly as he had arrived. As for my relationship with Lord Cawdor himself, I never felt it to be cordial but rather that there was a quiet resentment on his part. I had the clear impression that he regarded me as an unwelcome intruder. I did not doubt that Michael's initiative was planned to become an estate enterprise with Michael as nothing more than an estate employee as the leading hand.

Michael remarried, and his new wife, Fiona, came to live with him in the farmhouse, where Blair soon joined them. The work scene was unchanged, consisting mainly of the farmyard with a dilapidated barn providing the only poor cover for a very cold workshop and garage. A small caravan served as the office. The winter made life for Michael very tough as he struggled to find the work needed to justify the cost of running the tank vehicle and to make ends meet whilst, at the same time, doing the necessary work to maintain and keep it in a clean and serviceable condition; am unending task considering the nature of the work that also required the septic waste to be deposited on the ground of those farmers who were usually willing enough to have the beneficial fertiliser spread on their land for nothing. But the state of the vehicle needs little imagination and the task of hosing down the filthy tanker at the close of a miserable winter day. I was certainly not enviable of Michael's lot.

Against this background, the small undertaking became a limited company, a wise move made at the suggestion of Lord Cawdor, with himself and Michael as the directors; Michael designated managing director, and myself as company secretary. The Cawdor estate was to have the controlling interest with fifty-one per cent of the shares and Michael with the remaining forty-nine per cent. I prepared the necessary documentation but ensured that a local solicitor, who also obtained the company seal, did the legal process of registration. The company was given the name Nontox Limited, a name derived from non-toxic and suggested by Lord Cawdor. This was a move in the right direction, giving Michael a greater feeling of position in his relationship with the funding source. But it did nothing for the general state of things that I knew could never be improved without funding on a considerably larger scale that was certainly beyond the existing earning capability and probably beyond the acceptable limit of the estate interest. Certainly, there was not going to be any profitability from the present set-up and without funding, there could be no expansion.

We had unending discussions on the subject of profitability and funding. We went to the bank; the manager of the local branch being well known to me as a fellow member of the Nairn Rotary Club, and borrowed to the limit determined by him. This, whilst easing the overall financial situation, only increased the company's liability. The workload gradually increased, and it was obvious that Michael could no longer cope by himself. We hired a good man who was a licensed heavy goods vehicle driver and could also help with the maintenance work. The fact that we had to pay him absorbed the small profit from the increased work. The much higher capital costs were still out of reach, and I could see no improvement in the situation. I felt that Lord Cawdor was concluding that there was to be no profit for the estate in this venture, and I got the clear impression that no further investment was likely from that source. It did seem like a hopeless situation until, quite without prior warning, in the early autumn of 1979, the morning mail contained Lord Cawdor's resignation as a director of the company. There was no explanation, but after a short spell of incredulity, I got the impression that he must have had a fear of forthcoming bankruptcy and liquidation.

Although my first thought was that winding up the business may well have been the best move at that time, uppermost in my mind was the overriding thought of the probable effect for Michael if the estate should now seek to liquidate the company by its own action. After discussing the effect of the resignation with Michael on his return to the office, I found him, not surprisingly, unwilling to surrender to any threat to himself after the tremendous work and worry that the venture had so far demanded of him, but rather a grim determination to carry on by every possible means even if the estate forced the company's demise. So, I proposed that the best action would be to acknowledge the resignation immediately by letter and then create a record in the form of a minute of an extraordinary meeting of the company containing the declaration of intent to carry on business as usual. This I did without creating the impression of anything out of the ordinary. After a few days, I contacted the estate factor, Alan de Candia, of whom, from the very beginning, I had formed the opinion that he was not in favour of the estate involvement. I asked him to point blankly what the estate action was likely to be in regard to its now somewhat diminished financial investment? He said that the matter had been discussed but that Lord Cawdor would not under any circumstances pull the rug from under Michael's feet, as it were. I took some comfort in this and suggested that we should have a meeting about it at an early date and that he might consider what the estate would accept by way of disposing of their interest in the company. He said that he would discuss the matter in some detail with Lord Cawdor and convene a meeting as soon as possible. I thought it was better to have what lay in the immediate future clarified.

Amazingly, the future was made clear by an event that was to provide the means of a complete change in the fortunes of Nontox Ltd. We were approached by a major undertaking engaged in the development of the offshore oil industry located in eastern Aberdeen-shire. This would involve us in a contract that would require a small detachment of the company to work on location and live close by for a short period in order to assist in the preparation of a large site. Our task would be to clear liquid wastes. Michael successfully negotiated the contract that would bring in a single sum that would guarantee the easy clearance of our current financial liabilities and, perhaps, acquire the Cawdor interest. We kept the matter to ourselves and concentrated on the task before us. We had a meeting with George Milne, our bank manager, who was naturally delighted to learn of the turn of events. He agreed to assist in every possible way to extend assistance within the financial constraints imposed on him. Of course, we did not mention anything about the change in the company structure. Neither did we mention the Aberdeen-shire contract to Cawdor.

By the time we were invited to attend a meeting at the estate offices, the work on the new contract was well underway and proceeding satisfactorily. Lord Cawdor himself was most affable, and we were pleasantly surprised with what I thought was a generous settlement offer to which I readily agreed. Alan de Candia brought up another matter of an additional seven thousand pounds that I had intentionally not mentioned. It had to do with something that we had asked for in connection with assistance to improve the amenity of the farmhouse that was not an estate liability. So, I indicated agreement to the inclusion of that in the settlement sum. I asked for written confirmation of the share purchase option and was assured that this would follow in the course of the next few days. After a pleasant handshaking all around, we left that meeting and I find it difficult to adequately express our relief at an outcome that was below our expectations. We were also assured that there would be no change in the tenancy agreement of the farm property.

I went through the formal procedure to notify the resignation of the Registrar Of Companies. In a few days, I had the written confirmation of the share purchase offer and was able to secure a bank guarantee against the surety of the expected imminent income. I wrote to Lord Cawdor immediately, enclosing a cheque for the agreed sum and, on notification of final acceptance, registered the transfer of the entire shareholding to Michael. He now had the business, whatever it meant – and I know that it meant a great deal to him by way of reward for his determination, hard work and worry over the past two years or so. We had discussed the possibility of seeking support from the Highlands and Islands Development Board (HIDB). Providentially, I had an old RAF colleague who, in retirement from the active list, had taken up employment with the Board at their Inverness offices. He was well known to me as Jock Brown, and I lost no time in contacting him. He was not directly concerned with the development side of things but put me in touch with Peter Colinson. I had a brief chat with Peter who suggested that I submit a request for the Board's assistance to develop the company. The letter should set out the nature of the work being undertaken and all relevant historical details and progress to date and, of course, the need for assistance and the anticipated future effect. He would then arrange an on-site meeting at an early date. No problem; I was well-practised in the business of setting forth arguments for improvements and increases in establishments and funding.

We soon had Peter's response by telephone and his request for a visit to our site the very next day. He was not particularly impressed by the work conditions but wanted to see more of the nature of the past trading pattern and the last report of the auditors on the trading accounts for the previous financial year, together with anticipated growth in the current financial year and beyond. Fortunately, we had engaged one of the most reputable accountant firms in the Inverness area, and he seemed satisfied with their last report and was able to see immediately that the business was seriously underfunded in regard to the high capital outlay required for the kind of operation. I left him in no doubt about the operating difficulties in the light of our relationship with the local authority that seemed resentful of our existence, as were the local populations who lived close to the site and the farmlands on which we spread the septic waste. He was more concerned with our developing involvement with the offshore oil industry and our entry into the oil recovery aspects. He was most amicable and helpful and was interested in my RAF career, of which Jock Brown would, of course, have given him a brief. Together, we prepared the appropriate form of application, which I signed and off he went with an indication that the Board would make its decision without delay.

When the decision came, we could hardly believe the extent of the assistance that was being offered to us. It was in three stages: Firstly, there was a sizeable development grant that was not refundable. Then an equally sizeable loan that was repayable progressively with interest, all in exchange for forty-nine per cent of the share capital, leaving Michael with the controlling fifty-one per cent. Moreover there was a suggestion of help with relocation to an industrial area that was being developed at the former RAF Dalcross station site adjacent to its former airfield that had been Inverness Municipal Airport for the past several years. If we are interested, perhaps we would like to meet Peter there for a detailed survey and discussion. I knew the site well, having been involved in its final closure, and thought the former station equipment section would serve our purposes very well. It was still pretty much the same as I had last seen it, although the local farmer was making casual use of it as cover for some of his machines. The building was in reasonable order and would be adapted without major work, and Peter would take the necessary steps to ensure that there were no other claims for it. Its location was well separated from other buildings, and there was plenty of space around it that would facilitate external development.

By the end of 1979, the building and a designated space around it were assigned to us, and I had the whole deal tied up with regard to the formalities of title and the reallocation of the forty-nine per cent of the shares in favour of HIDB. All we had to do now was get the necessary conversion work done and move in as soon as possible. We now had funds in the bank to keep the bank manager happy and pay the bills, as the work was completed stage by stage. By the spring of 1980 the place was beginning to take on a different appearance inside and out. There was now a recognisable main entrance to an office suite with an inviting porch. Inside the office suite, the wartime single brick walls were hidden behind wooden panelling and the asbestos roof with a false ceiling. A wooden floor a few inches above ground level added much-needed additional insulation to a building that was intensely cold in the winter. Hardwearing carpeting and a background heating installation added an essential final touch. The office suite contained a good-sized reception area with general office facilities, whilst adjoining rooms provided separate offices for Michael as managing director, the maintenance manager and me as company secretary and director responsible for financial control and administration. We also had a well-planned toilet area, including a shower facility. In the spacious maintenance area, we had a pit and adequate facilities for vehicle maintenance. A space heating system added an essential degree of warmth to the central workshop and smaller adjoining rooms set aside for use as offices and stores.

We moved into our new domain in April 1980, my intended year of final retirement. But there were difficult days ahead, as Michael and I knew only too well. Whilst we now had a considerably improved company structure in which to work and develop, forces beyond our control were not in our favour. There were local protest groups who seemed intent on protesting for nothing more than protest itself without the slightest recognition of measures necessary to control environmental pollution. The local controlling authority seemed to be quite inept and concerned only about their political future. However, Michael had concluded negotiations for the purchase of an additional and much larger tanker vehicle that considerably increased our capability. We were already in the oil recovery business but had to rely on an outlet in Edinburgh for the processing of our waste oil, a good distance from us, involving a day's driving for the return journey. But it was all we could do at a small profit until we were able to get planning permission for the installation of a recovery plant of our own. The powers that be were somehow very slow to recognize the benefits that were likely to arise for the local economy. Eventually we got that authority and built a tank farm to store the reclaimed oil that was ideally suited for heating purposes. Of course, our workforce expanded with the business, and we became a rather busy little company. But we still had serious problems with the local authority, particularly when it came to the disposal of certain wastes to landfill facilities controlled by them. We were required to carry certain wastes of a toxic nature to distant facilities under other control with consequent expense to the local producers of that waste in the developing industrial Highland scene. Here again, there was evidence of some fear that the Highlands of Scotland should not have the economic advantage of any form of industrial development but should be dependent instead on its traditional tourist and agricultural industries that should themselves be expanded. They seemed not to realise that a measure of on-shore industrialisation had to follow to support the rapidly developing offshore oil activities. It

314

was an opportunity that should not be missed by the Highland communities of the Moray Firth coastal areas.

There was so much still to be done in the development of Nontox Limited that I felt that it would be most unfair to leave Michael to get on with it. I therefore agreed to postpone my final retirement for a further two years until July 1982. So the company continued to grow slowly against the difficult background. There were peaks and troughs in the pattern of work, and I well remember one occasion when we had to standoff four drivers/operators, which came as a rather sad blow for us. But things picked up again, and we were able to recall them. By the end of the 1980/81 financial year, we were showing marked progress, and our profit and loss account was well worth a second glance. HIDB were quite impressed. By the end of the next financial year, the beginning of April 1982, the turnover was comfortably in excess of the six-figure sum that I had hoped for, and I felt that I could pull out with an easy mind at the age of sixty-two. Michael and Fiona were nicely settled in a newly built house at Moss Side on the southern edge of Nairn. Their wee girl Laura Emily, a most lovable child, was at the primary school stage and I thought that Fiona, with her earlier experience in banking coupled with her natural acumen, could easily carry on as company secretary, thus placing the top management of the company firmly in their hands to their entire benefit. There was, of course, a full-time clerk/book-keeper and with the administration settled into a routine, it was really a matter of adequate management supervision with an essential degree of legal knowledge relating to the operation of the company in terms of financial and general administration, in any case, I would be on hand to advise if required. During 1987, the company had attracted the interest of a very large industrial waste undertaking based on the Manchester Ship Canal, to whom they eventually disposed of the company in a deal which, after settling all liabilities, including the HIDB interest, left Michael and Fiona with a capital sum that, wisely invested and controlled, would produce for them interest on which they would be able to live comfortably for the rest of their lives. Nontox Limited was, therefore, a successful, though very hard-won, enterprise, resulting in a well-deserved reward for Michael's unceasing efforts.

So, on the third of July 1982, two years later than initially intended, I came to the end of the much-advocated short second career following my retirement from RAF active duty. Looking back on my entire working life and times, of which the foregoing is intended to be an account, I believe I can say that it was truly A Life Worthwhile. Certainly, it was one of attainment far beyond whatever initial expectations I may have entertained at the age of seventeen. At that age, my education had been advanced to sound secondary standard with passes to school certificate standards in English, Mathematics, Science and Practical Drawing in preparation for training as an artisan in a wide range of technical skills. I was interested in three of the advancing technologies of that time: electricity, wireless and aviation, and was fortunate enough to be able to sample all of them. But my greatest wish had been to enter the Royal Air Force in a skilled trade with the initial prospect of a flying opportunity as a wireless operator progressing by planned stages to non-commissioned pilot. That wish was granted and opened my way to the satisfaction of doing that which I so much wanted to do. In every way, my subsequent efforts, though not always easily accomplished, were attended by success.

Passing my RAF qualifying examinations, as they arose, although needing a great deal of application to study, was never a real problem for me. As I compose these closing words (August 2003), I feel a great sense of satisfaction that whatever I had to do, I always tried to do it to the best of my ability without conscious effort to impress those set in authority over me. Many noticeably went to great lengths to impress and seemed to have the uncanny knack of always being on hand to get themselves noticed on chosen occasions, but the obsequious were seldom successful in gaining the genuine attention and approbation of those under whom they served. The system, though far from perfect, usually exposed those who could deceive, and I knew many in this category who fell by the wayside. I never forgot one of the early lessons learned at Cranwell; 'Apply yourself diligently to your duties; the progress of your career is in the hands of those at higher and will usually be appropriate and deserving of your efforts and assessed ability.' I never found myself in any situation that I felt was beyond my capability to manage. Perhaps I didn't take full advantage of the opportunities that my chosen field of endeavour offered. Perhaps I could have done better. Perhaps, possibly, if only this and that! Looking back on those of my contemporaries who I judged to have been capable of surpassing me and failed even to make my own level of achievement, I feel that I was fortunate in doing so well for myself. I could certainly have done much worse. My real reward has been found in the ability to make adequate and reasonably carefree provisions for the comfort of Rosemary and myself in our declining years. That is what, after a working life attended by an essential degree of satisfaction throughout, makes for the final happy ending of A Life Worthwhile.

EPILOGUE

I started to write these memoirs a good many years ago when, in the mid-1980s, I became virtually plagued by many enthusiasts seeking first-hand accounts of those who flew operationally during the Second World War. Usually, these were related to individual operations being researched through records held in the Public Records Office, which, of course, contained the names of personnel involved. I found it rather time-consuming and decided to compile my memoirs of flying with 102 Squadron between late 1938 and mid-1940. My sons encouraged me to expand my writing to cover my entire RAF career. Initially, the composition was a much-laboured business that had to be done using a typewriter designed for use by those blessed with two hands, each having five digits. I was soon to discover that no matter how I tried to follow the teachings of the more accomplished, I never did discover that I had more than a single finger on each hand. However, along came the Personal Computer to which I was introduced towards the end of 1999. This made progress somewhat faster with its greater ease of correcting my unlimited mistakes, but the keyboard only provides more confusion with its increased number of keys most of which I have yet to discover the use of. However, I think I can claim that I have not done too badly for a young feller of my age. I am just glad that I don't have to make a living by typing.

What I have written is the truth as I remember it, and I would hasten to add that I have not sought to embellish it in any way. I have read many accounts of operational flying that have been grossly overstated to the degree that is obvious to those who were also there. In my reminiscences of wartime flying, I have gone to great lengths to avoid anything that may be thought dubious.

I have often been asked if I intended to submit my memoirs for publication. I never seriously considered the matter except for chapters IV to VI, extracts from which have been published in the works of several authors of WW2 Historical Publications. A copy of these chapters covering my wartime flying memoirs is also held in the archives of The Aircrew Association at the Yorkshire Air Museum at Elvington, York.

What I have written was never intended to be more than a personal record of the family history, such as it may be. I can only hope that it may be the richer for my contribution to it.

Have I really got to the intended ending of my story? Certainly there have been many problems to overcome in typing it using my limited knowledge of PC word processing and keyboard manipulation. For me, the result is pleasing, but it has taken a long time, during which there have been inevitable problems, many of a technical nature. I have learned a lot about modern PC usage and technology, even to build my own computer successfully. Perhaps I owe a lot to my early interest in electricity and wireless and my training in the Youth Entry Wing of the Electrical and Wireless School at Cranwell all those years ago, which now allows me a more ready understanding of the technologies involved which, after all, are no more than developments of those of my own early interest and learning.

The End

Edited to End

By my son Michael Jacobs

June 2024

Photographs

A four-year-old Michael on the day he was to meet his father for the first time at Nairn
Railway Station on his return from the war in Burma 1947

Leaflets Dropped over Germany 1939 By 102 Bomber Squadron

A document came to me recently and had content that tells the tragic death of Flight Sargent George Oliver Maughan, first mentioned on page 58 as best man at Sgt W Jacobs's wedding in Nairn 1940. Although Sgt. Jacobs was aware his friend was killed in action, but he never knew the circumstances.

Letter written by P O Kenneth McKellar White (RAAF) POW 1942. Reference loss of Hunson AE523 No.62 Squadron on 9 Sept.1942

We were engaged in a bombing attack on Akyab, a port on the and flying at 2000 feet. There were a lot of clouds on and western coast of Burma, about 200 miles south of the Indian border. Unexpectedly, we flew into one of these and I became separated from the other two aircraft in the formation, when we were out of a cloud, I saw the other two a short distance ahead of me, and it was then our troubles began. I opened the engines to catch up with the other planes, but the port engine, instead of increasing its speed, it started coughing and cutting out no matter what I did, kept dying away. In the midst of this, Sgt. McNeil's voice came over the intercom, saying there were two Jap fighters above and were attacking. Mc was in the rear gun turret, and I could hear his machine guns firing. Mc never spoke again. I again opened the motors, and by this time, the port engine was useless. I started twisting and turning the plane in order to dodge the Jap fighters. One of them came diving down on my port side and pulled up underneath me, and a burst of cannon fire from its guns rocked the plane from one side to the other. The starboard motor was hit and stopped dead and burst into flames. Other cannon shells burst inside the plane, and in a matter of seconds, the whole front of the plane was a mass of flame and choking white smoke. The smoke was so dense and hard to breathe I was forced to hang out of the window and, at the same time, try to keep control of the plane, which was a difficult job.

Even had I wanted to control the plane by instruments, I could not as they also had been shot away, and the smoke was so thick that it was impossible to see them. All this happened in a matter of a few seconds, and all the time, I could hear Mc firing his guns as I said he never spoke again. As the Jap fighters continued to attack us by this time, the plane was almost out of control. Both engines were now dead, and we were diving to the ground at a hell of a speed. Immediately after Margolis, the observer came rushing back from his position in the nose with blood flowing down his face. He had been hit with shrapnel and started combating the flames with extinguishers and kept fighting the flames in the terrific heat and choking smoke until we crashed, and when I got his body out, he was still grasping a fire extinguisher in his hand.

Simultaneously, George Maughan was operating the radio messaging base about our plight and advising them of our rough position where we would crash. One of the last things I remember was George transmitting SOS continuously, and then we crashed. Margolis and George were killed instantly, and Mc died in my arms a couple of hours later. The best friends any man could have. What I did not lose is the conviction that it was not God's will for me to die then. Then and again later, I have faced death and very narrowly escaped and now know that my job in this world is not yet done as I have in these times of peril and, of course, at other times, resorted to prayers. These have been answered, so whatever my ultimate fate is to be, I know that it will be His will and that he is with me.